Trade Union Politics

TRADE UNION POLITICS

AMERICAN UNIONS AND
ECONOMIC CHANGE, 1960S–1990S

EDITED BY

GLENN PERUSEK AND KENT WORCESTER

HUMANITIES PRESS
NEW JERSEY

First published 1995 by Humanities Press International, Inc.,
165 First Avenue, Atlantic Highlands, NJ 07716.

This collection ©1995 by Humanities Press International, Inc.

Library of Congress Cataloging-in-Publication Data
Trade union politics : American unions and economic change,
  1960s-1990s / edited by Glenn Perusek and Kent Worcester.
    p.   cm.
    Includes bibliographical references and index.
    ISBN 0-391-03886-9. — ISBN 0-391-03887-7 (pbk.)
    1. Trade-unions—United States—History—20th century. 2. Trade-
  unions—United States—Case studies. 3. Industrial relations—United
  States—History—20th century. 4. United States—Economic conditions—
  1945-   I. Perusek, Glenn W. (Glenn Wesley), 1958-   . II. Worcester, Kent,
  1959-   .
  HD6508. T683   1995
  322'.2'0973045—dc20   94-37802
                                                                  CIP

A catalog record for this book is available from the British Library.

Printed in the United States of America

TO THE MEMORY OF CHRISTINA BERGMARK (1952–1986)

CONTENTS

ILLUSTRATIONS

ABBREVIATIONS

ACWA	Amalgamated Clothing Workers of America
AFL	American Federation of Labor
AFSCME	American Federation of State, County, and Municipal Employees
AFT	American Federation of Teachers
ALPA	Air Line Pilots' Association
CAW	Canadian Auto Workers
CIM	Computer Integrated Manufacture
CIO	Congress of Industrial Organizations
CLA	Communist League of America
COLA	Cost of Living Allowance
CP	Communist Party (U.S.)
CRS	Computerized Reservations Systems
CWA	Communications Workers of America
DNC	Democratic National Committee
EC	European Community
ERM	Exchange Rate Mechanism
ESOP	Employee Stock Ownership Plan
ETUC	European Trades Union Congress
FASH	Fraternal Association of Steelhaulers
FE	Farm Equipment Workers Union
FTA	Food, Tobacco, and Agricultural Workers Union
GMAD	General Motors Assembly Division
IAM	International Association of Machinists
IBT	International Brotherhood of Teamsters, Chauffeurs, Warehousemen, and Helpers of America
ICC	Interstate Commerce Commission
IHC	International Harvester Company
ILGWU	International Ladies Garment Workers Union
ILWU	International Longshoremen's Warehousemen's Union
IS	International Socialists (U.S.)
ISL	Independent Socialists League (U.S.)
IUE	International Union of Electrical Workers
IWA	International Woodworkers of America
IWW	Industrial Workers of the World

LPP	Labor Protective Provisions
LRBW	League of Revolutionary Black Workers
MEC	Master Executive Council
MFD	Miners for Democracy
NAACP	National Association for the Advancement of Colored People
NAFTA	North American Free Trade Agreement
NLRB	National Labor Relations Board
NMFA	National Master Freight Agreement
NMU	National Maritime Union
PATCO	Professional Air Traffic Controllers Union
PRCD	Professional Drivers Council, Inc.
QWL	Quality of Work Life
RLA	Railway Labor Act
RWDSU	Retail, Wholesale, and Department Store Union
SCLC	Southern Christian Leadership Conference
SFTU	Southern Tenants Farmers Union
SIU-SUP	Sailors International Union—Sailors Union of the Pacific
SP	Socialist Party (U.S.)
SPD	Social Democratic Party (Germany)
STAC	Steel Tripartite Advisory Committee
SWOC	Steel Workers' Organizing Committee
SWP	Socialist Workers Party (U.S.)
TCI	Tennessee Coal, Iron and Railroad
TDC	Teamsters for a Decent Contract
TDU	Teamsters for a Democratic Union
TPM	Trigger Price Mechanism
TURF	Teamsters United Rank and File
TWU	Transport Workers Union
UAW	United Automobile Workers Union
UCAPAWA	United Cannery, Agricultural, Packing, and Allied Workers of America
UE	United Electrical, Radio and Machine Workers of America
UMW/UMWA	United Mine Workers of America
UNC	United National Caucus
UPS	United Parcel Service
UPWA	United Packinghouse Workers of America
USS/USX	United States Steel Corporation
USW/USWA	United Steel Workers of America

Unions are big business. Why should truck drivers and bottle washers be allowed to make big decisions affecting union policy? Would any corporation allow it?

—Dave Beck, President of the
International Brotherhood of Teamsters

There is only one thing worse than a wildcat strike—A wildcat strike that succeeds.

—George P. Shultz, Secretary of Labor

PART I

THEORETICAL ISSUES

1

Introduction:
Patterns of Class Conflict in the
United States since the 1960s

Glenn Perusek and Kent Worcester

TRADE UNIONS CONSTITUTE ONE of the most distinctive and important expressions of interest-group association in modern America. Yet social scientists
have had relatively little to say about contemporary trade unionism in the
United States as a political, economic, and institutional phenomenon. In particular, social scientists have neglected two issue areas that are of critical importance in understanding organized labor's membership decline, political
powerlessness, and institutional decay in the current period: the impact of changes
in international and domestic political economy on the character of labor-
based conflict; and the multiple layers of interest conflict within trade unions,
that is, the microfoundations of internal conflict within industrial interest groups
and their impact on union politics.[1] It is our hope that this volume will help
to bring these problematics into focus among social scientists and others concerned with the role of trade unions in contemporary U.S. society.

The essays in this volume are marked by a common interest in trade unions
as institutions that operate in complex and dynamic environments that are
conditioned by other institutions (such as states, political parties, industries) as
well as by political and cultural values, economic incentives and constraints,
and other key variables. In particular, the approach developed in this volume
finds the *interest disjuncture* between leaders and members of bureaucratized
unions to be crucial in explaining the current paralysis of organized labor. We
define bureaucratized unions as unions with a stable corps of full-time salaried
officers. This definition draws upon a much-neglected tradition of theories of
union organization and behavior that can be termed the *classical political sociology* approach. This tradition can be traced to the pathbreaking work of Sidney
and Beatrice Webb and also includes the work of Robert Michels, Antonio
Gramsci, and others.[2] The analysis here extends this approach by examining
the socioeconomic and sociopolitical roles served by a variety of interests within

3

the bureaucracy—between elected national or international officers, appointed international staff representatives, and full-time local leaders. In this way we seek to contribute to the small but important body of recent social-theoretical literature that has examined the interest disjuncture between members and leaders in private associations as part of a generalized critique of the pluralist approach.[3]

In addition to emphasizing the bureaucratic contradictions of modern trade unions, we highlight the relationship between developments at the level of the global economy and the social and industrial organization of American workers. The impact of global economic change on U.S. trade unionism and working-class politics more generally cannot be easily overstated. The international economic context changed dramatically, especially from the mid-1970s onwards, as America's manufacturing base was eroded by international competition and increased capital mobility. In this period, the combined pressures of economic stagnation and an international restructuring of capital have devastated the traditional bastions of blue-collar unionism. By the 1980s, the "Thatcher model" of financial deregulation, technological innovation, privatization, and anti-union legislation had captured the imagination of international economic elites.[4] In the United States, the number of strikes fell dramatically, as workers conducted largely defensive battles over such issues as health care benefits, wage concessions, and unionization.

Scholarly responses to labor's current crisis have been heavily influenced by the pluralist approach to the study of politics and organizations.[5] As a result, the role of internal institutional dynamics and of international economic forces has received rather less attention than have the domestic cultural and political sources of trade union decline. Specifically, pluralist-inspired authors have tended to foreground such factors as America's individual-centered, pro-entrepreneurial civic culture, unfavorable labor legislation (for example, the Taft-Hartley Act of 1947 and the Landrum-Griffith Act of 1959), and the intransigent anti-unionism of business and other economic elites.[6] While acknowledging the importance of these factors, this volume seeks to identify ways in which internal organizational dynamics and broad economic tendencies have come to play significant roles in constraining the capacity of unions to mobilize effectively in defense of their members' interests. We intend, therefore, to go beyond the pluralist paradigm and to draw on more innovative approaches in explaining the genesis and dynamics of labor's decline in the postwar period.

Rather than viewing unions as undifferentiated organizational units, as pluralist analyses suggest, we highlight the existence of competing institutional and social interests within modern trade unions.[7] We are particularly concerned with the intra-organizational interest disjuncture dividing full-time union officers from dues-paying members. Depending on the concrete circumstances, such a cleavage of institutional interests can have profound consequences for the patterning of industrial conflict. For example, bureaucracies (or particular sections of them) may rationally decide to avoid the aggressive organizing campaigns or prolonged strike actions that may be necessary to secure contractual gains from employers in order to protect specific institutional advantages.

The near-hegemony of the pluralist approach may also have served to obscure the growing importance of international economic trends in shaping the political and socioeconomic environment within which trade unions operate. Pluralist theory, after all, was first developed in a period when key sectors of the U.S. economy were relatively isolated from international economic and political trends. Furthermore, pluralists have tended to view organizational dynamics strictly in terms of discrete local or national settings. As a result, the impact of a variety of international influences—particularly, but not exclusively, those generated in the sphere of political economy—have been overlooked by social scientists working on modern trade unionism. Sociologists have only recently considered the role of foreign-owned companies in the area of industrial relations; political scientists are only now becoming aware of the impact of international economic competition on the regulation of labor relations or on the contemporary transformation of political culture in America. One of a host of issues that remains little understood is the variable impact of international trends on competing interest blocs within interest groups such as trade unions—groups that were at one time seen as operating within purely national or local environments.

One reason why the pluralist approach retains its hold over the social sciences is that pluralists have appropriated the powerful if flawed concept of "American exceptionalism" to explain the relative political conservatism of the American working class. In this context, "conservatism" refers to the failure of workers to form an independent labor or social democratic party and develop "socialistic" consciousness. Following Louis Hartz, arguments that focus on the distinctiveness of American political culture (specifically, that culture's roots in Lockean liberalism) are often seen as the most satisfactory explanation for the relative weakness of trade unionism in America. This volume's focus on the modern bureaucratization of U.S. unions, on the existence of structurally based intra-organizational conflicts, and on the growing impact of international economic interdependence on U.S. socioeconomic structures, may help to provide components of an alternative approach to more traditional perspectives.

Whatever the explanatory merit of culture-centered analyses (such as arguments derived from the notion of American exceptionalism), it is important to recognize that at the very least institutional factors play an important intervening role. To give only one example: The relative size and organizational power of the multiple layers of full-time salaried officials in U.S. unions may have a profound effect on the character of social relations within specific unions and on the quality of labor-based militancy in the United States. It is important to recognize a key paradox in this context: One of the weakest union movements in the advanced industrial democracies sustains the largest and richest bureaucracy of full-time salaried officers in the entire world.[8] As Staughton Lynd has argued, the shortcomings of contemporary American unionism may in part reflect the failure of a particular model or practice of unionism: highly centralized, highly bureaucratized national organizations that engage in firm- or industry-specific bargaining.[9] It seems to us that there is nothing generically "American" about this model of trade union organization. Instead, the current hegemony of this form of labor organization may be said to reflect both the material interests of the labor bureaucracy and that bureaucracy's historical experiences vis-à-vis the mass corporatized industries that flourished in midcentury America. There are real questions, however, whether this model can be expected to cope with the challenges posed by the recent changes in the international political economy.

THE DECLINE OF AMERICAN UNIONS

The American union movement is sometimes said to suffer from a terminal disease. After labor's heroic revival in the 1930s and 1940s, when important sections of the industrial workforce were organized, organized labor found it harder to extend its gains and a deep paralysis set in. Despite the notable increases in public-sector unionization, overall union membership figures have experienced secular decline since the mid-1950s (see tables 1.1 and 1.2). Organized labor's political influence, similarly, has been both limited and on the wane. American unions have effectively been declared a "special interest," one beleaguered faction of the Democratic Party's shrinking liberal wing. The strengthening of the labor–Democratic Party connection during the postwar period generally served to mask the creeping suppression of labor's independent political voice. On the whole, loyalty to the Democratic Party has failed to produce the sorts of legislative gains that would have justified a strategy of subordination. It is significant in this context that even at the height of Lyndon Johnson's Great Society in the mid-1960s, with a strong liberal Democratic majority in both houses of Congress, the unions' confederation, the American Federation of Labor–Congress of Industrial Organizations (AFL-CIO), could not secure passage of a bill to repeal the Taft-Hartley Act's open-shop clause (section 14B).[10]

By the early 1980s the decline of American labor accelerated. After President Reagan broke the Professional Air Traffic Controllers union (PATCO) in 1981, workers in several industries were forced to accept concession contracts, which cut wages and curtailed work-rule protections won in previous rounds of negotiations. Union membership plummeted, particularly in industrial unions. As industrial America, once the heartland of CIO unionism, became a painful symbol of rust belt decline, unemployment soared in the coalfields and in the Flints, Akrons, and Youngstowns of the Northeast. The centers of manufacturing growth moved on, it appeared, to the American South and West, to Japan, and to the Asian boom economies. The fortunes of organized labor apparently paralleled those of industrial capitalism.

The heyday of American industrial unionism was the 1930s—the campaigns to unionize the automobile, steel, and rubber industries. From union leaders' point of view, this was the heroic, "amateur" phase of a movement that has

TABLE 1.1   Membership Density in the United States, (1945–1992, selected years, millions of workers)

YEAR	NONAGRICULTURAL EMPLOYEES	UNION MEMBERSHIP (IN THOUSANDS)	PERCENTAGE UNIONIZED
1945	40.4	12.3	30.4%
1950	45.2	14.3	31.5
1954	49.0	17.0	34.7
1960	54.2	17.0	31.4
1964	58.3	16.9	28.9
1970	70.9	19.4	27.3
1974	78.4	20.2	25.8
1980	85.7	20.2	23.6
1983	90.1	18.6	20.6
1992	108.5	16.4	15.1

Sources: For employees, U.S. Department of Labor, Bureau of Labor Statistics, *Handbook of Labor Statistics* (Washington, D.C.: U.S. Government Printing Office, June 1985), Bulletin 2217, p. 174; the series ended in 1978. Also, *Employment and Earnings*, July 1993, p. 81. For members, Leo Troy and Neil Sheflin, *Union Sourcebook* (West Orange, N.J.: IRDIS, 1985), 3–10; Michael Goldfield, *The Decline of Organized Labor in the United States* (Chicago: University of Chicago Press, 1987), 10–11; *Employment and Earnings*, January 1993, p. 238.

TABLE 1.2   Union Density by Industrial Sector

INDUSTRY	1947	1966	1970	1975	1980	1984
Manufacturing	40.5	37.4	38.7	36.0	32.3	26.0
Mining	83.1	35.7	35.7	32.0	32.1	17.7
Construction	87.1	41.4	39.2	35.4	31.6	23.5
Transportation	67.0	50.3	44.8	46.6	48.0	38.7
Services	9.0	na	7.8	13.9	11.6	7.3
Government	12.0	26.0	31.9	39.5	35.0	na
Total non-farm	32.1	29.6	29.6	28.9	23.2	19.4

na = not available
Source: Leo Troy and Neil Sheflin, *Union Sourcebook* (West Orange, N.J.: IRDIS, 1985), 3–15, table 3.63.

become more respectable as it has become professionalized. As long-time AFL-CIO president George Meany put it, the industrial strike—the key weapon of the 1930s—was no longer necessary, or even appropriate, given conditions of postwar prosperity.[11] Thus, in the view of most postwar social scientific analyses of unions and in the view of union leaders themselves, Herculean struggles became a thing of the past. This volume dissents from this overall interpretive framework, which we believe does an injustice both to the actual historical record and to the interests of American workers confronting a global competitive economy.

THE LATE 1960S-EARLY 1970S:
A PERIOD OF HEIGHTENED RANK-AND-FILE MILITANCY

Notions of a decline in the level of industrial-based social conflict during the postwar period obscure the explosion of rank-and-file militancy in the late 1960s and early 1970s. Two national wildcat strikes in 1970 may be seen as epitomizing the oppositional character of the 1967–1974 period. The nation-wide postal workers' wildcat strike, in March 1970, was perhaps the most dra-matic example of worker militancy in this era. Two hundred thousand postal workers, members of an eighty-year-old union that had never struck the United States Postal Service, wildcatted. The week-long illegal strike forced President Nixon to declare a national emergency and order thirty thousand national guards-men and army reservists into New York City, the heart of the action. The government was compelled to grant large numbers of public employees an immediate 6 percent wage increase; postal workers received a 14 percent raise. The postal workers, members of a timid, frail union organization with no his-tory of militancy, defied the president, Congress, federal law, injunctions, and their own union officials to engage in a nationwide wildcat strike, the first ever in the history of U.S. public employment. A second major wildcat strike began a week after the postal workers returned to work. Teamsters in major Mid-western and East Coast cities struck for over two months to win an average wage increase of 13 percent per year, "the highest nationwide increase for a leading union in the country's history."[12]

Little independent rank-and-file organization existed among postal workers or teamsters. But other groups of workers had begun to create formal rank-and-file groups in opposition to their union leadership. Among United Mine Workers (UMW) three organizations were formed: the Black Lung Associa-tion, the Miners for Democracy (MFD), and the Disabled Miners and Wid-ows organization. In February–March 1969, the Black Lung Association played a role in leading 43,000 West Virginia miners to wildcat until a Black Lung Bill was signed into law.[13] Eventually Arnold Miller, backed by the MFD, would become president of the UMW.

Strike activity in 1967–1974 was not confined to a single industry or group of workers. The level of activity was higher in these years than in any other period since the passage of the Taft-Hartley Act in 1947 (see table 1.3). More than this, workers acted against both employers and their own union officials.

In the 1940s and 1950s, American business leaders had grudgingly come to accept the existence of the CIO unions. Henry Ford II summarized the view of most employers when he said, in January 1946, "We of the Ford Motor Company have no desire to 'break the unions,' or to turn back the clock." Instead, he argued, "we must look to an improved and increasingly responsible [union] leadership for help in solving the human equation in mass produc-tion."[14] This "improved and increasingly responsible leadership," the stratum of salaried, full-time union officers, struck a broad accord with management in

TABLE 1.3   Work Stoppages Involving 1,000 Workers or More in the
United States (1947–1992)

YEARS	WORK STOPPAGES	WORKERS INVOLVED (THOUSANDS)	DAYS IDLE (THOUSANDS)
1947	270	1,629	25,720
1950	424	1,698	30,390
1953	437	1,623	18,130
1957	279	870	10,340
1960	222	896	13,260
1963	181	512	10,020
1967	381	2,192	31,320
1970	381	2,468	52,761
1973	317	1,400	16,260
1977	298	1,212	21,258
1980	187	795	20,844
1983	81	909	17,461
1987	46	174	4,481
1990	44	185	5,926
1992	35	364	3,989
1993	35	182	3,981
1994 (through August)	32	247	3,389

Source: U.S. Department of Labor, Bureau of Labor Statistics, *Compensation and Working Conditions* (Washington, D.C.: U.S. Government Printing Office, September 1994), p. 78.

the late 1940s and 1950s. During this era of steady expansion of American capitalism, employers in the primary industrial sector were able to offer contracts with steady wage and benefit improvements. The union leaderships thus obtained a secure source of dues income. In return, the unions guaranteed uninterrupted production for the life of signed contracts. The typical contract in this era was for two to three years and contained a no-strike pledge.[15]

However, this accord was predicated on the assumption that union leaders could convince their members to accept the contracts they negotiated and keep them on the job during the life of individual contracts. This assumption did not necessarily hold during the period from 1967 to 1974. Members no longer automatically passed negotiated contracts. The rate of contract rejections—where members voted against contracts negotiated by their union leaders—rose to one in eight by 1968.[16] This period witnessed a remarkable rise in wildcat strikes to force renegotiation of settlements deemed unsatisfactory by the rank and file. The number of strikes during the term of contracts also increased in this period, as did the number of job actions over production standards and working conditions. Wildcat strikes created a situation that was a mixed blessing for union officers. While union leaders could demand more at the bargaining table, they also had a harder job "selling" the deals they negotiated to the rank and file.

Ordinary workers' confidence in their ability to influence events through self organization and independent action—even against the policies of their own officers—was a prime factor in the nature of the period. This mood of confidence evaporated quickly in the recessionary period in the mid-1970s. After about 1974, workers believed less and less that militant action could improv wages and working conditions. In part, higher unemployment levels forced worker to think in terms of job security instead of wage increases. This strengthened employers in bargaining; they could now weather longer strikes to gain more favorable contracts. Workers' lack of confidence in the efficacy of their own action also appears to have been crucial in undercutting rank-and-file organiza tions. The cautious and defensive rank and file was no environment for th existence of militant rank-and-file organizations; with the lone exception of Teamsters for a Democratic Union (TDU), they withered and died.[17]

Strike action in general dropped off in the wake of the 1974-5 recession Those strikes that did occur were increasingly defensive. Wildcat strikes, com mon in the 1967–1974 period, became rare. Not coincidentally, real wage tracked closely with these changes in militancy. Workers made steady but rela tively low gains in the years of stable expansion from the early 1950s to th late 1960s. Then, even though rising inflation could have been expected to ea into workers' real living standards, the militancy of the late 1960s and earl 1970s kept real wages ahead of inflation. Only after 1974 did workers' rea wages drop. Worker militancy, coupled with economic growth, parallels th trend of real wages (see table 1.4).

The transformed mood on the shop floor provided an opportunity for em ployers to embark on a many-sided offensive against workers and their unions Although it is commonly believed that this employers' offensive coincided wit Ronald Reagan's presidency, it actually began much earlier. The Common Situ picketing bill, which would have weakened the Taft-Hartley ban on secondar boycotts, passed Congress in 1975 but was vetoed by President Ford.[18] Th bill came before Congress again in 1977. With a Democrat in the White House the AFL-CIO was confident of passage. But this time the bill failed in th House of Representatives, as key Democrats shifted against organized labor.

The 1977 defeat of the picketing bill only foreshadowed the more seriou defeat of the labor law reform bill in the Senate in June 1978. This bill woul have made it more difficult for large employers willfully to violate existin labor law. It would have barred such violators from federal contracts for thre years, expedited National Labor Relations Board (NLRB) representation elec tions, and awarded double back pay to employees illegally discharged in orgar izing drives, among other things.[20] Business groups organized a massive lobbyin effort against the bill.

The 1978 defeat of the labor law reform bill was the turning point in labo relations in the whole post–World War II period. Labor leaders considered th defeat as "that single crucial battle which marked the end of the labor accor that had prevailed throughout the post-war era."[21] Many analysts believed tha

TABLE 1.4 Average Weekly Earnings of Production or Nonsupervisory Workers on Private, Nonagricultural Payrolls, Selected Years, 1947–1993

YEAR	CPI-U 1982–4 = 100	TOTAL PRIVATE		MINING		CONSTRUCTION		MANUFACTURING		TRANSPORTATION AND PUBLIC UTILITIES		SERVICES	
		Nominal	Real	Nominal	Real	Nominal	Real	Nominal	Real	Nominal	Real	Nominal	Real
1993	144.5	374	259	647	448	552	382	486	336	540	374	350	242
1990	130.7	345	264	603	461	526	402	442	338	505	386	320	245
1985	107.6	299	278	520	483	464	431	386	359	450	418	257	239
1980	82.4	235	285	397	482	368	447	289	351	351	426	191	232
1975	53.8	164	305	249	463	266	494	191	355	233	433	135	251
1973	44.4	145	327	201	453	236	532	166	374	203	457	117	264
1970	38.8	120	309	164	423	195	503	134	345	156	402	97	250
1965	31.5	95	302	124	394	138	438	108	343	125	397	74	235
1960	29.6	81	274	105	355	113	382	90	304	N A		N A	
1955	26.8	68	254	90	336	91	340	76	284	N A		N A	
1950	24.1	53	220	67	278	70	290	58	241	N A		N A	
1947	22.3	N A		N A		N A		49	220	N A		N A	

Sources: CPI-U, the Consumer Price Index for Urban Areas, is from the United States Department of Commerce, Bureau of the Census, *Statistical Abstract of the United States* (Washington, D.C.: United States Government Printing Office, September 1994), 488. Wages are from United States Department of Labor, Bureau of Labor Statistics, *Handbook of Labor Statistics* (Washington, D.C.: United States Government Printing Office, August 1989), 317; United States Department of Labor, Bureau of Labor Statistics, *Employment and Earnings* (Washington, D.C.: United States Government Printing Office, September 1994), 44; 118; United States Department of Commerce, Bureau of the Census, *Historical Statistics of the United States*, part 1 (Washington, D.C.: United States Government Printing Office, 1970), 169.

this defeat would usher in a new period of militancy by union leaders. Ferguson and Rogers argued that

> by shattering the consensus on goals that has long guided much of industry and most of labor, the bill's demise heralds an end to the epoch of industrial relations that began in the later stages of the New Deal. By setting in motion powerful tides of interest and sentiment, it virtually insures a long period of turmoil in American society and politics.[22]

Indeed, the defeat of labor law reform did usher in a new era of labor relations. Labor's political defeats in 1977 and 1978 occurred in strongly Democratic Congresses, suggesting that the union movement's traditional link to the Democratic Party counted for little against the unified opposition of organized business.

Setbacks in the late 1970s gave way to a long period of direct economic attacks against organized labor. An ailing Chrysler Corporation, on the brink of bankruptcy, gained concession contracts from the United Automobile Workers (UAW) in 1979 and again in 1980.[23] In August 1981 a dramatic confrontation between President Reagan and the air traffic controllers' union, PATCO, capsulized the whole union movement's weakness in the era of concessions. When PATCO struck, Reagan issued a swift ultimatum: return to work within forty-eight hours or be terminated. PATCO members showed remarkable resolve. Only eight hundred crossed picket lines before the deadline. But the government carried through its plan, originally devised under the Carter administration, to replace the striking controllers with supervisory personnel, nonunion controllers, military controllers, and new hires. Within weeks, air traffic stabilized at 70–80 percent of prestrike levels. Faced with the most serious government attack on a union in decades, labor leaders mustered only passive, verbal support. Labor leaders explicitly rejected the idea of sympathy strikes to shut down the airlines, condemning PATCO to their fate.[24]

Concessions at Chrysler and the destruction of PATCO emboldened all of American business. There followed a long period of defensive struggles and defeats for organized labor. No single causal factor animated this new era of employers' attacks. Rather, several factors, including declining profitability and economic stagnation, deregulation, intensified competition from foreign industries, new production technologies and processes, and capital flight, all contributed to the new environment for capital-labor conflict in the United States starting in the mid-1970s. In industries facing intensified international pressure, such as auto and steel, unions were hard-pressed to forestall concessions and massive erosion of their membership base. In industries undergoing deregulation, such as the airlines, and transportation more generally, and communications, a period of turmoil upset traditional patterns of bargaining. In the airline industry, which was deregulated in 1978, reasonably paid union members were pitted against low-paid nonunion workers in newly established airlines.

Unprofitable firms were not the only ones who sought concessions. Although the major steel companies, Chrysler (in 1979 but not in 1984), and several airlines could justifiably argue that financial hardship necessitated wage cuts, many firms with no such problems secured concessions in the 1980s. Ford and General Motors (GM) secured concession contracts in the early 1980s even as they were making record profits. Managers for Greyhound and Hormel forced strikes, in 1983 and 1985 respectively, by demanding wage and work-rule concessions even as they posted strongly profitable years. As Kim Moody wrote in 1983, "The employers' push for concessions and the growing willingness to use union-busting tactics is not just a product of recession. Recovery is well under way, and employers' demands have escalated."[25]

The general picture by the mid-1980s was one of a steady fall in the overall level of unionization and reductions in wages and work standards that protected those workers who were still unionized. For instance, by 1985 only 30 percent of negotiated contracts contained cost-of-living clauses, a standard feature of large employers' union contracts in the period up to the mid-1970s. In appraising these transformations of American industrial relations, this volume emphasizes that the response of the leadership of American unions—as well as the response of ordinary members—was in no way predetermined. At crucial steps, union leaders were faced with distinctive choices about strategy. That they, for the most part, chose a cautious path in no way obviates the fact that they were confronted with choice situations. Rather, it suggests that their organizational interests—in maintaining a stable dues base, conserving strike funds, and preserving negotiatory relations with management wherever possible—were strong enough to influence their choices.

The union leadership's policy in the post-1975 period is characterized by three elements. First, in the face of the employers' economic offensive against wage and work-rule standards, union leaders have been passively acquiescent. Second, union leaders strove to restore full participation in the Democratic Party. The Democratic Party's 1972 nomination of George McGovern for president marked the apogee of AFL-CIO estrangement from the liberal wing of the party. But since Carter's election in 1976, the AFL-CIO has worked to reestablish its position alongside the corporate wing of the party's supporters. In 1981, fifteen of twenty-five at-large seats on the Democratic National Committee (DNC) were granted to the labor movement, along with four of thirty-five seats on the party executive. In return, the AFL-CIO became the institutional Democratic Party's single most important financial backer, providing the DNC with more than one-third of its operating budget ($2.5 million of $7 million).

The third element of top union leaders' approach has been an emphasis on an increasingly moderate legislative program, rather than reliance on workplace strength. Since the emasculation of the Humphrey-Hawkins Bill in 1978, the AFL-CIO leadership has retreated completely from full employment and instead has aimed at narrow protection of members' sectional interests. The large industrial unions have pressed for protectionist trade policy. The UAW sought

domestic content legislation in the early 1980s, the United Steel Workers (USW
pursued restrictions on foreign imports of steel, and the Teamsters have lo
bied for partial reregulation of the trucking industry as the airline unions ha
done for air transportation. Construction unions worked to preserve Davi
Bacon legislation, which effectively requires all federal construction projects
pay union scale regardless of whether workers are unionized. Thomas Byr
Edsall has noted that it is somewhat paradoxical that as organized labor's mer
bership base has eroded, it has become more protectionist and is increasing
perceived as a special interest group, with little capacity to represent the bro
working-class base of the Democratic Party coalition.[26]

The AFL-CIO leadership characterizes its failure to reverse the downwa
trend of union membership almost exclusively as a legal-political problem. Th
point to the rise in the use of union-busting law firms and the openly pr
business stance of the National Labor Relations Board. One AFL-CIO repo
contrasted the chilly legal climate in the United States with the warmer env
ronment in Canada:

> Canada has roughly the same type of economy, many similar employer
> and has undergone the same changes [as] in the U.S. But in Canada, unli
> in the U.S., the government has not defaulted on its obligation to prote
> the right of self-organization; rather, Canada's law carefully safeguards th
> right.[27]

The result, the authors went on to say, is that between 1963 and 1983, t
unionization rate in Canada has gone from approximately 30 percent to 4
percent, while in the United States it has dropped from 30 percent to abo
20 percent. The AFL-CIO leadership places most of the responsibility f
membership decline on the general political climate, absolving their own de
sory organizing efforts. Yet, as Paula Voos has shown, the real dollars devot
to organizing have remained remarkably constant since the mid-1950s, whi
money spent on legislative and publicity functions has greatly increased.[28] T
small amount of money devoted to organizing is the result of a conscio
choice by the union leadership rather than of the political climate.

Thus American union leaders pursued a cautious or "prudent" course in t
post-1974 period. At the same time, the rank-and-file confidence on which t
late 1960s–early 1970s militancy had been based evaporated. The threats
plant closings or relocation and other developments, such as "double-breasting
the establishment of low-wage, nonunion subsidiaries siphoning work away fro
established, unionized firms—threats that were rooted in the globalization
the American economy—all made it especially difficult for ordinary workers
regain the militancy of the earlier period. Nevertheless, a subsidiary element
this general picture has been the development of an alliance between the shrinki
minority of rank-and-file militants and an equally narrow wing of local unic
officials. The fight against steel mill closings that culminated in a one-day o
cupation of U.S. Steel headquarters in Youngstown, Ohio, the 1983 Greyhour

s drivers strike, the 1985–86 Hormel meatpackers strike in Austin, Minne-
ta, the 1985–1987 Watsonville strike, as well as the emergence of TDU and
e New Directions Caucus in the UAW all exhibit this pattern. Local acti-
ts in these cases became responsible for union locals and found that the
ly way to defend gains won in previous rounds of bargaining was to strike
ainst concessions or to actively oppose the policies of their national union
derships. This necessarily meant relying upon or even creating informal groups
rank-and-file militants, sometimes with ties to existing networks such as
ose sponsored by the Detroit-based journal *Labor Notes*. In some cases, re-
onding effectively to the demanding climate of the 1980s brought into the
en conflicts between local activists and more conservative national or inter-
tional union leaders. The qualitative difference between this pattern and the
ttern of cleavage between a much wider layer of rank-and-file militants and
relatively unified union bureaucracy in the late 1960s–early 1970s period is
ghlighted by several chapters in this volume.

APPROACH OF THIS VOLUME

is volume is animated by the conviction that the contemporary history of
e American labor movement needs to be studied in an interdisciplinary and
ethodologically innovative manner. Toward that end, the contributors have
und a number of social science literatures and methodological approaches to
useful in their analyses of the decline of organized labor. It should be noted
at no single approach could be expected to provide an integrated account of
set of issues that span economic, political, and cultural dimensions. Addi-
nally, the specific problem at hand, that of the decline of the U.S. labor
ovement, is one that calls into question conventional dichotomies, such as
e one that is often drawn between "domestic" and "international" spheres of
man activity. In this context, this volume emphasizes the need to go beyond
miliar pluralist approaches to interest group behavior.
A degree of eclecticism is not the same as assuming that all approaches are
ually valid, however. This volume emphasizes a consideration of organized
or in terms of two main approaches: neo-institutional, and class-conflictual.
addition, we have been enlightened by the contribution of social historians
the study of contemporary labor politics.
The neo-institutional paradigm has attracted considerable attention among
cial scientists in recent years. The emphasis here has been on the role that
stitutional structures and rules play in shaping political dynamics and politi-
l outcomes.[29] For our purposes, institutions will be defined as multitiered
ganizations whose rules, deliberations, conventions, and practices may con-
tute key ingredients in policy-making and other political processes. The best
rk in this neo-institutional paradigm draws on historical studies, understand-
g that institutional change takes place in a historical and political context
d that institutions themselves acquire histories that may be "opened up" for

examination and interpretation.[30] We also recognize the importance of the di
logue that has been recently generated between neo-institutionalist approach
and those that highlight the strategic quality of decision-making in politic
and economic activity, that is, the school of "rational choice."[31]

The class-conflictual approach does not have the special cachet that institu
tionalist analyses currently enjoy among social scientists. But it nevertheless h
much to recommend it in terms of comprehending the contemporary crisis
organized labor in America. The class-conflictual approach will be defined he
as a historical and sociologically oriented perspective that highlights the inhe
ent tension between different sectors of society as they respond to environmen
shaped by unequal distributions of resources and power.[32] In particular, tf
class-conflictual approach emphasizes the centrality of the workplace and tf
labor process in generating patterns of conflict—and collaboration—across cap
talist societies as a whole.[33] While it is important to recognize that politic
dynamics—such as, to take one example, the changing relationship between tf
Democratic Party and the AFL-CIO leadership—can hardly be reduced to cor
flicts centered around production, it is also important to acknowledge the con
plex role that such conflicts can play in conditioning wider political development
As will become apparent, the contributions to the present volume seek to d
ploy class-conflictual analyses in a nonreductive and nondogmatic manner.

Another important literature that is of obvious relevance to this project
the new social history that goes beyond descriptive studies of particular hi
torical episodes. With its emphasis on examining processes "from below," s
cial history has enjoyed a discernable impact on labor studies in North Ameri
and Western Europe.[34] Although much of this literature is unfamiliar to soci
scientists, a considerable portion of it is of direct relevance to political scie
tists, sociologists, economic historians, and others interested in the relationshi
between work, history, and politics. One reason many social scientists hav
been reluctant to integrate social history into their field of vision may be the
belief that social historians have neglected the political dimension to soci
action. Yet this is an issue that social historians have themselves recognize
and confronted.[35]

Some readers may already have noted that our focus is on trade unionism i
so-called primary sector industries such as auto, air transport, and steel. Fro
the 1930s onwards, these kinds of mass, privately owned industries have bee
regarded as the bastion of the unionized workforce and as the heartland
trade union politics. In the postwar period, of course, significant numbers
government employees—such as postal workers and blue-collar municipal worl
ers—also became durably fixed in the ranks of organized labor. This develo
ment has rightfully called into question the notion that unionized workers i
the private sector somehow have a more central role to play within trade ur
ion politics, and as a result the AFL-CIO has taken a number of steps t
ensure that leaders of public-sector unions are fully integrated into the highe
circles of the confederation.

While the emphasis in this volume is on developments in the private sector, we are clearly not wedded to a viewpoint that privileges non-public-sector employees. We have simply chosen to concentrate on some of the segments of the unionized labor force that arguably have taken the hardest hit in the past fifteen or so years. Our overall focus on primary-sector workers should not be seen as constituting a statement about which (if any) segment of the workforce is more central to the study of labor relations and the contemporary workplace, or to the creation of a new mode of progressive politics. This applies not only to local, state, and federal employees, but also to workers in the service sector, the vast majority of whom are unorganized at present.

In addition, our emphasis on specific industries and on specific sectors of the labor force is not intended to slight the work of those who have focused on the role of particular demographic groups, such as women, African Americans, Latinos, and so on. The same holds true for approaches that consider these questions in terms of religious or geographic-based cleavages. Indeed, several of our contributors pay special attention to issues of race and gender and their multifaceted impact on efforts to organize and mobilize sectors of the industrial labor force. With the exception of Michael Goldfield's chapter, however, they do so in the context of particular industries rather than looking at social groupings across industrial sectors or even across the economy as a whole.

ORGANIZATION OF THE BOOK

The essays collected here are tied together by their examination of two critical themes. The first theme is that the interest disjuncture between the layer of salaried, full-time officers—the union bureaucracy—and the rank and file is crucial to understanding union behavior. The second theme is that American capitalism has undergone a fundamental transformation, in part due to the globalization of production and financial markets, which has effectively undermined the preconditions for postwar-style American trade unionism. What emerges from the development of these themes is a distinctive portrait of American unionism during the past thirty years.

This volume is divided into two major sections. The first provides a theoretical overview of the economic and organizational dynamics that have helped undermine the capacity of labor interests to revive their institutions, expand their membership bases, and assert their political demands. While the importance of international and domestic political economy to this topic is widely recognized, the importance of organizational factors is perhaps less understood. This first section develops the major themes of the volume and looks at some of the ways that economic change and interest disjuncture within unions have contributed to the crisis of organized labor in the United States.

The second section provides case studies that emphasize political, economic, and organizational factors in the development of trade union politics in a number of different contexts. Particular attention is paid to organized rank-and-file movements, and their interaction with industrial and economic structures, in the trucking, steel, auto, and airline industries. The chapter that opens this section explores the applicability of the concept of "social unionism" to the prewar and wartime experience of the CIO in a way that raises important questions for contemporary trade unionism. The penultimate chapter considers the political implications of the "European Model" as it has been developed by progressive forces in the United States, and the closing chapter revisits the book's themes and advances some provocative solutions to some of the key problems currently facing organized labor.

Notes

1. As Grant McConnell, *Private Power and American Democracy* (New York: Vintage, 1966), chap. 5, has pointed out, this inattention is part of the wider failure to come to terms with the problem of the internal governance of private associations.
2. Sidney Webb and Beatrice Webb, *The History of Trade Unionism* (London: Longman's, Green and Company, 1920); Sidney Webb and Beatrice Webb, *Industrial Democracy* (London: Longman's, Green and Company, 1926); Robert Michels, *Political Parties* (New York: Free Press, 1962); Antonio Gramsci, *Selections from Prison Notebooks* (New York: International Publishers, 1971); *Leon Trotsky on Trade Unions* (New York: Monad, 1969).
3. McConnell, *Private Power*, chap. 5; Theodore Lowi, *The End of Liberalism*, 2nd ed. (New York: Norton, 1979), chaps. 2 and 3, especially pp. 57–60; J. David Greenstone, "Group Theories," in *Handbook of Political Science*, vol. 2, ed. Fred Greenstein and Nelson Polsby (Reading, Mass.: Addison-Wesley, 1975), 243–318.
    The pluralist tradition has had great influence on the social scientific examination of unions. For instance, there is a long tradition in labor economics that treats union organizations as unitary actors seeking to maximize something, usually wages. Classic statements include Henry C. Simons, "Some Reflections on Syndicalism," *Journal of Political Economy* 52 (March 1944): 1–25; John Dunlop, *Wage Determination under Trade Unions* (New York: Macmillan, 1944); Arthur Ross, *Trade Union Wage Policy* (Berkeley and Los Angeles: University of California Press, 1948). See also William J. Fellner, *Competition among the Few* (New York: Knopf, 1949); Allan M. Carter, *Theory of Wages and Employment* (Homewood, Ill.: R. D. Irwin, 1949); H. Gregg Lewis, "Competitive and Monopoly Unionism," in *The Public Stake in Union Power*, ed. P. D. Bradley (Charlottesville: University of Virginia Press, 1959), 181–208. Richard Freeman and James Medoff, in *What Do Unions Do?* (New York: Basic Books, 1984, chap. 14), argue that unions are democratic, member-dominated institutions.
    Orley Ashenfelter and George Johnson, "Bargaining Theory, Trade Unions, and Industrial Strike Activity," *American Economic Review* 59 (March 1969): 39–49, is widely considered to be an advance on orthodox economists' two-party bargaining model, as it appears to take into account differences of interests between members and union leaders. But, as Brian Hirsch and John Addison, *The Economic Analysis of Unions: New Approaches and Evidence* (Boston: Allen and Unwin, 1986), 92–93, point out, the failure to state explicit hypotheses of union leadership behavior that result from this divergence collapses the model back into two parties: "Despite

the authors' discussion pointing to a dissonance between the goals of the leadership and the rank and file, the Ashenfelter-Johnson model is in fact a two-party model involving management profit maximization subject to the union constraint. Union leaders do not pursue their own special interests independent of their members' preferences; indeed, they act as perfect agents for their . . . principles." As such, this model remains the functional equivalent of that advanced by pluralist political scientists and orthodox economists. For reviews of this literature, see Jeff Borland, "The Ross-Dunlop Debate Revisited," *Journal of Labor Research* 7 (Summer 1986): 293–307; and Henry S. Farber, "The Analysis of Union Behavior," National Bureau of Economic Research, Working Paper No. 1502, Cambridge, Mass., November 1984.

4. On the Thatcher model see, *inter alia*, Colin Crouch, "Conservative Industrial Relations Policy: Towards Labour Exclusion?" in *Economic Crisis, Trade Unions, and the State*, ed. Otto Jacobi, Bob Jessop, Han Kastendilk, and Marino Regini (London: Croom Helm, 1986); Andrew Gamble, *The Free Market and the Strong State: The Politics of Thatcherism* (London: Macmillan, 1988); Peter A. Hall, *Governing the Economy: The Politics of State Intervention in Britain and France* (Cambridge: Polity Press, 1986); and Kent Worcester, "Ten Years of Thatcherism: The Enterprise Culture and the Democratic Alternative," *World Policy Journal* 6, no. 2 (Spring 1989).

5. Seymour Martin Lipset, *Political Man: The Social Bases of Politics* (Garden City, N.Y.: Doubleday, 1960) offers an influential statement of the pluralist position. The research focus that flows from its theoretical framework is developed in Seymour Martin Lipset, Martin Trow, and James Coleman, *Union Democracy: The Internal Politics of the International Typographical Union* (Glencoe, Ill.: Free Press, 1956).

6. As Seymour Martin Lipset, "North American Labor Movements: A Comparative Perspective," in *Unions in Transition* (San Francisco: Institute for Contemporary Studies, 1986), 452, argues, "The American social structure and values foster the free market and competitive individualism, an orientation which is not congruent with class consciousness . . . or a strong trade union movement."

7. One of the founders of the pluralist school, David Truman, acknowledged the existence of competing interests within organizations, but other pluralists did little with his insight. See David Truman, *The Governmental Process: Political Interests and Public Opinion* (New York: Knopf, 1951).

8. Seymour Martin Lipset, "Trade Unions and Social Structure," *Industrial Relations*, no. 1 (October 1961): 75–89, and no. 2 (February 1962): 89–111.

9. Staughton Lynd, "Trade Unionism in the USA," *New Left Review*, no. 184 (November/December 1990): 76–87.

10. Graham Wilson, *Unions in American National Politics* (New York: St. Martin's Press, 1979), 104–5.

11. Meany: "You can be quite radical if you are involved in a labor dispute where people are getting 30 cents an hour, because [if you pull a strike] all you lose is 30 cents an hour. But [when] you have people who are making $8,000 or $9,000 a year—paying off mortgages, with kids going to college . . . you have an entirely different situation. . . . They have obligations that are quite costly—insurance payments and all that sort of thing. So this makes the strike much less desirable as a weapon. Naturally, we wouldn't want to give it up as a weapon but I can say to you quite frankly that more and more people in the trade union movement—I mean at the highest levels—are thinking of other ways to advance without the use of the strike method." Quoted in Archie Robinson, *George Meany and His Times* (New York: Simon and Schuster, 1981), 294–95.

12. "Back behind the Wheel," *The Economist*, 11 July 1970, p. 46. See also Jeremy

Brecher, *Strike!* (San Francisco: Straight Arrow Books, 1972), 271–74.

13. Paul John Nyden, "Miners for Democracy: Struggle in the Coal Fields" (Ph.D. diss., Columbia University, 1974); Paul Clark, *The Miners' Fight for Democracy: Arnold Miller and the Reform of the United Mine Workers* (Ithaca: New York School of Industrial and Labor Relations, 1981).

14. Quoted in Howell John Harris, *The Right to Manage: Industrial Relations Policies of American Business in the 1940s* (Madison: University of Wisconsin Press, 1982), 146.

15. U.S. Department of Labor, Bureau of Labor Statistics, *Characteristics of Major Collective Bargaining Agreements, January 1, 1980* (Washington, D.C.: U. S. Government Printing Office, 1981), chart 1, table 2; Michael Piore, "American Labor and the Industrial Crisis," *Challenge* 25 (March/April 1982): 5–11.

16. Mike Davis, *Prisoners of the American Dream* (London: Verso, 1986), 126.

17. Although these developments created confusion among militants, they were not unprecedented. In a similar context in Britain in 1922, shop steward leader J. T. Murphy argued: "In England we have had a powerful shop stewards' movement. But it can and only does exist in given objective conditions. These necessary conditions at the moment do not exist in England. . . . You cannot build factory organizations in empty and depleted workshops, while you have a great reservoir of unemployed workers." Quoted in Tony Cliff, "Patterns of Mass Strikes," *International Socialism* 29 (Summer 1985): 26.

18. Davis, *Prisoners of the American Dream*, 133–34; Wilson, *Unions in American National Politics*, 51, 100–102.

19. Thomas Byrne Edsall, *The New Politics of Inequality* (New York: Norton, 1984), 135.

20. D. Quinn Mills, "Flawed Victory in Labor Law Reform," *Harvard Business Review* 57 (May/June 1979): 93.

21. A. H. Raskin, "Big Labor Strives to Break Out of Its Rut," *Fortune*, 27 August 1979, p. 33. Davis, *Prisoners of the American Dream*, 135, terms "the destruction of its legislative program in the Democratic Congress . . . the biggest debacle in the AFL-CIO's history."

22. Thomas Ferguson and Joel Rogers, "Labor Law Reform," *The Nation*, 6 January 1979, p. 1.

23. Harry Katz, *Shifting Gears: Changing Labor Relations in the U.S. Automobile Industry* (Cambridge: MIT Press, 1985), 49ff.

24. AFL-CIO president Lane Kirkland sent a letter to affiliates attacking the idea of nationwide job action in support of PATCO: "I personally do not think that the trade union movement should undertake anything that would represent punishing, injuring or inconveniencing the public at large for the sins or the transgressions of the Reagan administration." International Association of Machinists (IAM) head William Winpisinger could probably have ended the PATCO strike victoriously simply by calling out IAM ground crew for a few days, bringing most air travel to a grinding halt. But he declined such a course of action as too risky. "Our attorneys warn us," he wrote in the Boston *Globe*, "that if I, as International president, should sanction, encourage or approve a sympathy strike under these conditions, I would risk the IAM's entire financial reserves." Quoted in "PATCO: The Time to Strike Is Now," and "Solidarity Forever," *Socialist Worker*, October 1981, pp. 3, 15.

25. Kim Moody, "Behind Greyhound's Union Busting," *Labor Notes*, 20 December 1983, p. 8. See also Kim Moody, "Who Says Concessions Are a Thing of the Past?" *Labor Notes*, June 1986, p. 1.

26. Edsall, *New Politics of Inequality*, 171.

27. AFL-CIO Committee on the Evolution of Work, *The Changing Situation of Workers and Their Unions* (Washington, D.C.: AFL-CIO, 1985), 15.

28. Paula Voos, "Labor Union Organizing Drives, 1954–1977" (Ph.D. diss., Harvard University, 1982).

29. See James March and Johan Olsen, "The New Institutionalism: Organizational Factors and Political Life," *American Political Science Review* 78, no. 3 (September 1984).

30. See, *inter alia*, Hall, *Governing the Economy*; Gary Marks, *Unions in Politics: Britain, Germany, and the United States in the 19th and Early 20th Centuries* (Princeton, N.J.: Princeton University Press, 1989).

31. Unfortunately, much of the recent work within the rational choice school is characterized by a highly abstract, ahistorical modeling of choice situations. Instead of proceeding in this manner, this volume recognizes the value of rationality as a metaphor for political action that takes place in a strategic environment. Case studies guided by rational choice can help us to understand how political actors face specific choices in particular situations, making decisions that influence the nature of future choices. See, *inter alia*, Russell Hardin, "Rational Choice Theories," in *Idioms of Inquiry: Critique and Renewal in Political Science*, ed. Terence Ball (Albany: State University of New York Press, 1987), 67–91; Margaret Levi, *Of Rule and Revenue* (Berkeley and Los Angeles: University of California Press, 1988). One interesting attempt to reconcile rational choice and institutional approaches is Ruth Lane's "Concrete Theory: An Emerging Political Method," *American Political Science Review* 84, no. 3 (September 1990).

32. See the editors' introduction in Ira Katznelson and Aristide Zolberg, eds., *Working Class Formation: Nineteenth Century Patterns in Western Europe and North America* (Princeton, N.J.: Princeton University Press, 1985); and Gosta Esping-Andersen, Roger Friedland, and Erik Olin Wright, "Modes of Class Struggle and the Capitalist State," *Kapitalistate*, nos. 4–5 (1976).

33. See, for instance, Richard Hyman, *The Political Economy of Industrial Relations: Theory and Practice in a Cold Climate* (London: Macmillan, 1989); John Kelly, *Trade Unions and Socialist Politics* (London: Verso, 1988); and Jonathan Winterton and Ruth Winterton, *Coal, Crisis, and Conflict: The 1984–85 Miners' Strike in Yorkshire* (Manchester: Manchester University Press, 1989).

34. We can only refer to a few of the better-known titles that have appeared in the field of social history. See Joshua Freeman, *In Transit: The Transport Workers Union in New York City, 1933–1966* (New York: Oxford University Press, 1989); Martin Glaberman, *Wartime Strikes* (Detroit: Bewick, 1980); James Green, *The World of the Worker: Labor in Twentieth-Century America* (New York: Hill and Wang, 1980); Nelson Lichtenstein, *Labor's War at Home: The CIO in World War II* (New York: Cambridge University Press, 1982); and Ruth Milkman, *Gender at Work: The Dynamics of Job Segregation by Sex during World War II* (Urbana: University of Illinois, 1987). A useful article that considers the possibility of synthesizing new studies of consciousness and language with older institutional studies is Howard Kineldorf, "Bringing Unions Back In (Or Why We Need a New Labor History)," *Labor History* 32 (Fall 1991): 91–103.

35. Geoff Eley and Keith Nield, "Why Does Social History Ignore Politics?" *Social History* 5 (May 1980).

2

Political Economy After Reagan

Chris Toulouse

INTRODUCTION

Caterpillar's Trump Card Threat
of Permanently Replacing Strikers Gave Company
Advantage Against Union

THUS RAN A FRONT-PAGE lead in the *New York Times* on 16 April 1992. The report began with an unusually forthright remark about the meaning of Caterpillar's victory in its battle to end pattern-bargaining with the UAW: "The abrupt end of a five-month strike against Caterpillar Inc. showed that management can bring even a union so mighty and rich as the United Automobile Workers to its knees by asserting that experienced machinists, tool makers and technicians add no more value to the products they make than an untrained job hunter who comes in off the street." Caterpillar chairman Donald V. Fites "said he needed greater flexibility to set wages, benefits and working conditions to protect Caterpillar's pre-eminent position in competition with companies in Japan and Europe."

This is the harsh reality for unions in the early 1990s. With their right to fire striking workers affirmed, corporations have now enjoyed the power to compete in global markets by running down the cost of labor for over a decade (since the Reagan administration set the precedent by firing the PATCO strikers in 1981). The results are well known. The context in which unions organize in the United States has been transformed. Whereas a generation ago, unions like the UAW were in the vanguard of a high-wage manufacturing economy and a union job was a route to middle-class status, today they look on in bewilderment as corporations cut wages in their American plants and shift investment in manufacturing abroad. With the service economy generating mainly low-wage work and a college degree emerging as the only guarantor of upward mobility, the core belief of American identity—that anyone can make it because America is basically a middle-class society—is increasingly the subject of anguished public debate.[1]

FIGURE 2.1   World Trade Flows U.S.-EC-Southeast Asia

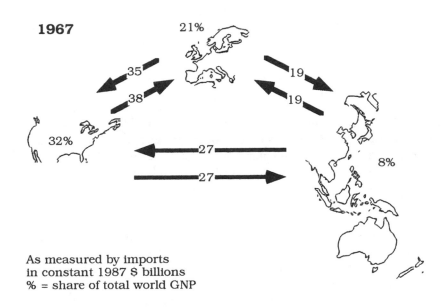

1967

21%

35

38

19

19

32%

27

27

8%

As measured by imports
in constant 1987 $ billions
% = share of total world GNP

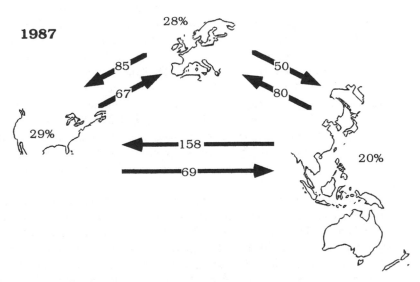

1987

28%

85

67

50

80

29%

158

69

20%

Source: *The Economist*, 24 December 1988.

CHANGING PATTERNS OF GLOBAL TRADE

Figure 2.1 illustrates changes in the flow of global trade since the late 1960s. As the work of Wallerstein and his followers has shown, the world system in itself is not a new phenomena: Indeed, trade between states strung around the globe predates the emergence of modern nations, and àn international division of labor for the production of goods was a hallmark of nineteenth-century imperialism.[2] However, it is clear that the restructuring of economic relations around the world in the last twenty-five years has produced a qualitatively new kind of global economy.

The figure illustrates the rise of Japan and the Newly Industrializing Countries (NICs) of Southeast Asia. Their share of total world gross natural product (GNP) rose from 8 percent in 1967 to 20 percent by 1987, in comparison to a rise in the European Community's (EC's) share from 21 percent to 28 percent, and a slight fall in the share of the U.S. and Canada from 32 percent to 29 percent. This reflects the success of Japanese corporations in American and European markets for electronic goods, computers, automobiles, and machine tools. It also reflects the success of corporations from South Korea, Taiwan, Hong Kong, and Singapore, which, with the aid of some highly authoritarian state policies, have inserted themselves into the production chains of American and Japanese corporations. By 1987 a greater volume of trade flowed across the Pacific than across the Atlantic.

The essential characteristic of the new global economy is interpenetration. Goods are still designed and, for the most part, marketed in the advanced capitalist societies, but typically they are now assembled where labor is cheap and readily disciplined (for example, in Mexico or Spain) from components manufactured by subcontractors in parts of the world where labor is cheaper and more readily disciplined still (for example, Thailand or China). The global market for capital, facilitated by information technology and financial deregulation, has induced a global market for labor. As multinational corporations have come to make their investment decisions on a global scale, national governments have lost the leverage they once had over macroeconomic policy (over interest rates and capital flows), and cities and regions—and the working people tied to them—now find themselves in increasingly cutthroat competition for jobs.

These are the key features of the new global economy as far as unions and their members are concerned. This chapter addresses the wider social and political forces behind this transformation. It is about the restructuring of the global economy since the 1960s and the polarization of American society that has come in its wake, particularly during the 1980s. Its central contention, like that of many chapters in the rest of the book, is that much of what has happened to unions and working people over the last generation is less the preordained result of economic forces and more the outcome of political responses to global economic change: in this case, the strategic responses of the

Reagan administration and its success in shaping the impact of global restructuring and engineering social polarization for its own political purposes. The opening section reviews the leading theoretical approaches to restructuring. After reviewing some problems with these approaches, it presents a fourth alternative that focuses on the Reagan and Thatcher governments' responses to restructuring in terms of a particular "hyper-capitalist" strategy. This strategy was aimed at reconstructing the economic growth and political stability of the 1950s by concentrating the benefits of prosperity on a narrower political majority. The second section traces the links between the hyper-capitalist strategy and social polarization and looks at some of the major social and political trends of the 1980s. The third section examines the consequences of social polarization for union organizing in the United States in the 1990s and looks at the question of how far the Clinton presidency might go toward reversing social polarization in the 1990s.

THEORIES OF RESTRUCTURING

The fate of the Caterpillar strikers outlined above is clear, but how can this fate be apprehended theoretically, that is, apprehended in a way that will offer us some insight into the future? A broad range of approaches have addressed the question of where American society is heading in the 1990s and beyond. However, three approaches have been particularly influential in addressing the strategic situation of unions: postindustrial theory, research on the role of high technology, and post-Fordist theory. It is beyond the scope of this chapter to provide a thorough review of all three. In what follows we will look simply at the major characteristics of each and note some of the problems that commentators have highlighted. With these problems in mind, we will then be in a position to consider an alternative approach.

Postindustrial Society

The most important proposition of postindustrial theorists is that American society is undergoing a transformation as profound as the Industrial Revolution. The current shift from the primacy of manufacturing in the economy to the primacy of services matches the importance of the nineteenth-century shift from agriculture to manufacturing. A new epoch in human civilization is coming about. Global restructuring and its impact on American society must be seen in this context.

The second major proposition concerns the centrality of services and theoretical knowledge. The postindustrial transformation is seen as a consequence of the growing complexity of industrial society and the increasing reliance of corporations and government on scientific research, technical problem-solving, and administrative proficiency. In Bell's original formulation,[3] in which preindustrial society was based on extraction and industrial society on manufacturing, postindustrial society is based on information processing. Knowledge replaces human labor as the primary source of value. Expert professionals replace entrepreneurs as the primary group in society. White-collar work situations become typical, and the key growth sectors are corporate services, government agencies, not-for-profit organizations, universities, and hospitals. As a more recent proponent of the approach puts it: "Boiled down, post-industrialism is a broad phenomenon that can be gauged along multiple dimensions. It encompasses a change in what we do to earn a livelihood (processing or services rather than manufacturing) as well as how we do it (brains rather than hands) and where we do it (offices rather than factories)."[4]

The third proposition concerns the political ramifications of the postindustrial transformation. It is on this question that the general idea of postindustrial society is best known. Here it is popularly used in conjunction with the idea of Progress (what you can't stand in the way of) to denote an evolutionary change in the character of society—change that is leaving left-wing parties and unions behind. In this guise, the term "postindustrial society" focuses on a range of phenomena associated with computerization that are held to make work more challenging, home life more fulfilling, and politics more a matter of personal choice and rational calculation than of group loyalties and worldviews. In 1992 Ross Perot's presidential candidacy played on these themes.[5]

The debate on postindustrialism has highlighted a number of significant problems. Critics have been harsh about the proposition that postindustrialism represents a new epoch in human civilization. As one sympathetic critic noted, the theory "has been perceived as deterministic, evolutionary, and essentialist in a period when these are seen as serious intellectual errors."[6] After the failure of governments to manage the crises of capitalism in the late 1970s and 1980s, it is difficult to be as confident of planning and progressive evolutionary change as many commentators were in the 1950s and 1960s.

The second proposition about services and theoretical knowledge has been subject to fierce scrutiny. The proposition implies a natural progression from an economy based on agriculture to one based on manufacturing to one based on services. Historical research has discounted this view: Only in Britain did manufacturing employment ever constitute a majority of the workforce, and even there, only in the first twenty years of this century. Everywhere else, manufacturing employment has hovered around 30 percent of the workforce, and the great transition has been from agriculture to services.[7] The proposition also implies that white-collar working conditions represent an advance on blue-collar conditions. The evidence here is complicated. In both white- and blue-collar jobs, there has been an increase in the level of skills required of full-time employees. However, this increase in skill has not always been met with commensurate increases in pay or, more importantly for postindustrial theory, by increases in work satisfaction. In addition, deskilling (the erosion of worker autonomy) remains a potent phenomenon in management efforts to exert control in the workplace—especially for low-paid part-time positions.[8]

Two further arguments can be made against the centrality of services and theoretical knowledge. The first is the argument made by economists Stephen Cohen and John Zysman in their book *Manufacturing Matters*. They argue that manufacturing is no more out-of-date than agriculture. Although agricultural employment has fallen, agricultural productivity has shot up, and modern agribusiness provides huge markets for manufacturers and services. Similarly with manufacturing. Cohen and Zysman estimate that up to one-third of business services are dependent on manufacturing: "Services are compliments to manufacturing, not potential substitutes or successors. The wages generated in services that are tightly linked to manufacturing exert an enormous effect on wage levels in services quite independent of manufacturing, activities as distant as teaching, government work, hairdressing, and banking."[9] Neither is high technology a substitute for manufacturing. Most new technologies produce intermediary goods that go into the finished product, and most of the value is derived from manufacturing the product itself.

There is also the argument that theoretical knowledge can hardly become the basis of a new epoch if knowledge is turned into a commodity like the manufactured goods that were the basis of the epoch before it. Bell held out hope that professional expertise would prevail and that the competition that characterized relations between entrepreneurs would give way to cooperation between experts dedicated to the public good. Unfortunately, it is all too easy to argue that corporations, having seen the uses to which information technology can be put, have rushed to redefine the laws on intellectual property in order to protect the application of theoretical knowledge for their own private purposes.

Finally, there is the issue of postindustrial theory and politics. As we have seen, there are strong arguments against the idea that the postindustrial transformation is a necessary evolutionary change, and these undermine the conservative political conclusions that are popularly associated with it. However, as a theoretical interpretation, postindustrial theory has a larger problem with politics: namely, that there is no particular role for politics in it. In Bell's original formulation, society is divided into three autonomous institutional realms: social structure, polity, and culture; and the postindustrial transformation is primarily a matter of change in the social structure. Other writers have used the idea of a postindustrial transformation as an economic backdrop against which they can evaluate specific government policies.[10] Either way, post-industrialism tends to lack a theoretical grasp of group conflict that provides the driving force of social change in other approaches.

High Technology and Global Restructuring

A second approach to global restructuring and its impact on American society comes from research on the role of high technology. Research has come from a variety of perspectives, within postindustrial and post-Fordist theory as well as from other schools of thought. Our purpose here is simply to highlight some major points from research findings. This will serve to address the question of technology raised by postindustrial theory and also to prepare the way for an assessment of post-Fordism.

The precise role of high technology in global restructuring is often misunderstood.[11] A number of points should be made to put it in proper perspective.

First, it is not a matter of high technology driving the restructuring process. This may have been the way reorganization was experienced by individual corporations and their managers as they were compelled to react to the innovations their competitors used to cut costs. But this view ignores the wider social and political context in which new technologies were being introduced, and the interest that really drove the process forward: corporations' drive to take advantage of a conservative pro-business political climate to reorganize the labor process and to lower the cost of labor. Innovation did not drive restructuring; innovation was put to the service of restructuring. Many of the technologies that facilitated this reorganization in the 1970s and 1980s had their origins in corporate research and development (R&D) for military use; It was only later that these innovations found civilian application.[12]

Second, we should be clear about what innovation means. it is not simply the invention of new devices; it can also be the assembly of existing devices into new products or, just as importantly, the development of new techniques of production. Take, for example, the invention of "mechatronics" that produced the numerically controlled (NC) machine tool:

> Three separate industries came together as midwives for its birth. Fujitsu, a leading supplier of communications equipment at the time, developed a compact little controller based on a cheap but highly accurate stepping-motor instead of the usual feedback controller (which suffered from wear and tear in the works). A bearing manufacturer, Nippon Seiko, perfected a ball-screw with friction low enough for the stepping motor to do its job. And a materials company came up with a Teflon-like compound for coating the machine tool's sliding bed—so both controller and bearing could work much more smoothly than ever before. Separately, each was merely a modest advance; together, they fused to become a powerful innovation.[13]

NC machine tools held out the promise of greater precision and adaptability than their electromechanical counterparts were capable of (instead of changing dyes to produce a new part, a different program could be run through the computer controlling the machine). More importantly, when generally applied— either to mass production or small-batch production—mechatronics gave corporations the opportunity to reorganize the labor process on the shop floor: to change work rules, training standards, lines of authority, and hiring practices.

Third, the opportunity to reorganize labor on the shop floor meant that the role of high technology in global restructuring was to a large extent less a matter of its actual introduction (new processes take time to perfect) than of the possibility that it would be introduced. The option of new technology gave added leverage to corporations in their relations with labor (in the office as well as on the shop floor), with consumers, and with national governments.

In the office, new technologies gave corporations the capacity to massively extend the range of their operations. In the 1950s and 1960s the national telephone network and the mainframe computer had made it possible for corporations to keep track of branch plants and stores supplying markets all over the country. After 1970 developments in telecommunications, like fiber-optic networks for data transmission and the fax machine, together with the introduction of the desktop computer, made it possible to orchestrate production systems stretching around the globe. After relocating manufacturing wherever labor was cheaper, corporations in many industries devoted substantial energies to integrating new technologies into their administrative and executive functions at home and to restructuring their white-collar workforce accordingly. These functions became increasingly specialized and grew most quickly outside of corporations in the rapidly expanding business-service sector (advertising, marketing, accounting, legal services, management consultancy).[14]

On the shop floor, new technologies gave corporations the opportunity to reduce their reliance on large unionized workforces and to upgrade what manufacturing they chose to retain in their home countries. The option of introducing robots and automated manufacturing systems made it possible to extract concessions from unions. The training and kind of labor required to operate the new systems divided workforces into high- and low-skilled groups in a way that made them much more difficult to unionize. The new office technologies made it easier to coordinate with low-wage nonunion subcontractors. In the meantime, computerized machines and processes, with their tremendous levels of precision, made it possible to open up markets for high value-added specialty products—for example, high-grade alloys instead of sheet steel and special insecticides instead of bulk fertilizer.

It is also important to consider what high technology meant away from work, in the home, for people as consumers as well as workers. High technology gave corporations the option of restyling all of the consumer durables of the early postwar period: washing machines, automobiles, and televisions all appeared with digital control panels and added functions. New technologies also made possible a second generation of consumer durables for consumers to aspire after and acquire: the VCR, the microwave oven, cable television, the CD player, the camcorder, the home computer. New technology made possible a proliferation of new consumer styles, and through databases and direct mail, producers were able to define and target new and narrower markets.[15]

Perhaps most important of all, however, were the new options that high technology gave corporations with regard to government. The political economy of the early postwar period was based on a significant degree of government influence over the flow of capital. In the broadest macroeconomic terms, exchange rates were fixed and governments set interest rates. There were specific regulatory frameworks establishing clear divisions between types of financial institutions and markets, and in many countries there were also controls over the import and export of capital.

In the 1970s this regulatory structure was weakened by the collapse of fixed exchange rates. In the 1980s it effectively collapsed under the advance of computerization and government deregulation. At the time, governments were motivated less by orthodox arguments about the benefits of free markets than by an interest in diverting some of the windfall from the explosive growth of computerized financial instruments through their own money centers. Nevertheless, the upshot was that governments lost many of the constraints they had once used to influence investors, and particularly the investment plans of large corporations.[16]

In summary then, high technology facilitated global restructuring. For the causes of the restructuring and for a sense of the direction social trends might take, we must look beyond research on technology to theories of the economic and political climate in which it was introduced.

Post-Fordist Capitalism

According to post-Fordist theory, high technology is being used to bring about a transition to a new stage in the organization of capitalism. Post-Fordist theory starts from Marx's belief in the chronic instability of markets in capitalist economies. According to post-Fordist theory, if capitalist economies are to function effectively they require a particular organization of supply and demand (a regime of accumulation), which is enforced and upheld by government (a mode of regulation). The regime that built the capitalism of the long postwar boom is Fordism, named after Henry Ford's invention of the mass-production assembly line. Mass production made mass consumption possible, mass consumption made mass production viable, and the two were brought together by government intervention after World War II. In the late 1960s and early 1970s, as a result of heightened global competition and industrial and social conflict at home, the Fordist regime experienced a regulation crisis. Out of that crisis a new regime of accumulation is emerging—a post-Fordist stage of capitalism. The first proposition of post-Fordist theory, then, is that this is a distinctly new organization not of human civilization but of capitalist society.[17]

The second proposition concerns the most important distinguishing feature of this new stage: flexible production. New technology and the breakdown of Fordist modes of regulation have given capital much more flexible machines, which in turn have allowed corporations to "flexibilize" their workforces, that is, to concentrate skills in a core work group and to use more part-time and short-term employees, either directly or indirectly through subcontractors. In Michael Piore's and Charles Sabel's version of this thesis, the transition represents *The Second Industrial Divide*. The crisis of Fordism has been resolved by political forces in favor of a new paradigm: The mass production of assembly lines is now being superceded by flexible production. Smaller firms, using flexible computerized production to meet specialized markets, are becoming the driving force of the economy.[18]

The third proposition characterizing post-Fordist theory was added to the body of thought by subsequent theorists and relates to the cultural consequences of the transition. For Fredric Jameson, postmodernism is the "new cultural logic of capital."[19] In place of modernism's rebellion against traditions, postmodern culture is characterized by nostalgia for the past, a pastiche of different styles from all periods of history, and an ironic disengagement from politics. Advanced capitalist economies now produce such a plethora of products from a global range of cultural sources that people's identities have become increasingly fluid and fragmentary. The British social commentator Stuart Hall sums up this view as follows: "We can no longer conceive of 'the individual' in terms of a whole, centred, stable and completed Ego or autonomous rational 'self'. The 'self' is conceptualized as more fragmented and incomplete, composed of multiple 'selves' or identities in relation to the different social worlds we inhabit, something with a history, 'produced', in process."[20]

The debate on post-Fordist theory has highlighted some significant problems. The first problem is whether we are really entering a distinctly new stage of capitalism. Many critics have their doubts. Given the severity of the recession in the early 1990s, it is tempting to argue that flexible production was a temporary fix to the crisis of Fordism, and that the crisis of the 1970s has now reemerged. Others have argued that many of the hallmark characteristics of post-Fordism are not new at all. Urban planners Susan and Norman Fainstein have pointed out that the decentralization of manufacturing, the rise of new industrial economies, the revitalization of city centers, and the dependence of cities on services are all trends that go back beyond the turn of the century.[21] Further along this line of thought is the idea that the welfare state represents a historical aberration in the history of capitalism, born out of the exceptional conjuncture that followed World War II. According to this view, there is nothing new about the social polarization of the 1980s. Now that global restructuring has broken the back of organized labor, capital is free to return to type.

More serious problems arise with the idea of flexible production. Robots and automated manufacturing systems are at the heart of post-Fordist theory, but surveys show that they have yet to be adopted on any great scale anywhere in the advanced capitalist economies. Where they have been adopted, they are often used to reduce the costs of producing existing products rather than to expand a product range. Their introduction is also severely disruptive of established routines, and they often meet with fierce resistance from management, let alone workers.[22] There are greater problems with the conceptual division between mass production and flexible specialization. Economist Karel Williams and his colleagues have argued that Piore and Sabel's distinction is impossible to sustain empirically. The majority of industries, and in particular the automobile industry, actually use a mixture of production techniques, and it is often difficult to decide just how inflexible a technique has to be to fall to either side of the divide.[23] As geographer Andrew Sayer puts it: "Capitalist industry has always combined flexibilities and inflexibilities, and what are possibly emerging now are new permutations of each rather than a simple trend towards greater flexibility, period."[24]

Similar arguments can be made against postmodern culture. Post-Fordist theory may mistake market fragmentation for product differentiation; that is, it may mistake a global range of producers for a global range of products. Even when the significance of such phenomena as CNN, MTV, Benetton, and Madonna is conceded, it is possible to question whether the multiple social worlds of postmodern consciousness exist in groups other than young music fans and the intellectual elite. After all, even if the global village and global celebrities are more immediate, they are hardly new phenomena, and the majority of cultural products are still bounded by distinctively national cultural styles (detective shows, soaps, sitcoms, the NFL). The fact that cultural analysis shows that media messages try to construct their audiences in new ways, or that certain groups use a wider range of sources in constructing their identities, does not mean that that majority of viewers apprehend those messages or use them in any different way than they used to.

There is a further problem with post-Fordist theory, which provides the point of departure for the approach outlined in the rest of the chapter. This is the problem of economic determinism. Post-Fordist ideas can be very useful in the construction of ideal types by which to compare the changes associated with global restructuring in the different advanced capitalist societies. However, post-Fordist theory often reads as if it were constructed after the fashion of the base-superstructure model of society, whereby global restructuring (changes in the economy) inevitably leads the state to accede to capital's demand for a reconstruction of the government-business-labor relations (changes in politics), which in turn leads inexorably to social polarization and cultural fragmentation (changes in ideology).

In other words, there often appears to be an implicit assumption that global restructuring is economically driven and that it is essentially a universal process with uniform results. The problem here is that post-Fordist theory neglects the role of politics and economic policy-making in shaping economic conditions in the first place. It also makes little allowance for differences in government responses to restructuring. In the words of geographer Nigel Thrift: "The French Regulation School parallels a regime of accumulation with a mode of regulation which leaves little room for the indeterminacies of social and political struggle."[25] According to Thrift, this bias may be fatal:

> What if the assumption implicit in many commentators' accounts, that the important trigger of change must be found in the productive sphere, is wrong? Changes during the 1980s can be described equally well as the result of the growth of fictitious capital combined with restructuring of financial and commercial capital, the redistribution of income, a massive consumer binge fuelled by easy credit, and an associated engineering of class and consumption.[26]

An Alternative Approach

An alternative approach to global restructuring takes this observation as a point of departure. The changes of the 1980s "can be described equally well" because in the United States and Britain that was what the politics of restructuring was all about. The approach adopted here focuses on the strategic response of the Reagan administration to the political opportunities created by global restructuring. It does not deny that the globalization of capital demanded a response from the state in all Western nations, but in order to analyse what has happened in any one society, it concentrates on the effects of the strategy the U.S. government actually adopted. It focuses on the way the party in power used government policies to shape the impact of the restructuring process, and it looks at the consequences for the economy, social life, and politics.

Political scientists Teresa Arnott and Joel Krieger have described the Reagan administration and its ideological soul mate the Thatcher government as hyper-capitalist regimes.[27] Their response to restructuring involved going much further than other governments were prepared to go to facilitate global restructuring. In West Germany and France, the social rights built up in the course of the postwar period were threatened during the 1980s, but they still survived. In spite of the *tendenzwende* ('turn-around') that saw Helmut Kohl's Christian Democrats assume power in 1982 and the defeat of François Mitterand's reflationary experiment in 1983, West German and French policy toward, for example, public investment, industrial policy, and unions remained very different from the analogous Anglo-American policies. In the United States and Britain, by contrast, the hyper-capitalist governments set out to challenge social rights and effectively to abrogate the implicit social compact that characterized the relations of government, corporations, and unions in the early part of the postwar period. As the next section will show, this had enormous consequences for the shape of things to come: for the impact of global restructuring on American society and the situation unions and working people find themselves in today.

THE POLITICS OF SOCIAL POLARIZATION

The Hyper-capitalist Response

Reaganism and Thatcherism were essentially defensive responses to the challenges presented by global restructuring. Both fed off the acute status anxiety of middle-class households. Although both were committed to restoring the rate of profit, this was not an end in itself but primarily a means of restoring rising living standards to their suburban electoral bases. Both were also essentially backward-looking. Reaganism in particular was driven by a fixation on Pax Americana and an idealized picture of the orderly society America was supposed to have been in the 1950s: It promised not so much to build a new America as to rebuild former glories. By the late 1970s this kind of appeal could elect Ronald Reagan president because the same fixation was shared by many blue-collar households. Their living standards were under threat from inflation, they bore the brunt of civil rights remedies through court-ordered bussing and affirmative action, and they, too, looked in vain for answers from the Democratic Party.[28]

It is important to distinguish intention and rhetoric from effect and outcome when analyzing the consequences of Reaganism and Thatcherism. The intention was to restore prosperity and political stability that had been shattered by the crises of the 1970s. The rhetoric claimed that this could be done by getting government off the backs of the people and letting the market decide. The effect, however, was to give advantages to those groups and areas of the country that were already strong. The outcome was to accentuate the social polarization associated with global restructuring and to restore prosperity and stability only on the basis of a much narrower political majority.

At the level of intention, both governments sought a redistribution of wealth and opportunities to shore up the living standards of the upper and middle classes. Where governments had once undertaken to provide prosperity for all, they now pledged only to secure prosperity for those who earned it. As Arnott and Krieger point out, this led the hyper-capitalist regimes to repudiate "the integrative strategies" used by their predecessors to incorporate unions and working people into the national political process. No longer did governments launch policies on the basis of improving the conditions of citizenship and extending rights to previously excluded groups. Now governments sought "an anti-welfarist legitimation" by promising to safeguard the privileges of some groups against the claims of others. As Arnott and Krieger put it: "Appeals to denominational, fundamentalist, or racist constituencies replace[d] the more common postwar egalitarian and universalistic claims of welfarism."[29]

At the level of effect, it is important to appreciate that in spite of the rhetoric about withdrawing government from the market, the hyper-capitalist strategy involved the concerted use of state intervention to favor some groups at the expense of others. This is true not only in the more obvious sense of tax and spending changes, which favored groups and areas of the country where government support was already strong. It is also true where the state deregulated and relinquished its role as referee. In the ideal world of free-market economics, the result of free and open competition between individuals is the enablement of the strong and the ennoblement of the weak. Eventually there is equilibrium and social harmony because the greater wealth of the strong "trickles down" into new opportunities for the weak. In the real world, however, deregulation only served to reinforce the advantages of the strong, and the enablement of the strong resulted in the enfeeblement of the weak.

Reaganism and Restructuring:
Tax Cuts, Spending Cuts, and Deregulation

The outcome of the hyper-capitalist strategy was a creeping polarization of American society. This will be reviewed later. First, we will look in more detail at the key aspects of the strategy as it was employed by the Reagan administration. We can see a pattern of strengthening above and weakening below running as a central theme through all the major policy changes of the so-called Reagan Revolution: through tax cuts, changes in federal spending, and deregulation.

The effect of the Reagan tax cuts is by now well known and only the major trends need be recalled here. The 1981 cuts were the first since the 1920s to redistribute wealth up the income scale. The immediate effect was to give a one-time boost to the better-off, but over the course of the decade, the tax changes exacerbated income inequality caused by occupational polarization and the growth in investment income. According to House Ways and Means Committee figures, from 1980 to 1990 the pretax incomes of the top quintile rose by 26.4 percent, but the after-tax gain was 29.85 percent. The equivalent figures for the bottom quintile are 5.35 percent and 6.85 percent, respectively. At the very top, in the richest 1 percent, the equivalent figures were 75.5 percent and 87 percent. In spite of the rhetoric of tax cuts, the vast majority of working Americans wound up paying more to the federal government by the end of the decade because of increased deductions for social security. According to Congressional Budget Office figures, the proportion of federal government tax receipts from social security taxes increased from 30.5 percent in 1980 to 36.7 percent in 1989.[30]

The changes in federal spending offered military Keynesianism for the suburbs and cuts in welfare support and urban spending for the cities. Between 1980 and 1986 defense spending more than doubled, from $134 billion to $282 billion, or from 23 percent of the federal budget to 28 percent. By 1987 Americans were paying sixty cents of every tax dollar to the Pentagon.[31] It should be clear what this meant to Orange County, California. In the 1980s the Los Angeles area alone received "about seventeen percent of total defense spending, and the local association of prime contractors likes to boast that the Southern Californian aerospace-electronics complex is a larger economy than India's."[32] By contrast, federal grants to state and local government (in 1982 dollars) fell from $109.7 billion in 1978 to an estimated $90.2 billion in 1987. It should be clear what this meant for New York City. Federal aid fell from 22 percent of the city's budget in 1976 to 10.8 percent in 1988.[33] Although aid from a booming New York State economy made up some of this shortfall in the mid-1980s, it could not close the gap. Mayor Ed Koch, like many other mayors and governors, made a higher priority of upgrading infrastructure and subsidizing commercial development than of reinforcing social support.[34]

Two policies stand out in the area of deregulation: the deregulation of banking and finance and of labor relations. The first area was essential to the hypercapitalist strategy. The deregulation of banking and finance, through the medium of the revolution in information technology, unleashed an explosive growth of financial instruments. The ease of touch-of-a-button trading made capital hyper-mobile. This had a number of important political effects. First, it made it much easier for the top 1 percent to protect the value of their investments. Second, corporations found it much easier to go into debt, while the emergence of the junk-bond market and the collapse of regulation in the savings and loan sector made mergers and acquisitions possible on a previously undreamt of scale.

Third, the growth of these new markets created hundreds of thousands of high-income computer-literate jobs in the cities, which in turn generated hundreds of thousands of construction jobs in the "renaissance" of city downtowns and suburban office parks.[35] Fourth, deregulation permitted the colossal expansion of personal credit that helped to underpin middle-class living standards in the 1980s. Some of the statistics on this phenomenon are salutary. Whereas in 1980 there were 12 million credit cards in circulation, by 1990 there were 289 million. Over the same period, the average credit card holder's debt rose from $853 to $2,350.[36] The very rapid growth of this market must have played an important part in creating the aura of suburban prosperity that served the Republicans so well in the 1984 and 1988 presidential elections.

The impact of deregulation in labor relations is dealt with extensively in the rest of this book. For the present purposes, we need simply note the Reagan administration's leading role in weakening labor's right to organize in the workplace: the PATCO debacle, with its public sanction of replacement workers, and the NLRB's lurch toward business interests. Suffice to say that corporations acted decisively on these precedents and pursued their restructuring strategies secure in the knowledge that they had the federal government's full support for breaking up pattern-bargaining, for busting unions, and for otherwise reducing the hourly wage bill as far as it would go.

In summary, the overall effect of the Reagan response to restructuring was to transfer wealth, public subsidies, and the benefits of government regulation from the bottom of the income distribution to the top, from the cities to the suburbs, and from working people to corporations. The restructuring necessitated by the globalization of capital was always going to have an enormous impact on American society, but the effect of the hyper-capitalist strategy was to intervene decisively to strengthen the hand of those at the top while weakening the defenses of those at the bottom. Three key social trends capture the outcome of the restructuring strategy: deindustrialization and uneven development; social polarization in the cities and suburbs; and the definition and demonization of the "underclass."

Social Trends in the 1980s

The 1981–1983 "Reagan recession" turned the deindustrialization of American manufacturing into a full-scale wipe out. Political economists Barry Bluestone and Bennett Harrison cite an estimate that between 1978 and 1982 the United States lost about 25 percent of the employment in large manufacturing plants (3.5 to 4 million jobs).[37] In one industry after another, corporations ran down their plants in the United States, often milking unions for givebacks on the way, before shutting up shop and investing in new production facilities where labor was cheaper—partly in "right-to-work" southern states but mainly in Mexico and in Southeast Asia. A large number of jobs were swept away in the tide of imports sucked in while the dollar was riding high on the wave of the "Reagan recovery." However, many more jobs were lost to outsourcing (sub-contracting) and to asset-stripping, which was used to finance many mergers and acquisitions, as corporations like USX (earlier called the United States Steel Corporation) and General Electric (GE) moved out of their old core businesses and diversified into more profitable businesses in the energy and service sectors.

Deindustrialization had devastating effects on traditional industrial communities. Laid-off workers lost pensions and health benefits, suffered higher rates of illness and family breakdown, and even when they did manage to find work, rarely found it with wages and benefits to match their former jobs. In company towns the effects were particularly traumatic.[38] The collapse of demand hit the local service sector and falling incomes hit tax collections and city services. Union leaders who had grown used to a life of comfortable cooperation with the firm were reluctant to recognize that management, their partners in social control, would break agreements made in good faith. Slowly the attributes of middle-class status began to drain away from many families and the atmosphere of a depression settled in.

One of the foremost obstacles in mobilizing any collective response to deindustrialization was the uneven character of recession and recovery in the early and mid-1980s. The recovery came first to the East and West Coasts, but the Midwest and parts of the South were susceptible to what became known as the "rolling recession" throughout the decade. More than this, however, mobilization was inhibited by the fact that different parts of the same state or even the same city could be experiencing very different economic fortunes at the same time. It was difficult to make common cause when economic experiences differed so much. Geographer Robert Beauregard sums it up: "Organizers' need restructuring to be dramatic. The nature of the process is frequently, if not always, the opposite."[39] In the absence of firm political leadership articulating any kind of explanation or alternative, from union leaders or from the Democratic Party, many blue-collar households became demoralized and cynical about politics.

Looking back from the end of the decade, however, it is clear that the twin growth poles of the "Reagan recovery" were the new city downtowns and the outer suburbs. Both benefited from the upside of corporate restructuring: the reorganization of executive and administrative functions. In the downtowns, new office towers accommodated growth in banking and finance, as well as those business services that expanded rapidly to meet the increasingly sophisticated needs of corporations trying to coordinate global production systems. At the summit of the urban systems, New York and Los Angeles became global cities, the key hubs in the electronic networks of global capital and entry points for the foreign investment and immigration attracted by rapid economic growth.[40]

In the outer suburbs corporations concentrated back office and R&D facilities in new campuslike office parks. Some of these became meccas of reindustrialization, as economic development officials flocked to decipher the synergies that made Silicon Valley, Route 128, Durham–Raleigh–Chapel Hill, and the Princeton Corridor centers for the new high-technology industries in microelectronics, software, biotechnology, composite materials, and so on.[41]

However, in both the new downtowns and the outer suburbs, the hyper-capitalist strategy intersected with the global restructuring to produce a creeping polarization. At work and in the neighborhood, out shopping and in the media, people's chances of prosperity, with all that that entails for the fulfillment of the rights of citizenship, began to drift in opposite directions, subtly and slowly in everyday life, but quickly and clearly when seen across the society as a whole over the course of the decade.

At work, on both the shop floor and in the office, there was a polarization in the types of jobs created through restructuring and reorganization. In factories where firms chose to upgrade their plant and move their product upmarket, regular line jobs disappeared in favor of smaller numbers of more highly trained technicians on the one hand and larger numbers of low-wage, often part-time or short-term workers on the other. Similarly, in the office, the ranks of middle management were whittled down, as firms concentrated on creating highly skilled project teams, serviced by lower-grade administrative assistants, and banks of low-wage, often part-time or short-term data processors.[42]

These trends show clearly where most of the new jobs were produced in the 1980s: in the service sector. Between 1980 and 1988, 15.2 million jobs were created, 26.9 percent of these were in retail, 16.3 percent in business services, 12.3 percent in health services, and 11 percent in restaurants. All are traditionally nonunion sectors paying low wages. According to a Senate Budget Committee Report in 1988, up to half of the new jobs created between 1979 and 1987 paid less than the poverty level for a family of four. Somewhere in the region of a third to a half of them were part-time or short-term. About a quarter of job holders now work part-time or short-term. Over 60 percent of the new jobs went to women.[43] By 1990 they still earned only seventy cents for each dollar men earned, which goes a long way toward explaining why moonlighting is increasing among women while it is falling among men.[44]

Global restructuring and occupational polarization had important effects on the geography of neighborhoods and the relationship between them. New types of spatial relationships were generated. Urban planner Peter Marcuse writes about the way in which New York City was quartered by the forces of global restructuring. These forces pulled the city apart into a series of discrete neighborhoods: the luxury city of the international elite, the gentrified city of high-income office workers, the suburban city of white-collar workers and blue-collar ethnics, the tenement city that they had fled and that now houses low-wage workers ready to get out, and finally the ghetto ("the abandoned city") of the trapped and dispossessed:

As residential locations, the quarters of the modern city might almost be described as being four separate cities, coexisting in time and space, interrelated with each other and often directly related as well with outside spaces (the users of the World Financial Center in New York City have as direct a relationship with the City of London or the hallways of Washington as they do with the Bronx or Harlem).[45]

It takes no great leap of the imagination to picture a similar process of quartering dividing up the suburbs, underlining the differences between counties with elite addresses and executive mansions, "edge city" office parks, commuter towns, struggling industrial suburbs, and minority projects.[46]

People's experience of shopping and the way they utilize media messages are two areas that are very difficult to quantify, and yet in qualitative terms they are probably as influential on political beliefs as are experience at work or in the neighborhood. Two general changes of circumstance are worth considering: in shopping, the proliferation of shopping malls, their gradation by status, and the bifurcation of the retail sector into upmarket boutiques and downmarket discount marts; and in the media, the dispersion of cable television through the suburbs. In both cases, the mass market represented on the one hand by Sears and on the other by the big three television networks has been superseded by the division of the market into outlets catering either to the needs of the many or the tastes of the few. The better-off (say, the 40 percent of households making $32,000 or more in 1990) have always been able to seclude themselves from the rest of the population at work and in their neighborhoods. The point is that increasingly they can do so when they go shopping and when they switch on the TV.

Economist Robert Reich has written of "the secession of the successful,"[47] the "fortunate fifth" who work for multinationals and business service firms and who help to manage worldwide operations. These are the people who live in the wealthiest suburbs. Their high salaries and investment income allows them to support what are, in effect, their own school systems and privately funded municipal services. They have the skills, confidence, time, and money to defend their neighborhoods from all comers, from the state to multinational property developers and energy companies. Mike Davis vividly dissects the frenetic nimbyism ("nimby": "not in my back yard") of reactionary white homeowners in the Los Angeles suburbs, and the laager mentality of the Los Angeles Police Department (LAPD) in his book *City of Quartz*. Urban sociologist Manuel Castells evokes the other-worldy feel of the privatized enclave, while at the same time raising the key theoretical issue when he writes:

> Secluded individualistic homes across an endless suburban sprawl turn inward to preserve their own logic and values, closing their doors to the immediate surrounding environment and opening their antennas to the sounds and images of the entire galaxy. The issue arises that in such a structure organized around flows, people, activities, and cultures that are not valued (or priced) could easily be switched off the network.[48]

This effect can be witnessed every night when local news shows broadcasting from downtown office towers report on city life through the prism of suburban fears about what's going on in the streets below.[49]

One group that was clearly switched off the network in the 1980s was the inner-city minority population. The gap in life chances between poor blacks and Hispanics and the white and minority middle classes grew at an alarming rate. A litany of indicators show a steep downward trend in male labor force participation and a steady rise in the incidence of female-headed households.[50] The poverty rates for black and Latino female-headed households are particularly horrifying: In New York City in 1987, 67 percent of single black mothers lived in poverty; the rate for Latinos was 80 percent. Nearly 40 percent of all the children in the city—500,000 of them—lived in poverty (twice the rate of the elderly). The value of public assistance in New York State fell so far that in 1986, public assistance and food stamps together were worth only 83 percent of the poverty level.[51] On a national scale, "for black families with children, in the bottom quintile, average annual income (measured by after-tax income and including housing assistance and food stamps), in 1987 was $5,112, or $98.30 a week—56 percent of the official poverty level."[52]

For white suburbanites, however, this was not the most pressing issue. The media pictured the poor as an "underclass," perpetually mired in poverty, living off welfare and drugs, filling up the prisons and the welfare rolls. In *Chain Reaction: The Impact of Race, Rights, and Taxes on American Politics*, journalists Thomas Byrne Edsall and Mary Edsall reason that for white suburbanites, the rise of the black middle class (their appearance at work, in the mall, and on TV) has broken up the old racial stereotypes and helped persuade whites that their's is no longer a racist society. Since racism no longer exists for whites, they now believe that black poverty must be the result of individual character failings and a pervasive refusal to accept personal responsibility. We may add that it is through this door that the Republicans stalked new racial stereotypes—most notoriously through the Bush campaign's Willie Horton commercial in the 1988 presidential race—and fostered new prejudices to take the place of the old and to explain away the causes of poverty.

Political Trends in the 1980s

Politically, however, it is important to appreciate that for the most part the hyper-capitalist strategy was a great success. The rate of profit was revived and economic growth was restored, at least for those who counted. In domestic politics, the 1980s were also considerably more stable than preceding decades. There were scandals (some, like Iran-Contra and the saving and loan bailout, of epic proportions) but no long-running crises to match the ghetto rebellions of the 1960s or the "malaise" of the 1970s. On the international stage, Americans and their way of life emerged as clear victors in the Cold War (in everyone else's eyes if not their own), and by the end of the decade, with wage rates and the dollar down and productivity cranked up, U.S. exporters were showing new competitive strength in the global economy.

Political stability was reconstructed, but on a much narrower basis than before. It was not only that government used state power on behalf of a smaller segment of the population and began to justify its policies by reference to the rights of individuals rather than the obligations of citizenship. It was also a matter of the effect of the "Reagan recovery" on public discourse and the political system. The 1980s saw a substantial contraction of the representative function of American democracy. As political commentators Thomas Ferguson and Joel Rogers document in their book *Right Turn*, by the time of the 1984 presidential campaign serious opposition to the direction that the country was taking had been effectively marginalized.[53]

The contraction of the polity is highlighted by the performance of two major indicators of the health of the political system: voter turn-out and incumbency reelection rates. Voter turn-out fell to its lowest point since the 1920s; only half the eligible electorate voted in the 1988 presidential election. Sociologists Francis Fox Piven and Richard Cloward counter the argument that this rate equals the regular 70–80 percent turn-out seen in Western Europe when it is figured as a percentage of those registered. In *Why Americans Don't Vote*, they show that regulations on voter registration are patently discriminatory against low-income voters. Inside the political system, politicians became ensnared in a web of highly paid professional campaigners, staff, and lobbyists. By the late 1980s, the iniquities of the campaign finance system and face-slapping politics of negative campaigning were producing incumbent reelection rates (of over 90 percent) seen elsewhere only in one-party states.

It is interesting to speculate about why there was no serious backlash against the hyper-capitalist strategy before the 1992 presidential election. A number of factors have been mentioned already: the uneven character of the recovery in the 1980s, the absence of any alternative to Reaganism, the fact that many families in the top 50 percent did quite well out of the boom in personal credit in the mid-1980s—certainly better than they remember doing in the 1970s. Certainly the character of the early 1990s recession accounts for much of the backlash; this recession hurt the ranks of middle management in the way the recession of the early 1980s hit blue-collar workers. At the same time, it is sobering to note that for all the populist overtones of the 1992 campaign, on the criteria noted above, American democracy did not become notably healthier. Turn-out improved, but only to 54 percent of the eligible electorate, and of congressional incumbents who sought reelection, over 90 percent were still reelected.

We will return to the question of the Clinton administration and what might replace the hyper-capitalist strategy at the close of the chapter. First we will look more closely at two emerging consequences of social polarization that will shape union efforts to organize in the 1990s: the character of the new political economy and the decline in working-class mobility chances.

THE NEW CONTEXT FOR UNION ORGANIZING

The difficulties that unions face in organizing in the 1990s are dealt with extensively in the rest of this book. The purpose of this section is to look at some key aspects of the social and political context—the strategic climate—in which unions will be attempting to organize. It will ·be argued here that this climate is likely to be quite different from that experienced in the recent past, or at any time in the postwar period. In some ways—thinking in particular of the industrialization of China and the North American Free Trade Agreement (NAFTA)—the climate will be just as bleak for working people as during the 1980s. In other ways, however, the 1990s may provide the scope for union organizing and activism not seen in many decades, with the continued decline of working-class life chances and a set of constraints that may well make it difficult for elites to respond effectively to popular discontent.

The New Political Economy

There are increasing indications that global restructuring and social polarization have brought what might be characterized as "a new political economy" to American society, and a new terrain to American politics. Although there is an obvious danger of stereotyping in using broad dichotomies, the transformation of the American political economy over the last generation can be outlined in the following terms.

In the old political economy, working people (typically men) faced corporations based primarily in national markets. They worked hard for their leisure time, but until the mid-1970s the economy was prosperous, and their wage packets brought more into the home each year. Their security was underpinned by an implicit social compact, by which the firm provided a career ladder from the shop floor into middle management and the government underwrote the costs of old age, housing, and education.

The new political economy is decidedly different from the old. In the new political economy, working men and women face corporations based primarily in global markets (or they work for firms dependent on these corporations). They work longer hours for less leisure, the economy is not so prosperous, and they are fortunate if their wage packets bring the same into the home this year as they did last year. The social compact no longer underpins their security, there are few career ladders left for those who did not go to college, and the government has slashed its support for all but the politically powerful elderly.[54]

In the old political economy life was characterized by what we might call (following historian John Alt) the "work-for-leisure bargain." In return for steadily rising real wages and material abundance on an unprecedented scale, workers were willing to accept management's domination in the workplace. In Alt's words, in contrast to the primacy of work over leisure under the brutal conditions of industrial capitalism, "labor ceased to have a determinant influence on the experience of daily life and gave way to the private gratifications of family life and consumerism."[55] For the first time, a majority of Americans were able to enjoy a level of material security reserved in previous generations for the middle class.

Now the Reagan administration's hyper-capitalist one-sided intervention in the restructuring process has enabled the strong to improve their chances of prosperity at the expense of the weak. For the top 20 percent, and particularly the top 1 percent, life has never been so prosperous. Their skills have never been so highly prized, and their investments have never been so well protected. For the bottom 20 percent, and particularly the bottom 10 percent, by contrast, chances of prosperity have diminished significantly in the last twenty years.

The effects of the new political economy show up in indicators of the health of two core premises of the social compact: the work-for-leisure bargain and the possibility of mobility into the middle class. The work-for-leisure bargain is being eroded. Americans are working longer hours. Between 1980 and 1990 the proportion of the labor force working more than forty-nine hours per week increased from 18 percent to 24 percent. Correspondingly, the median number of leisure hours has been falling, from 26.2 hours a week to 16.6 between 1973 and 1987.[56] More importantly, the ranks of the middle class are being squeezed, on the one hand by the whittling down of middle management and on the other by the collapse in middle-income job creation. Bluestone and Harrison report that nearly 90 percent of new jobs created between 1963 and 1973 fell into the middle of the income distribution. Between 1979 and 1986, the proportion fell to 50 percent. The effect was particularly marked for men. Between 1963 and 1973, 78 percent of new jobs taken by men paid middle-level earnings (which they define as $11,000–$44,000 a year). Between 1979 and 1986, that proportion fell to an astonishing 26 percent.[57] Whatever the merits of the traditional middle-class nuclear family as a forum in which to raise children, clearly this trend is decreasing the numbers of men able to play a traditional role in forming these families.

The effect of the new political economy also shows up in the statistics on inequality. Indicators of inequality all showed a marked decrease from the late 1940s until the mid-1970s, through the peak years of the postwar boom. After that the picture becomes more complicated, but over all, the trend is clearly toward increasing inequality.

In real terms, average weekly wages have now fallen back to the level of the early 1960s. Average household income, by contrast, is still at its 1973 level, but this is only because more women have gone out to work. In 1960, 18 percent of women with children under eighteen worked; by 1987 the rate was 65 percent.[58] Steady real incomes, however, do not mean steady expenses: increases in housing costs and college tuition have run way ahead of the rate of inflation, and two-earner households also incur extra expenses as a result of having the extra person working. A 1988 study for the Democratic

Party concluded that for the average family 20–30 percent of the money brought in by a second earner went straight out again in extra costs for travel and child care.[59]

In the meantime, average real income per capita in the United States has continued to increase. But this is only because those at the top did so well. The top 1 percent made 60 percent of all the gains in after-tax income in the 1980s. Because of the fall in weekly wages for the bottom quintile and the struggle for those in the middle to hold their own, the broadest measure of inequality—the GINI coefficient, which measures the degree of concentration of wealth—has now fallen back to its late-1940s level. As far as the distribution of income is concerned (let alone the distribution of wealth), American society is back to where it started in 1947.[60]

The Decline in Social Mobility

Perhaps the most important factor for union organizing in the 1990s will be the long-term impact of the decline in occupational mobility chances. It is important to recall the importance of the myth of social mobility (in the anthropological sense) for postwar American politics. Sociologically, there are reasons to doubt whether it was ever true: At least one comprehensive multinational study of mobility data from the 1960s and 1970s shows that when data are controlled for the rate of growth in white-collar jobs, American mobility rates fall back into the middle ranks of the advanced capitalist countries.[61] However, politically, the idea that any one can make it because America is basically a middle-class society was the keystone of political culture in the old political economy. It defined what it meant to be American.

Today that definition of American identity is increasingly the subject of anguished public debate. As political commentator Kevin Phillips argues in an analysis of the 1992 national election results, middle-class defections from the Republican Party can be traced to the disproportionate impact of the recession on white-collar jobs and housing prices. This impact was much greater than in previous recessions, and in some parts of the country it was greater in the suburbs than in the cities.[62]

There is also the matter of the swelling numbers of the working poor. In *The Forgotten Americans* sociologists John Schwarz and Thomas Volgy show that if the poverty rate had been measured according to the original concept of poverty pioneered by the Johnson administration (updated for changes in the relative costs of basic necessities), then the rate in 1989 would have been 22.8 percent instead of the government's official 12.8 percent: "At 56 million, the total number of Americans unable to afford basic necessities was nearly double the number of Americans—31.5 million—who the government's official poverty figures said lived in poverty in 1989."[63] According to Schwarz, in that year there were 5.9 million Americans in households containing eighteen million people who worked year round, full time, but who still lived below what he defines as a self-sufficiency threshold: "That is four to five times more Americans than are often defined to be in the 'underclass,' and more than half again as many people as were on welfare at any one time that year."[64]

As Schwarz also points out, there is nothing new about working poverty in the United States. However, there are at least three factors that distinguish the situation under the new political economy in the 1990s from the old political economy in the 1960s: the increase in raw numbers, with around 60 million people living below the self-sufficiency threshold today as opposed to 40 million in the early 1960s;[65] the apparent rise in the incidence of downward mobility from the middle class; and the poorer prospects working people now have of escaping what one of Schwarz's respondents (a young mother with two children) called "the treadmill to oblivion."[66]

This is particularly the case for the so-called baby bust generation. Mobility chances for younger Americans are in precipitous decline. Real median family income for families headed by persons under thirty is 13 percent lower than in 1973; for those headed by people with no more than a high school education it is 16 percent lower. A college education is still the surest route into the middle class, but only because of the contribution of working wives. In inflation-adjusted terms, the income of college-educated men has fallen 2 percent since 1973, while the income of college-educated families as a whole has risen 16 percent.[67]

The consequences of declining real incomes show up on a range of indexes of mobility and middle-class status. It is taking longer for young people to find steady work. In 1973 the majority of high school dropouts had found steady work by the age of twenty-two. By 1991 the equivalent age was twenty-six.[68] The proportion of people twenty-five to thirty-four years old living at home with their parents rose from 16 percent in 1970 to 23 percent in 1990.[69] The proportion of the same age range owning their own homes fell from 52 percent in 1973 to 44 percent in 1990. "The problem, unsurprisingly, can be summed up as one of cost versus income. In the twenty years from 1970 to 1990, the median price of a starter home for a typical married couple between 25 and 29 years old rose by 21 percent in constant dollars, while the income of this typical couple declined by 7 percent."[70] The contrast with the 1950s is dramatic. Then, a thirty-year-old man typically spent 14 percent of his gross income on housing costs; by 1973 that figure had risen to 21 percent; by the mid-1980s it was 44 percent.[71]

The impact on the generation to come has been particularly brutal. The rate of child poverty in the United States increased from 14.4 percent in 1973 to 20 percent in 1991. Over the same period, the erosion of benefit levels and tightened eligibility requirements reduced the proportion of children in poverty receiving welfare from 81 percent to 50 percent.[72]

If present trends continue, not only will the next generation be less secure than the baby boomers—as health costs continue to climb and pension coverage shrinks—they will also be materially less well off, as the cost of home ownership follows the cost of a college education up the income scale and age range and out of sight. At the same time, this is the generation that is supposed to become more flexible and productive than ever as America scrambles to keep up payments on the national debt.

It takes no great foresight to envision a new generation gap opening up in American politics along the class lines. The new political economy simply cannot deliver the same levels of mass mobility as the old. The gap between classes and generations will become ever more obvious as producers and advertisers continue to chase discretionary spending as it retreats into the suburban bastions of the older and better educated. Icons of the old political economy will come to seem increasingly out of place: television ads that once reinforced consumerism will instead come to highlight the gap between splendid sexy imagery and squalid dull reality. It is possible that the whole nature of the work-for-leisure bargain, and even the centrality of consumerism in American culture, may be thrown open for question in a way that they have never been before.

Beyond Hyper-Capitalism

This brings us to the questions of what will replace the hyper-capitalist strategy and how far the Clinton administration and its successor might go toward reversing social polarization in the 1990s. Will the American political system once again display its famed adaptability and accommodate popular discontent, as it did in the 1930s and 1960s, the last junctures at which it faced a popular upsurge? It is tempting to make the analogy between these periods and the 1990s, and Kevin Phillips popularized the idea of a new reckoning in his book *The Politics of Rich and Poor: Wealth and the American Electorate in the Reagan Aftermath.* The election of Bill Clinton would seem to bear out his forecast. On the campaign trail, Clinton made a point of reaching out to younger Americans, with talk of a new kind of national service to pay back college loans, as well as talk of an industrial policy to get the economy growing again by pressing government into the service of global competitiveness.

It is not difficult to foresee the general form that the new governing strategy must take. It will have to be a reintegrative strategy, aimed at persuading groups that were excluded by Reaganism that the government is aware of their interests and ready to address them. In light of the federal budget deficit, the leading theme is likely to be one of shared sacrifice, perhaps with some corporatist overtones (business, tax payers, and government sharing the burden). Government will take two main approaches to shape economic restructuring: investment in human capital, focusing on education and training and health care reform; and investment in infrastructure and R&D, focusing on defense conversion.

Although it is difficult to predict the exact content of the new reintegrative strategy (that will depend on the course of political conflict), it is possible to discern five factors that will constrain the ways in which it can develop.

1. SUSTAINING THE ELECTORAL COALITION. Support for the Democrats in 1992 was not strong, and much of it was conditional on government delivering specific benefits to particular constituencies. This will have to happen at a time when financial markets will be keen to see the president and Congress cut spending in order to reduce the federal budget deficit. An immediate problem for the Democrats is that different constituencies support their two main approaches to restructuring. Broadly speaking, support for the human capital approach is greater among consumers (the young, the working poor, and the frightened middle class), while support for infrastructure investment is greater among big producer groups (corporations, state and local governments, and unions). Since the federal government has rather more control over infrastructure spending than over education or health, it will be tempted to concentrate more of its efforts in that direction, leaving consumers disappointed.

2. THE LACK OF PRECEDENTS. Then there is the problem of having no clear precedent to follow. It is not simply a matter of avoiding the pitfalls of the Johnson and Carter administrations. Two examples from the 1980s do offer partial alternatives to the hyper-capitalist strategy. For the human capital approach, there is the example of West German meso-corporatism—collaboration between business, labor, and government at the regional level to upgrade the existing manufacturing base in an effort to capture and dominate niche markets for highly specialized products. For the infrastructure approach, there is the example of French investment in such high-tech projects as the *Train à Grande Vitesse* (TGV) high-speed rail network and the technopoles (high technology centers) around French cities.[73]

Unfortunately for the federal government, vital ingredients are missing from the American case: the strong unions that were essential in West Germany, and the capacity of local government to run up huge debts that was essential in France. In any case, although both approaches were relatively successful in sustaining growth and living standards in the late 1980s, this was mainly for people in work. Neither did very much for those out of work, and both countries continue to face considerable problems with youth and long-term unemployment.

3. MAINTAINING INVESTOR CONFIDENCE. More than ever this is a matter of maintaining the confidence of foreign investors, since U.S. corporations can now move their capital in and out of the country as readily as can foreigners and have the same general interests. As long as the recession persists in the global economy, it seems likely that major institutional investors from the United States and abroad will be prepared to finance further deficit spending in the hope that it will kick start the great growth engine of American middle-class demand. However, if and when there is a global upturn, it appears equally likely that other investment opportunities will arise offering investors more attractive rates of return—China and Southeast Asia, Latin America, and even Eastern Europe. The relative weight of the American economy in global trade will continue to decline, and in that case, the federal government could well find itself subject to the kind of capital flight and currency crises that have crippled the economic programs of left-leaning governments in Britain and France.

4. CONFLICTING DEFINITIONS OF THE PROBLEM.   This is the issue of deciding what the reintegrative strategy is for. To the majority of working people who voted for Bill Clinton, the major problem to be addressed is the deterioration in life chances that has come in the wake of the hyper-capitalist response to global restructuring. The majority of the nation's economic and political elites, however, more often see social polarization as an unfortunate side effect, and declining American competitiveness in the global economy as the major problem. This difference in definitions has crucial implications for the way the human capital and infrastructure approaches will be put into practice and for the politics of sustaining the electoral coalition.

It is very important to put elite anxiety about American competitiveness in the proper perspective. It can be argued that by the late 1980s, the hyper-capitalist strategy—by so drastically changing the balance of power in the American workplace and in the political system—had done a remarkable job of pushing American corporations back on top again. Although the proportion of the labor force employed in manufacturing fell during the 1980s, the contribution of manufacturing to the gross domestic product (GDP) actually rose. On the back of a cheap dollar and low wages, America's share of world trade in manufactured exports increased from 14 percent in 1987 to 18 percent in 1991, 1 percent higher than Japan's. According to the weekly news journal *The Economist* (in many ways the house organ of international finance), American iron and steel, aircraft, pharmaceuticals, electrical machinery, telecommunication equipment, and clothing are all highly competitive on world markets.[74]

Much media coverage of the issue puts the accent on falling rates of productivity growth. But the fixation on productivity growth overlooks the fact that America has high rates of productivity to start with. In the mid-1980s America had higher productivity across the whole economy than did any of its large rivals. This is partly because the personal computer (PC) revolution has spread so much further in the United States than in Japan or Western Europe and because America has higher productivity in services (even if it is difficult to measure). But it is also because productivity growth in American manufacturing recovered in the 1980s and was actually higher than Japan's or Germany's (Britain was highest, followed by France). Contrary to received wisdom, output per hour in American manufacturing is equal to Japan's and half as high again as Germany's.[75]

Contrary to elite assertions, then, American corporations are in fact very competitive in the global economy. It is hardly surprising that the major problem for economic elites is how to sustain that competitiveness. Their own incomes and wealth are directly at stake. For political elites, however, sustaining competitiveness may not be the most pressing problem. What they are more likely to be judged on by the majority of working people is how well they can mitigate the social costs of competitiveness.

A reintegrative strategy aimed at the one without addressing the other will not be up to the task of sustaining the electoral coalition. One of the gravest dangers for the Clinton administration would come from following an elite definition of the problem and pursuing an industrial policy that, while it may, in time, boost economic growth and increase the quantity of jobs, would do nothing to improve the quality of employment and the way American corporations use labor. Such a strategy might help sustain profits and business support, but it will not in itself do anything to reverse the decline of real wages and improve working-class life chances.

The most obvious way to improve the quality of employment would be to strengthen unions' rights to organize in the workplace, to contest the rampant abuse of low-skilled labor, and to force employers to accord as high a priority to the needs of their workers as they do to their shareholders, executives, and bankers. After Reaganism, however, the balance of power will have to be shifted a long way back to the left if unions are to effectively improve working conditions. And there are powerful corporate donors in the Democratic Party ready to lobby hard against such measures every step of the way.

5. THE INSULARITY OF THE ELITE.   Finally, there is the issue of how adaptable the nation's economic and political elites are likely to be if the constraints outlined above prevent the Clinton administration from generating a viable reintegrative strategy. Although elites can respond swiftly when they feel threatened, there are good reasons for arguing that the hyper-capitalist strategy has produced an elite that is more insulated from the rest of society than it has been in the past.

Both multinational corporations and the "fortunate fifth" who work for them have lost the direct connection they once had with the economic fortunes of the rest of the population. It has become a truism that if capital takes a dislike to the local business climate it can quickly move on. The point is that when it moves on, the jobs of the top 20 percent (households making more than $64,000 in 1990) do not go with it. They stay where they are in the big cities, in corporate headquarters and the firms that service them. Even when they do lose their jobs in a corporate reshuffle, the elite have little fear of downward mobility. They are cushioned by investment income and have the kind of highly prized skills that quickly find them work elsewhere.

Elite experience of the decline of middle-class society and of the country's most pressing social problems is therefore very different from that of the rest of the population. Commuting between privatized enclaves, patrolled by private security forces, the elite are well protected from the collapse of public safety in America's cities. At home they live among a clutter of electronic gadgets that seem to provide ample evidence of the creative genius of capitalism:

they are hooked up to HBO and America Online; they can summon up Mozart as if they were in a concert hall or *Top Gun* as if they were in a movie theater. Even where they are socially progressive ("yes, let everyone make their own choices about how to spend their money"), they will always have a strong material incentive to remain economically conservative ("but let everyone be free to make as much money as they want"). After all, if it was simply a matter of hard work for them, why should it not be a matter of hard work for everyone else?[76]

There is also the matter of just how strong the elite have become. For the most part, multinationals are still headquartered in America, but (as with Caterpillar, Inc.) they now make their investment decisions on a global scale. The hyper-capitalist strategy, combined with the impact of information technology, has massively increased the leverage of corporations over government, unions, and consumers. It is important to see that this is not only a matter of the mobility of capital; it is also a matter of the power to collect, analyze, and act on information. Multinationals are at the hub of the networks and are the gatekeepers to some of the most powerful databases. This is true not just in marketing products but also in marketing political ideas, as in direct-mail fund-raising and mass lobbying. They are adept and rehearsed at defining the way politicians understand economic issues and make economic policy.

For these reasons, it is arguable that an elite response may not be forthcoming to accommodate popular discontent, and in that case, the famed adaptability of the American political system will fail, and we may be in for a period in which a much more profound challenge to the system can take shape.

CONCLUSION

This chapter looked at the broad sociological context in which unions organize. It analyzed the way in which global restructuring and social polarization have transformed American society and politics.

We began by looking at theories that might explain some of the key features of the conflict at Caterpillar, Inc., outlined in the introduction. Three leading approaches were assessed—postindustrial theory, research on the role of high technology, and post-Fordist theory—and problems were noted with each. We then looked at an alternative approach: one that focuses on the Reagan administration's hyper-capitalist response to the challenge of global restructuring. In the second section we looked at some of the major policy changes of the Reagan administration and noted that each of them had the strategic effect of strengthening the hand of those at the top while weakening the defenses of those at the bottom. We traced the outcome of this process in a creeping polarization: at work, in the neighborhood, out shopping, and in the media. We noted that in political terms at least, the hyper-capitalist strategy was a success, at least for those who counted.

The third section dealt with key aspects of the context for union organizing

in the 1990s. A contrast was made between the new political economy brought
by global restructuring and social polarization and the old political economy
of the postwar boom. It was argued that the most important development
arising from the transition for unions will be the decline of working-class mobility
chances. This factor may give unions the opportunity to organize on a new
scale, especially if—as anticipated—multinational corporations and the suburban elite succeed in defining declining mobility as a problem of global competition and productivity to be fixed by more sacrifices on the part of working
people.

There remains one essential issue that must be addressed. This chapter has
concentrated on the changing politics of social class. If the strategic political
climate in the next decade is to seed the ground for a new generation of working-class organization, then that organization will have to find a path through
the deep thicket of racism in American society. Already increased competition
for jobs whose wages will support a family is eroding Americans' commitment
to affirmative action. For all the success of the civil rights movement in establishing a black middle class, it is more likely than not that it will shrink in the
next generation. There is an equally serious likelihood of a new nativist backlash against migrant labor. The United States has not thus far seen the kind of
anti-immigrant fervor that has driven much of French and West German politics in the last few years, but if the new reintegrative strategy fails, then a
whites-come-first politics (already aired by the likes of David Duke, Jesse Helms,
and Patrick Buchanan) would be any easy resort for elements of the Republican Party and a seductive diversion for the political mainstream.

Two of the leading positions on the question of race and working-class organization are represented by the views of political economist Mike Davis and
journalists Thomas and Mary Edsall. At the conclusion of *Prisoners of the American
Dream* Davis argues that since American capitalism is a global empire, it can
only be effectively challenged by an alliance of the most oppressed groups,
both at home (in links between the trade union left and the minority working
classes) and abroad (in links to insurgents in the developing world): "My thesis is that, if there is to be any popular left in the 1990s, it will develop in the
first instance through the mobilization of the radical political propensities in
the Black—and, perhaps, Hispanic—working classes. . . . This is the nation
within a nation, society within a society, that alone possesses the numerical
and positional strength to undermine the American empire from within."[77]

The analysis put forward by Thomas and Mary Edsall in their book *Chain
Reaction: The Impact of Race, Rights, and Taxes on American Politics* effectively
rules such a strategy out. Even if a new left alliance did succeed in organizing
the many fragments marginalized by Reaganism, it would soon run up against
the impenetrable racial antipathy of the bulk of the white working and middle
classes. For the Edsalls, this is the tragic legacy of liberalism: "Among Democrats and liberals, the stigmatization—that is, the discrediting—of racism in
the 1960s had the unintended, detrimental, and paradoxical consequence of

stigmatizing the allegiance of many voters to a whole range of fundamental moral values."[78]

There are problems with both positions. The Edsalls' portrait lends too much credence to the conservative stereotype that the Democrats clung to liberalism in the 1980s (conspicuous by its absence in their 1984 and 1988 presidential campaigns) and neglects the Democrats' failure to address the economic interests of their traditional constituencies. The Edsalls' assertions about the potency of race-baiting over issues like taxes and quotas may also be overdrawn: At times, they make it sound as if white Americans are now so suffused with racial superstition that they have become utterly incapable of judging their own self-interest. More likely, for every vote that race-baiting decides, it puts somebody else off voting all together. As far as the Republicans were concerned in the 1980s, the effect was the same, but for the possibility of overcoming racial divisions in the 1990s, it may mean something quite different.

The problem with Davis's solution is that it might allow reactionary elements to inflame racist sentiments at the very point at which such sentiments might be superseded by divisions of class. It is unlikely that the question of race will ever be entirely resolved in American politics. The continual reconstruction of racial categories is too bound up with deep-rooted institutional and cultural practices.[79] Indeed, the very meaning of freedom under the present Constitution is defined by the experience of slavery. However, it may be that the collapse of the myth of middle-class mobility in the next two decades will provide the opportunity to push race and race-baiting back from its dominant position on the electoral agenda and to attach questions of social morality ever more firmly to economic issues instead.

Notes

1. Witness the public response to the series of articles by Donald Barlett and James Steele in the *Philadelphia Inquirer* in Fall 1991, subsequently published as *America: What Went Wrong* (Kansas City: Andrews and McCee, 1992).
2. See Christopher Chase-Dunn, *Global Formation: Structures of the World Economy* (Oxford: Blackwell, 1989).
3. Daniel Bell, *The Coming of Post-Industrial Society* (New York: Basic Books, 1973).
4. H. V. Savitch, *Post-Industrial Cities: Politics and Planning in New York, Paris, and London* (Princeton, N.J.: Princeton University Press, 1989).
5. There is a more radical interpretation of postindustrialism in the work of Alain Touraine, *The Post-Industrial Society* (New York: Random House, 1971); and Andre Gorz, *Farewell to the Working Class* (Boston: South End Press, 1982). This interpretation is not addressed here.
6. Fred Block, *Postindustrial Possibilities: A Critique of Economic Discourse* (Berkeley and Los Angeles: University of California Press, 1990), 7.
7. See for example John Urry, "Some Social and Spatial Aspects of Services," *Environment and Planning D: Society and Space* 5 (1987): 5–26.
8. See Block, *Postindustrial Possibilities*, chap. 4; and Krishan Kumar, *Prophecy and Progress: The Sociology of Industrial and Post-Industrial Society* (New York: Penguin, 1978), 7.

9. Stephen Cohen and John Zysman, *Manufacturing Matters: The Myth of the Post-Industrial Economy* (New York: Basic Books, 1987), 7.

10. See, *inter alia*, Savitch, *Post-Industrial Cities*; and John Mollenkopf, *The Contested City* (Princeton, N.J.: Princeton University Press, 1983).

11. On the relation between technology and politics see Donald MacKenzie and Judy Wacjman, eds., *The Social Shaping of Technology* (Milton Keynes, England: Open University Press, 1985), particularly chap. 1, Langdon Winner, "Do Artifacts Have Politics?," 26–38.

12. Gareth Locksley, "Information Technology and Capitalist Development," *Capital and Class*, no. 27 (1987): 81–105.

13. Nicholas Valery, "Thinking Ahead: A Survey of Japanese Technology," *The Economist*, 2 December 1990. Other useful (and unsigned) articles that have appeared in *The Economist* include "The Endless Road: A Survey of the Car Industry," 17 October 1992; "A Question of Communication: A Survey of Information Technology," 16 June 1990; and "Minds in the Making: A Survey of Artificial Intelligence," 14 March 1992.

14. For a recent account of this process, see Saskia Sassen, *The Global City: New York, London, Tokyo* (Princeton, N.J.: Princeton University Press, 1991).

15. See, for example, "Almost Grown: A Survey of the Music Business," *The Economist*, 21 December 1991; and "Fast Forward: A Survey of Consumer Electronics," *The Economist*, 13 April 1991.

16. See Adrian Hamilton, *The Financial Revolution* (London: Penguin, 1986); and Susan Strange, *Casino Capitalism* (Oxford: Blackwell, 1986).

17. The equivalent of Bell's seminal work for post-Fordist theory is Michel Aglietta, *A Theory of Capitalist Regulation* (London: New Left Books, 1979).

18. Michael Piore and Charles Sabel, *The Second Industrial Divide: Possibilities for Prosperity* (New York: Basic Books, 1984). See also D. Leborgne and A. Lipietz, "New Technologies, New Modes of Regulation: Some Spatial Implications," *Environment and Planning D: Society and Space* 6 (1988): 263–80.

19. Fredric Jamieson, "Postmodernism, or the Cultural Logic of Late Capitalism," *New Left Review* 146 (1984): 53–93.

20. Stuart Hall, "The Meaning of New Times," in ed. Stuart Hall and Martin Jacques, *New Times: The Changing Face of Politics in the 1990s* (London: Lawrence and Wishart, 1989), 116–34.

21. Susan Fainstein and Norman Fainstein, "Technology, the New International Division of Labor, and Location: Continuities and Disjunctures," in *Economic Restructuring and Political Response*, ed. Robert Beauregard (Beverly Hills, Calif.: Sage, 1989), 17–39.

22. See Harley Shaiken, *Work Transformed: Automation and Labor in the Computer Age* (Lexington, Mass.: Lexington Books, 1986).

23. Karel Williams, Tony Cutler, John Williams, and Colin Haslam, "The End of Mass Production?" *Economy and Society* 16, no. 3 (1987): 405–39.

24. Andrew Sayer, "Postfordism in Question," *International Journal of Urban and Regional Research* 13, no. 4 (1989): 666–93.

25. Nigel Thrift, "New Times and Spaces? The Perils of Transition Models," *Environment and Planning D: Society and Space* 7 (1989): 127–30.

26. Thrift, "New Times and Spaces?"

27. Teresa Arnott and Joel Krieger, "Thatcher and Reagan: State Theory and the 'Hypercapitalist Regime,'" in *New Political Science* 4 (1982): 9–37.

28. For a comparison of Reaganism and Thatcherism see Joel Krieger, *Reaganism, Thatcherism, and the Politics of Decline* (New York: Oxford University Press, 1986). On Thatcherism see Kent Worcester, "Ten Years of Thatcherism: The Enterprise

Culture and the Democratic Alternative," *World Policy Journal* 6, no. 2 (1989): 297–330; and Chris Toulouse, "Thatcherism, Class Politics, and Urban Development in London," *Critical Sociology* 19, no. 1 (1992): 55–77.

29. Arnott and Krieger, "Thatcher and Reagan," 17.

30. Thomas Byrne Edsall and Mary Edsall, *Chain Reaction: The Impact of Race, Rights, and Taxes on American Politics* (New York: Norton, 1991), 9–37.

31. John Walton, *Sociology and Critical Inquiry*, 2nd ed. (Belmont, Calif.: Wadsworth, 1990), 244; and Barry Bluestone and Bennett Harrison, *The Great U-Turn: Corporate Restructuring and the Polarizing of America* (New York: Basic Books, 1988), 147.

32. Mike Davis, "Chinatown, Part Two? The Internationalization of Downtown Los Angeles," *New Left Review* 164 (1987): 73.

33. Ray Bahl, "Federal Policy," in *Setting Municipal Priorities, 1988*, ed. Charles Brecher and Raymond Horton (New York: New York University Press, 1988), 82; and James Krauskopf, "Federal Aid," in *Setting Municipal Priorities, 1990*, ed. Charles Brecher and Raymond Horton (New York: New York University Press, 1990), 117, 125.

34. Norman Fainstein and Susan Fainstein, "Governing Regimes and the Political Economy of Development in New York City, 1946–1984," in *Power, Culture, and Place: Essays on New York City*, ed. John Mollenkopf (New York: Russell Sage Foundation, 1988), 161–200.

35. Neil Smith and Peter Williams, eds., *Gentrification of the City* (Lexington, Mass.: Lexington Books, 1986).

36. "The Big Squeeze," *The Economist*, 2 November 1991, pp. 107–8.

37. Bluestone and Harrison, *The Great U-Turn*, 37.

38. See Bluestone and Harrison, *The Great U-Turn*; and also their *Deindustrialization of America: Plant Closings, Community Abandonment, and the Dismantling of Basic Industry* (New York: Basic Books, 1982). Also see June Nash, "Community and Corporations in the Restructuring of Industry," in *The Capitalist City: Global Restructuring and Community Politics*, ed. M.P. Smith and Joe Feagin (Oxford: Blackwell, 1987); and Kim Moody, *An Injury to All: The Decline of American Unionism* (New York: Verso, 1988).

39. Robert Beauregard, "Space, Time, and Economic Restructuring," in *Economic Restructuring and Political Response*, ed. Beauregard, 209–40.

40. See Mike Davis, *City of Quartz: Excavating the Future in Los Angeles* (New York: Verso, 1990); and Sassen, *The Global City*.

41. See Anna Lee Saxenian, "The Urban Contradictions of Silicon Valley: Regional Growth and the Restructuring of the Semiconductor Industry," in *Sunbelt, Snowbelt: Urban Development and Regional Restructuring*, ed. Larry Sawers and William Tabb (New York: Oxford University Press, 1984), 163–99.

42. See in particular the chapters in Stephen Wood, ed., *The Transformation of Work? Skill, Flexibility, and the Labor Process* (Boston: Unwin Hyman, 1989); Heidi Hartmann, Robert Krause, and Louise Tiffy, eds., *Computer Clips and Silicon Chips: Technology and Women's Employment* (Washington, D.C.: National Academy Press, 1986); and Thomas Stanback, *Computerization and the Transformation of Employment: Government, Hospitals, and Universities* (Boulder, Colo.: Westview Press, 1987).

43. William Serrin, "The Myth of the New Work: A Great American Job Machine?" *The Nation*, 18 September 1989.

44. "Tales from the Digital Treadmill," *New York Times*, 3 June 1990.

45. Peter Marcuse, "Dual City: A Muddy Metaphor for a Quartered City," *International Journal of Urban and Regional Research* 13, no. 4 (1989): 697–708.

46. Joel Garreau, *Edge City: Life on the New Frontier* (New York: Doubleday, 1991).

47. Robert Reich, "The Seccession of the Successful," *New York Times Sunday Magazine*, 20 January 1991.
48. Manuel Castells, "High Technology, Economic Restructuring, and the Urban-Regional Process in the United States," in *High Technology, Space, and Society*, ed. Manuel Castells (Beverley Hills, Calif.: Sage, 1985), 19.
49. "A Grim Wasteland on News at Six: New York's Bleak Image Is Played Out Nightly," *New York Times*, 14 June 1992, p. B2.
50. See William Julius Wilson, *The Truly Disadvantaged: The Inner City, the Underclass, and Public Policy* (Chicago: University of Chicago Press, 1987); and Michael Katz, *The Undeserving Poor: From the War on Poverty to the War on Welfare* (New York: Pantheon, 1989).
51. Elizabeth Durbin, "Public Assistance," in *Setting Municipal Priorities, 1990*, ed. Brecher and Horton; and Philip Weitzman, *Housing, Race/Ethnicity, and Income in New York City* (New York: Community Service Society, 1988).
52. Edsall and Edsall, *Chain Reaction*, 232.
53. On American politics in the 1980s, see Thomas Ferguson and Joel Rogers, *Right Turn: The Decline of the Democrats and the Future of American Politics* (New York: Hill and Wang, 1986); Thomas Byrne Edsall, *The New Politics of Inequality* (New York: Norton, 1984); Mike Davis, *Prisoners of the American Dream* (New York: Verso, 1986), pt. 2; and Frances Fox Piven and Richard Cloward, *Why Americans Don't Vote* (New York: Pantheon, 1990).
54. This understanding follows the line of thought established by the following: Kesselman and Krieger's use of the rise and fall of the postwar settlement in Mark Kesselman and Joel Krieger, eds., *European Politics in Transition*, 2nd ed. (Lexington, Mass.: D. C. Heath, 1992); Samuel Bowles, David Gordon, and Thomas Weisskopf, *Beyond the Wasteland* (Garden City, N.Y.: Anchor Press, 1984); Scott Lash and John Urry, *The End of Organized Capitalism* (Oxford: Polity Press, 1987).
55. John Alt, "Beyond Class: The Decline of Industrial Labor and Leisure," *Telos* 28 (1976): 73.
56. "Tales from the Digital Treadmill," *New York Times*.
57. Bluestone and Harrison, *The Great U-Turn*, chap. 1.
58. "American Living Standards: Running to Stand Still," *The Economist*, 10 November 1990, pp. 19–22.
59. "American Living Standards," *The Economist*.
60. Bluestone and Harrison, *The Great U-Turn*, chap. 1.
61. Anthony Heath, *Social Mobility* (London: Fontana, 1981), chap. 7.
62. Kevin Phillips, "Down and Out: Can the Middle Class Rise Again?" *New York Times Sunday Magazine*, 10 January 1993.
63. John Schwarz and Thomas Volgy, *The Forgotten Americans* (New York: Norton, 1992), 62.
64. Schwarz and Volgy, *The Forgotten Americans*, 65.
65. Schwarz and Volgy, *The Forgotten Americans*, 62.
66. Schwarz and Volgy, *The Forgotten Americans*, 60.
67. "Whatever Happened to the American Dream?" *Business Week*, 19 August 1991, pp. 80–85.
68. "Whatever Happened to the American Dream," *Business Week*, p. 81.
69. "More Young Single Men Hang On to Apron Strings," *New York Times*, 16 June 1991.
70. "Homeownership—A Receding Dream," *New York Times*, 20 October 1991.
71. "American Living Standards," *The Economist*.
72. "Why Marginal Changes Don't Rescue Welfare," *New York Times*, 1 March 1992.
73. See Richard Fogelsong and Joel Wolfe, eds., *The Politics of Economic Adjustment:*

Pluralism, Corporatism, and Privatization (Greenwich, Conn.: Greenwood Press, 1989).

74. "Can America Compete?" *The Economist*, 18 January 1992, pp. 65–68.
75. See "Can America Compete?" *The Economist*.
76. See also Barbara Enhrenreich, *Fear of Falling: The Inner Life of the Middle Class* (New York: Harper Perennial, 1990).
77. Davis, *Prisoners of the American Dream*, 311, 314.
78. Edsall and Edsall, *Chain Reaction*, 258–59.
79. See Barbara Jeanne Fields, "Slavery, Race, and Ideology in the United States of America," *New Left Review* 181 (1990): 95–119.

3

Classical Political Sociology and Union Behavior

Glenn Perusek

ONE OF THE THEMES of Grant McConnell's contemporary classic, *Private Power and American Democracy*, is the undemocratic character of "private governments." Interest organizations, in other words, are not necessarily homogeneous between leaders and members—leaders and members might very well have opposed interests.[1] This was not a theme that pluralist political scientists were likely to develop. An important assumption of the pluralist or interest-group liberal perspective is precisely the democratic character of such groups.[2] After all, large membership groups, such as trade unions, are precisely the organizations expected to act as a countervailing force to the concentrated economic power of business and its organizations. If they are undemocratic in some systematic way, the whole pluralist cosmology might come apart. Interestingly, most critics of pluralism also tend to neglect the problem of leaders and members within union organizations. For those who seek a rejuvenated liberal-labor alliance in American politics, it would hardly do to suggest that significant interest conflicts exist between trade union leaders and members.

Such considerations lead to a critical examination of the work of a very different analytical tradition, what can be called classical political sociology. A central theme of the work of Sidney and Beatrice Webb, Michels, Lenin, and Trotsky is that the interests of union leaders diverge from those of members as soon as organizations achieve any stability and permanence. They contend that union leaders are immutably conservative in the pursuit of union aims. It will be argued that the broad position of these theorists is a salutary corrective to the pluralist viewpoint. However, the categorical imperative of the Michelsian position is too strong. The conservatism of the union bureaucracy is more contingent on economic and political circumstances than Michels and the others argued. Additionally, both pluralism and classical political sociology can be interpreted as offering functionalist explanations for the existence of bureaucratized unions. Collective action theory's intentionalist framework, examined at the end of this chapter, provides stronger explanations because it focuses on the activity of structurally constrained agents.

SIDNEY WEBB AND BEATRICE WEBB

Sidney and Beatrice Webb were the first to analyze the impact of the growing layer of full-time officers on union behavior in major studies. They termed the condition of unions before the advent of full-time officers "primitive democracy": "The members of each trade, in general meetings assembled, themselves made the regulations, applied them to particular cases, voted the expenditure of funds, and decided on such action by individual members as seemed necessary for the common weal."[3] With no full-time officers delegated to handle the affairs of these early nineteenth-century trade clubs, general meetings decided on business and conducted affairs for themselves.[4] The Webbs argued that this basic democracy hindered efficiency as trade societies grew. For such organizations to survive, full-time officers were needed. They ascribed great importance to

> the setting apart of one man to do the clerical work [that] destroyed the possibility of equal and identical service by all the members, and laid the foundation of a separate governing class. . . . Once chosen for his post, the general secretary could rely with confidence, unless he proved himself obviously unfit or grossly incompetent, on being annually re-elected.[5]

This passage contains two important ideas. First, the apparently innocuous act of delegating a single member as full-time clerical worker was profoundly important. Nothing less than the establishment of a "separate governing class" was foretold. Second, upon election, the full-time officer became a permanent fixture, even though he had to face annual electoral competition. Why? For one reason, the new "clerical officer" rapidly developed administrative skills that made him indispensable. The Webbs point to the cotton industry, where mountains of precise paperwork were required. So taxing were these duties that the cotton workers' societies developed competitive examinations to screen potential secretaries. In short, the officers' special skills were beyond the average worker's capacity. Organizational efficiency bade unions to choose the most able among them to serve as secretary. It would not do to rotate such a position.

But more important, the full-time general secretary possessed considerable resources to effect his permanence. In a society with only a single full-time officer, that officer could publicize his name more widely than anyone else. Although the Webbs did not put it in this language, the membership of such unions had a collective action problem when confronted with the full-time secretary's power. Only the grossest malfeasance aroused the membership sufficiently to depose an official. Thus, "the annual election of the general secretary by a popular vote, far from leading to frequent rotation of office . . . has, in fact, invariably resulted in permanence of tenure exceeding even that of the English civil servant."[6] Internal elections between candidates with unequal resources resulted in entrenchment of the powerful.

Such permanence in office of a differentiated governing class was not, in itself, cause for concern. But the Webbs showed that full-time officers' interests were necessarily at variance with their members'. In the Amalgamated Society of Engineers, preservation of the organization's financial base became the full-time leadership's overriding concern.[7] Full-time officers became guardians of growing financial affairs. Their special concerns for this money affected their industrial policy—to strike or not to strike. The officers' *social role* distorted their vision of strategy and tactics. An inbuilt conservatism went with the administration of large unions. The Webbs showed that the main craft societies' leaders during the 1860s and 1870s sought to make no great change in workers' wages and conditions. Their "distinctive policy . . . was the combination of extreme caution in trade matters and energetic agitation for political reforms" that would fully legalize the unions, and thus solidify their own leadership positions. "The trade policy was . . . restricted to securing for every workman those terms which the best employers were willing voluntarily to grant."[8]

The Webbs distinguished between full-time, salaried union officers and those who continued to work at their trade. Beneath the layer of salaried officers was a larger number of working branch officers and shop stewards. As top officials "got more and more out of touch with the men in the shop," stewards were increasingly seen as the real member representatives.[9]

One of the most striking elements of the Webbs' work on the union bureaucracy was their precise portrayal of the *social differentiation* of this layer of full-time officers from their members.[10] The full-time officers who governed the unions were distinguished from those they purportedly represented by their social role.[11] If members came into conflict with leaders over union policy, they might suppose he has been bribed by his new neighbors, but distinctive and potentially antagonistic interests went along with the particular role of the full-time officer.

Disturbed by this outcome, the Webbs spent considerable time in *Industrial Democracy* discussing potential remedies. How can the organizational efficiency of full-time salaried officers be reconciled with democratic, popular control? How can the salaried officers be overseen so that their policies do not deviate significantly from rank-and-file wishes and interests? In turn, they considered, and rejected, referendums and initiatives, full-time executives, popular election of salaried officers, and mandated delegate bodies. Full-time officers can unduly influence referendums and initiatives which they oversee and administer. Additionally, the Webbs were acutely aware that such ballots could decide only a narrow range of questions, leaving full-time officers with wide discretion over complex day-to-day decisions. They rejected mandated delegate bodies because it is physically and technically impossible to vote, beforehand, on every potential issue that would face delegates. Sooner or later, delegates would have to deviate from the direct instructions of their electors, if only because they have been presented with new problems or nuances on old ones. Then the full-time leadership could unduly affect their decisions. If the delegates stuck only to their instructions, then by default the salaried officers would enjoy great discretion in implementing policy.

While executives composed of workers could remain in touch with membership wishes, the Webbs rejected them because they would not be competent to supervise full-time officers. The full-timers devoted their entire energies to the union's business. A body of tired workers, meeting in the evening after a full day of work, could not be sufficiently familiar with these affairs to criticize and supervise full-time secretaries' policies and proposals. These same constraints doomed the efforts of periodic conventions of working members.[12]

The opposite problem plagued full-time executives. While competent to supervise the work of full-time administrators, such bodies would lose touch with rank-and-file attitudes. Popular election of all salaried officers brought its own problems. In contrast to Seymour Martin Lipset (a leading post-WWII American pluralist) the Webbs commented that annual elections led salaried officers' tenure to be more permanent than that of "an English civil servant," and they dismissed mere elections as a means of popular control. Salaried officers could manipulate the resources of their positions to enhance their popularity, and so electoral contests between full-time officers and rank-and-file members could not be equal. The full-time officer could spend more time campaigning and could use his office to put his name before the entire union. The member could not. Additionally, the popular election of all salaried officers led them to be uncritical of each other. Salaried officers "would naturally be indisposed to risk their offices by appealing, against their official superior, to the uncertain arbitrament of an aggregate vote."[13] Full-time officers became absorbed in a conspiracy of silence. None wished to risk his own position by criticizing one of his fellows and appealing to the membership.[14]

The Webbs charged true representatives with three duties: to reflect the wishes of the membership, to oversee the full-time "civil service" of the union, and to formulate organizational policy. In attempting to fulfill all three functions simultaneously, union representatives ran up against a contradiction. The Webbs argued that full-time professionals would lose the ability to reflect accurately their electors' will. But the alternative—worker-delegates to a convention or similar body—was no better. While such delegates could fulfill the first duty of genuine representation, they could not carry out the other two. Worker-delegates could not stand on equal ground with professional functionaries in policy formulation and could not criticize the functionary's activities.[15] Either the representative is a professional, who can oversee salaried officers and formulate policy but not reflect the electorate's will, or he can reflect the will but not oversee officers and formulate policy.[16]

ROBERT MICHELS

Robert Michels's *Political Parties* is probably the best-known study within classical political sociology of the internal politics of large membership organizations. It has been widely influential, in particular on American pluralist writers, who interpret Michels to be a defender of democracy. To Lipset, for example, *Political Parties* warns that even the most avowedly democratic organizations can succumb to the disease of oligarchism. But this abstracts this work from Michels's political evolution. To fully understand *Political Parties*, it is necessary to place it within the context of Michels's political trajectory.[17] *Political Parties* occupied a transition phase for Michels from revolutionary syndicalism to fascism. Until 1907 an active member of the German Social Democratic Party (SPD), Michels wrote extensively in the international press of the Second International. He was a left-wing critic of SPD conservatism, but from inside the organization, attempting to reform its policies and activities. Michels wrote *Political Parties* only after he abandoned this project as hopeless. The work contained analytic elements Michels developed while an active SPD member, but it also provided his justification for abandoning socialist politics. The theme throughout is that truly democratic large-scale organizations are unachievable, largely because of the "incompetence of the masses" to govern themselves. A logical conclusion of arguing that large organizations were a necessary feature of modern society, but could not be self-governing, was Michels's drift to fascism after World War I.

Stated briefly, Michels's thesis in *Political Parties* is this: Democracy is the self-rule of the mass of workers. This must be based on small, face-to-face groups. But modern society requires that workers combine in large organizations. Self-rule is impossible in these large organizations, for reasons technical, psychological, and material.[18]

The tendency to conservative oligarchy is a universal phenomenon in modern society. In earlier writings Michels attempted to understand SPD conservatism by reference to particular historical and national circumstances. Now he argued that the tendency to oligarchy subsumed all other factors—it was present in every large organization. Michels elevated the tendency to oligarchism to the status of universal law. The very strength of modern organizations spelled the demise of democracy.[19] What caused oligarchy?

> The incompetence of the masses is almost universal throughout the domains of political life, and this constitutes the most solid foundation of the power of the leaders. Incompetence furnishes the leaders with a practical and to some extent with a moral justification. Since the rank and file are incapable of looking after their own interests, it is necessary that they should have experts to attend to their affairs.[20]

Psychological factors, affecting masses and leaders alike, were central to Michels's explanation of the rise of oligarchy. The masses were apathetic and had a weakness for spectacles. Great orators hypnotized them. The orator developed a greatly expanded ego, corresponding to his actual fame.[21]

There thus developed a cultural separation between leaders and members in modern organizations. Formal education was the first element of this separation, but other members of the "political class" affected the new leader, even if he was originally of working-class origin.[22] Here Michels trod a fine line between offering a social explanation for the union bureaucracy's behavior based

upon interests that separated it from the rank and file and a cruder psychological explanation of the effects of leadership on the individual leader. Michels
did not so much argue that union leaders developed interests distinct from
those of the mass of members. Rather, leaders presumptuously identified their
own individual interests with those of the organization. What was good for
the leader was good for the organization.[23] Most of *Political Parties* conceived
of. union and party bureaucracy conservatism as based on mass psychology—
the incompetence of the masses, their gratitude to leadership, and the effect of
the leadership process on individual leaders. Throughout *Political Parties*, the
tendency toward conservative bureaucracy was immutable. For Michels, there
appears to be no force that arrests this development, and no circumstances
under which the bureaucracy would be anything but conservative. Note the
difference between this unequivocal stance and that of Lipset. For Lipset, the
union bureaucracy exists only as an unchallenged political machine, while for
Michels it was an immutable tendency of all large-scale organizations, the structural
trend toward the differentiation of leaders from members and the subordination of the latter to the former. The existence of elections would hardly have
impressed Michels that the "iron law of oligarchy" had been refuted.

Lenin and Zinoviev

The writings of Lenin/Zinoviev during World War I were far superior to any
Marxist writings on the union movement to that time.[24] Zinoviev acknowledged the Webbs' original 1890s contribution on the British labor movement.[25]
Like Michels, Lenin and Zinoviev concluded that the bureaucratization of unions
was a universal tendency. The failure of the parties and unions associated with
the Second International to oppose World War I forced Lenin and Zinoviev
to generalize from British experience. The shorthand for this problem was:
"What caused the conservatism of the German Social Democratic Party?" Zinoviev
argued that there were three related causes of the SPD's conservatism: the rise
of the union bureaucracy, the influence of the petty bourgeoisie in the party,
and the influence of the labor aristocracy, that is, the thin layer of skilled and
well-paid workers from which the bureaucracy drew most of its members. Let
us take these in turn.

Lenin's and Zinoviev's wartime writings argued that the union bureaucracy
is a social layer above the working class as a whole. They no longer conceived
of disputes between reformists and revolutionaries as purely political. Now the
relatively privileged position of union officials constituted the social roots of
this divide. Of course, revolutionaries still had the task of politically convinc-
ing the majority of workers that capitalism was not in their interest and that
workers' self-activity would be necessary to transform the society. But the union
bureaucracy had a material interest in arguing against such a transformation,
for it would eliminate their distinctive social role (negotiation between capitalists and workers) and thus ruin their material privilege.

Zinoviev distinguished between the subjective beliefs of the officials and their objective social role.[26] He strove to distinguish the labor bureaucrats' interests from those of the working class as a whole. The war proved, from the officials' perspective, that workers did not have the international and homogeneous interests that the Second International had previously proclaimed. Instead, workers fell in behind their own governments and capitalist classes. This confronted the bureaucrats with a dilemma—remain with the principles of the International (and face the wrath of those they represented, who were now, in the main, marching off to war) or go along with workers. The bureaucracy's social position, institutionally strong but still not strong enough to resist the government's war drive, was vividly illustrated here. Thus, the Lenin/Zinoviev writings relate the organizational power of the union bureaucracy to wider political conflicts in a way that the Webbs and Michels did not.

Zinoviev and Lenin wrote that the German government understood the usefulness of the union bureaucracy in stabilizing their rule, under certain circumstances.[27] They thus conceived of the bureaucracy as a social caste between workers and employers. Its prime function was to negotiate, and any actions from either side that would upset that function—threatening the very existence of the bureaucracy itself—would have to be opposed by the bureaucracy. A workers' uprising against the government and employers would upset this relationship and so would be opposed by the officials regardless of their ideological commitments. Likewise, employers and the government could threaten to outlaw union organizations, motivating the officials to favor the war to preserve their organizations. It is thus with the writings of Lenin and Zinoviev that Marxists first comprehend the Janus-faced position of the union bureaucracy as a caste with contradictory apparent loyalties between the major social classes.

Alongside this analysis of the union bureaucracy, Lenin and Zinoviev contended that the influence of the petty bourgeoisie conservatized the SPD. Zinoviev's prime example of petty bourgeois influence in the SPD is somewhat comical: innkeepers in parliament. In 1912, 12 of the 110 SPD Reichstag deputies were innkeepers. "In the critical moments of history it is the petty bourgeois and not the proletarian tendencies in the social democracy that win the upper hand."[28] But Zinoviev never explained how the petty bourgeoisie articulated its influence over the party. In any event, this was a secondary part of his and Lenin's explanation for party and union conservatism.

More central was the contention that a "labor aristocracy" stood alongside the union bureaucracy in conservatizing the SPD. "The worker-functionaries very often hail from the circles of the labor aristocracy. The labor bureaucracy and the labor aristocracy are blood brothers. The group interests of the one and of the other very often coincide." Interest conflict was not between the labor bureaucracy and the working class but between the labor bureaucracy and aristocracy together against the rest of the working class. The union bureaucracy's rise was "intimately bound up with the victory of the narrow, group interests of the relatively small group of labor aristocrats over the genuine interests of the . . . mass of workers."[29]

This argument rested upon a conception of imperialism that contended that advanced countries extracted "super profits" from backward countries, and from these "threw crumbs" to a thin layer of skilled workers, the labor aristocracy. This layer of privileged workers then had an objective material interest in imperialism; its support for the war stemmed from the advantage it derived from imperialism. Only one layer of the working class benefited: "It would be false to believe that the magnanimity of the British capitalists was extended in equal measure to the entire working class. No, with these crumbs they bought off mainly the upper stratum of the working class—the labor aristocracy." Thus, reformism and support for war stood "on a common economic basis—the interests of a thin crust of privileged workers and of the petty bourgeoisie, who defend . . . their privileged position, their 'right' to some modicum of profits that their 'own' national bourgeoisie obtain from robbing other nations, from the advantages of their Great Power status, etc." The argument rested on a conception of privileged workers' interests.[30]

Lenin and Zinoviev combined the aristocracy-of-labor argument with the theoretical conception of the union bureaucracy because they wanted to account for the political backwardness of organized workers in the most advanced capitalist countries. By 1914 it was clear that American and British unionists were not necessarily politically more advanced than those of central, southern, and eastern Europe. The labor-aristocracy argument was a way to explain the apparently anomalous development of the relatively conservative workers' movements where workers had exhibited enough class consciousness, solidarity, and self-confidence to organize strong economic organizations.

There is good reason to distinguish the two arguments. The labor-aristocracy argument ran up against fairly strong empirical refutation in the aftermath of World War I. It cannot account for the role that skilled workers played in the 1916–1923 revolutionary upsurge that swept Europe. But its idea of the union officials as negotiators between classes was generalizable to other cases beyond the original problem situation in which it was advanced. Finally, Lenin developed a stronger argument that, coupled with the theory of the union bureaucracy, accounted in a superior fashion for much of the course of interwar labor movements in the advanced industrial societies: the theory of the revolutionary party.[31] Lenin and Trotsky conceived of a revolutionary party as the organization of the most far-seeing and class-conscious section of the working class, able to lead workers in struggle. They thought it was an indispensable instrument of workers' revolutionary struggle. Where such a mass party was *absent*, the working class would remain under the sway of reformist organizations and leaders. In such places, the union bureaucracy, with a material interest in maintaining its own negotiatory role within democratic capitalism, would have a relatively free hand to operate. This seems like a superior way of accounting for the failure of the revolutionary upheavals in Europe after World War I.

TROTSKY'S WRITINGS OF THE 1920s AND 1930s

Trotsky's essential contribution to the classical conception of the union bureaucracy was his analysis of its behavior under conditions of economic contraction. Under economic stability or expansion Trotsky thought the bureaucracy could maintain itself as a significant, independent political force. Since union leaders could continue to win wage and working condition improvements, they would remain legitimate to their members. But economic crisis eroded the material basis for such reformism.[32] Now employers and the state would slash workers' living standards to restore profit rates. Unions could either be transformed into revolutionary organizations implacably opposed to capitalism or become the "economic police of capital," working to aid the intensification of the exploitation of the working class.

This "policing" role would be particularly important in conditions of economic crisis.[33] Trotsky suggested that the union bureaucracy was the crucial factor in stabilizing political democracy under capitalism in economic crisis. The union bureaucracy is unique among the institutional supports for democratic capitalism in its great prestige and organizational resources to influence workers. It subsumes large segments of the working class into the system, ideologically and organizationally. The unions are a crucial instrument for enforcing austerity on the working class.

The French Popular Front in the mid-1930s confirmed this argument. Union leaders, many of them Communist Party cadres, served capital by reigning in the spontaneous workers' movement. They acted as a mask for capitalism and its politicians, shielding them from workers' wrath. This forestalled the necessity of using force against the strikers, which could well have exacerbated the situation. However, in serving the capitalists in this crisis situation, the Popular Front exhausted its raison d'être so that a year later it could be dispensed with.

Politically, the union bureaucracy was interested in the maintenance of bourgeois democracy, for its social function was dependent on the continued existence of class antagonism and on the possibility of negotiatory solutions to the clash between labor and capital. Authoritarian capitalism would outlaw the unions or incorporate them into the state, destroying their independent role. Working-class revolution would do away with bargaining over wages and conditions, thus also making the union leaders superfluous. Since the union bureaucracy has a corporate interest in the maintenance of bourgeois democracy, employers and bourgeois democratic politicians thus have an important commonality of interests with the union officials.

The experiences of Germany, Austria, and Italy suggested that in the 1930s the old bourgeois democratic social equilibrium was increasingly impossible for the advanced societies. Trotsky deemed rising international economic competition and heightened domestic class conflict to be fundamental features of advanced political economies of the 1930s. A parliament became irrelevant as

a political factor. Classes would increasingly confront each other in open are-
nas, rather than through the mediation of a parliament. Half measures and
compromises could not provide lasting solutions. Economic crisis was eroding
the very basis for capitalist democracy. The capitalist democracies were faced
with contradictions soluble only by revolutionary or counterrevolutionary measures.
Centrifugal pressures were ripping the advanced democracies apart.

Under such circumstances, reformist political institutions, especially the unions,
would increasingly have their base cut from beneath them. Union officials,
under conditions of economic decline, could remain independent of the state
for only so long. Partly this was a result of raw economic forces. Falling profit
rates forced individual capitalists to rationalize production. Labor costs, especially, had to be slashed, eventually necessitating an all-out attack on the union
bureaucracy itself. As the attack would come from highly centralized and powerful capitalists, increasingly fused with the state itself, the union leadership
was unlikely to be able to resist. Unions would soon be transformed into institutions of the state themselves, functioning to enforce new, worse, terms on
their members.

Trotsky thus portrayed the unions as institutions that to save themselves
would effectively represent the interests of capital in the labor movement. The
union leaders would struggle, in futility, to free the state from the employers'
powerful influence. The trend to incorporation of the unions into the state
and for the unions to represent the interests of the capitalist class were, for
Trotsky, universal.[34] Again, the bureaucracy's ideological views seemed entirely
secondary—the parameters of their behavior were determined by economic
trends and by their special social position as a negotiatory stratum between
classes. If reformist unions refused to serve capital, they would be transformed
into revolutionary unions, utterly opposed to capitalism, or swept away by the
rising tide of fascism. Reformist unions, like stable political democracy, were a
thing of the past.

The bureaucracy's function as a negotiatory layer between the classes predis-
posed it to subvert mass actions, such as the 1926 British general strike or the
wave of sit-in strikes in France in 1936. Trotsky argued that *regardless* of the
bureaucracy's formal politics, it was forced to oppose militant action. Left-
wing officers would speak militantly only until obliged to translate militancy
into action. The union bureaucracy as a whole functioned to hold workers
back from militant struggle.[35] Militant mass action that challenged the very
foundations of the government itself threatened to unleash elemental, uncon-
trollable forces in the working class. To union officials, this was tantamount to
wrecking the union movement, since it would supersede their negotiations and
compromise with employers and the state.[36]

Although highly suggestive, Trotsky unfortunately did not draw many of
the logical implications of his analysis. He suggested that the union bureaucracy's conservatism, while rooted in "reactionary" ideological notions in British
political conditions, was determined by its social function as negotiator. But

Trotsky appears to have overplayed the independent role of ideological factors. If the bureaucracy's social role was such a strong determinant of its behavior, then its backward ideology must have been secondary. In addition, Trotsky probably misassessed the degree of revolutionary consciousness among European workers in the 1920s and 1930s.[37]

Nor did Trotsky confront one important implication of his analysis—how it bore on the labor-aristocracy argument. It appears that the bureaucracy should be considered as distinct from the skilled, highly paid workers. Economic decline would force the bureaucracy to attack this aristocracy in particular. Union members' wages would be cut along with those of the rest of the working class. There is no reason to believe any section of workers would be exempt from such an attack by the employers. Finally, Trotsky's epigrammatic "either/or" choice for the bureaucracy under conditions of economic decline does not specify the precise *form* of "incorporation" of the bureaucracy into the mechanism of the state.

COLLECTIVE ACTION THEORY

Classical political sociology portrayed the development of a layer of salaried full-time officers whose interests were necessarily at odds with those of their members. For Michels, the union bureaucracy was immutably conservative; for Trotsky it worked toward the stabilization of capitalist democracy, particularly in the economic and political crises of the 1920s and 1930s. Interestingly, pluralism and classical political sociology share a mode of explanation: The behavior of union leadership is stable over time, and *functional* for democracy under capitalism.

There are both empirical and theoretical problems with this account. Empirically, the union bureaucracy does not appear to be as immutably conservative as the Michelsian thesis would have us believe. In the 1980s across Western Europe and North America, militant union action was often initiated by leaders of bureaucratized unions, not by a restless rank and file. It appears that the conservatism of the union bureaucracy is more contingent on economic and political factors than Michels allowed.

Theoretically, functionalist explanations in general have recently come under attack. Elster argues that much Marxist-influenced sociology, in particular, argues in weak functionalist terms. "In Marxist writings on education, bureaucracy and indeed on most topics there seems to be an implicit regulative idea that 'Every institution or behavioral pattern in capitalist society serves the interests of capitalism and is maintained because it serves these interests.'"[38] Such explanations are wrongly based upon the analogy of biology.

One way to account for the often contradictory behavior of the union bureaucracy and to counter the tendency to argue in functionalist terms is to cast an explanation of the union bureaucracy's behavior in explicitly *intentionalist* terms. This entails emphasizing those elements in classical political sociology that focus on the aims of particular actors within and outside unions and applying elements of collective action theory to the strategic problems that these actors have within bureaucratized unions.

The rise of bureaucratized unions can be seen as the result of a set of choices made by different actors. Processes that crystallized the interest division between union members and leaders and fostered bureaucratic power resulted from the unintended outcomes of intentional action. For example, in the CIO unions, militants fought for full-time committeemen and the dues check-off as organizational security measures. Unfortunately, they also became measures that insulated leaders from members. Political factionalism, the systematic struggle for elected leadership positions, fosters union democracy. But individual leaders or factions are interested in eliminating factionalism to safeguard their own power—this, too, furthered bureaucratism.

Leadership behavior at variance from members' interests is possible because members have a collective action problem in monitoring their leaders. It is costly (in time, money, and organizational resources) for members to check leadership behavior. Every individual member would prefer that other members bear the cost of keeping their leaders in line. Since noncontributors cannot be excluded from the benefits of this effort, there exists a strong incentive to take a free ride. But if enough members become free riders, no effective monitoring will occur.

A handful of economists have begun to develop such ideas.[39] They accept that members and leaders have distinctive interests owing to their distinctive organizational positions. Union leadership behavior at variance from member preferences is possible to a great degree in unions because members' collective action costs to monitor union leaders are so great. Such a view of unions allows these theorists to develop some provocative and useful hypotheses about union behavior. For example, Jean-Jacques Rosa argues that it is a mystification to believe that union leaders exist as member representatives. Instead, "unions' services are demanded not only by wage earners but also by companies. Firms need unions to substitute for or act as a complement to personnel policy, or as a way to monopolize or attain vertical control in an industry."[40] Or, as Wallace Atherton argued, union leaders' concern for maximizing net dues revenue leads them to favor strike lengths that are shorter than the optimal for membership interests.[41] Or, as Donald Martin argued, even though monitoring union leaders presents union members with a collective action problem, union leaders will anticipate membership challenges and competition for their own positions. This will lead them to devote some organizational resources to securing their own tenure.[42]

While economists proceeding from such an understanding have developed the most promising line of analysis for modeling union behavior in the whole postwar period, problems with the approach remain. First, these theorists are not particularly sensitive to qualitative transformations in the character of relations between union members and leaders through time. The interests and behavior of union members and leaders should be conceived as distinctive, but it is also true that the opportunities and constraints on their behavior change with changing economic circumstances. Second, these theorists make no clear distinction between layers of the union bureaucracy, between national leaders and local full-time officers, in the first instances. A comprehensive interpretation of the behavior of bureaucratized unions appears to rest upon this distinction. Third, these theorists have a limited view of the scope of possible actions that constitute rank-and-file monitoring of union leadership.[43] Finally, these theorists are preoccupied with ownership. They do not acknowledge that their useful insights rest on an examination of the social relations of control inside union organizations, not on juridical foundations.

CONCLUSIONS

Classical political sociologists all accepted that the union bureaucracy, once formed, would be profoundly conservative, industrially and politically. Indeed, for Michels and the Marxists, the union bureaucracy's conservatism was immutable, not contingent on political or economic factors. For the Webbs, the social and role differentiation of leaders from members gave rise to an interest disjuncture. Leaders' positions, resting on the union's financial base, imparted to them a different calculus from that of union members on industrial questions. Officials' social conditions cemented this difference. Removed from the dirt and dangers of the shop floor and from constant conflict with the employers, union leaders no longer faced their members' employment uncertainties— the possibilities of periodic layoffs, disciplinary firing, injuries, and so on. They were conservatized. For Trotsky, the union bureaucracy was the single most important institutional stabilizer for democratic capitalism under conditions of economic crisis. The bureaucracy had an organizational connection to the most important sections of the working class. Unfortunately, this Marxist writing never shed the connection of the union bureaucracy to the putative labor aristocracy of skilled, highly paid workers.

All of these classical theorists understood the union member-leader division to be structural—that is, systematic deviations from the "iron law of oligarchy," the conservatization of the bureaucracy, were impossible. For the Webbs, this signified the coming of age of union leadership, something to be welcomed more than decried. For the classical Marxists, the union bureaucracy was a necessarily conservative support for capitalism and imperialism, an obstacle to revolutionary objectives. For Michels, the emergence of the union bureaucracy signaled the demise of genuine democracy. Post–World War II writers took up the theme of the antithesis of democracy and bureaucracy inside unions. For Lipset, the existence of regular electoral competition, such as the institutionalized two-party system of the International Typographical Union (ITU), was sufficient to circumvent union bureaucracy. While for the Webbs the union bureaucracy could become entrenched—with "more tenure than a judge"—even under regular elections, for Lipset such elections dissolved bureaucracy.

The Webbs suggested that a fundamental distinction be drawn between salaried, full-time union officers and the local officers who continued to work at their trade. The latter, by dint of their continued contact and shared position with working members, would reflect rank-and-file wishes and interests to a much greater degree than the salaried top officers. But today, there are salaried, full-time officers at both the national level and at the local level. If we take the Webbs' argument that the social role and position of these salaried officers makes it inevitable that they deviate from the interests of the rank-and-file, we must also note that the interests of these different layers of the union bureaucracy may also be different in some circumstances. Lower levels of the union bureaucracy are more susceptible to removal by the rank and file; they are also more vulnerable to employers' attacks. Thus we must draw an analytic distinction between layers of the union bureaucracy.

A serious problem with the classical theorists is their tendency to argue in functionalist terms. Recently some social scientists have started applying collective action theory to union behavior. These theorists accept the salience of the member-leader distinction in unions. Yet these theorists take too little account of economic and political determinants of particular configurations of power between union members, union leaders and employers. Additionally, the range of membership behavior to monitor union leaders is conceived too narrowly. Still, these theorists have developed a fruitful line of argument that deserves to be pursued.

Notes

1. Grant McConnell, *Private Power and American Democracy* (New York: Vintage, 1966), chap. 5.
2. Theodore Lowi, *The End of Liberalism* (New York: Norton, 1979).
3. Sidney Webb and Beatrice Webb, *Industrial Democracy* (London: Longman's, Green and Company, 1920), 3.
4. Webb and Webb, *Industrial Democracy*, 8: "The early trade club was thus a democracy of the most rudimentary type, free alike from permanently differentiated officials, executive council, or representative assembly. The general meeting strove itself to transact all the business, and grudgingly delegated any of its functions either to officers or to committees."
5. Webb and Webb, *Industrial Democracy*, 15.
6. Webb and Webb, *Industrial Democracy*, 16.
7. Webb and Webb, *The History of Trade Unionism* (London: Longman's, Green and Company, 1920), 320–21: "The rapid growth of the society brought with it a huge volume of detailed business. . . . The quantity of routine soon became enormous; and the whole attention of the General Secretary was given to coping with the mass of details which poured in upon him by every post. This huge friendly society business brought with it, too, its special bias. Allan [the General Secretary] grew more and more devoted to the accumulating fund, which was alike the guarantee and the symbol of the success of his organization. Nothing was important

enough to warrant any inroad on this sacred balance. The Engineers' Central Executive, indeed, practically laid aside the weapon of the strike. 'We believe,' said Allan before the Royal Commission in 1867, 'that all strikes are a complete waste of money, not only in relation to the workmen, but also to the employers.'"

8. Webb and Webb, *History of Trade Unionism*, 240–41.

9. Webb and Webb, *History of Trade Unionism*, 577–78, put the number of full-time union officers in the 1890s at six to seven hundred, rising to three to four thousand by 1920. By 1920, they estimated there were 100,000 branch officers and working stewards in Great Britain.

10. Webb and Webb, *History of Trade Unionism*, 465–66, contrast top leaders to the branch officers and stewards who "form the backbone of the Trade Union world, and constitute the vital element in working-class politics. Dependent for their livelihood on manual labor, they retain to the full the workman's sense of insecurity, privation and thwarted aspirations. Their own singleness of purpose, the devotion with which they serve their fellows in laborious offices with only nominal remuneration, and their ingenuous faith in the indefinite improvement of human nature by education and better conditions of life, all combine to maintain their enthusiasm for every kind of social reform. . . . This class of non-commissioned officers it is which has, in the main, proved to be the progressive element in the Trade Union world, and which actually determines the trend of working class thought."

11. According to Webb and Webb, *History of Trade Unionism*, 467, the actual government of the Trade Union world rests exclusively in the hands of a class apart, the salaried officers of the great societies: "The salaried official . . . occupies a unique position. He belongs neither to the middle nor to the working class. The interests which he represents are exclusively those of the manual working class from which he has sprung, and his duties bring him into constant antagonism with the brain-working property owning class. On the other hand, his daily occupation is that of a brain-worker, and he is accordingly sharply marked off from the typical proletarian, dependent for his livelihood on physical toil. . . . The promotion of a working man to the position of a salaried brain-worker effects a complete and sudden change in his manner of life."

Webb and Webb, *History of Trade Unionism*, 469–70, also quotes, at length, a skilled worker who described the impact of social differentiation on the bureaucracy's policies: "As Branch Secretary, working at his trade, our friend, though superior in energy and ability to the rank and file of his members, remained in close touch with their feelings and desires. . . . He believes, almost as a matter of principle, that in any dispute the capitalist is in the wrong and the workman in the right." But when he becomes a full-time officer, "the point at issue no longer affects his own earnings or conditions of employment, any disputes between his members and their employers increase his work and add to his worry. The former vivid sense of the privations and subjection of the artisan's life gradually fades from his mind; and he begins more and more to regard all complaints as perverse and unreasonable." Concurrent with the new position of the trade union full-timer was a change in lifestyle, cementing the new viewpoint: "With this intellectual change may come a more invidious transformation. Nowadays the salaried officer of a great Union is courted and flattered by the middle class. . . . He goes to live in a little villa in a lower middle-class suburb. The move leads to his dropping his workmen friends; and his wife changes her acquaintances. With the habits of his new neighbors he insensibly adopts more and more of their ideas. Gradually he finds himself at issue with his members, who no longer agree to his proposals with the old alacrity. All this comes about by degrees, neither party understanding the cause. . . . He begins to look down upon them all as 'common workmen.'"

12. Webb and Webb, *Industrial Democracy*, 17–18.
13. Webb and Webb, *Industrial Democracy*, 32.
14. Webb and Webb, *Industrial Democracy*, 27, concluded: "We see, therefore, that almost every influence in the Trade Union organizatiǫn has tended to magnify and consolidate the power of the general secretary. If democracy could furnish no other expedient of popular control than the mass meeting, the annual election of public officers, the Initiative and the Referendum, Trade Union history makes it quite clear that the mere pressure of administrative needs would inevitably result in the general body of citizens losing all effective control over the government."
15. Webb and Webb, *Industrial Democracy*, 56: "Directly the working man representative becomes properly equipped for one-half of his duties, he ceases to be specially qualified for the other."
16. As a solution to this quandary, the Webbs proposed that the union representatives' multiple functions could only be carried out in a body that *combined* professional representatives with worker-delegates. The workers could bring the popular will and the professionals an oversight and policy-formulation ability. Given the way they posed the problem, they were understandably dissatisfied with this solution. They admitted that in such mixed bodies, the full-time, professional representatives would tend to dominate, just as salaried secretaries dominated over part-time executives.
17. See David Beetham, "From Socialism to Fascism: The Relation between Theory and Practice in the Work of Robert Michels," *Political Studies* 25 (March): 3–24; and *Political Studies* 25 (June): 161–81.
18. Robert Michels, *Political Parties* (New York: Free Press, 1962), 70: "Organization implies the tendency to oligarchy. In every organization, whether it be a political party, a professional union, or any other association of the kind, the aristocratic tendency manifests itself very clearly. The mechanism of the organization, while conferring a solidity of structure, induces serious changes in the organized mass, completely inverting the respective position of the leaders and the led. As a result of organization, every party or professional union becomes divided into a minority of directors and a majority of directed."
19. Michels, *Political Parties*, 71: "Democratic evolution has a parabolic course. At the present time . . . democracy is in the descending phase. It may be enunciated as a general rule that the increase in the power of the leaders is directly proportional with the extension of the organization. . . . Where organization is stronger, we find that there is a lesser degree of applied democracy."
20. Michels, *Political Parties*, 111–12.
21. Michels, *Political Parties*, 100–101: "The quality . . . which most of all impresses the crowd is the prestige of celebrity. . . . The crowd always submits willingly to the control of distinguished individuals. The man who appears before them crowned with laurels is considered *a priori* to be a demi-god."
22. Michels, *Political Parties*, 282–84: "The new environment exercises a potent influence upon the ex-manual worker. His manners become gentler and more refined. In his daily association with persons of the highest birth he learns the usages of good society and endeavors to assimilate them. . . . Inspired with a foolish self-satisfaction, the ex-worker is apt to take pleasure in his new environment, and he tends to become indifferent and even hostile to all progressive aspirations in the democratic sense. He accommodates himself to the existing order, and ultimately, weary of struggle, becomes even reconciled to that order. What interest for them has now the dogma of the social revolution? Their own social revolution has already been effected."

23. Michels, *Political Parties*, 221–23: "The bureaucrat identifies himself completely with the organization, confounding his own interests with its interests. All objective criticism of the party is taken by him as a personal affront. This is the cause of the obvious incapacity of all party leaders to take a serene and just view of hostile criticism. . . . When in any organization the oligarchy has attained an advanced stage of development, the leaders begin to identify themselves, not merely with the party institutions, but even the party property."

It is worth nothing, parenthetically, that a somewhat different argument found its way into one of Michels's concluding chapters. Here (if not in the rest of the book), Michels drew quite close to the Marxists (*Political Parties*, 353): "The party . . . is not necessarily identifiable with the totality of its members. . . . The party is created as a means to secure an end. Having, however, become an end in itself, endowed with aims and interests of its own, it undergoes detachment, from the teleological point of view, from the class which it represents. In a party, it is far from obvious that the interests of the masses which have combined to form a party will coincide with the interests of the bureaucracy in which the party becomes personified. The interests of the body of employees (bureaucrats) are always conservative, and in a given political situation these interests may dictate a defensive and even a reactionary policy when the interests of the working class demand a bold and aggressive policy; in other cases, although these are very rare, the roles may be reversed. By a universally applicable social law, every organ of the collectivity, brought into existence through the need for the division of labor, creates for itself, as soon as it becomes consolidated, interests peculiar to itself. The existence of these special interests involve a necessary conflict with the interests of the collectivity. . . . In the long run they tend to undergo transformation into distinct classes."

24. Lenin and Zinoviev were close collaborators during the war. Their arguments concerning the union bureaucracy were essentially identical.

John Scheidmann, *Unions in Post-Industrial Society* (University Park, Penn.: Penn State University Press, 1979), is one of a long line of writers who considers Lenin's *What Is to Be Done?* (New York: International Publishers, 1969) as Marxism's definitive final word on trade unionism. But *What Is to Be Done* could not develop an analysis of trade unionism that included an appraisal of the union bureaucracy because no developed bureaucracy existed in the Russian labor movement at the time. As late as the 1905 revolution, only 7 percent of St. Petersburg workers were organized. Throughout Russia there were no city councils, uniting all workers in a locality, until 1905. Of six hundred union organizations, only twenty-two had more than two thousand members. During the years of reaction following 1905, unions practically ceased to exist—there were no national organizations and less than thirty thousand members of locals. There were no union officials with a vested interest in the maintenance of trade unions and the stabilization of capitalist democracy in Russia. See S. M. Schwarz, *Labor in the Soviet Union* (New York: Praeger, 1952), 338.

Similarly, Rosa Luxemburg, *The Mass Strike, the Political Party, and the Trade Unions* (New York: Harper & Row, 1971), failed to make a social critique of the rising trade union bureaucracy. Luxemburg's political criticism was not grounded in any understanding of the causes of official conservatism. Luxemburg's main wartime work, *The Junius Pamphlet* (in Luxemburg, *The Mass Strike*, 97–222), written in 1915, does not move far analytically beyond her earlier work. This work, an implacable and eloquent protest against the war and the SPD's failure to oppose it, is a normative and not an empirical critique. It provides us with no social causes for the union bureaucracy's conservatism, even though it poses a political strategy that is quite similar to that of Lenin and Zinoviev in the same period.

25. Grigory Zinoviev, "The Social Roots of Opportunism," in *Lenin's Struggle for a Revolutionary International* (New York: Monad, 1984), 480.

26. Zinoviev, "Social Roots," 484: "Subjectively, many members of this caste are still convinced that they have been acting exclusively in the interests of the working class, that their conduct was dictated by their better understanding of proletarian interests. When we speak of the 'treachery of the leaders' we do not mean to say by this that it was all a deep-laid plot, that it was a consciously perpetrated sell-out of the workers' interests." Similarly, Claus Offe and Helmut Wiesenthal, "Two Logics of Collective Action: Theoretical Notes on Social Class and Organizational Form," *Political Power and Social Theory* 1 (1980): 67–115, have called for the development of a "sociology of opportunism." The terms "treachery" and "sell-out" should be stripped of their pejorative sense.

27. Zinoviev, "Social Roots," 484: "The most far sighted of the German reactionaries knew long before the war that the official organization of German Social Democracy had become thoroughly 'bourgeoisified.' And they said quite openly that at the critical moment they would appeal to the heads of the SPD against the laboring masses.

28. Zinoviev, "Social Roots," 477.

29. Zinoviev, "Social Roots," 485, 487.

30. Vladimir Ilyich Lenin, *Lenin on the United States* (New York: International Publishers, 1970).

31. Chris Harman, *Party and Class* (Chicago: Bookmarks, 1985), argues that Lenin's Bolshevik Party was highly flexible in practice and in response to changing circumstances but was a staunch defender of central principles. Such a view of the party was far different from either the social democratic mode of the Second International (of which the German SPD was the prototype) or the Russian Communist Party of the Stalin era.

32. Leon Trotsky, *Leon Trotsky on the Trade Unions* (New York: Monad, 1969), 54: "The decay of British capitalism, under conditions of decline of the world capitalist system, undermines the basis for the reformist work of the trade unions."

33. This bears on the contemporary social scientific debate over the governability of democracy. See for example, Michael Crozier, Samuel Huntington, and Josi Watanubi, *The Crisis of Democracy* (New York: New York University Press, 1975); Juan Linz, ed., *The Breakdown of Democratic Regimes* (Baltimore, Md.: Johns Hopkins University Press, 1978); and Philippe Schmitter, "Interest Intermediation and Regime Governability in Contemporary Western Europe and North America," in *Organizing Interests in Western Europe: Pluralism, Corporatism, and the Transformation of Politics*, ed. Suzanne Berger (Cambridge: Cambridge University Press, 1983), 287–330. For an overview of the literature see Anthony Birch, "Overload, Ungovernability, and Delegitimation: The Theories and the British Case," *British Journal of Political Science* 14 (April 1984): 135–60.

34. Trotsky, *Trotsky on the Unions*, 68–69: "There is one common feature in the development . . . of modern trade union organization in the entire world. It is their drawing closely together with the state power. This process is equally characteristic of the neutral, the Social Democratic, the Communist and the "anarchist" trade unions. This fact alone shows that the tendency towards "growing together" is intrinsic not in this or that doctrine as such but derives from social conditions common for all unions."

35. Leon Trotsky, "Trotsky on Problems of the British Labour Movement," *International*

Socialism 48 (June/July 1971), 30; Leon Trotsky, *Trotsky on Britain* (New York: Monad, 1973), 80–81.

36. During and after the British general strike, for example, officials often expressed their fear that the strike would evolve out of their control. For example, Charles Duke, of the Municipal Workers: "Every day that the strike proceeded the control and the authority of that dispute was passing out of the hands of responsible Executives into the hands of men who had no authority, no control, no responsibility, and was wrecking the movement from one end to the other" (TUC General Council, *The Mining Crisis and the National Strike*, 1926 [London: Trades Union Congress, 1927] 185). Walter Citrine, General Secretary of the Trades Union Congress (TUC), wrote that "the outstanding lesson of the General Strike of 1926 is that authority must be invested exclusively and entirely in the directing body. . . . Never again will the Congress undertake the custodianship of any movement without the clear, specific, and unalterable understanding that the General Council, and the General Council alone, shall have the free and untrammelled right to determine policy" (quoted in Chris Farman, *The General Strike, May 1926* [London: Rupert Hart-Davis, 1972], 229).

37. Richard Hyman and James Hinton, *Trade Unions and Revolution: The Industrial Politics of the Early British Communist Party* (London: Pluto Press, 1975), argue that the failure of the British Communist Party to create a solid cadre of organizers resulted from their misassessment of political conditions in Britain. The party, in short, set for itself the wrong tasks because it perceived a revolutionary situation where none existed. Particularly in the late 1930s, Trotsky wrote of the working class as a necessarily revolutionary agent, "betrayed" by its current leadership and waiting only for the correct political guidance from the Fourth International. In France, wrote Trotsky in June 1936, "the revolution has begun" (*Trotsky on the Unions*, 162–67). Trotsky was not the only observer of French politics to hold this view. *Le Temps* and the London *Times*, two of the most respected newspapers in Europe, agreed. Thus, the judgment of writers such as Jean LaCouture, *Leon Blum* (New York: Holmes and Meier, 1982), 257, that Trotsky's political perspective was responsible for his mistaken view is false. Still, the consensus with important capitalist papers does not make the premise any less problematic.

38. Jon Elster, *Ulysses and the Sirens* (Cambridge: Cambridge University Press, 1979), 34.

39. Indeed, it was a tiny handful until the 1980s. Donald L. Martin, *An Ownership Theory of the Trade Union* (Berkeley and Los Angeles: University of California Press, 1980), counts only Orley Ashenfelter and George Johnson, "Bargaining Theory, Trade Unions, and Industrial Strike Activity," *American Economic Review* 59 (March 1969): 35–49; and Wallace N. Atherton, *Theory of Union Bargaining Goals* (Princeton, N.J.: Princeton University Press, 1973) among those economists who took the leader/member distinction seriously in attempting to model union behavior.

40. Jean-Jacques Rosa, "Toward a Theory of the Union Firm," in *The Economics of Trade Unions: New Directions*, ed. Jean-Jacques Rosa (Boston: Kluwer-Nijhoff, 1984), 158.

41. Atherton, *Theory of Union Bargaining Goals*, 75.

42. Martin, *Ownership Theory*, 93. This corresponds with the Webbs' observation on British trade unions at the end of the nineteenth century, discussed above.

43. John Burton, "The Economic Analysis of the Trade Union as a Political Institution," in *The Economics of Trade Unions*, ed. Rosa, 123–54, suggests that political voice—*pace* Albert Hirschman, *Exit, Voice, and Loyalty* (Cambridge: Harvard University Press, 1970)—inside union organizations could consist of increased

participation in union affairs, that is, increased voter turn-out, committee participation, and so on, or support for alternative candidates. Martin's list of member
threats to the existing leadership appears distorted by the neoclassical economists'
political agenda. Decertification campaigns, raiding efforts by rival unions, and
support for rival candidates within the organization comprise a narrow list of alternatives for union members, and they tend in the direction of individualist rather
than collectivist solutions (Martin, *Ownership Theory*, 94).

PART II

CASE STUDIES

4

Was There a Golden Age of the CIO? Race, Solidarity, and Union Growth during the 1930s and 1940s

Michael Goldfield

INTRODUCTION

AMERICAN UNIONS ARE AS weak today as they have been at any time since before World War I. The union density (percentage of the labor force organized) in the private sector is now less than since the beginning of the Great Depression.

The recent decline of unions may be traced statistically from the peak of union density in 1953 or the earlier all-time high union density in 1945. Since then, union density has declined continuously. The United States is the only economically developed capitalist country to suffer such a continuous decline in the last four decades. Despite renewed traumas and attacks—including the rise of anti-union consultants in the 1960s and 1970s, the forced concessions, the destruction of pattern-bargaining, and the generally heightened anti-unionism of the Reagan and Bush administrations in the 1980s and early 1990s— the decline over the last forty years has been relatively steady.[1] These trends suggest that the major causes for the weakness and decline of U.S. unions are not to be found in this or that problem of recent decades but, rather, in the period before the decline began, that is, in the 1930s, 1940s, and early 1950s.

In looking at these trends there is a tendency to view this earlier period of rapid union growth as something of a "golden age." There is a tendency to see the early CIO unions in general as militant and dedicated to new organizing, rather than merely being committed to the narrow material interests of their members. CIO unions as a whole supposedly had a broader social vision, struggling for the class interests of all American workers. They were allegedly solidaristic, antiracist, and characterized by "social unionism." Others, noting the narrow-mindedness and bigotry of some CIO unions, have dismissed these claims entirely, suggesting that there was little to recommend the CIO unions, especially on issues of race. The truth, however, as is often the case, is more complex.

78

In this essay, I wish to examine the claim that the CIO as a whole was characterized by social unionism, that there was a golden age to which the CIO as a whole can rightly lay claim. I wish to do this by focusing on one set of issues, the racial practices of CIO unions. This focus is not as restrictive as one might think, since the sine qua non of solidarity and class perspective in this country has always revolved around the axis of race.[2] I will attempt to show here that there was no golden age, that there were tensions within the CIO even during its heyday in the 1930s and 1940s, and that those segments of the labor movement that were most committed to racial egalitarianism, and were as a consequence the most dynamic, were largely destroyed by those more moderate forces who have led the labor unions into their current state.

HOW RACIALLY EGALITARIAN WAS THE CIO?

Historiographic Traditions

If one views the traditional, mainstream industrial relations and labor history literature, one finds hardly a reference to this question.[3] One may more fruit-fully look at the rich tradition that focuses specifically on African-American labor, a tradition that was largely ignored during its heyday by mainstream labor historians and industrial relations writers. W.E.B. DuBois, Charles Wesley, and Lorenzo Greene and Carter Woodson, for example, document the condi-tion of black labor in the United States and the many unions that played an important role in denying employment and promotional opportunities to Afri-can-American workers.[4] The classic pre-CIO work is Sterling Spero's and Abram Harris's *The Black Worker*, which analyzes both the exclusionary, oppressive role of the AFL and the degree to which the UMW, other unions, and a number of left-wing groups were and were not more racially egalitarian than the ma-jority of AFL unions.[5]

Those writing in this latter tradition naturally turned their attention to the CIO in the 1930s and 1940s. While not without their criticisms, these writers were remarkably positive in their evaluations of CIO racial practice. DuBois, for example, states:

> Probably the greatest and most effective effort toward interracial understand-ing among the working masses has come about through the trade unions. The organization of the CIO in 1935 . . . As a result, numbers of men like those in the steel and automotive industries have been thrown together, black and white, as fellow workers striving for the same objects. There has been on this account an astonishing spread of interracial tolerance and under-standing. Probably no movement in the last 30 years has been so successful in softening race prejudice among the masses.[6]

Horace Cayton and George Mitchell, Herbert Northrup, and Robert Weaver, while unrelenting in their criticisms of many AFL craft unions and even some CIO practices, are similar to DuBois in their overall enthusiastic evaluation of CIO racial practices.[7]

Many of these writers assume that there was a racially egalitarian logic to industrial unionism in this country. Herbert Gutman and Spero and Harris, to take several seminal, quite perceptive labor historians, have argued that there is a certain inevitability to egalitarian unionism where African-American workers make up substantial portions of the workforce and where the union has a "broad social philosophy."[8] It is argued by many that the logic of successful industrial unionism requires the organization of inclusive, solidaristic unions when the industries are composed of low-skilled, racially and ethnically heterogeneous workforces. To act otherwise is to plant the seeds of failure before the journey is begun. I will discuss later the degree to which these structural determinants have proved necessary or sufficient for the formation of racially egalitarian unions.

Highly critical evaluation of industrial unions emerged in full force in the 1960s. The most across-the-board rejection of the above positive evaluations may be found in the work of Herbert Hill.[9] Hill's work, filled with scathing criticisms and exposures of many supposedly racially egalitarian unions, provides a dramatic wake-up call to complacent acceptance of the older, established wisdom on the CIO. Hill argues that even the most "racially progressive" industrial unions have inevitably become white job-control organizations; these unions often espoused egalitarian rhetoric for expediency, where blacks had substantial percentages in an industry, particularly during early periods of new organizing. After becoming established, the unions then used their organizations to lock African-American workers out of access to superior jobs. Hill argues that there were few exceptions among unions, including those with left-wing leadership.[10]

Hill and many others assume that the exclusive, primary, or major reasons for racial inequalities at the workplace and within the labor market are the racial privileges or advantages that white workers gain from such arrangements and the racist attitudes that they express. Thus, the natural expectation one would have for labor unions (be they all-white or racially integrated unions— presumably overwhelmingly African-American and other minority organizations would be an exception) is that they would be discriminatory.[11]

My argument in this essay will be that each of the two major alternative theories—the one that concentrates on the logic of industrial unionism and the other that emphasizes the racial attitudes of white workers—have identified an important aspect of reality. Yet each theory is inadequate, as a comprehensive argument or even combined with the other. To get to the root of things, we must recognize that there is now and was during the 1930s and 1940s a range of racial practice by unions (how wide we shall try to determine). One must disaggregate union practice, not merely by union and industry. One must look at the percentage of African-American workers in a union, industry, and area; one must take into account the locale, especially the percentage of the workers in the South; one must distinguish between the attitudes and practices of local officers, the international union, and rank-and-file members; finally, one must look at the historical development of particular unions, for some unions improved their racial policies while others deteriorated. Only by considering all these factors can one make a considered judgment. Although I will refer here to racial practices of CIO unions in all parts of the country, my focal point will be on the South, for it was in the South that racial discrimination was arguably harshest, the system of white supremacy most rigidly entrenched in law, custom, and social practice, and the commitment to egalitarianism most severely tested.

EARLY INTERRACIAL LABOR ORGANIZATION

Interracial labor struggles, organization and varying degrees of egalitarian practice existed in the United States in isolated, atypical instances long before the rise of the CIO. A characteristic of all these early cases was a significant proportion of African-American laborers, whose joint organization with whites in some fashion or another was seen as a prerequisite for obtaining bargaining leverage against employers. Yet the racial mix of the potential constituency, while seemingly a necessary condition, was never sufficient by itself to insure that interracial organization would be attempted, since it was only in rare circumstances that it was even tried. Nor was successful interracial organization sufficient to insure minimal success, because the weight and wrath of challenged white supremacy, in addition to normal opposition to unions, was usually enough to crush such struggles. Nevertheless, this heritage was not without its influence during the 1930s.

Black and white farmers and rural poor in the South united and struggled together briefly during the Reconstruction (circa 1866–1876) and the Populist eras (circa 1888–1896). Both were defeated by a combination of racist hysteria, intense economic and social pressure against individuals in the movements, voter fraud, physical intimidation, violence, and murder, leaving the lower classes cowed and defeated; white supremacist hegemony reemerged, after the defeat of both movements, more dominant than ever. The reaction to Reconstruction and Populism in the South made clear to all that whatever the compelling logic of lower-class, interracial organization in the abstract, the likely consequences in practice would be harsh indeed. Nevertheless, interracial working-class movements continued to emerge in the South.

Recent scholarship has uncovered extensive organization of black and white workers in the South by the Knights of Labor during the 1880s and 1890s. Melton McLaurin describes not merely joint organization but integrated struggles against segregation and successful political activities. Peter Rachleff's study of Richmond in the 1880s and 1890s shows the strength of solidaristic interracial unions and the rise of black political power and influence, as well as the occasional forthright stands of the Knights on racial issues.[12] At the 1886 Knights convention, for example, held in Richmond, the capital of the old Confederacy, national leaders successfully insisted that Richmond theaters and hotels accept African-American delegates, causing a stir throughout the whole South. In 1886, in the Fourth Congressional district of North Carolina, made up of the eight counties centered in the Raleigh-Durham area, state master workman John Nichols, a pro-Union printer (that is, he defended the North during the Civil War because he was an abolitionist) and outspoken supporter of the Knights' liberal racial policies, was elected to Congress.[13] The policies of the Knights were, to be sure, highly contradictory, but their activities in Richmond and elsewhere—especially their commitment to integrated unions—often necessitated a frontal challenge to white supremacy.

Varying degrees of interracial unity were also achieved by New Orleans waterfront workers from the end of the Civil War in 1865 until the crushing of union organization in the Crescent City in the 1920s.[14] Tens of thousands of African-American and white woodworkers in Louisiana and Texas organized by the Brotherhood of Timberworkers, affiliated for a while with the Industrial Workers of the World (IWW), also achieved impressive solidarity and organization from 1910–1913.[15] And the mine workers (who will be discussed below) were committed to interracial organizing in the Deep South from the 1890s on. These cases were, of course, atypical, although it is unclear to what extent more was possible had there been additional energy and commitment directed toward such attempts.[16]

In contrast to these exceptional cases, most craft unions were openly racist, excluding black members either formally or by custom. Many AFL unions with industrial jurisdictions, be they in the North or South, even where a so-called logic of industrial unionism dictated that they organize African-American workers, rejected interracial unionism, thus giving up on successful industrial organization from the start. Those who found it necessary to accept black members because of their high percentage in a trade—for example, in longshore and many of the trowel trades in the South—generally organized them into separate locals and gave them inferior status. Primarily northern industrial campaigns under AFL auspices in steel (1919) and meatpacking (1917–1922) failed in good part because of their inability to convince African-American workers that their interests would be served by AFL unions. The AFL and independent railroad unions, prior to the 1930s, with several important exceptions, only varied in the degree and forms of implementation of extreme racist practices. Even the socialists within the AFL were hardly any different. Despite the antiracism of some left socialists at this time and even occasionally a few socialists on the right, the range of socialist principles varied by and large from the outright racism of Victor Berger to the benign neglect of Eugene Debs.[17]

THE CIO BREAK WITH AFL RACIAL PRACTICES

From its beginning in 1935, the CIO espoused racially egalitarian rhetoric. The question naturally arises of the degree to which its practice represented a break from AFL racial policies or was merely a continuation of these practices in a new setting, that is, an industrial setting in which white workers—who could not control the labor market for themselves in unskilled industrial workplaces without enlisting the support of their black fellow workers—made the necessary opportunistic overtures. To answer this question one must first look at the roots of the egalitarian stance in the CIO.

Aside from structural imperatives, the impetus for egalitarianism in the CIO came from two sources. The first and initially defining source was the ex-AFL unions that came to form the CIO. Primarily this meant the 600,000-member United Mine Workers of America (UMWA) and secondarily the needle trades unions centered in New York City, particularly the International Ladies Garment Workers Union (ILGWU) and the Amalgamated Clothing Workers of America (ACWA). The second source was the left organizations, primarily the Communist Party (CP), whose members were central to, and in many cases the only important organizers, in most of the key unorganized industrial sectors (including auto, longshore, steel, electrical, maritime, and tobacco). Secondarily were a small number of other leftists, most of whom were associated with A. J. Muste or with the left-wing of the Socialist Party (SP), the latter group including Myles Horton, Highlander Folk School director, and the leaders of the Southern Tenant Farmers Union (STFU).

Evaluative Criteria

Any attempt to evaluate the racial practice of the CIO as a whole, of its component unions, and of various fractions within it must be multidimensional and systematic, not merely anecdotal. Five criteria seem pertinent in this regard.

First is the degree of union access itself. The independent railroad and many AFL craft unions totally excluded blacks and other minorities. These unions served to control jobs for whites (or a particular white ethnic group), denying representation and jobs to all others, enforcing their claims by job actions, contracts, state licensing and apprenticeship requirements, and even occasionally (as was the case in the early 1930s with the railroad unions) by murder. Other unions accepted black members but put them in inferior, subordinate, separate black locals. A further level of access was the degree to which black workers occupied leadership and paid staff positions within a formally open, interracial union and at what levels. The mine workers, for example, had numerous African-American local officals and even a number of district staff and organizers, but almost no blacks in national positions or on national staff.

Second, one wants to know the degree to which a union defended the rights of employed black workers. Equal pay for equal work was the most elementary principle, doing away with differentials by race or gender for the same type of job. Even with equal pay for equal work, however, equal rights were often denied. A higher-level principle demanded equal access to upgrading, especially to the most skilled and desirable jobs, often designated informally as the province of white males. These first two criteria involved defending the formal rights of already employed African-American workers.

Third, there were additional substantive concerns, beginning with discrimination in the hiring and job placement process. In many industries, blacks were excluded from hiring (as in textile or electrical) or when hired were sent to the worst areas and jobs (foundry work in many industries or coke plants in steel). With only department seniority—with no plant-wide bidding on open jobs—African-American workers were usually frozen from the better jobs from the beginning. This type of discrimination was difficult to challenge successfully, since attacks against it confronted basic issues of management rights, of which the right to hire was central.

Fourth is the degree to which a union supported or took the lead in civil rights activities. In the South especially, the more egalitarian industrial unions mobilized their members for the abolition of the poll tax, antilynching legislation, and the right to vote for African-Americans.

Fifth is the extent of egalitarian education and the involvement of workers, particularly whites, in the struggles for equality both inside and outside the workplace.

Finally, the union may be judged by the extent to which social equality was practiced among members and their families in union social affairs.

Some qualifications in applying these standards must be made for time and place. Unions that held integrated meetings and had any black officers at all in the Deep South in the 1930s were often taking far more audacious steps and presenting greater challenges to the system of white supremacy than were many unions in the 1960s which had these characteristics and took highly visible, public civil rights stances but did little to combat discrimination at the workplace.

With these criteria in mind, let us turn our initial attention to the UMWA influence on CIO racial policy. We shall then look at several other mainstream CIO unions, which also had substantial percentages of African-American workers.

THE MINE WORKERS' TRADITION IN THE CIO

The United Mine Workers of America

Coal mining during the 1930s was a highly competitive, labor-intensive industry. Its workforce was extremely heterogeneous both ethnically and racially, although this varied a good deal by region.[18] There were only small differentials in pay, skill, and general occupational status; to the extent that these existed, however, black workers were underrepresented at the top. Coal miners generally lived in highly controlled, repressive, isolated company towns. During strikes, there was often widespread violence and occasionally massive attempts to use strikebreakers, sometimes of a different racial or ethnic group from the strikers. Coal miners the world over throughout history have had a high propensity to strike;[19] the U.S. coal fields were no exception. These characteristics make coal mining in this country the archtypical case, where the logic of industrial unionism should have made labor organization interracial and egalitarian.

Before the turn of the century, the defeat of large-scale miners' struggles had made clear both to broad cross sections of miners and the leadership of their union that successful organization required intense solidarity, especially across racial and ethnic lines.[20] It also required great physical risks and exceptional militancy. Some have argued that building unions in such circumstances required a pragmatic—some might say opportunistic—commitment to include all workers and to make a minimal show of concern for the grievances of all groups. It is, as Stanley Greenberg notes, a "plausible scenario," but one that is far from inevitable. The rejection of white-only unions put workers, particularly but not only in the South, in open opposition to the whole system of white supremacy, hence to key economic interests in the South, the mores of the community, and in many places, the unrestricted power of the state. In the face of such opposition, many unions, despite the "logical" requirements of organization, chose other strategies. The Amalgamated Association in iron and steel, the International Association of Machinists (IAM) in many industries, the International Longshoremen's Association (ILA) in southern longshore, and the Mechanics Educational Society of America in auto all chose racially exclusionary strategies, while the International Woodworkers of America (IWA) after a right-wing leadership seized control of the union in 1940 with the active aid of the CIO national office, abandoned any attempt to organize its largely southern black constituency.

Thus the UMWA, from the time of its founding, embarked on a course that, whatever its flaws and defects, put it into conflict with many aspects of the system of white supremacy. Unlike certain left-led unions that were organized later, the UMWA did not start with a commitment to an all-around struggle for racial equality or an analysis of the importance of this struggle for class solidarity and consciousness. Rather, starting from a commitment to organizing all workers equally, the UMWA was led to challenge white supremacy in important ways and to fight for certain interests of its African-American members. In Alabama, they fought against the poll tax. They engaged in extensive voter registration efforts, first registering white miners, then mobilizing them in large numbers to assist in the registration of their African-American coworkers. They held integrated meetings and social activities, often in areas where these were illegal.[21] Despite the racist attitudes of many white miners, especially in the northern coal fields, and the hesitancies by some national leaders, the early UMWA was unique in the AFL with its many black officials, staff, and organizers.[22] At a time when virtually all middle-class African-American organizations were anti-union, one National Association for the Advancement of Colored People (NAACP) fieldworker who visited Birmingham in 1922 was extremely impressed by the number of black UMWA organizers, the lack of salary differentials vis-à-vis their white counterparts, and the general egalitarian atmosphere of union meetings. The UMWA fought for the destruction of racially based pay differentials in the South and maintained a principled, determined opposition to the Ku Klux Klan (KKK) at the local and national levels.[23] The national office of the UMWA from the beginning espoused a rhetoric of racial equality. John L. Lewis himself was an outspoken advocate of civil rights issues, often promoting black leadership. The UMWA continued its antidiscriminatory practices during the 1930s after they had successfully organized virtually all of the nation's coal miners, including those in the South. Wherever they were located, highly mobilized black and white coal miners were the shock troops in other interracial organizing efforts.

The accomplishments of the UMWA are impressive, especially in the South. Despite the defects of the UMWA at both the local and national levels with respect to its racial policies (and there were many), black coal miners left no doubt how they tallied the balance sheet. As Ronald Lewis argues, "Whatever local discrimination blacks encountered in their dealings with white miners, in the context of southern society the UMWA was the most progressive force in their lives."[24] African-American UMWA coal miners were the most steadfast and committed of unionists. They refused to scab and were involved in many of the most heroic and violent battles waged by the union, including the armed march of thousands of Appalachian coal miners on Blair Mountain.[25] Their contributions were duly recognized by their white union compatriots.

In spite of—or alongside of—the racially egalitarian thrust of the UMWA, there was a continuing thread of antiegalitarianism in many levels of the union. A number of the defects of the UMWA with regard to its racial policies have been described by Herbert Hill. The UWMA paper at times had racist jokes. The attitudes toward African-American strike breakers were both harsher than the attitudes toward white strike breakers and totally out of proportion to their frequency in comparison to nonblacks, reflecting the general racism of society.[26]

The UMWA was highly variegated, with a range of racial practices by district and leaders, even under the Lewis regime. Many of the worst attitudes and practices, including the exclusion of black union miners from jobs by white unionists, took place in the overwhelmingly white northern fields.[27] A number of the officials who were to become central to the CIO leadership in the late 1930s and in the 1940s were among those who were least firm on racial issues. Van Bittner, later a vice president of the United Steel Workers and the head of the CIO's Operation Dixie—the CIO's post–World War II campaign to organize the South—is a case in point. Bittner's appeal to black miners in Alabama during the 1908 strike smacks of racial insensitivity at best: he warned black miners that if they did not support the strike the union would abandon them forever, letting them "live in slavery the rest of their days.[28]" At the 1924 UMWA convention, Bittner tried to weaken the union's anti-Klan position in an attempt to appease racist whites, particularly in the northern fields. The overwhelming majority of white delegates, as well as the small number of black delegates, vehemently rejected the committee proposal advocated by Bittner. UMWA vice president Philip Murray—later steel workers and CIO president—himself rooted in the northern fields, denounced interracial "mingling" during a 1928 strike in Pennsylvania, attacking African-American strike-breakers in highly racist terms.[29] Although the halo of racial egalitarianism hung over all ex-UMWA officials for a long time, it is clear that Phillip Murray, Van Bittner, and Adolph Germer, to name only three of the more prominent ex-UMWA, CIO officials, were among the least committed, ranking other more conservative concerns more highly, even before the anticommunist purges of the late 1940s. Their attitudes were in sharp contrast not only to those of black miners and officials but to those of more progressive white miners and officials as well, especially those on the left.

In the end, the UMWA failed its ultimate test. As the industry began heavily automating after World War II, the union did not defend the interests of its African-American members. When their manual jobs were eliminated in greater proportion than those of whites, the union did not demand that they have priority in gaining newly created jobs over recently hired, lower-seniority white employees. By not making minewide and companywide seniority rights central to its demands, by not believing that it had a responsibility to fight the many racially discriminatory policies of the companies in changing their workforces as employers eliminated manual jobs and added new machine jobs, the UMWA completely abandoned its black members, allowing them to be driven out of the industry. Miners won minewide seniority in the late 1940s, but by the time they had won companywide seniority in many districts in the 1960s, most black workers were already gone from the industry.[30]

Steel

The campaign to organize steel in the 1930s was a direct outgrowth of the activities of the UMWA. UMWA and CIO president John L. Lewis saw the organization of steel as critical to the stability of the miners' union; thus, he gave it the highest priority within the CIO, assigning hundreds of organizers and numerous high-ranking UMWA officials and allocating it a large budget. Lewis and his lieutenants also assumed day-to-day, hands-on control. Thus, the initial activities of the Steel Workers' Organizing Committee (SWOC) seemed to be infused with the same racial idealism as that associated with the UMWA.[31]

Steel workers had higher wages and more extreme occupational differentials than coal workers; job hierarchies were stratified ethnically, but even more so racially. Still, the multiethnic, multiracial nature of the workforce, especially in the steel centers of Pittsburgh, Chicago, and Birmingham, seemed to require both an interracial and an egalitarian approach. To facilitate such a campaign and the building of racially egalitarian unionism, the Steel Workers' Organizing Committee developed an alliance with the left-wing National Negro Congress (NNC), which made special appeals to African-American workers.[32] John L. Lewis directly enlisted the support of the Communist Party, which, according to William Z. Foster, contributed sixty of the initial two hundred organizers, a number of whom were black. Without these alliances and the many African-American organizers, most with left-wing affiliations, it is doubtful that the SWOC campaign would have been successful. As a conscious part of its interracial strategy, there were many racially egalitarian activities that characterized the initial SWOC organizing in many places.

In some situations, white workers instinctively recognized that antiracist demands were at the root of strong solidaristic unions. White steelworkers joined with their black comrades in their own "civil rights revolution" in the late-1930s in newly organized steel towns lining the Allegheny, Monongahela, and Ohio rivers, desegregating everything in sight, from restaurants and department stores to movie theaters and swimming pools.[33] Thus, even in the North, for many white industrial unionists, even when there were not large percentages of African-American workers, the fight for racial equality was seen as a key to their own struggles for justice, dignity, and a living wage. Parallel accounts emerge from other steel centers.

Unlike in the UMWA, however, this racially egalitarian thrust was to disappear quickly as a defining characteristic of the union once organization was completed. Here and there, battles against discrimination burst forward after the steel industry had been organized. Invariably led by black workers, these struggles usually received at best only minimal, reluctant support from the leadership and had little resonance within the union.[34] This outcome is only partly explained by the racial hierarchy of wages and jobs and the associated entrenched racial privileges of an important segment of white workers. Equally important was the stifling of rank-and-file organization, militancy, and democratic control of the union by the highly bureaucratic Murray leadership. The establishment of the first contract with U.S. Steel without the types of struggle that took place in auto, longshore, meat packing, and other industries allowed CIO-appointed United Steel Workers of America (USWA) president Philip Murray to assert top-down control, appointing all initial officials and stifling opportunities for democratic rank-and-file influence. This too was an important legacy of the UMWA as nonelected, former Lewis supporters controlled all the top positions in the new steelworkers union. Communist and other leftist organizers, their services now unnecessary, were quickly removed. No longer needing to mobilize all segments of the workforce to engage in successful struggle against the company, demands that were designed specifically to enlist the support of African-American workers dropped in priority. The privileges of white workers were frozen, and highly discriminatory job classification systems were strengthened with the acceptance of departmental, rather than plantwide, seniority. These discriminatory provisions, contractually codified by the union, were successfully challenged in court during the 1970s, one of the most important cases being the consent decree at the Sparrows Point, Maryland, Bethlehem Steel plant, forcing the union and the company to pay aggrieved black workers millions of dollars in pay equity.

The union congealed along its nonegalitarian path in 1949 and 1950 with its destruction of Mine Mill, a largely black union; the USWA made racist, anticommunist appeals to white workers, attacking African-American workers, their leaders, and their white supporters (the Mine Mill case will be discussed in more detail below).

Auto

Some of the same impulses that led to the abandonment of egalitarianism by the USWA existed in the UAW, although the situation was not nearly so extreme for a number of reasons. First, there was more initial rank-and-file democracy in the UAW than in steel. The union had strong locals and a history of struggle, necessitated by the more prolonged battle to establish and maintain the union. Second, though communist influence—with the exception of certain indigenous black members like Hosea Hudson in Birmingham and in isolated locals in Little Steel—was eliminated quickly in the USWA, in the UAW communist influence and pressure for racial equality had a longer history. Third, the social democratic Reuther group was more committed in principle to racial equality than was the relatively conservative group of leaders who were placed in the leadership of the USWA. As a result, the Reuther group's tolerance for overtly racist behavior was much lower than that of the steel leadership group.

Still, in the factional struggles in the auto industry of the 1930s and 1940s, black workers tended in large majority to support the CP-led caucuses. Reuther had his strongest base of support among privileged white skilled workers, who were, to say the least, not moved to take the lead or support struggles for racial equality. Thus the Reuther leadership had little motivation to advance the cause of black workers in the shop. At Local 6 UAW, a large Chicago-area construction equipment plant of the International Harvester Company (IHC), where a strong CP-led left opposition existed in the post–World War II period, for example, racial equality was an issue pushed by the left caucus and largely opposed by the pro-administration Reuther caucus. When the plant reopened for civilian production in 1946 (during the war it had been a Buick engine plant), black workers were initially confined to janitorial jobs, mostly below the shop floor cleaning the washrooms. The left caucus, which had the allegiance of the majority of black workers, led the successful fight for opening machining and assembly-line jobs to black workers. The nearby left-wing Farm Equipment Workers Union (FE) local at IHC's Tractor Works in Chicago, which had a better civil rights record and a far more aggressive stance on such issues, won complete plantwide seniority for job bidding and layoffs at an early time. Local 6, despite UAW rhetoric, never won or fought for full plantwide seniority.[35]

It is important to note that the establishment of racially egalitarian unions was not an easy task, even with the best of intentions and efforts. The discriminatory hiring and job placement and racially circumscribed opportunities for upgrading in industrial workplaces were not primarily a consequence of the activities and attitudes of white workers. Rather, this discrimination was part of the general system of white supremacy, promulgated and reinforced by large agricultural interests in the South, whose desires and needs for cheap agricultural labor required poor, powerless black labor and racial hierarchies that kept African-Americans on the bottom and blacks and whites divided. Southern plantation owners had political power and influence, not merely in the black belt areas of the South that they dominated economically but in the rest of the South as well, and even in the politics of the country as a whole.[36] This system, backed by economic and political power, legal and illegal repression, and much public opinion, could not always be confronted head-on, although it is easy to see that the reticence of racial conservatives was mainly an excuse for inaction rather than a measured analysis of reality. There was often very strong resistance from white workers, which was real but whose permanence over time is often exaggerated. With these caveats, it is instructive to look at several left-led unions to see whether their commitment and practice were different from that of the UMWA and the more mainstream CIO unions.

LEFT-LED UNIONS

Mine, Mill, and Smelter Workers

The International Union of Mine, Mill, and Smelter Workers of America (referred to as Mine Mill) had its roots in the left-wing Western Federation of Miners, a mainstay of the Industrial Workers of the World at the time of the IWW's founding in 1905. Such a tradition, it should be noted, did not necessarily lead to egalitarian practice or even to a commitment to the organization of African-American workers. One organization that had IWW roots, the Sailors International Union–Sailors Union of the Pacific (SIU-SUP) is a case in point. SIU-SUP's syndicalism, while rooted in IWW tradition, developed an all-white, eventually racist, job-control orientation. The right wing of the International Woodworkers of America in the Northwest also had its roots in the IWW, but its syndicalism emphasized local control, turning it towards provincialism, anticommunism, and abandonment of the South and that region's largely African-American woodworkers. Mine Mill's tradition was less provincial. At the time of the union's revitalization, there was an active minority of communists, committed to interracial unionism and the vigorous organization of African-American workers. This influence was particularly strong among the overwhelmingly black metal miners in the Birmingham area. The communists, a distinct minority in 1934, highly critical of both the local and international Mine Mill leadership, gained dominant influence in the union after Reid Robinson was elected president in 1936; Robinson, elected as a noncommunist, quickly gravitated toward communist politics after his election.

Metal mining in the Birmingham, Alabama, area, like coal mining there, was done by a workforce whose pay and occupation classifications were not highly differentiated. In the early 1930s, 80 percent of this workforce was black. Paylines, mine cars, and work areas were integrated with both black and white foremen, although integrated crews and whites working for black foremen were eliminated after Mine Mill became established.[37] From the beginning of organizing in 1933, Mine Mill had far greater support from black workers than from whites, although at certain times, for example, in 1938, when Mine Mill won reinstatement of all 160 workers fired in the 1936 strike, there was also significant white support. In part because of the preponderance of black workers but also because of the growing role of communists (many of whom were black), Mine Mill from the outset had "an air of civil rights activism."[38] Mine Mill not only fought in the workplace for better working conditions and racial egalitarianism, it also campaigned actively in the community. Along with Alabama miners and steel workers, Mine Mill members engaged extensively in voter registration and in campaigns against the poll tax and lynching, giving it the character of a broad-based social movement as well as a workplace union. Kelley claims: "More blacks were elected to leadership positions within Mine Mill than any other CIO union, and its policy of racial egalitarianism remained unmatched," although he gives no figures or comparative measures.[39] Mine Mill's record with regard to Chicano workers in the Southwest was of a similar character.[40]

Even after the defeat of Mine Mill in workplace representation elections in the Birmingham area in 1949 and 1950, the union continued to be heavily involved in civil rights activity. In Bessemer, large numbers of Mine Mill members joined the NAACP chapter en masse, taking it over, carrying out an aggressive set of civil rights activities throughout the early 1950s.[41]

Mine Mill made a strategic mistake in not attempting to challenge more vigorously the change in hiring policy of Tennessee Coal, Iron, and Railroad (TCI, the largest mine and steel company in the Birmingham area). After the 1938 NLRB victory, white workers joined Mine Mill in large numbers. TCI then attempted to divide the workforce. Whereas they had previously hired mostly black workers, after 1938 TCI began hiring predominantly whites. The company also gave better jobs to those workers who did not join Mine Mill.[42]

The successful attempt of the steel workers in 1949 and 1950 to take over Alabama Mine Mill locals relied on overtly racist appeals to white workers. A CIO representative who told an all-white meeting of Mine Mill members that they would have to accept blacks when they joined the USWA was quickly replaced by one who promised all white locals in the Steelworkers' Union. Just before the 1949 TCI election between the steelworkers and Mine Mill, the KKK staged a large rally in support of the steelworkers. Despite the early antiracism of the SWOC, the leadership of the union, led by CIO president Philip Murray, barely complained. In demogogic fashion the steel workers attempted to hide their activities by accusing Mine Mill of fomenting racism and further claiming that this overwhelming black local union with its black leadership was itself allied with the KKK. The steel workers, in tactics reminiscent of the KKK during Reconstruction and in the counterattack on the Populist movement, attempted to isolate black workers by physically attacking the small number of whites who remained loyal to Mine Mill. In at least one instance, at the Muscoda Local 123 in Bessemer, black Mine Mill members rallied armed contingents from the black community to successfully defend their white union brothers from USWA-led assaults. These racist activities and assaults by the USWA were among many things that moved the CIO as a whole from an incipient antiracism to acquiescence, if not open support for discrimination against black workers.[43]

One could, of course, argue that the structure of metal mining employment and the high percentage of African-American workers in the Birmingham area led Mine Mill initially to interracial, egalitarian unionism and that the reaction of the increasing percentages of white workers to union policies was also inevitable. Such an analysis, however, while containing an important grain of truth, would belittle two important factors. One is the conscious choices of alternative leadership groups. The CP-led Mine Mill leaders chose to emphasize demands for racial equality, appealing directly to the interests of African-American workers. The conservative Murray leadership was willing to make racist appeals to white workers and abandon the interests of black workers in order to defeat the communists. Both leadership groups made conscious choices that were not predetermined. Second, the victory of the Murray leadership in Birmingham was not preordained either. They only won during the highpoint of Cold War anticommunism, supported by local and regional white supremacists in the South, Dixiecrat politicians, the CIO national office, the might of the federal government, and USWA violence against Mine Mill members and officials. And, even then, the critical election votes were close. The significance of structural factors and the racial attitudes of white workers cannot be assessed without taking account of these decisive components.

Food, Tobacco, and Agricultural Workers Union

The Food, Tobacco, and Agricultural Workers Union (FTA), unlike Mine Mill, USWA, UMWA, and the UAW, was an almost totally southern union. It was led and staffed by communists from its inception. In 1937, John L. Lewis appointed the highly energetic, recently fired economics instructor, and open communist, Donald Henderson to form the United Cannery, Agricultural, Packing, and Allied Workers of America (UCAPAWA), the forerunner of FTA (which became the name of the union in 1944). FTA's southern membership was initially overwhelmingly black with two main bases of support. The first was in an area of the Mississippi delta, emanating from its strongholds in the Memphis area, made up of workers in cotton compress plants, cottonseed plants, feed mills, and wholesale grocers.[44] The second stronghold was in the tobacco processing plants of Virginia and North Carolina. In both places, the union had strong black leadership. The most important local in Memphis was Local 19, led by a black man, John Mack Dyson, also an FTA executive board member. The anchor of FTA strength in tobacco was Winston-Salem Local 22 which had over ten thousand members in the R. J. Reynolds plant there. The national union helped train and promote Moranda Smith, a black female leader of the local, to become the director of the Southeast region. FTA was especially notable for its many black female officers and organizers, a striking anomaly within the CIO.[45]

In both main areas of FTA strength, conditions were considered inhospitable to unionism. As Herbert Northrup argues: "In few industries have conditions been so unfavorable as in the tobacco industry."[46] CIO activity began there in 1937, when four hundred African-American women stemmers walked out at the I. N. Vaughan Company in Richmond. Shunned by the AFL's Tobacco Workers International Union, the women finally gained support from the Southern Negro Youth Congress, a CP-led youth section of the NNC. "Within forty-eight hours the strikers had secured wage increases, a forty-hour week, and union recognition. . . . What is even more remarkable is that the strikers were considered absolutely unorganizable before they walked out."[47] Other victories followed, with the tobacco workers eventually affiliating with the UCAPAWA, CIO.

FTA organizing of tobacco workers had many of the characteristics of a "crusade" with civil rights struggles occupying a central place.[48] They had extensive educational activities involving both black and white workers, including a large library for members of Local 22. They also held a wide array of integrated social and athletic affairs, including picnics involving thousands of workers.[49] Local 22 was a center of oppositional cultural and political activity. Paul Robeson in particular appeared frequently in support of strikes and major events. FTA members also received entertainment and encouragement from Zephilia Horton, Woody Guthrie, and Pete Seeger. The union attempted to gain civil rights and greater political power in Winston-Salem and in North Carolina generally, by extensive voter registration campaigns and by supporting "pro-labor" candidates. Hundreds of FTA members also poured into the Winston-Salem NAACP, turning it into a large branch with over a thousand members, militantly committed to civil rights actions.[50] A correspondent for the black newspaper, the *Pittsburgh Courier*, wrote in June of 1944, "I was aware of a growing solidarity and intelligent mass action that will mean a New Day in the South. One cannot visit Winston-Salem and mingle with the thousands of workers without sensing a revolution in thought and action. If there is a 'New' Negro, he is to be found in the ranks of the labor movement."[51]

In Memphis, the UCAPAWA began organizing large numbers of black workers who had also previously been thought to be unorganizable. CIO organizers quickly found that African-American workers were generally far more ready to join and become active in industrial unions than white workers, particularly in the South. This often led moderate CIO leaders, like Van Bittner and others, to refrain from organizing black workers first, for fear of alienating whites, who they believed would not join largely black organizations. The CP-led UCAPAWA, however, had no such hesitancies and began building an overwhelmingly black membership in Memphis. The militancy of Local 19 and its almost unbroken string of organizing successes stimulated the organization of white workers in both integrated workplaces and in those that were overwhelmingly white[52]—thus showing that the fears of racially conservative CIO leaders were, at the very least, exaggerated. The differences in alternative racial practices are placed in sharp contrast in Memphis.

Conservative Memphis CIO director W. A. Copeland, who owed his position largely to national CIO leader and Murray-ally John Brophy, opposed integrated meetings of black and white workers and had special venom for FTA's racial policies.[53] Black workers, led by UCAPAWA Local 19, engaged in militant actions during World War II, in defiance of no-strike pledges, not merely for wage increases but for the elimination of racially discriminatory wage scales and job classification systems like those at the Buckeye Company, which, to take one instance, "kept blacks in the lowest positions in the plant, forcing them to do the same work as whites for half the pay."[54] In these activities they were opposed by more conservative Tennessee CIO leaders like Copeland and Forrest Dickenson. Copeland and fellow–Memphis Newspaper Guild leader Pete Swim did little to attempt to overcome the racism of white workers and opposed virtually all civil rights activities of local unions. Swim fought national CIO directives to combat racial discrimination. Copeland criticized FTA Local 19 for hiring a black office secretary, opposed the use of blacks as negotiators, and denounced "racial mixing" of whites and blacks at CIO union parties. Copeland also insisted on calling blacks by their first names while addressing whites as Mr., Mrs., or Miss. He and other conservatives attacked the proposal of white moderate state CIO director Paul Christopher to hold integrated CIO meetings at the Highlander Folk School in the spring of 1945.[55] Yet it was these extremely anticommunist and racially conservative southern CIO leaders that the national CIO office was to promote and back in Operation Dixie, other post–World War II organizing, and the battle to purge leftists. Racist leaders were supported by the CIO national office, not so much because the CIO national leaders agreed completely with their racist attitudes but because the desire to eliminate communist influence and to achieve respectability among business leaders and national political elites far outweighed their commitments to building interracial solidarity or even to building a dynamic growing labor movement—a legacy for which today's dwindling union organizations are still paying dearly.

The expulsion of FTA from the CIO in 1950 and the attacks on its locals were to parallel the attack on Mine Mill. Tobacco unionism was crushed when the CIO onslaught against FTA led to the complete destruction of unionism at the Winston-Salem Reynolds plant. The CIO's racism there was to haunt it in the future. In 1956, when the newly merged AFL-CIO made a major effort to organize that plant, they lost the election because black workers refused to support the AFL-CIO tobacco union.[56] In the early 1950s Local 19 was destroyed in Memphis. Antiracist white communists were also expelled from the union movement. These actions, combined with the activities of southern Dixiecrats and segregationists, effectively ended the upsurge of working-class civil rights activity in the South during the late 1940s and early 1950s.

United Packinghouse Workers of America

The United Packinghouse Workers of America (UPWA) operated in an industry with a racially and ethnically highly differentiated workforce, ranging from all white, largely Protestant areas, including the radical Hormel plant in Austin, Minnesota, to the heavily African-American and white Eastern European labor forces in Chicago, the center of the meat packing industry. The meat packing industry as a whole, however, was majority white.

The failure to organize the more recently hired African-American workers in Chicago had proven central to the defeat of the 1917–1922 union organizing campaign.[57] In contrast, the "crusading on the race issue" by the CIO-established Packinghouse Workers Organizing Committee (PWOC) during the late 1930s was the key, according to David Brodie, to the successful organization of packinghouse workers in Chicago.[58] The struggle to forge interracial unity took place over many years and was long and tortuous. The groundwork was laid, according to the seminal works of Eric Halpern and Roger Horowitz, by the extensive interracial unemployed organizing of communists in Chicago and other cities. This interracial unity and sensitivity to the mutual concerns of various groups was forged, sometimes in opposition to and often in the face of the obtuseness of many mainstream CIO leaders, including Van Bittner, the first appointed head of the PWOC.[59] Bittner's role was to foreshadow his insensitivity on questions of race and the repressive, bureaucratic orientation that were two factors that would quickly doom Operation Dixie.

The UPWA was in certain ways more successful in building stable, interracial, egalitarian, antiracist unionism than any other CIO affiliate. Their success, compared to other left unions, was based on several factors. First, unlike the case of Mine Mill, the racial composition of the meat packing industry became increasingly black during World War II, as white workers left to find more desirable jobs. Thus the strong civil rights stand of the union, supported initially by numerous whites, gained greater strength after the 1930s both from the increased number of African-American and from the growing contingent of Hispanic packinghouse workers. Second, although communists played a central role in the union, especially in Chicago, they did not dominate the national leadership of the union. The UPWA president, Ralph Helstein, was a noncommunist radical who had the respect of all factions in the union, including conservatives. Helstein sheltered and appreciated the communists and was himself highly committed to civil rights. The union thus escaped expulsion from the CIO but did not completely change its character like other CIO unions that purged their left-wing leaders.

Unlike in various FTA and Mine Mill workplaces, African Americans remained a minority, although a large one; they were, however, strategically placed as a majority on the all-important killing floors. Nevertheless, UPWA shared many of the antiracist commitments and activities of these other two unions. Although Chicago was a racist, highly segregated city, white supremacy was

not as all-encompassing there as in Memphis or Birmingham.[60] From the beginning, union committees and executive boards were racially and ethnically
integrated.[61] In 1938 a key to the organization of the large Armour plant, with
its high percentage of black workers, was the successful union demand to remove the stars on the time cards of blacks, which easily identified them as the
first to be laid off.[62] The union had a broad range of fully integrated social
activities in Chicago, including baseball, basketball, and bowling leagues, child
care and recreation facilities, dances, and picnics.[63] Along Ashland Avenue, in
the heart of the meat packing district, groups of white and black workers de-
segregated all the formerly whites-only taverns. The first contracts in Chicago
contained language guaranteeing that hiring of black workers be at least in
proportion to their percentage in the Chicago population.[64] During the war,
the union led successful job actions to integrate formerly all-white departments;
in 1948 it forced the hiring of blacks in sales and supervisory positions. The
1945 UPWA convention gave up the air-conditioned comfort of an Omaha
hotel, which had refused to house black members, and met in a sweltering
union hall.[65] By 1952 the UPWA had obtained the desegregation of its facilities in all its southern plants.[66] The active and enthusiastic militancy of African-American workers had direct, positive impact on southern white workers.
African-American Chicago Armour workers proved to be the key to abolishing
the lower wage differentials for largely white southern workers. Like the FTA
in Winston-Salem, UPWA joined and energized the NAACP. According to
Michael Honey, UPWA was the major supporter of the Southern Christian
Leadership Conference (SCLC) and other civil rights activities in the South
during the 1950s and early 1960s.[67] Unlike the UAW, which contributed money
to Martin Luther King from its treasury with little publicity or education among
members, UPWA mobilized members for activity and education, soliciting
contributions in all its locals. Its increasingly aggressive stance on civil rights
issues in the late 1940s and throughout the 1950s energized its black and
Hispanic members but led to diminished activity in the union from white
members, although the union continued to receive tacit support from the
overwhelming majority of the whole membership.[68] It is tempting to speculate
that white workers might have continued their high level of activity within
the union (as they did at the FE's civil rights–oriented Chicago IHC Tractor
Works local) if other larger unions had chosen the path of the relatively small
UPWA.

Clearly in all three unions, FTA, Mine Mill, and UPWA, the egalitarian
policies of the union were a result not only of the policies of the union leadership but of the active involvement and pressure from the high percentages of
African-American workers in these unions. It is reasonable to ask about the
commitment and activities of those left unions with only small percentages of
African-American workers.

United Electrical Workers

The United Electrical Workers (UE) has, for good reason, been a favorite target for those critical of the CP's racial policies in unions. Until its removal from the CIO in 1949, the UE was a stable union with successful organization of its major jurisdictions. In addition, a skilled CP leadership had consistent support from a majority of the membership. Herbert Hill uses the UE as his example to substantiate his assertion that "those industrial unions with a predominantly white membership that were controlled for many years by leaders loyal to the Communist Party were substantially no different in their racial practices than other labor organizations."[69] Hill gives examples of UE indifference to discriminatory hiring practices at the Allen-Bradley plant in Milwaukee, represented by UE Local 1111 since 1937. He also cites a case of International Longshoremen's and Warehousemen's Union (ILWU) battles against discrimination charges over ILWU practices in Portland, Oregon.[70] Donald Critchlow also discusses weaknesses in the UE's commitment to fighting discrimination during World War II. He compares UE unfavorably to the largely white, CP-led National Maritime Union (NMU), which he feels was far more consistent in its fight for egalitarianism. Although the electrical industry was only several percent black, Critchlow argues that UE districts in the New York/New Jersey area and the St. Louis area were exceptions to the UE national organization. New York UE Local 1225 developed a program to combat discrimination in hiring, which yielded a significant increase in the number of blacks in the electrical industry there.[71] Critchlow attributes this activity in New York and St. Louis to higher percentages of black workers in the electrical industry there, although in New York, the figure was probably never much over 10 percent. Critchlow claims that the UE national office never gave much support to or publicized the efforts of these districts, despite UE lip service to antidiscrimination and its official involvement in a host of civil rights activities.

Ronald Schatz, in a more sympathetic account of the UE, confirms both the lack of aggressiveness of UE leaders on issues of discrimination as well as their inability to counter management discrimination and the racial prejudices of their white members.[72] Mark McColloch, on the other hand, claims that the UE was miles ahead of the International Union of Electrical Workers (IUE), the CIO union set up to replace the UE. UE, McColloch claims, had successfully fought for the job rights of already employed black and women workers. One of the keys to this struggle was the winning and maintaining of plantwide seniority for job bidding and layoffs. Throughout the 1950s, UE successfully struggled to retain plantwide seniority, while the IUE retreated to department seniority, locking women and minority workers into inferior job and promotion paths and thus replicating the discriminatory practices supported by the USWA in the steel industry.[73] Still, the UE leadership does not appear to have been nearly as aggressive or committed to racial egalitarianism as their rhetoric suggested or as were the left leaderships of a number of other unions.

National Maritime Union

Critchlow finds NMU racial practices during World War II much different from those of the UE. The NMU was a CP-led union with no more than 10 percent black membership. The union was formed in 1937, as militant workers broke from the segregated International Seamens Union (ISU). The unified black and white sit-downs that formed the union became, according to Critchlow, a part of the union tradition. The union elected a black secretary-treasurer and had large numbers of black delegates at conventions.[74] The NMU also cautiously but steadfastly struggled for the full rights of blacks on ships. They did this even in the face of racist appeals to white workers by the SIU-SUP, a syndicalist union that was supported by the third camp Workers Party, whose virulent anticommunism led them to support an overtly racist union against the CP-led NMU. The NMU conducted education campaigns on the role of blacks in the industry and reported extensively on civil rights activities. Its education department, headed by Leo Huberman, widely publicized successful struggles for integration and carried on a steady stream of educational activities through its newspapers, pamphlets, books, organized discussions on ships, and in-port lectures. The CP-led Inland Boat division of the NMU, representing a 100 percent white constituency on the southern Mississippi River, not only agitated around civil rights issues, but successfully mobilized its membership to support the struggles of overwhelmingly black longshoremen in Memphis and other southern river ports. The inland boat workers opposed the poll tax and lynching and even expelled a member for stirring up racial prejudice. They did not, however, during this period attempt to change the racist hiring practices of the inland boat companies.[75]

The NMU began to break down the racial division of labor during the war on ocean vessels (according to both Critchlow and Honey) and in the Deep South on river vessels after the war, but this activity came to a complete halt when anticommunists gained control of the NMU and purged the communists in the late 1940s.[76]

Local 1199

As a final gloss on this question, we might examine the activities of New York Local 1199. During the anticommunist purges, 1199 was expelled from the Retail, Wholesale, and Department Store Union (RWDSU). At that time it was mainly an all-white organization of Jewish druggists in New York City under CP leadership. Local 1199, according to Michael Honey, was the only labor organization besides the UPWA that both gave money to SCLC and mobilized its membership actively in support of civil rights. In the early 1960s their hundreds of members were a fixture at major civil rights rallies along the East Coast. During the 1960s this small union successfully organized low-paid, overwhelmingly black hospital workers in the New York City area, growing into a union with tens of thousands of members.

Without minimizing the deficiencies of certain left-led unions and the wide range of commitments and activities, it is clear, contrary to Hill's assertions, that the racial practices of many were decisively more egalitarian than those of the best non-left CIO unions, which in turn were themselves different from some of the least egalitarian unions.[77]

DEFINING THE ISSUES

What can we reasonably conclude from this brief summary of certain aspects of CIO experience?

The Logic of Industrial Unionism Thesis

STRUCTURAL FACTORS.   It is clear that structural characteristics play an important role in laying the basis for interracial unionism. Low-skilled workforces with high percentages of African-American workers—especially where they have crucial leverage within the labor process—are more likely to be organized on an interracial basis into unions that have varying degrees of commitment to racial egalitarianism. While these structural features would seem to be necessary prerequisites, there are some noted exceptions, that is, largely white workforces with interracial unions with strong commitments to racial equality. NMU, FE, the CP-led Fur and Leather Workers Union,[78] and the early Local 1199 are cases in point. However necessary such structural prerequisites may be generally, it is absolutely clear that they are never sufficient. Rather, the structural factors represent only the greater degree of potential for racially egalitarian unions. Unions such as the Amalgamated Association of Iron and Steel Workers and the SIU-SUP adopted openly racist stances, insuring their ultimate failures.[79] The ILGWU, which started as a racially progressive union, became more discriminatory as its membership became more nonwhite and as its increasingly isolated white leaders strove to maintain complete control.[80] The IWA under right-wing leadership abandoned organizing the largely black, low-paid southern woodworkers, despite the potential they showed for organization. Other unions, including the steel workers, organized interracially and had rhetorical commitments to civil rights, yet still found ways to continue and even deepen discriminatory practices. Thus, while acknowledging the importance of the racial and ethnic composition of a workforce, the skill level of jobs, the nature of job hierarchies, and the character of the labor process in an industry, we must reject the thesis that these characteristics determine the degree of racial egalitarianism of a union.

EGALITARIANISM AS A PREREQUISITE FOR SUCCESS.   What is clear is that in a number of industries successful industrial organization was impossible unless it was interracial and had at least an initial egalitarian stance. Ford could not have been organized by the UAW without extensive efforts to appeal to the interests of black workers. Such a policy was also necessary in steel. In places where CIO unions were not able to make this appeal convincingly to black workers, they sometimes failed to establish a union. Such was the case in New Orleans in 1937, when white organizers from the left-wing ILWU, insensitive to the concerns of black waterfront workers, were unable to win these workers in competition with the AFL.[81] Such was also the case with a number of campaigns in the South in the post–World War II period.[82]

Racial Job Privileges and the Racism of White Workers

There is a good deal of evidence that workers with special privileges, especially across more skilled and higher-paying jobs, tend to defend these privileges and exclude access to them by other workers. Where the privileges are in part or whole racially based, then racial exclusion plays an important role. One might begin looking at the history of U.S. craft unionism, including the driving of African-American workers out of skilled construction trades and railroad jobs. One can also focus on the numerous industrial settings, from the exclusion of card-carrying African-American miners from union jobs in the northern fields by white union miners, to the exclusion of black workers from docks in the Northwest by ILWU longshoremen. One could note the perpetuation of racial job hierarchies in steel or the World War II "hate strikes" in auto, where white workers protested the upgrading of African-American workers to jobs to which they were entitled. As important as these antiegalitarian activities were, they were only part of the picture. Unions such as the UPWA, Mine Mill, FTA, NMU, FE, and even the UMWA, among others, engaged in significant racially egalitarian struggles on behalf of their African-American members.

Even where racial privileges existed to significant degrees, there was always a trade-off as to what could be achieved by white workers using exclusive strategies and what could be achieved by a broad, inclusive, solidaristic stance, because the existence of a racial division of labor in industrial settings was rarely primarily a result of the activities of white workers themselves. The system of white supremacy was designed and enforced to serve other interests, and these other interests did not view the wages and working conditions of even the most privileged white workers as their highest priority. Thus, in the late 1960s and 1970s, when large employers decided to break the power of the construction unions via the Business Roundtable organization, the whiteness of the employees was little help.[83] For many white industrial workers, the benefits of successful solidarity, even on a day-to-day level, usually outweighed the benefits of racial exclusion and division. And in the long run, antiegalitarianism was a losing strategy for almost all workers. These contradictory factors meant that for most white workers, racial attitudes, stances toward solidarity, and racially egalitarian unions were variables, not pre-existing frozen-in-stone, constants. Under certain sets of circumstances, these attitudes had a high degree of variance.

DID WHITE WORKERS EVER OVERCOME RACISM THROUGH STRUGGLE?   There is much evidence that solidaristic interracial struggle helped mitigate racist attitudes among white workers and even at times led them to support and even join the battles of African-American workers for equality. Many accounts of early organizing in steel, for example, suggest as much. I have already described Davin's account of early SWOC organizing in the Pittsburgh area. Cayton and Mitchell assert: "One of the most striking phases of the entire SWOC's campaign was the extent to which the union had been able to modify racial prejudice within the ranks of white laborers."[84] Many observers give anecdotes and general descriptions, as well as personal testimonies from white workers themselves, to support such claims. There were also numerous cases where white workers reacted against the egalitarian concerns of their fellow black workers, often in opposition to the antidiscriminatory stances of their union leadership. Examples abound in almost every union. Bruce Nelson's account of the Mobile shipyards during World War II suggests some of the difficulties in gaining minimal equity for black workers in the face of white worker intransigence.[85] Even in the Fort Worth meat packinghouses, the UPWA was often forced to move slowly and in a round-about fashion because of the resistance of many white workers.[86]

Although white workers were more likely to support the demands of black workers when they fit in with broadly accepted job rights and union principles, the circumstances in which white workers would be fully supportive and those in which they would break ranks were not always easily predictable in advance. Often dramatic changes and reverses took place. Solidarity was sometimes achieved in places where there had previously been antiblack riots; such was the case in New Orleans after the race riots of 1893, in a number of coal fields, and in Chicago after the 1919 riots.[87] Sometimes the changes took place abruptly, in dramatic fashion when white and black workers struggled together or when impressive black orators spoke to white audiences. It is also clear that those unions that were most successful in converting white workers had interracial leaderships that were committed in principle to full equality for black workers.

LIMITS TO EGALITARIAN UNIONISM.   The limits to egalitarian unionism and to full solidarity of white workers with blacks are in many cases clear from the historical record. While it would seem at first glance that egalitarian unionism was more easily approached in those unions where blacks were a substantial percentage of the workforce (as in coal and metal mining in the South) and had clear leverage in the work process (as in meat packing), there are industries with high percentages of African-American workers where whites opposed the elementary demands of blacks to the detriment of their unions and other such industries where organizing never took place. Solidarity was harder to achieve during periods of social conflict and racial competition (as in Mobile during World War II). It was more difficult during periods of intense anticommunism (for example, during the 1939–1941 period and during the McCarthy era). It was perhaps easier to achieve during World War II (for example, in Memphis, Tennessee, and Gadston, Alabama) when racist antagonisms of local authorities were held in check by antifascist ideology and fair practice federal government commitments enforced by government contracts. But even these factors were not always decisive.

THE HILL MODEL. Herbert Hill's model—that interracialism was a purely opportunistic strategy, designed to better defend the privileges of white workers—seems at first glance to be applicable to certain .unions. But the racial practices of even these unions must be looked at historically so we can understand why they developed the way they did. The UAW and the UMWA evolved from organizations with various degrees of commitment to egalitarian unionism into organizations that tacitly accepted discriminatory practices that were to the detriment of their black members. The steel workers accepted discriminatory practices, particularly in terms of white access to better job lines, by failing to attain broad seniority rights for all workers. It is no accident, however, that these unions were under right-wing CIO leadership. Left-wing unions with large African-American constituencies and more extensive minority leadership had significantly different practices from those with more conservative leaders. Thus Hill's model seems ill suited to describe the practice and evolution of the FTA, Mine Mill, and the UPWA. A number of left-led unions with largely white memberships, including the NMU, FE, Local 1199, and the Fur and Leather Workers Union were not only decisively different than non-left white unions but more egalitarian in many ways than even those non-left unions with substantial minority memberships. Because it refuses to accept the important differences that alternative leadership groups made on various union racial policies and because it does not examine their historical development, the Hill model ultimately fails to give us a comprehensive understanding of the racial dynamics of even the most inegalitarian industrial unions.

The Role of Leadership

The strongest proponents and the motor forces for egalitarian unionism were organized African-American workers. Yet a large percentage of black workers in a union was almost never sufficient, particularly for solidaristic attitudes by white workers. In general, as the cases we have examined so far suggest, it was left, usually integrated leaderships that proved to be a necessary ingredient for the development of interracial solidarity and egalitarian unionism. Left-wing unions, organizers, officials, and cadre were in general more committed in principle and practice to racial egalitarianism than non-leftists. There are a number of reasons why this was the case.

The first reason had to do with principles. Leftists in general were committed to broad, solidaristic organizing, since they tended to believe that only such a movement would lead to socialism and radical social change. Thus leftists usually favored the broadest forms of job rights, since narrow conceptions like departmental seniority invariably proved divisive. They tended to believe that this solidarity also required identification with and support for the most oppressed segments of the population, at home and abroad. African Americans and other minorities were clearly included in this latter category. Communists, in addition, saw the "Negro Question" as central to their strategy in the United States: African-Americans were more potentially revolutionary than other segments of the population, the struggle for civil rights had a revolutionary galvanizing potential for the whole population, and the support of white workers for this struggle was *the* key to their development of class consciousness.[88] Thus, communists in general showed more interest in organizing African-American workers (although there were exceptions, as the UE and ILWU demonstrate), as their efforts in metal mining, coal, steel, tobacco, meat packing, auto, farm and construction equipment, and other industries suggest. They tended to have and to promote more extensive black leadership and organizers and the general involvement of nonwhite workers than did non-left leaders, even in unions like Fur and Leather and the NMU, where there were not large percentages of African-American workers.

Conservative leaders tended to be far more committed to bureacratic control and anticommunism than antiracism. Left unions thus tended to push egalitarian measures in situations where conservatives balked. As in the NMU, leftists often widely publicized successful attempts at fighting discrimination and believed that membership should be actively educated and won to antiracism. Because of their antiracist stance, left leaderships and organizers were more proportionately black than were non-left leaderships. In most unions they also had the disproportionate support of black members. Thus in the struggle against communists in industrial unions in the late 1940s, non-left leaders usually relied upon the more privileged, mostly white, often racist segments of the unions. This was to be the case not only in the struggle against Mine Mill, FTA, and the NMU, but also in steel, rubber, and auto.

Leaders, of course, were often constrained in what they could advocate by their constituencies. Racially conservative white leaders were occasionally forced by African-American workers into egalitarian activity. Leftists were often inhibited by racially conservative white workers, as even happened in the UPWA. Yet leaders also made decisive choices, including the degree to which they wanted to "crusade on the race issue," to organize, develop, and empower African-American constituencies, who would themselves become a force for racial egalitarianism in their own right. And, I have been arguing, there were a wide range of choices that distinguished many left unions and factions from non-leftists.

A further reason that made conservative-led unions and conservative leadership invariably inadequate to the task of developing racial egalitarianism involves their attitudes and commitments on a series of separate but ultimately related questions. In most instances, the forging of strong interracial bonds was accomplished via shop struggles. Where black and white workers struggled together over common grievances, white workers were more likely not merely to appreciate the value of their black compatriots but to join with them in active opposition to the myriad forms and instances of racial discrimination. Frequent shop floor activity *tended* to be the province of the left for various reasons. Conservative leaders prefered stable, top-down organization that discouraged democratic control.[89] They also prefered and were often able to achieve closer, more cooperative relations with companies. Left unions, which believed in the organization of workers for broad class goals, were more highly committed to the mobilization and involvement of workers in day-to-day struggles. The NMU and the UPWA saw frequent job actions as important for maintaining their organizations, as did the FE and the UAW before the ascendancy of the Reuther leadership. While job actions and union democracy did not insure interracial solidarity (and have sometimes been the province of racist unions), they provided a necessary ingredient. When Phillip Murray, for example, decided that racism had gone too far in locals in the southern district of the steel workers, he ordered the removal of all Jim Crow signs, without attempting to organize and educate white steel workers. Much to his surprise, his initiative drew resistance and had to be withdrawn.[90]

Thus, by bureacratic inclination, by lesser commitment to egalitarian principles, by their anticommunist stances, by their consequent lack of support among black workers, and by their strongest bases of support being among the whiter, most conservative, more privileged elements in their unions and industries, non-left unions and leaderships were almost preordained to abandon the struggle for racial equality and to become part of the problem, rather than part of the solution. In contrast, the left unions, particularly UPWA, Mine Mill, FTA, NMU, and FE tended to be more inclusive and egalitarian, providing the seeds for both interracial solidarity and the civil rights struggle.

CONCLUSION

The development of broad, interracial working-class support for egalitarian demands might have substantially transformed the politics of the country, as well as made the achievement of those demands more likely. There were the beginnings of such a movement in the 1930s and 1940s among the UMWA and certain left unions in the CIO. These beginnings were rightly, although perhaps overoptimistically, touted by scholars, civil rights activists and organizations, and black newspapers during this period, many of whom had been highly critical of interracial unionism in the past. The history of the CIO during the 1930s and the 1940s suggests that the achievement of interracial working-class solidarity and racial egalitarianism in unions is a difficult task. Though there was neither a golden age nor a universal commitment to social unionism, the CIO's accomplishments and potential need not be belittled. The crushing of left-wing unionism, however, destroyed whatever possibilities existed for racially egalitarian unionism, congealed the CIO in a bureaucratic, conservative mold, and laid the basis for the long, continuous decline in U.S. union strength which continues to this day.

Notes

This chapter is a revised version of an article that originally appeared in *International Labor and Working Class History*, September 1993.

1. See Michael Goldfield, *The Decline of Organized Labor in the United States* (Chicago: University of Chicago Press, 1987) for a more detailed argument.
2. See Michael Goldfield, "Class, Race, and Politics in the United States," *Research in Political Economy* 12 (1990), for an extensive argument to this effect.
3. Despite often copious and informative material, Walter Galenson, *The CIO Challenge to the AFL: A History of the American Labor Movement, 1935–1941* (Cambridge, Mass.: Harvard University Press, 1960), and J. Raymond Walsh, *C.I.O.: Industrial Unionism in Action* (New York: Norton, 1937), for example, are most notable for the absence of any discussions of racial discrimination. Sumner Slichter in his foreword to *Organized Labor and the Negro*, by Herbert R. Northrup (New York: Harper and Brothers, 1944), seems to feel that all unions (including those in the AFL) were making "progress" and that "in nearly all instances the influence of the national officers of unions is thrown against discrimination" (p. xii). Though such assessments do great violence to the facts, they should not surprise us, since as Herbert Hill, in "Black Labor and Affirmative Action: An Historical Perspective," in *The Question of Discrimination*, ed. Steven Shulman and William Darity, Jr. (Middletown, Conn.: Wesleyan University Press, 1989), 216, quite accurately notes, "although racial issues were and are a crucial factor in American labor history, racist practices of labor organizations were either ignored or justified by dubious rationalizations in most of the important studies of that history, particularly in those works based in concept on the Commons-Taft tradition." In this context, it is worth noting the deep racism of many industrial relations practitioners trained by this school, especially William Leiserson, who was to become head of the NLRB and later the Industrial Relations Research Association; Northrup, *Organized Labor and the Negro*, 58–59.
4. See W. E. B. Du Bois and Augustus G. Dill, eds., *The Negro American Artisan* (Atlanta: Atlanta University Press; New York: Quadrangle, 1912); Charles H. Wesley, *Negro Labor in the United States, 1850–1925* (New York: Russell and Russell, 1927); and Lorenzo J. Green and Carter G. Woodson, *The Negro Wage Earner* Wash., DC: (The Association for the Study of Negro Life and History, 1930). For further specifics, see also F. E. Wolfe, *Admission to American Trade Unions* (Baltimore, Md.: Johns Hopkins University Press, 1912), 112–34; Ira De A. Reid, *Negro Membership in American Labor Unions* (New York: Negro Universities Press, 1930); and Northrup, *Organized Labor and the Negro*.
5. Sterling D. Spero and Abram L. Harris, *The Black Worker* (New York: Columbia University Press, 1931).
6. W. E. B. Du Bois, "Race Relations in the United States, 1917–1947," *Phylon* 9 (Third Quarter, 1948): 236.
7. Horace R. Cayton and George S. Mitchell, *Black Workers and the New Unions* (Westport, Conn.: Negro Universities Press, 1939); Northrup, *Organized Labor and the Negro*; and Robert C. Weaver, *Negro Labor* (New York: Harcourt, Brace and Company, 1946), especially 219–20. One could compile a very thick book of optimistic predictions from the African-American press, civil rights activists, and scholars, especially during the late 1940s.
8. Spero and Harris, *The Black Worker*, 347; Herbert G. Gutman, "The Negro and the United Mine Workers of America: The Career and Letters of Richard L. Davis and Something of Their Meaning. 1890–1900," in *The Negro and the American*

Labor Movement, ed. Julius Jacobson (Garden City, N.Y.: Anchor Books, 1968), 83.

9. For similar arguments see Robert J. Norrell, "Caste in Steel: Jim Crow Careers in Birmingham, Alabama," *Journal of American History* 73, no. 3 (1986); Robert J. Norrell, "Labor Trouble: George Wallace and Union Politics in Alabama," in *Organized Labor in the Twentieth Century South*, ed. Robert H. Zeiger (Knoxville: University of Tennessee Press, 1991); and Alan Draper, "A Sisyphean Ordeal: Labor Educators, Race Relations, and Southern Workers, 1956–1966," *Labor Studies Journal* 16, no. 4 (Winter 1991): 3–19; unlike Hill, who indicts both white workers and union leaders, both Draper and Norrell put their main emphasis on the former.

10. Ibid. Hill, "Black Labor and Affirmative Action," 245–48, *passim*.

11. See Goldfield, "Class, Race, and Politics in the United States," 89, 120 for references to this literature.

12. Melton A. McLaurin, *The Knights of Labor in the South* (Westport, Conn.: Greenwood Press, 1978); Peter Rachleff, *Black Labor in Richmond, 1865–1890* (Urbana: University of Illinois Press, 1989).

13. McLaurin, *The Knights of Labor in the South*, 82–84.

14. David P. Bennets, "Black and White Workers: New Orleans, 1880–1900" (Ph.D. diss., University of Illinois, 1972); Daniel Rosenberg, *New Orleans Dockworkers: Race, Labor, and Unionism, 1892–1923* (Albany: State University of New York Press, 1988); Roger W. Shugg, "The New Orleans General Strike of 1892," *The Louisiana Historical Quarterly* 21, no. 2 (April 1938): 547–60; Eric Arnesen, *Waterfront Workers of New Orleans: Race, Class, and Politics, 1863–1923* (New York: Oxford University Press, 1991).

15. See James R. Green, "The Brotherhood of Timberworkers, 1910–1913: A Radical Response to Industrial Capitalism in the Southern U.S.A.," *Past and Present* 60 (1973): 161–200; Melvyn Dubofsky, *We Shall Be All* (New York: Quadrangle Press, 1969), 209–20; and Philip S. Foner, *The Industrial Workers of the World, 1905–1917* (New York: International Publishers, 1965), 233–57.

16. Dubofsky, *We Shall Be All*, 209, even suggests that much more such organization was possible for those who were audacious enough to try.

17. See Spero and Harris, *The Black Worker*, for an informed discussion.

18. As Ronald L. Lewis, *Black Coal Miners in America: Race, Class, and Community Conflict, 1780–1980* (Lexington: University of Kentucky Press, 1987), comprehensively points out, the composition and racial dynamics were quite different in the overwhelmingly white central fields of Pennsylvania, Illinois, Ohio, and Indiana, from that of the majority black coal areas of Alabama, or from the more racially and ethnically diverse fields of Appalachia, especially southwest West Virginia, making generalizations with respect to race difficult for the union and industry as a whole. There are literally hundreds of highly informative books and articles on mine worker unionism and on the coal industry. For recent controversies, see Gutman, "The Negro and the United Mine Workers of America"; Stephen Brier, "The Career of Richard L. Davis, Reconsidered: Unpublished Correspondence from the *National Labor Tribune*," *Labor History* 21, no. 3 (Summer 1980); Herbert Hill, "Myth-Making as Labor History: Herbert Gutman and the United Mine Workers of America," *International Journal of Politics, Culture, and Society* 2, no. 2 (Winter 1988): 132–200; the rejoinders to Hill in *The International Journal of Politics, Culture, and Society* 2, no. 3 (Spring 1989); Herbert Hill, "Rejoinder to Symposium on 'Myth-Making as Labor History: Herbert Gutman and the United Mine Workers of America,'" *International Journal of Politics, Culture, and Society* 2, no. 4 (Summer 1989): 587–96; Joe W. Trotter, Jr., *Coal, Class, and Color: Blacks in Southern West Virginia, 1915–32* (Urbana: University of Illinois

Press, 1990); David A. Corbin, *Life, Work, and Rebellion in the Coal Fields: The Southern West Virginia Miners, 1880–1922* (Urbana: University of Illinois Press, 1981); and Judith Stein, "Race and Class Consciousness Reconsidered," *Reviews in American History* 19 (1991): 551–60. Spero and Harris, *The Black Worker*; Cayton and Mitchell, *Black Workers and the New Unions*; Philip Taft, *Organizing Dixie: Alabama Workers in the Industrial Era* (Westport, Conn.: Greenwood Press, 1981); and Paul Nyden's pathbreaking work on black workers in coal, "Black Coal Miners in the United States," Occasional Paper no. 15, American Institute for Marxist Studies, 1974, are all highly informative. For an insightful review, critical of recent work of both Trotter and Corbin, see Stein, "Race and Class Consciousness Reconsidered." For extensive references and overview, especially about the career of John L. Lewis, see Melvyn Dubofsky and Warren Van Tyne, *John L. Lewis* (New York: Quadrangle Press, 1977).

19. Clark Kerr and Abraham Siegel, "The Interindustry Propensity to Strike: An International Comparison," in *Industrial Conflict*, ed. Arthur Kornhauser, Robert Dubin, and Arthur M. Ross (New York: McGraw Hill Press, 1954), 189–212.
20. The UMWA was founded in 1890 from a merger of Knights of Labor National Assembly 135 and the National Federation of Miners and Mine Laborers. From the beginning it was explicitly committed to racial egalitarianism. See Lewis, *Black Coal Miners in America*, 137; Spero and Harris, *The Black Worker*, 355.
21. Cayton and Mitchell, *Black Workers and the New Unions*, 323; Lewis, *Black Coal Miners in America*, 46, 54–55; Ray F. Marshall, *The Negro and Organized Labor* (New York: John Wiley and Sons, 1965), 97.
22. Nyden, *Black Coal Miners in the United States*, 2; Spero and Harris, *The Black Worker*, 355–56.
23. Lewis, *Black Coal Miners in America*, 47, 63; Spero and Harris, *The Black Worker*, 371; Northrup, *Organized Labor and the Negro*, 165.
24. Lewis, *Black Coal Miners in America*, 64. Further evidence is presented in the testimonies of black miners surveyed by Cayton and Mitchell, *Black Workers and the New Unions*, 201; and Spero and Harris, *The Black Worker*, 375–76.
25. Lewis, *Black Coal Miners in America*, 49, 94, 104, 164; Spero and Harris, *The Black Worker*, 376.
26. Nyden, *Black Coal Miners in the United States*, 23–28; Lewis, *Black Coal Miners in America*, 81, 86.
27. Spero and Harris, *The Black Worker*, 361; Lewis, *Black Coal Miners in America*, 101–6.
28. Quoted in Spero and Harris, *The Black Worker*, 361.
29. Lewis, *Black Coal Miners in America*, 106, 117–18.
30. Nyden, *Black Coal Miners in the United States*, 10, 17–19; Northrup, *Organized Labor and the Negro*, 171; Lewis, *Black Coal Miners in America*, 170–76.
31. Note, for example, the extremely positive early evaluation by Cayton and Mitchell, *Black Workers and the New Unions*, 224.
32. Cayton and Mitchell, *Black Workers and the New Unions*, 205.
33. Eric Leif Davin, "The Littlest New Deal: SWOC Takes Power in Steeltown. A Possibility of Radicalism in the Late 1930s," unpublished manuscript, 1989.
34. For opposite evaluations of the progress of the union and its commitment to racial egalitarianism in Birmingham during the 1940s and 1950s, see Norrell, "Labor Trouble," and Judith Stein, "Southern Workers in International Unions, 1936–1951," in *Organized Labor in the Twentieth Century South*, ed. Zieger.
35. In the 1970s the pro-administration Local 6 president put out a racist leaflet in the plant, calling some African-American local union officials "fugitives from the watermelon patch," enraging not merely the over one thousand black workers but

large numbers of Hispanic and white workers as well. When the local Fair Practices Committee unanimously filed charges for the local president's impeachment, over five hundred workers attended a union meeting demanding his removal; it was the Region 4 UAW office that rose to the president's defense (leaflets and material from Local 6, in author's possession). This was, of course, the same regional leadership that marched with Jesse Jackson and Operation Push in Chicago.

36. V. O. Key, *Southern Politics in State and Nation* (New York: Alfred A. Knopf, 1949); W. E. B. Du Bois, *Black Reconstruction* (New York: Quadrangle Press, 1935); Stanley B. Greenberg, *Race and State in Capitalist Development* (New Haven, Conn.: Yale University Press, 1980); Jack M. Bloom, *Class, Race, and the Civil Rights Movement* (Bloomington: University of Indiana Press, 1987); E. E. Schattschneider, *The Semisovereign People* (New York: Holt, Rinehart, and Winston, 1960).

37. Horace Huntley, "Iron Ore Miners and Mine Mill in Alabama: 1933–1952" (Ph.D. diss., University of Pittsburgh, 1977), 20–26.

38. Robin D. G. Kelley, *Hammer and Hoe: Alabama Communists during the Great Depression* (Chapel Hill: University of North Carolina Press, 1990), 66, 145.

39. Kelley, *Hammer and Hoe*, 145, 147, 151.

40. See Cletus Daniel, *Chicano Workers and the Politics of Fairness* (Austin: University of Texas Press, 1992).

41. Huntley, "Iron Ore Miners and Mine Mill in Alabama," 215–18.

42. The new hiring policy was "the subject of a heated debate" in 1941 at the Wenonah local. The issue was raised by a rank and filer, who expressed the concerns of other black miners that so few blacks were being hired. One proposal was that the union demand that the company hire equal numbers of blacks and whites. The black vice president of the local opposed this suggestion, much to the pleasure of the white newcomers and the chagrin of black miners. Although the vice president was subsequently voted out of office, attempts to get the company to change its hiring policies failed. Huntley, "Iron Ore Miners and Mine Mill in Alabama," 96–98.

43. Huntley, "Iron Ore Miners and Mine Mill in Alabama," 110, 162, 189, 208–9.

44. Karl Korstad, "Black and White Together: Organizing in the South with the Food, Tobacco, Agricultural, and Allied Workers Union (FTA-CIO), 1942–1952," in *The CIO's Left-Led Unions*, ed. Steve Rosswurm (New Brunswick, N.J.: Rutgers University Press, 1992), 76; Michael Honey, "Labor and Civil Rights in the South: The Industrial Labor Movement and Black Workers in Memphis, 1929–1945" (Ph.D. diss., Northern Illinois University, 1988), *passim*.

45. Korstad, "Black and White Together," 86; Robert R. Korstad, "Daybreak of Freedom: Tobacco Workers and the CIO, Winston-Salem, North Carolina, 1943–1950" (Ph.D. diss., University of North Carolina, 1987), xvii, 5.

46. Herbert R. Northrup, "The Tobacco Workers International Union," *Quarterly Journal of Economics*, 56, no. 4 (August 1942): 606.

47. Northrup, "The Tobacco Workers International Union," 616, 617.

48. Korstad, "Daybreak of Freedom," 201–2.

49. Korstad, "Daybreak of Freedom," 208.

50. Korstad, "Daybreak of Freedom," 209–28, 228–30.

51. Korstad, "Daybreak of Freedom," 230.

52. Honey, "Labor and Civil Rights in the South," 261, 379; Lucy Randolph Mason, letter to CIO Organization Director Allan S. Haywood, 5 October 1940, quoted in Honey, "Labor and Civil Rights in the South," 379.

53. Korstad, "Black and White Together," 76; Operation Dixie papers, Duke University Library, *passim*.

54. Honey, "Labor and Civil Rights in the South," 500.
55. Honey, "Labor and Civil Rights in the South," 527, 528–29, 530.
56. Ray F. Marshall, *Labor in the South* (Cambridge, Mass.: Harvard University Press, 1967), 172.
57. David Brodie, *The Butcher Workman: A Study of Unionization* (Cambridge, Mass.: Harvard University Press, 1964), 88; Eric B. Halpern, *"Black and White Unite and Fight": Race and Labor in Meatpacking, 1904–1948* (New Haven, Conn.: Yale University Press, 1989), 257.
58. Brodie, *The Butcher Workman*, 176.
59. Halpern, *"Black and White Unite and Fight"*; Roger Horowitz, "The Road Not Taken: A Social History of Industrial Unionism in Meatpacking, 1920–1960" (Ph.D. diss., University of Wisconsin, 1990), 440–48; Rick Halpern, "Interracial Unionism in the Southwest: Fort Worth's Packinghouse Workers, 1937–1954" in *Organized Labor in the Twentieth Century South*, ed. Zieger, 163.
60. Leroi Jones, *Blues People* (New York: Morrow Quill, 1963), 96, 106, makes this point compellingly in his discussion of the wider social space in Chicago in the 1920s, which allowed for the flourishing of jazz there.
61. Halpern, *"Black and White Unite and Fight,"* 338.
62. Brodie, *The Butcher Workman*, 176; Halpern, *"Black and White Unite and Fight,"* 365.
63. Halpern, *"Black and White Unite and Fight,"* 383.
64. Brodie, *The Butcher Workman*, 176.
65. Halpern, *"Black and White Unite and Fight,"* 507, 509, 534.
66. Horowitz, "The Path Not Taken," 642.
67. Michael Honey, "Coalition and Conflict: Martin Luther King, Civil Rights, and the American Labor Movement," unpublished manuscript, 1992.
68. Halpern, "Interracial Unionism in the Southwest," 158–59.
69. Hill, "Black Labor and Affirmative Action," 245.
70. Nancy Quam-Wickham, "Who Controls the Hiring Hall? The Struggle for Job Control in the ILWU during World War II," in *The CIO's Left-Led Unions*, ed. Rosswurm, argues that the ILWU during the 1940s was insensitive to racial issues despite the ideological commitments of the union's leaders. Eventually, but much later, she argues, the union evolved in a more racially egalitarian direction, in part because of the stance of the leadership.
71. Donald T. Critchlow, "Communist Unions and Racism: A Comparative Study of the Responses of the United Electrical Radio and Machine Workers and the National Maritime Union to the Black Question during World War II," *Labor History* 17, no. 2 (Spring 1976), 237; Weaver, *Negro Labor*, 221.
72. Ronald W. Schatz, *The Electrical Workers: A History of Labor at General Electric and Westinghouse, 1923–60* (Chicago: University of Illinois Press, 1983), 127–31.
73. Mark McColloch, "The Shop-Floor Dimension of Union Rivalry: The Case of Westinghouse in the 1950s," in *The CIO's Left-Led Unions*, ed. Rosswurm, 193–99.
74. Critchlow, "Communist Unions and Racism," 238.
75. Honey, "Labor and Civil Rights in the South," 254, 256, 261, 292, *passim*.
76. Honey, "Labor and Civil Rights in the South," 343.
77. Such an assessment is supported by virtually all fair-minded observers. Ray Marshall, for example, who believed that the expulsions of communists and left-led unions were extremely positive for the CIO (*Labor in the South*, 350), still acknowledged that the CP was an important force for racial equality in the CIO (*The Negro and Organized Labor*, 36, 46).
78. Northrup, *Organized Labor and the Negro*, 131.
79. Cayton and Mitchell, *Black Workers and the New Unions*, 81.

80. Robert Laurentz, "Racial Conflict in the New York City Garment Industry, 1933–1980" (Ph.D. diss., State University of New York, Binghamton, 1980). Northrup, *Organized Labor and the Negro*, 128, written in 1944, cites the ILGWU as one of the most racially egalitarian of unions. Herbert Hill, "The Racial Practices of Organized Labor: The Contemporary Record" in Julius Jacobson, ed., *The Negro and the American Labor Mood* (Garden City, NY: Doubleday, 1968), documents their degeneration into narrow bigotry.

81. Bruce Nelson, "Class and Race in the Crescent City: The ILWU, from San Francisco to New Orleans," in *The CIO's Left-Led Unions*, ed. Rosswurm; Marshall, *Labor in the South*, 210.

82. Marshall, *Labor in the South*, 272, 281; Michael Goldfield, *Race, Class, and the Nature of American Politics: The Failure of the CIO's Operation Dixie*, unpublished manuscript.

83. Goldfield, *The Decline of Organized Labor in the United States*, 110, 191, 192.

84. Cayton and Mitchell, *Black Workers and the New Unions*, 212.

85. Bruce Nelson, "Mobile during World War II: Organized Labor and the Struggle for Black Equality in a 'City That's Been Taken by Storm,'" unpublished manuscript, 1991.

86. See also Brodie, *The Butcher Workman*, 176.

87. Lewis, *Black Coal Miners in America*, 87–88.

88. See Michael Goldfield, "The Decline of the Communist Party and the Black Question in the U.S.: Harry Haywood's *Black Bolshevik*," *Review of Radical Political Economics* 12, no. 1 (1980): 44–63.

89. Judith Stepan-Norris and Maurice Zeitlin, "Insurgency, Radicalism, and Democracy in America's Industrial Unions," working paper series 215. Institute of Industrial Relations, University of California, Los Angeles, 1991.

90. Norrell, "Labor Trouble," 256–57.

5

Rank-and-File Teamster Movements in Comparative Perspective

Aaron Brenner

INTRODUCTION

IT IS WELL KNOWN that from the later 1960s through the early 1970s Europe was rocked by a great wave of mass workers' struggles—from May 1968 in France to the Hot Autumn of 1969 in Italy to the British miners' strike that brought down a conservative government in 1974 to the Portuguese Revolution of 1975 to the great mobilizations for democracy in Spain in 1976. What has gone almost unnoticed is that the United States had its own—admittedly more modest yet nonetheless significant—counterpart to these events. As the long postwar economic boom entered its final stages, U.S. workers began to challenge the system of stabilized collective bargaining that had ruled American industrial relations since World War II. For a decade after 1966, collective action on the part of ordinary workers shook virtually every major U.S. industry—mining, steel, auto, communications, trucking, post office, longshore, and many more. Workers engaged in official and unofficial strikes, slowdowns, boycotts, work-to-rule campaigns, plant occupations, sabotage, and demonstrations, all to win better contracts, higher wages, and improved working conditions. The new militancy attacked not only the employers but the union leadership as well. In several of the nation's largest unions, rank-and-file workers built their own autonomous organizations that both challenged the existing union leadership *and* organized broad-based collective action against the employers on the shop floor.

The Teamsters for a Democratic Union (TDU) was one such organization. Emerging in 1975, near the end of the broad labor upsurge, it was nonetheless nurtured by many of the same conditions that fostered other rank-and-file struggles. Beginning in the late 1960s, teamsters, like other workers across the economy, faced a mounting employers' offensive. Very serious downward pressure on profits gripped much of the economy beginning in 1966. Trucking employers, like those in other industries, responded by cutting costs and boosting productivity. The changes fell heavily on teamsters, who were forced to work harder and longer. Meanwhile, top leaders of the International Brotherhood of Teamsters, Chauffeurs, Warehousemen, and Helpers of America (IBT), like officials in other unions, largely failed to organize collective opposition to the speedup. Still confident in their abilities after two decades of improving conditions, rank-and-file teamsters, like workers across the country, organized on their own. They won wage and benefit increases, protected some of the job privileges won during the postwar boom, and organized a challenge to IBT officials.

What made rank-and-file teamsters different from workers in other unions was that they created a permanent, national, independent rank-and-file organization. TDU was the only group of its kind to survive more than a few years. Almost from the start it was an institution of rank-and-file power inside the country's largest labor union. Within a few years, ten thousand of the IBT's 1.5 million members had joined TDU. Its influence was especially strong among the 700,000 workers in the IBT's core jurisdictions—freight trucking, carhauling, grocery delivery, and United Parcel Service. By 1991, TDU was the organizational backbone of a reform campaign that swept the first one-member-one-vote elections in IBT history. Though they held neither of the union's two highest offices—general president and general secretary-treasurer—TDU members were, in 1993, a majority of the IBT's seventeen-person international executive board, giving them the power to shape much of the union's activity.

Precisely because TDU has similar origins to the other rank-and-file struggles of the period, yet has such a unique ulterior history, its experiences are instructive. On the one hand, TDU is symptomatic of the rank-and-file upsurge of the late 1960s and early 1970s. On the other hand, TDU's experience as the lone survivor of the period suggests the specific conditions that give rise to *permanent* rank-and-file organization.

THE GENERAL UPSURGE

The rank-and-file upsurge in the period between 1967–1976 came suddenly and struck very broadly. The most general evidence comes from strike statistics. The average number of strikes per year for those ten years was 35 percent higher than it had been between 1948–1966. The average number of workers on strike each year rose 30 percent compared to the previous period, while the average number of days lost to strikes increased by 40 percent. Not included in these statistics is the number of "unofficial" strikes. While statistics on such job actions are not gathered by the government, anecdotal evidence indicates that wildcats increased in the late 1960s and early 1970s compared to the 1955–1965 period. This sudden burst of rank-and-file activity represented a break with the past twenty years of relatively stable labor relations. The new phase, characterized by a higher level of conflict, affected virtually every major industry.[1]

Strike activity was not the only expression of rank-and-file discontent during the 1967–1975 period. Absenteeism, tardiness, insubordination, drug use, turnover, and sabotage were also constant problems for employers. Combined with the strikes, this behavior represented a rather sharp break with the past twenty years of relatively stable labor relations. Workers in virtually every category of employment rejected contracts, confronted union leaders, and challenged the authority of management on the shop floor.[2]

At the root of the new militancy was a generalized employers' offensive triggered by falling profitability. Between 1966 and 1974, the return to capital declined dramatically. The average rate of return on tangible assets for the nonresidential, nonfarm business sector fell from approximately 12.5 percent in 1966 to about 8.75 percent in 1973 and 6.75 percent in 1974. In manufacturing, the decline was even steeper. The average inflation-adjusted, before-tax rate of return on assets in manufacturing fell from a peak of 12 percent in 1965 to around 10 percent in 1966 to around 4 percent in 1970, with a rise to 6 percent in 1973, and a further fall to under 3 percent in 1974. By all measures, profit rates have yet to recover the average levels reached during the twenty years after World War II.[3]

Faced with falling profitability as the postwar boom slowed to a crawl and finally collapsed, employers increasingly sought methods to cut costs and boost productivity. Before the mid-1970s they were only partially successful in cutting real wages and benefits.[4] They were more successful on the shop floor. Across the economy work intensified. The most famous example was the auto industry, where workers tried to cope with a more quickly moving assembly line. Other examples included the steel and mining industries, where plant reorganization, new technology, and consolidated personnel management sped production, reduced the workforce, and diluted workers' control over the labor process. Similar changes were at work throughout the economy. Rising concern over job safety, an increased number of union health grievances, and reports of a rising number of job accidents indicate that speedup was widespread.[5]

Union officials proved to be unable to stem the tide of deteriorating working conditions and slowing wage growth. Their collective bargaining strategy, successful during the period of unprecedented economic growth after the war, was ineffectual in the changed economic and social circumstances. Employing the practices of business unionism, officials had grown used to bartering labor peace for wage and benefit increases.[6] Generally, workers had supported the results of business unionism, reelecting union leaders and ratifying the contracts they negotiated. By the late 1960s, however, the economic rewards of compliance were diminishing at precisely the same time as the encroachments on workers' control of the labor process were advancing.

Continuing the strategy of the last two decades, union leaders sacrificed workers' job control for dwindling economic improvements. United Steel Workers officials, for example, signed the Experimental Negotiating Agreement in 1973 which prohibited strikes—even after contract expiration—and called for binding arbitration of grievances in exchange for a 3 percent floor on wage increases and cost-of-living provisions in future contracts.[7] Teamsters leaders won large wage increases in the 1970 National Master Freight Agreement but relinquished the right to strike for twenty-four hours for any reason, a significant diminution of rank-and-file power. Similar exchanges took place in other industries.

For many workers, long accustomed to wage increases, the official strategy was inadequate. When they took actions into their own hands, however, union leaders refused to support them. One dramatic example of union officials' opposition to independent rank-and-file militancy occurred in the auto industry. On 16 August 1973, Douglas Fraser, head of the UAW's Chrysler division and later its president, led one thousand UAW officials and loyalists in an assault upon UAW members walking a wildcat picket line in front of Chrysler's Mack Avenue Stamping Plant. While police looked on, the UAW officials forcibly broke the strike by removing picket signs and beating those who resisted. Bill Bonds, a Detroit television reporter, noted that "for the first time in the history of the UAW, the union mobilized to keep a plant open." Fraser said, "The wildcat violated our constitution, the law, the contract, and it really upset our bargaining strategy."[8]

For failing to stand with the membership, the leaders of practically every major industrial union in the country faced an organized challenge from below. In the UAW, black members created the Revolutionary Union Movements and the League of Revolutionary Black Workers in Detroit and the United Black Brothers and the Linden Auto Workers in New Jersey. Some of their union brothers organized the United National Caucus and several other local rank-and-file groups with the purpose of confronting the UAW leadership not just over their handling of wages and working conditions but on issues of internal union democracy and politics.[9] In the bituminous coal industry, the Miners for Democracy, the Disabled Miners and Widows of southern West Virginia, and the Black Lung Association fought and defeated the corrupt leadership of UMW president Tony Boyle, while also winning health and safety improvements from mine operators.[10] Telephone workers created a group called Bell Ringer to channel rank-and-file anger against the leadership of the Communications Workers of America (CWA) and AT&T, and rank-and-file groups were also formed in the National Association of Letter Carriers, the United Steel Workers Union, the Rubber Workers Union, and the American Federation of Teachers (AFT).[11]

In 1970, *Business Week* complained about the threat to orderly collective bargaining represented by so much rank-and-file dissent. Citing the fact that one of every seven union-employer agreements was being rejected by the ranks, the magazine went on to say:

> The hard fact is that union leaders who heeded pleas to act responsibly and moderate their demands almost certainly would run into trouble with their own unions. However solidly entrenched they may be, today's union officers know, from sore experience, that the days of unchallenged leadership are history. . . . There is less orderliness now within labor ranks.[12]

Like *Business Week*, the *Wall Street Journal* identified a common interest between union officials and employers. It viewed the rank-and-file challenge to union leadership as a threat to employers and praised those company bargainers who understood the positive function of "union-management cooperation." As the *Journal* saw it, wildcats, slowdowns, sabotage, and other forms of collective rank-and-file protest threatened the organizational stability of the union. Such protest jeopardized orderly shop floor relations and smooth collective bargaining. Both union leaders and employers stood to lose, so where possible they should cooperate to restrict independent rank-and-file activity.[13]

The employers' offensive and the union bureaucracy's failure to confront it gave workers the motivation to fight. The confidence needed came from two decades of nearly constant increases in living standards. Workers expected to win improvements in wages, benefits, and working conditions. Under the implicit capital-labor accord of the postwar era, these were their rewards for cooperation in the labor process. High employment, buttressed in part by the war in Vietnam, further reinforced confidence by reducing the fear of job loss.

Workers were also confident because they were organized on the job. Before the employers' productivity drive reached high gear, workers enjoyed a considerable degree of control over production. This control, usually enforced by informal work groups, bolstered workers' confidence for two reasons. First, job control meant greater freedom and creativity in the performance of work and was worth protecting. Second, the practices of job control could be used to defend workers and win improvements at the workplace. Through the activity of informal work groups, workers had experience in uniting, challenging, and defeating the employers on the job. In short, they already knew how to win. Job control, which was the first target of the employers' offensive, became both motivation and mechanism for workers' collective struggle.[14]

Workers' willingness to fight back was further reinforced by the concomitant antiwar, black power, and feminist movements, which radicalized many. These movements raised the political awareness of ordinary people by putting such issues as racism, sexism, and imperialism in the forefront of their consciousness. Workers then confronted these issues as they were manifested on the job and in their unions. Tens of thousands became activists. Many became revolutionaries. In a number of cases, it was these working-class political militants who, by replicating their experience from the social movements in the movements in the workplace, led the rank-and-file groups that challenged the employers and the union bureaucracy.

The pattern of rank-and-file organization in the late 1960s and early 1970s can be summarized. Facing a crisis of profitability, employers began to chip away at workers' working conditions and living standards. Union officials were unable to organize a collective response, preferring instead to protect the security and stability of their organizations by negotiating concessions. Flush with confidence from two decades of rising income and improving employment conditions, buoyed by the concomitant black power, antiwar, and feminist movements, and with their job control still partly intact, rank-and-file workers began to fight back. Usually their efforts were spontaneous or temporary, but at times they created groups that could organize both resistance on the shop floor and political challenge within the union. Often political radicals were instrumental in the creation and maintenance of such groups. In virtually all cases, they were organized and led exclusively by working union members, not full-time union officials, and the shop floor was the main but by no means exclusive arena of their activity.

Nonetheless, despite the militancy of rank-and-file workers, rank-and-file organizations were unable to sustain themselves. By 1977, every one disintegrated under the combined pressures of the employers, the union leadership, and internal factionalism, except the Teamsters for a Democratic Union.

TRUCKING AND THE ROOTS OF TEAMSTER MILITANCY

As a rank-and-file organization, TDU was not unique. It shared most of the characteristics of other rank-and-file organizations of the period. Like them, it was a response to the employers' offensive and the inadequacy of the union bureaucracy. But more than most sections of the U.S. working class, rank-and-file teamsters[15] maintained a level of autonomy and militancy that gave them the confidence to fight and the strength to win. Teamsters retained an inordinate amount of power vis-à-vis the employers and the union. This power was rooted in the peculiar political economy of trucking and the unique history of the IBT.

Two Teamster Traditions

Since the 1930s, two traditions have coexisted uneasily within the International Brotherhood of Teamsters. On the one hand, militant, democratic, and at times politically radical rank-and-file activity was the basis for the union's transformation during the late 1930s and 1940s from a small, exclusive craft association into one of the most powerful industrial unions in the country.[16] On the other hand, extreme business unionism, bureaucratic centralization, corruption, sweetheart contracts, gangsterism, and even murder have given the IBT its well-deserved reputation as the "biggest and baddest" union in the country.[17] This paradoxical combination of rank-and-file militancy and bureaucratic business unionism was made possible by the unique structure and uninterrupted growth of the trucking industry from the early 1930s to the late 1960s.[18] This growth provided both the space for rank-and-file activity to win improvements on the job and the wherewithal for budding labor bureaucrats to become Mafia kingpins.

The growth of the trucking industry was extraordinary, increasing by a factor of six between 1948 and 1968. Direct and indirect government support was crucial. Trucking companies received an enormous subsidy in the form of the federal interstate highway system, which made trucking more competitive with the railroads. Technological innovations like the air-filled rubber tire had the same result. More directly, since the 1930s the Interstate Commerce Commission (ICC) has regulated virtually every aspect of trucking operations, including rates, routes, safety procedures, equipment, entry into the industry, mergers, and acquisitions. Rate and route regulation eliminated price competition and virtually guaranteed profits.[19]

Despite growth, the trucking industry was populated by thousands of small firms even as late as the mid 1970s. In 1971, there were 64,737 trucking companies, of which only eighty-eight employed five hundred or more workers. Total trucking industry employment was over one million. The trucking company with the most workers in 1973 was Roadway, with 16,701 employees. It operated 246 terminals, for an average of sixty-eight employees per terminal. Trucking companies were small for two reasons. First, the financial requirements for entry were extremely small, amounting to little more than a few trucks and a place to park them. Second, ICC regulation kept firms small by limiting their access to new routes and their ability to acquire or merge. Route limitations also had the peculiar effect of forcing trucking companies to cooperate with each other in a process called "interlining." To get customer shipments from one area to the next, one company had to "hand off" its cargo to another. This made for extensive trucking company interdependence, something teamsters would quickly learn to exploit.[20]

Industry growth, small firm size, ICC regulation, and company interdependence made the over-the-road trucking industry vulnerable to unionization and rank-and-file organization. The first to recognize this vulnerability were members of the Communist League of America (CLA), later the Socialist Workers Party (SWP), a small revolutionary group expelled from the Communist Party in 1928.[21] They won leadership of IBT Minneapolis Local 574 (later 544) during the city's general strike in 1934.[22] Once secure in power, they introduced a radical strategy, called leapfrogging, to organize intercity trucking throughout the Midwest. Teamsters in a unionized city or terminal boycotted trucks from nonunion cities and terminals until the employers recognized the union. This tactic, essentially a secondary boycott, took advantage of industry conditions.

Given their small size, trucking firms did not possess the resources to withstand a boycott for long. Route regulation further reduced their options; nonunion firms faced with a boycott could not switch routes to avoid the boycott without application to the ICC. Nor were trucking firms highly motivated to resist unionization. Given interdependence, boycotted firms faced the possibility of losing the aid of cooperating companies in the future. More importantly, industry growth and rate regulation eased the financial pain associated with the union, the former by providing the revenue to meet workers' demands, the latter by incorporating wage increases into shipping rates and thereby passing the cost of unionization to customers. Exploiting these conditions, the IBT "leapfrogged" along the routes traveled by truck drivers, organizing terminal after terminal.[23]

In carrying out the leapfrog strategy, Farrell Dobbs, teamster, CLA member, and leader of the North Central District Drivers Council, encouraged teamsters to participate in strikes, mass and roving pickets, mass meetings, demonstrations, any activity that gave them collective control over their working lives. He hoped to develop a form of "class-struggle unionism" that emphasized the collective activity of workers on the broadest possible scale.[24] Although IBT general president Daniel Tobin attempted to stifle Dobbs, the CLA, and Local 574, the innovative tactics of the Minneapolis leaders proved popular and effective, winning the IBT its first ever areawide contracts.

The form of leapfrog organizing, however, proved more durable than the content introduced by Dobbs and the CLA, who were purged from the IBT in the early 1940s.[25] Young and rising IBT leaders like Dave Beck in the Northwest and Jimmy Hoffa in the Midwest soon recognized another, more coercive aspect of the strategy. In their hands, leapfrog organizing was stripped of its militancy. They pitted employers against each other by using "organized threats," not actual activity. Like Dobbs, they ordered teamsters to refuse to unload nonunion trucks until employers recognized the union. But unlike Dobbs, they did not organize the rank and file. As Joseph Gritten, secretary of the Christian Labor Association, complained in a letter to Daniel Tobin dated 11 June 1945, Hoffa would "simply call employers from a hotel room and tell them that they must sign a closed shop contract by a certain time or their business place will be picketed, their trucks stopped, etc. In brief, these employers are told that they must sign up or be put out of business."[26] In this way, workers, as well as employers, were coerced into the union. They joined the union without any organizing effort on the part of the union. If they did not like it, they often faced physical threats and intimidation.[27]

Essentially, Beck and Hoffa used Dobbs's strategy to serve the goals of business unionism, preferring to harness rank-and-file militancy rather than unleash it. Like Dobbs, the two leaders pushed to centralize areawide bargaining and establish uniform wages, hours, and working conditions. Unlike Dobbs, they emphasized employer rather than employee organization. While the trucking industry grew, the strategy was extremely effective. Hoffa and Beck organized hundreds of trucking employers into regional (and later national) associations, which then signed contracts with the IBT that guaranteed uniform wages and working conditions. Both the rank and file and the employers benefited from the elimination of competition, the rank and file from increasing wages and benefits (administered by a bloated bureaucracy), the employers from uniform costs. As a result, the union grew rapidly, using its base in trucking to expand into new jurisdictions—warehouse, grocery, food supply, department stores, airlines, education, municipal government, and many more. By 1950, membership had passed the million mark; by 1970, the two million mark.[28]

The unique economic conditions of the trucking industry also proved ideal for labor racketeering, extortion, bribery, pension ripoffs, and the other forms of union corruption that have made the IBT (in)famous. Small employers could not and did not stand up to the union, nor did they necessarily wish to. As Daniel Bell has pointed out with regard to the longshoremen's union, racketeering can stabilize a labor market where the presence of so many employers creates chaos.[29] Walter Galenson concurs, pointing out that the business unionism of IBT leaders had "quite a different set of ethical standards from traditional American business unionism. Beck and Hoffa made no bones about the fact that they were in business—the business of selling labor—and if alongside their main wares they were engaged in selling other goods which yielded personal profits, what harm to the members?"[30] As businessmen, IBT leaders were ruthless, using any means necessary to extend their market share, that is, to expand the union.

Teamster Job Control

Despite the domination of corrupt business unionism at the top of the IBT, the rank-and-file traditions of autonomy and militancy begun in the Midwest under Dobbs were never eradicated. The favorable economic circumstances of trucking accommodated both business unionism and rank-and-file job control. Through their collective activity at the workplace, ordinary teamsters were able to decide the content and pace of work. For example, at an Earl C. Smith barn in Detroit in the late 1960s, elected stewards in Local 299 still insisted on taking ten minutes on the clock daily to check that all trailers were blocked to assure that they would not roll away from the dock during loading. Moreover, when jobs entered the dock, the stewards assigned them, not the terminal manager. If dock workers were displeased by a foreman, they slowed the pace of work to a crawl until he was replaced. They did the same if the company violated seniority rules or health and safety regulations or tried to reduce benefits. When dock workers believed a fellow teamster was fired unjustly, they walked out until he was rehired, even if the dismissal was allowed under the contract.[31]

Rank-and-file control like that at Earl C. Smith existed in thousands of IBT-organized barns across the country, with or without official union sanction.[32] In fact, few of the practices of teamster job control were formally recognized by the company or the union in contract language. Rather, they were reproduced daily by informal work groups that came together as needed. Consisting of workmates or friends, these groups enforced their own set of unwritten work rules through collective action on the job. Usually, such action was simple. For example, a group of teamsters might confront a foreman over the treatment of a workmate or over how a truck should be unloaded. Occasionally, a "quickie" strike would be necessary.[33] In either case, when successful, such practices were self-perpetuating. They reinforced teamsters' confidence in their own ability to win and protect their job privileges. Over time, many teamsters took that ability for granted.

Teamsters' practices of job control were made possible by the unique nature of the trucking industry. Truck driving was an occupation that encouraged independence, freedom, and informal organization. Drivers were free, within broad limits, to determine their own route, the speed with which they completed a job, and the time and place of their breaks. In moving from terminal to terminal, they developed friendships, which became the basis of informal communication networks. In essence, an activist driver could be a part-time rank-and-file organizer simply by doing the job.[34]

Trucking employers were reluctant to attack teamster job control for the same reasons that they were unwilling to challenge the union. Economic growth, industry regulation, and periodic rate increases assuaged the inconvenience of higher costs associated with teamsters' command of the work process. Firms' small size and geographic frontiers limited the resources with which they could neutralize pressure from organized workers. In a labor-intensive industry and with minimal capital, trucking firms found it difficult to substitute technology for labor. They could not easily eliminate jobs and exploit the resultant fear to discipline remaining workers. Nor could they easily employ technology to reorganize the labor process in such a way as to erode teamsters' job control. In sum, trucking employers had little motivation and few resources with which to confront the rank and file at the workplace.

The structure and politics of the IBT also reinforced teamsters' practices of workplace control. Despite the centralization caused by regional contracts, the union developed through the 1940s and 1950s as a collection of local and regional "baronies," each in the hands of a small group of union officials. These officials were autonomous from the international on most questions, including strikes, collective bargaining, grievances, and in many cases, pension investments. Only Jimmy Hoffa was powerful enough to unite these baronies, and even then only for a short time. The result was a high level of local independence.

Regional and local baronies were themselves divided by the existence of many trucking terminals spread among many trucking employers. Only the largest trucking workplaces saw union business agents on a regular basis. There were just too many work sites for them to cover. For the rank and file, IBT decentralization and the lack of union presence at the workplace meant independence. Local agents were often unavailable to settle disputes or enforce work rules.[35] Workers had to defend themselves and impose their own regulations, further reinforcing their informal organizations and practices of job control.

As long as trucking firms remained small, did not have to compete, and continued to have guaranteed profits, rank-and-file teamsters and IBT leaders could expect little resistance from employers to their respective demands. Under such circumstances, the two sets of practices were mutually reinforcing. Rank-and-file militancy provided the muscle with which IBT leaders could threaten employers. The decentralization, political simplicity, and tough stance of IBT business unionism gave rank-and-file teamsters the space and confidence to establish and maintain control at the workplace.

Three institutional expressions of teamsters' inordinate power were the "open-ended" grievance procedure, the right to veto company "changes of operation," and the right to strike for twenty-four hours for any reason. Whether or not teamsters exercised these rights, all three were potent weapons for the defense of their prerogatives on the job. The very fact that they possessed the rights demonstrated their power vis-à-vis the employers.[36]

The circumstances of the trucking industry and the IBT were uniquely conducive to rank-and-file organization. Yet trucking was not so different that it was immune to the general crisis of profitability that struck the U.S. economy in the late 1960s, nor was the IBT so different that it could avoid the consequences of this development. These changes set the stage for the Teamsters for a Democratic Union.

INDUSTRY CHANGES AND THE RESPONSE TO THE EMPLOYERS' OFFENSIVE

By the late 1960s, changes in the trucking industry were forcing the IBT to choose between its two traditions of corrupt business unionism and rank-and-file militancy. The fortunes of the trucking industry were closely tied to those of the economy as a whole. Thus when the rate of economic growth fell in the late 1960s, the trucking industry's rate followed. The total growth of ton-miles carried by trucking slowed from 25 percent in the five years between 1960 and 1965 to 14 percent in the five years between 1965 and 1970.[37] Intra-industry competition, long suppressed by regulation, intensified under these conditions as trucking firms fought to keep their share of a stagnating market. Competition from outside the industry also intensified. Railroads still sought trucking's freight business. More threatening were air freight and nonunion trucking firms. As the price of air freight fell, it took more and more business from the trucking companies.

Nonunion trucking firms represented the potentially greatest threat to the union. As long as the IBT did not organize them, they could be used to "whipsaw" teamsters—companies could threaten to make their operations nonunion (using various legal and illegal methods) if the IBT refused to match the wages and working conditions at the nonunion firms. In some cases, unionized trucking firms opened nonunion subsidiaries and demanded that the unionized workers match the conditions in the nonunion subsidiaries, a process called "double-breasting." In some of these cases, IBT officials reached deals to look the other way. For various reasons, nonunion companies were not a serious threat to the union until well into the 1970s. Still, their existence indicated new conditions were emerging in the industry.[38]

A second manifestation of the new competition was an increase in mergers and acquisitions, which led to the creation of several national freight trucking firms with the wherewithal to stand up to the competition and the IBT. These included Consolidated Freightways, Roadway, and Yellow Freight. In the early 1970s these companies were still relatively small, employing a combined 40,000 of the 500,000 unionized drivers and dock workers in the freight industry. Though they did not dominate the industry, they played a leadership role in several employer associations and set some of the work-rule patterns for the industry as a whole. With several hundred terminals spread across the country, each company was better equipped to withstand local or regional strikes than were the vast majority of trucking firms. They could also use the process of regional supplemental contract bargaining to whipsaw terminals in one area against those in another.[39]

Industry competition prompted trucking companies to mount an offensive against working teamsters. The employers' primary target was the set of traditional job-control practices in the hands of rank and filers. Managers increasingly emphasized cost-cutting and productivity increases rather than expansion as the way to maintain profitability. New sophisticated management techniques and technological improvements were introduced to streamline operations, especially in the larger firms that could afford the necessary investment. Routing, loading, and dispatching, traditionally run by teamsters, were put under tight management control. Computers were used where possible to plan operations, removing any debate over how things should be done within the terminals or on the road. New, more efficient terminals were built to move freight more quickly. These were equipped with chain-pulled carts and larger forklifts that required more frequent use of pallets. This equipment eliminated jobs (pallets could only be moved by machine) and raised productivity, as did larger trucks. Tractor-trailer combinations, called "semis," increasingly replaced "bobtails," trucks with connected tractor and trailer. Semis allowed the tractor to be used elsewhere while the trailer was loaded. Where legal, "doubles" (two trailers, one tractor) were used, and employers lobbied for laws allowing "triples."[40]

Companies' labor relations were also streamlined during the 1960s. Personnel departments had been introduced during the 1940s, but few companies had full-time labor relations experts to handle union-management problems and grievances. In most places grievances were handled by the local employer association, since management did not have the personnel and expertise necessary. By the 1960s, many trucking companies were large enough and smart enough to employ full-time experts. Many of these experts were retired IBT business agents who used their experience to teach employers how to exploit the contract. Employers also learned from the IBT the advantage of unity. Following the example of larger firms, they began to consolidate their associations during the 1960s. While this consolidation was initially foisted upon them by Hoffa's drive for a National Master Freight Agreement (NMFA), employers quickly adapted, so much so that they were able to enforce an almost total lockout in 1967.[41]

The effect of the new industry conditions on ordinary teamsters was pronounced. Teamsters began to lose the informal control they had previously enjoyed. Strict work rules were implemented for each task. Standards were introduced and enforced. United Parcel Service (UPS), the largest single teamster employer, became known as the Big Brown Machine during this period, when it pioneered such practices as setting daily delivery goals, clocking drivers, and firing those who did not meet standards. While UPS was not covered by the National Master Freight Agreement, its practices were admired and imitated by management in the freight industry.[42]

Teamsters worked harder and under worse conditions. New equipment and new management techniques eliminated jobs but forced those still employed to pick up the slack. Companies realized that two teamsters doing the work of three and paid overtime to do it still cost less, since the third would have to be paid health and pension benefits. Increased use of casuals, which cut the number of full-time teamsters and companies' overall wage bill, produced similar results. Cutting corners made work more hazardous. Larger loads, longer hours and distances, and quicker safety checks increased the likelihood of accidents and injury. Flextime, as opposed to a regular schedule, was increasingly used, keeping teamsters guessing as to when they would have to work and forcing them to sit by the phone without pay.[43]

Trucking employers could not alter the balance of power in the workplace overnight. The processes that reduced teamster job control were uneven. Industry consolidation took time, as did the introduction of new technology and personnel management procedures. Few companies adopted all the techniques described. Some did nothing at all, while many others struck at teamsters' job control in piecemeal fashion. ICC regulation, firms' small size, and teamsters' resistance also slowed the onslaught.

Nevertheless, the trend was clear to many working teamsters. They were losing command of their jobs. Their working conditions were deteriorating.

The Bureaucracy's Response

In response to the employers' offensive, the leadership of the IBT proved helpless. In National Master Freight Agreement negotiations with the employers, Frank Fitzsimmons, Jimmy Hoffa's hand-picked replacement, tried to trade teamsters' job control for higher wages, but he usually failed. According to a 1967 *Business Week*, "The employers' sights are on a 5 percent settlement before a March 31 deadline—if the union will agree to a number of cost-cutting changes in work rules."[44] That year the IBT's original demand was for wage and benefit increases of 6 percent to 7 percent in each of three years. In the end the settlement called for an average 5 percent increase over three years, and the employers won the work-rule changes they wanted. Where flextime was already in use it was maintained. In some areas where premium pay for weekends existed it was phased out, thereby spreading flextime. The employers also won a virtual freeze on mileage pay, increasing their ability to assign long-distance routes.[45]

In 1970, the NMFA negotiations were little different. Fitzsimmons began with a demand for a $3-per-hour wage increase, nearly 75 percent for the average truck driver, over three years, but made no demands dealing with the erosion of rank-and-file job control. His first settlement, however, called for only $1.10 per hour over three years *and* it eliminated teamsters' right to strike for twenty-four hours. He had traded one of the teamsters' most powerful weapons in exchange for a relatively small wage gain.[46]

IBT officials further undermined rank-and-file wages and working conditions by negotiating an increasing number of supplemental contracts to the National Master Freight Agreement. These contracts covered specific types of work (carhaulers, chemical drivers, oil drivers) or particular regions of the country. While they differed only slightly from the NMFA, the differences usually provided better terms for the employers.[47] After the first NMFA in 1964, the number of supplements to it increased each time it was negotiated. To make matters worse, teamsters did not vote on the supplements that covered them, only on the national contract, and a two-thirds vote was required to reject.[48]

The union's willingness to stand up to the employers was weakened by the corruption of its officials. With Hoffa in jail from March 1967, no individual leader was capable of controlling the union's regional baronies. With Hoffa gone, IBT officials engaged in the biggest expansion of union corruption in history, an orgy of embezzlement, crooked loans from IBT pension funds, employer extortion, sweetheart contracts, physical intimidation, and murder, all of which left union members poorer, weaker, and angrier.[49]

The Rank-and-File Reaction

While IBT leaders sat idle in the face of the employers' offensive, rank-and-file teamsters did not. Wildcat strikes in 1967 and 1970 demonstrated as much. Directly following Fitzsimmons's announcement of the National Master Freight Agreement in April 1967, teamsters in Chicago went on strike demanding more money from Chicago trucking companies. In a matter of days they won a wage increase higher than that won by Fitzsimmons, forcing him to renegotiate the national agreement to better the terms won in Chicago (but not to eliminate the work-rule concessions).[50] The strike demonstrated the inadequacy of the IBT leadership and the strength of rank-and-file action.

The 1970 national wildcat strike was the largest wildcat in IBT history. Close to fifty thousand teamsters participated. As in 1967, the strike began in Chicago right after the national contract was agreed upon. It quickly spread until the major break bulk centers in the Midwest and California were shut. Fitzsimmons immediately tried to stop the strike by sending telegrams to three hundred locals urging strikers to return to work. But teamster rank-and-file organization was too strong. In Ohio, crowds of teamsters battled and at times defeated National Guard troops. In St. Louis, teamsters held out for a month against court injunctions until they were cited so many times they had to return. In Los Angeles, strikers avoided court injunctions by calling in sick, part of a strategy to raise their local demand for sick leave. After twelve weeks on strike, Chicago teamsters won a wage raise of $1.65 per hour over three years. This forced Fitzsimmons to renegotiate the NMFA, giving teamsters across the country an additional seventy-five cents per hour over three years.[51]

Wildcat actions were not the only rank-and-file response to deteriorating

job conditions and inadequate union representation. Local and regional teamster dissident groups began to form during the late 1960s. These included the
Fraternal Association of Steelhaulers (FASH), the Unity Committee, the 500
at 50 clubs, Teamsters United Rank and File (TURF), and the Professional
Drivers Council, Inc. (PROD). Most of these groups lasted only a short time
and were able to initiate little militancy. FASH initiated wildcat strikes among
steelhaulers in 1967 and 1970 but managed little activity thereafter. PROD
was a lobbying group stimulated by Ralph Nader; it eventually merged with
TDU.

Several other local groups formed in the early 1970s. With handfuls of members,
these groups met on a regular basis and engaged in activity in several cities.
They ran in local union elections but stressed rank-and-file education and activity. They held small, local demonstrations, made arguments in union meetings, and distributed literature. In Pittsburgh a group called Concerned Rank-
and-File Teamsters published a paper called *From the Horse's Mouth*. In Cleveland the local rank-and-file newsletter was called *Membership Voice*, in San
Francisco it was *The Fifth Wheel*, and in Los Angeles it was *Grapevine*, with
the slogan "All the News That Fitz Won't Print." All these groups were tiny
minorities within their locals, yet they survived because dedicated militants,
many of whom were organized socialists, kept a core of supporters active.[52]

The International Socialists

The socialists at the center of the local rank-and-file organizations inside the
IBT were members of the International Socialists (IS), a small revolutionary
socialist organization with roots in American Trotskyism.[53] The IS, with its
headquarters in Detroit, had several hundred members and a newspaper called
Workers' Power. Most members were recruited from college campuses, but the
group focused its activity on the working class. The IS's strategy for intervention in the labor movement centered on the rank-and-file caucus. Dave
Wolfinsohn, a member of the IS and an early participant in TDU, explained
the goals of the caucus:

> What the IS hoped to do was stimulate a level of struggle out of which rank
> and file workers could develop the capacity to cohere their own fighting
> organizations, hopefully on a union-wide basis. Such organizations would
> aim to build up enough influence among the membership of the union so
> that they would take on the employers. The minimum precondition of such
> rank and file groups would be an acute consciousness of the need for self-
> reliance and independence from the bureaucracy and an understanding of
> the need to build the broadest sort of connections, within the unions and
> beyond them, to other groups of workers—most especially, to begin to con-
> front the divisive effects of racism and sexism within the working class.[54]

The IS would organize workers around the issues they confronted at the
workplace—wages, benefits, job control, working conditions, pensions, safety,
and health. This would require a conscious challenge to union officials who

refused to support rank-and-file demands. More importantly, it would require leading the struggle at the workplace to demonstrate to workers, through experience, the rank and file's collective power to win concessions from the employers.

The IS hoped to recruit industrial workers through its activity in the rank-and-file groups. Nonetheless, adherence to IS's socialist principles was not a requirement for participation, membership, or leadership in the organizations. They were not front groups, nor were they socialist caucuses inside the union, nor were they dual unions. They were alternative workers' organizations with the double purpose of leading the struggle against the employers and vying for political power within the unions on the basis of that leadership. The common political denominators would be concentration on workplace issues, an insistence on coordinated militancy at the workplace as the primary weapon for confronting the employers, radically democratic rank-and-file organization, and independence from the union machinery. Where necessary, rank-and-file groups would take stands on contested political issues, such as affirmative action. Aside from these general principles, which in practice turned out to be rather flexible concepts, the precise role of IS members in the rank-and-file groups was left unclear.[55]

IS members took jobs in "strategic" industries deemed central to the group's overall revolutionary project, including auto (UAW), steel (USWA), teaching (AFT), public service American Federation of State, County, and Municipal Emloyees (AFSCME), telephone (CWA), and trucking (IBT). As it turned out, they were successful in implementing their rank-and-file caucus strategy only among teamsters.[56]

TEAMSTERS FOR A DEMOCRATIC UNION

In August of 1975, at the initiative of those in the IS, activists from the various local rank-and-file groups inside the IBT met in Chicago to form Teamsters for a Decent Contract (TDC), the forerunner to Teamsters for a Democratic Union. TDC was a national contract campaign designed to pressure IBT general president Frank Fitzsimmons into supporting certain demands in the upcoming 1976 National Master Freight Agreement negotiations. These included cost-of-living wage, pension, and health adjustments, a two-year contract (instead of three), an additional week of vacation, no forced overtime and double pay for voluntary overtime, paid sick leave, separate votes on all supplements and riders to the national contract, maintenance of seniority in mergers and acquisitions, elimination of casual, probationary, and replacement employees, restoration of the right to strike for twenty-four hours, amendment to the grievance procedure to hold teamsters innocent until proven guilty, elimination of flextime, and health, safety, and comfort improvements for all new trucks. TDC supporters circulated petitions pledging teamsters to vote against any contract that did not contain TDC's demands. Local chapters were formed.

These organized on a barn-by-barn basis, in part by distributing TDC's national newspaper *Convoy* and in part by holding educational meetings.[57] In the months leading up to the national contract, TDC won thousands of supporters by holding a series of coordinated national demonstrations in cities across the country, including one in front of the IBT's "Marble Palace" in Washington, D.C., that received national media attention.[58] TDC's growing popularity forced Fitzsimmons to call the first official national freight strike in teamster history on 1 April 1976. Though the strike lasted only two days and won little from the employers, it led to wildcat strikes in several cities, some led by TDC or future TDC members. These strikes cemented TDC's presence in the IBT's freight jurisdiction, its core jurisdiction with nearly a third of the IBT's 1.5 million members. The most important of these wildcats was in Detroit Local 299, the home local of Jimmy Hoffa and Frank Fitzsimmons. It established TDC as a force in one of the IBT's most important and powerful locals. The freight wildcats also prepared the way for wildcats in other important IBT jurisdictions. On 1 May United Parcel Service workers in the Midwest wildcatted when their contract expired, and on 1 June, 450 carhaulers from Cincinnati sent roving pickets around Ohio and Michigan, leading to wildcats in Detroit and Flint. TDC supporters played key roles in most of the wildcats.[59]

The wildcat strikes gave TDC notoriety, which was enhanced by events at the June 1976 IBT national convention. TDC activists from Los Angeles organized a small demonstration, and IBT leaders overreacted. Fitzsimmons first responded in a speech to the entire convention, promising that "no damned Communist group is going to infiltrate this union" and shouting "but for those who would say that it's time to reform this organization, that it is time that the officers quit selling out the membership of their union, I say to them: Go to Hell!"[60] If that were not enough to get teamsters talking about TDC, IBT goons beat Pete Camarata, a TDC activist from Detroit Local 299 and the lone convention delegate TDC had managed to elect, in front of a Las Vegas hotel. Partly as a result, Camarata, already well known as a leader of the Detroit wildcat, drew large audiences during a TDC speaking tour of the West right after the convention.[61]

The momentum built during the spring wildcats and at the summer IBT convention convinced TDC leaders that they had the basis for a permanent rank-and-file organization. During the summer they started calling their organization Teamsters for a Democratic Union and planned a founding convention, held 18–19 September 1976, at Kent, Ohio. It was attended by 250 teamsters from forty-four locals in fifteen states.[62]

The convention drafted a constitution and a set of resolutions. The two documents set out the way TDU would operate and its political program. TDU was to be a collection of branches with the highest power vested in a yearly national convention. A national steering committee, elected by the convention, would run the organization between conventions. All TDU members attending the convention were eligible to vote on steering committee members and on all resolutions before the convention.[63]

TDU's political program reflected the influence of the IS. In essence, TDU would be a caucus of the type IS imagined. It would be an independent rank-and-file organization of teamsters, open to all teamsters agreeing with the basic tenet of building "a national, unified movement of rank and file teamsters that is organized to fight for rank and file rights on the job and in the union. We aim to bring the Teamsters Union back to the membership."[64] TDU founders hoped their organization would someday become the leadership body of the IBT, giving teamsters democratic control of their union and reinvigorating it with the principles of class struggle unionism.[65]

Toward this end, the convention adopted resolutions pledging TDU to rely strictly on rank-and-file self-organization and to avoid reliance on union elections, the courts, or politicians. Other resolutions pledged support for affirmative action for minorities and women, an end to casual work, restoration of the right to strike, the election of stewards, democratization of the union, and an innocent-until-proven-guilty grievance procedure. Most of the resolutions, save those dealing with internal union democracy, did not mention the IBT. Rather, TDU concentrated its fire at the employers, as TDC had done during the 1976 NMFA campaign.[66]

TDU addressed the concerns teamsters cared about most: their rights and privileges on the job. In emphasizing the employers, TDU stressed the necessity of rank-and-file organization's confronting employers at the workplace. By making demands of the employers, TDU was also implicitly making demands of the IBT, insisting that IBT officials put the needs of the rank and file ahead of all others. As TDU leaders saw it, union corruption and totalitarianism were not the major problems but were symptoms of a more general disease: The union had ceased to function by and for its members. Writing in *Convoy*, Ken Paff, national secretary of TDU since its inception, said,

> The real issue is RANK AND FILE POWER. That's what Fitzsimmons and the TEI [employers association] were against. . . . YOU CAN'T WIN RANK AND FILE POWER BY RELYING ON THE COURTS, FEDERAL JUDGES, POLITICIANS OR UNION OFFICIALS. We will win our right to vote by continuing to organize the rank and file until we have OUR OWN POWER. That's how our union was built in the first place. That's how it will be rebuilt now. . . . The only way to win is to be so well organized they have to deal with us.[67]

Following this logic, TDU developed a two-pronged strategy: rank-and-file power to confront the employers *and* the union.

In carrying out its strategy, TDU recognized that it would have to play the role of the union since IBT officials refused to do so. The group would have to be a workers' organization for the protection and promotion of teamsters' rights and privileges, just like a union; yet TDU would have to remain inside the IBT where teamsters had the power to fight.

Advancing the interests of rank-and-file teamsters took several forms. First, TDU tried to stimulate rank-and-file self-organization at the workplace, to reinvigorate the informal work groups that teamsters had employed in the 1940s, 1950s, and 1960s. For example, local TDU chapters organized support for teamsters with grievances. They attended grievance hearings en masse or passed petitions to demonstrate the grievance's widespread support.[68] When teamsters were unjustly fired, TDU organized rank-and-file protests to win their jobs back. In some cases this required little more than a meeting with management. In others it meant a wildcat strike.[69] Activities like these demonstrated to ordinary teamsters that they could improve their working lives through their self-activity and that TDU could help them do it.

TDU's attempt to democratize the IBT was part of its strategy to mobilize rank-and-file teamsters. One of its initial tactics for building local TDU chapters was a campaign to reform local bylaws. TDU hoped that by opening the structure of the locals it could encourage rank-and-file participation, and that the campaign itself, which consisted of passing petitions to put various proposals on the local ballot, would do the same. TDU's proposals for bylaws reform included elected rather than appointed union business agents and stewards, lower salaries for local officers, elected rather than appointed union committees, and dues reduction. Given that a two-thirds majority was required to pass bylaws changes, it was rare that TDU was able to win, as it did in Flint Local 332.[70] Even where bylaws campaigns fell short, they schooled teamsters in confronting union officials.

TDU's two-pronged strategy was successful because the group was able to initiate militant activity. Though victories were few, TDU led many battles, involving thousands of teamsters in collective struggle, including job actions, bylaws campaigns, strikes, union elections, worker education, legal defense, and contract campaigns. This activity drew consciously upon the traditions of teamster rank-and-file militancy and autonomy. At the workplace, TDU exploited the informal work groups that teamsters had traditionally formed.[71] Where possible, they formalized these through membership in TDU. With regular meetings, TDU activists developed strategies for taking on the employers in any small way possible. Given the continued weaknesses of some employers, victories were occasionally possible. The same was true within the union. The group exploited its decentralized structure, organizing a few locals to adopt all or part of its program.[72] These successes, usually at the local level, gave TDU a reputation that sustained it through periods of waning rank-and-file militancy.

TDU activity was not simply an extension of teamsters' traditional practices. TDU developed a much higher level of organization than that of teamster informal work groups. It was a national organization that by 1978 had a full-time staff. It had a well-developed program and committed, activist leadership. As a coordinated national organization, TDU reduced the negative effects of local isolation and presented a more credible alternative to rank-and-file teamsters. The group's national scope provided practical and psychological support.

Through the national office, national meetings, and the national newspaper, *Convoy*, activists in various areas exhanged information, strategies, and stories. They also celebrated each other's successes and commiserated with each other's failures. Though TDU most often succeeded on a local level, it did so largely due to support from the national organization.

IS members played an essential role in developing and maintaining TDU's leadership. Their dedication was crucial to TDU's survival. Teamsters may have had a higher degree of confidence in their own self-activity than did most other American workers, but it took the ideas and organization of a few socialist militants to turn that confidence into constructive activity. That so many teamsters joined TDU and participated in its leadership proves that IS alone was not responsible for the group's success. Without the IS, however, it is doubtful that TDU would have started or survived. To borrow a popular analogy, teamster rank-and-file militancy and informal organization provided the steam to drive the piston of TDU activity, while the IS program and its members' dedication provided the cylinder to channel that activity in a positive direction.

The TDU Trajectory

TDU's road to IBT leadership did not follow an even upward arc. The group was able to maintain a high level of activity and growth during its first four years. Membership grew. The circulation of *Convoy* increased. Each yearly convention drew more teamsters. As a result, TDU was able to establish institutional permanence. A small staff was hired and a small internship program instituted. A nonprofit foundation was created to solicit donations from friends of teamster reform, a cause aided by continued exposure of IBT official corruption and Mafia ties. By 1979, it was pretty clear that TDU would survive as long as the core group of militants remained active.

The 1980s proved more difficult. The group continued to grow but was unable to initiate the same level of activity against the employers. The balance shifted toward union electoral campaigns. TDU activists continued to inform teamsters of their rights on the job, helped them file grievances, and aided them in navigating the tricky waters of the IBT pension system, but they were unable to stimulate more militant activity on the job. Despite building high levels of militancy around the contract campaigns of 1976 and 1979, TDU received little response in 1982 and 1985. The reason was clear. Trucking deregulation, initiated in the late 1970s, followed by recession in the early 1980s, had dramatically tilted the balance of power toward the employers.

Stepping up the productivity drive begun in the late 1960s, teamster employers expanded their attack on teamster wages, benefits, working conditions, and job control. Following the lead of United Parcel Service, they instituted productivity standards and disciplined workers who failed to meet them. They opened more nonunion subsidiaries (double-breasting) and whipsawed union and nonunion workers against each other. Their two-tier wage systems threatened living standards and undercut teamster solidarity. Finally, they instituted flexible work weeks and increased the use of casuals. As the IBT leadership retreated even further into the underworld, rank-and-file teamsters were defenseless.

Despite the attacks, TDU maintained itself and cultivated a national network of activists. By the late 1980s, conditions for a qualitative leap in TDU's membership and activity were emerging. Though the number of teamsters in the IBT's core trucking jurisdictions had shrunk, those that were left began to regain confidence. In 1987–1988, TDU was able to organize three straight contract rejections—UPS, master freight, and carhaul—which embarrassed IBT leaders and employers. But the biggest stimulus to TDU's reinvigoration in the early 1990s was the 1989 settlement of the government's Racketeering Influenced Corrupt Organizations Act (RICO) suit against the IBT. Along with measures to eliminate corruption, the settlement called for an open, one-member-one-vote election of the IBT international executive board. TDU played an active role in the government's suit and deserves some of the credit for the inclusion of the election stipulation. TDU argued that the best way to rid the union of corrupt officials was to give the union back to its membership through democratization.

Once the settlement was approved, TDU leaders immediately recognized the opportunity. At the end of 1989, fully two years before the election, they endorsed a presidential candidate, Ron Carey, a longtime New York local president who had maintained independence from the international leadership. Though not a TDU member, Carey accepted TDU support and included seven TDU members on his sixteen-member reform slate. TDU then became the backbone of the campaign. Reinvigorated by the electoral opportunity, the group's network of activists pulled thousands of rank-and-file teamsters to rallies, meetings, demonstrations, and other campaign activities. The result of the December 1991 election was a resounding victory for the Carey slate, winning every seat for which it ran, sixteen of seventeen spots on the IBT international executive board.

Since the election, TDU has grown rapidly. The key question now is whether teamsters so eager to democratize their union are as willing to take on the employers. Can TDU combine its position among the IBT leadership with its rank-and-file organization to stimulate a level of teamster militancy that can challenge the employers' offensive?

TDU AND THE RANK-AND-FILE UPSURGE

The type of activities undertaken by American workers during the decade after 1966 was significantly different from that of the preceding decades. In the context of a world economy, with huge multinational corporations and large international unions, on the cusp of sustained crisis, U.S. workers did things they had rarely done before. Never during the post–World War II period had workers struck against their employers *and* their unions on such a scale. In doing so, they threw into question the relationship between individual workers and their unions. They challenged the pattern of industrial relations upon which the success of unionism was supposedly built during the previous twenty-five years. And they did it in virtually every major industry.

Teamsters for a Democratic Union was the only rank-and-file organization to survive the period. As shown, the circumstances of this success were unique. Given the organization and activity associated with their high degree of job control, teamsters retained an inordinate level of confidence in their ability to fight and defeat the employers. Teamsters' job control was itself fostered by the particular political economy of the industry (small-sized firms, regulation, limited competition), the nature of the labor process (the independence of truck driving and relatively small, tight work groups), and the unique internal development of the IBT (decentralization, simplicity, corruption). When economic conditions put teamsters on the defensive, they were better able to resist than workers elsewhere. They could actually protect some of the privileges they had won during the postwar boom. To do so required a much higher level of organization than previously achieved, and here the intervention of the International Socialists proved crucial.

Having said this, however, it must be acknowledged that many of the circumstances facilitating the rise of TDU also existed in other industries. The employers' offensive and the weak response of the union bureaucracy were ubiquitous. Other unions enjoyed long traditions of rank-and-file militancy at least as impressive as that of the teamsters. Various sorts of socialists, including members of the IS, intervened in several unions with the hope of creating rank-and-file organizations. In a few cases, organizations like TDU were actually built, but only among teamsters did one survive for any length of time. Clearly, the experiences of TDU beg comparative analysis of a type beyond the scope of this essay. Nonetheless, some tentative arguments can be put forward that may perhaps provide a point of departure for later, more systematic work on the rank-and-file upsurge of the late 1960s and early 1970s.

In the final instance, TDU's success depended on its ability to deliver the goods. But what allowed it to deliver the goods was the unusual capacity of locally organized rank-and-file groups to win gains for their members. Because TDUers acting at the local, or sometimes regional, level could secure certain gains, TDU could retain and build a following on an incremental basis. National organization made possible local successes; local successes allowed for the gradual construction of an ever stronger national organization. But relatively few other major industries in the last third of the twentieth century had the sort of decentralized structure of ownership and effectively decentralized structure of the union to permit such an evolution. The point can be well illustrated—though not of course yet proved—by reference to the industry that was, in a sense, the polar opposite to trucking, that is, automobile manufacturing.

Between 1967 and 1973 the auto industry shook with one rank-and-file revolt after the next: the Dodge Revolutionary Union Movement and the League of Revolutionary Black Workers, the United National Caucus, the United Black Brothers, the Linden Auto Workers, huge strikes against speedup in Lordstown and Norwood in 1972, and waves of wildcat strikes in 1973. Behind each instance of militancy lurked the speedup, the most famous example of which was the General Motors Assembly Division (GMAD) program, which had workers in some factories cranking out a hundred cars per hour. But despite nearly universal opposition to the productivity drive and the high level of rank-and-file militancy of the period, auto workers were unable to create and sustain a permanent rank-and-file organization.

Why were the auto rank and filers unable to convert a level of militancy and political consciousness that was in some respects even higher than that of the teamsters into more successful rank-and-file organization? As with TDU's success, the answer seems to lie in what the rank-and-file groups in auto were able to do for their followers. Unlike TDU, these groups were unable to deliver the goods, and their difficulty appears to lie in the nature of their opponents—companies and a union that, quite unlike those in trucking, were highly centrally organized and highly organizationally sophisticated.

When the auto companies unleashed their speedup campaigns in the later 1960s and early 1970s, they did so on a national basis. Given the size of the companies, their ability to sustain economic losses, and their capacity to shift production from plant to plant, the rank and file faced a very difficult task in winning demands at the local level. To make matters much worse from the rank-and-file standpoint, the national union, unsympathetic to resistance, exerted the tightest centralized control over the locals. The UAW was very well organized to discipline, and ultimately to eliminate, militant local leadership that sought to struggle in isolation. The result was that even relatively successful rank-and-file organizing tended to be short-lived. It might succeed for a brief time at the local level, but the company and the union would soon reduce or destroy its capacity to secure gains for its members. The group would soon lose support, as its followers came to see the futility of their local fight. This made it impossible for any national rank-and-file organization to consolidate itself at the local level and build on the basis of incremental local organizing.

This fundamental problem was very well exemplified, as local resistance to the GMAD speedup reached its apex in 1972–1973. In this period, big local strikes were waged at Norwood and Lordstown, and powerful local resistance was launched in many other plants around the country. The locals succeeded in forcing the International to call a national council about how to respond nationally to GMAD. But, at that point, the locals' failure to create *their own* national rank-and-file organization, à la TDU, left them at the mercy of the International.

UAW president Leonard Woodcock implemented the infamous "Apache" strategy, which essentially played on the union's weakness. The International launched short, local strikes, announced in advance. These played directly into the strength of General Motors and were easily defeated. The locals' militancy was dispersed, and the opportunity for broader organization dissipated. Whereas TDU had the important insight that national organization was needed from the start, it also had the luxury, in the face of a decentralized union and small companies, of building over an extended period, from the localities up. The rank-and-file oppositionists in auto had no such breathing space, and the need for coordinated national organization from the start is perhaps the primary lesson, albeit a negative one, that oppositionists in the major industries can learn from the experience of TDU.

Notes

1. U.S. Department of Labor, Bureau of Labor Statistics, *Handbook of Labor Statistics*, bulletin no. 2175 (Washington, D.C.: Government Printing Office, 1983), 380; Kim Moody, *An Injury to All* (London: Verso, 1988), 86; David Brody, *Workers in Industrial America* (New York: Oxford, 1980), 209.
2. On the general level of struggle during these years, see Jeremy Brecher, *Strike!* (Boston: South End Press, 1972), 264–91. See also Peter Henle, "Some Reflections on Organized Labor and the New Militants," *Monthly Labor Review* (July 1969); Stan Weir, "The Conflict in American Unions and the Resistance to Alternative Ideas from the Rank and File," *Radical America* 6, no. 3 (1972); Barbara Garson, "Luddites in Lordstown," *Harper's*, June 1972, p. 68; Agis Salpukis, "Young Workers Disrupt Key GM Plant," *New York Times*, 23 January 1972, p. 24; "Violence in the Factory," *Newsweek*, 29 June 1970; and Dan Georgakas and Marvin Surkin, *Detroit: I Do Mind Dying* (New York: St Martin's, 1975), 9–12.
3. Barry Bosworth, "Capital Formation and Economic Policy," *Brookings Papers on Economic Activity* (1982), no. 2, 293; President's Commission on Industrial Competitiveness, *Global Competition: The New Reality*, vol. 2 (Washington, D.C.: Government Printing Office, 1985), 12. See also Thomas Weisskopf, "Marxian Crisis Theory and the Rate of Profit in the Postwar U.S. Economy," *Cambridge Journal of Economics* 3 (1979): 349; Dale N. Allman, "The Decline in Business Profitability: A Disaggregated Analysis," *Economic Review of the Federal Reserve Bank of Kansas City* (January 1983), 19–26; G. Dumenil, M. Glick, and J. Rangel, "The Rate of Profit in the United States," *Cambridge Journal of Economics* 11 (1987): 331–59.
4. Average real weekly earnings for production and nonsupervisory workers in private nonagricultural employment, measured in constant dollars, rose 3.8 percent between 1965 and 1969. They fell 1.6 percent in 1970, reached an all-time high in 1973, and then fell back to their 1966 level by 1975. The long-term trend was toward moderation. Between 1947 and 1962, real hourly earnings of production or nonsupervisory workers in the private nonfarm economy increased at an average of 2.5 percent annually. During the following fifteen years, annual growth averaged only 1.2 percent. After 1973, stagnation followed moderation. Real compensation per hour, wages plus benefits, has gone virtually unchanged to the present. Council of Economic Advisors, *Economic Report of the President* (Washington, D.C.: Government Printing Office, 1978), 299; H. M. Douty, "The Slowdown in Real Wages: A Postwar Perspective," *Monthly Labor Review* 100, no. 8 (August 1977): 7; President's Commission, *Global Competition*, 10.
5. Glenn Perusek, "The Internal Politics of the United Automobile Workers, 1967–1985" (Ph.D. diss., University of Chicago, 1988), 243–45; Paul Nyden, "Miners for Democracy: Struggle in the Coal Fields" (Ph.D. diss., Columbia University,

1974), 156, 175; Philip W. Nyden, *Steelworkers Rank and File: The Political Economy of a Union Reform Movement* (New York: Praeger, 1984), 42–49; "Untangling the Mess in the Post Office," *Business Week*, 28 March 1970.

6. Brody, *Workers in Industrial America*, chap. 4; Moody, *An Injury to All*, chap. 3.

7. James R. Green, *The World of the Worker*, (New York: Hill and Wang, 1980) 214; Perusek, "The Internal Politics of the UAW," 78–79.

8. Perusek, "Internal Politics of the UAW," 259; Moody, *An Injury to All*, 93; Bill Bonds, WXYZ-TV News, 16 August 1973, quoted in Georgakas and Surkin, *Detroit*, 227. Fraser quoted in Perusek, "The Internal Politics of the UAW," 252.

9. James A. Geschwender, *Class, Race, and Worker Insurgency: The League of Revolutionary Black Workers* (Cambridge: Cambridge University Press, 1977), 83–137; Georgakas and Surkin, *Detroit*, 29–157; Perusek, "The Internal Politics of the UAW," 205–63.

10. Nyden, "Miners for Democracy," 518–717.

11. International Socialists, "Perspective Document, June 1975," 1975 Convention Folder, International Socialist Collection, Tamiment Institute Library, New York University (hereafter cited as IS Collection, TIL).

12. "The U.S. Can't Afford What Labor Wants," *Business Week*, 11 April 1970, 104.

13. *Wall Street Journal*, 20 October 1970.

14. Brody, *Workers in Industrial America*, 205; Rick Fantasia, *Cultures of Solidarity: Consciousness, Action, and Contemporary American Workers* (Berkeley and Los Angeles: University of California, 1988), chap. 3. On informal work groups see Stan Weir, "A Tale of Two Cities: Gdansk and San Diego," *Against the Current*, 1st ser., 1, no. 2 (Winter 1981): 12–13; Sam Friedman and Stan Weir, "Informal Work Groups: Invisible Power in the Work Place—An Exchange," *Against the Current*, 1st ser., 1, no. 4 (Spring 1982): 45–48; Michael Burawoy, *The Politics of Production* (London: Verso, 1985), 128–37; Brecher, *Strike!* 233–42.

15. Here and throughout, "teamsters" refers to those IBT members in the union's core local and intercity trucking, warehouse, grocery, and United Parcel Service jurisdiction. Other IBT jurisdictions include airlines, education, and municipal government.

16. The classic works on the IBT's transformation from craft to industrial union are Farrell Dobbs's four volumes: *Teamster Rebellion, Teamster Power, Teamster Politics*, and *Teamster Bureaucracy* (New York: Monad, 1972, 1973, 1975, 1977). See also Steven Brill, *The Teamsters* (New York: Simon and Schuster, 1978), 361–64; Ralph James and Estelle James, *Jimmy Hoffa and the Teamsters: A Study of Union Power* (Princeton, N.J.: Van Nostrand, 1965), 89–116; Dan La Botz, *Rank and File Rebellion: Teamsters for a Democratic Union* (London: Verso, 1990), chaps. 8, 9.

17. The literature on IBT corruption is overwhelming. The best examples are James and James, *Hoffa and the Teamsters*; Dan Moldea, *The Hoffa Wars: Teamsters, Rebels, Politicians, and the Mob* (New York: Paddington Press, 1978); Clark R. Mollenhoff, *Tentacles of Power: The Story of Jimmy Hoffa* (Cleveland, Ohio: World Publishing Company, 1965); Walter Sheridan, *The Fall and Rise of Jimmy Hoffa* (New York: Saturday Review Press, 1972); Lester Velie, *Desperate Bargain: Why Jimmy Hoffa Had to Die* (New York: Reader's Digest, 1977).

18. Charles R. Perry, *Deregulation and the Decline of Unionized Trucking* (Philadelphia: The Wharton School, University of Pennsylvania, 1986), 12, 51; Samuel Friedman, *Teamster Rank and File: Power, Bureaucracy, and Rebellion of Work in a Union* (New York: Columbia University Press, 1982) 116–18; James and James, *Hoffa and the Teamsters*, 344.

19. Freight transportation is measured by the ton-mile, which is one ton of cargo transported one mile. Between 1940 and 1968, the number of intercity ton-miles

moved by truck increased by a factor of six. Trucking's share of total ton-miles increased from 10 percent to 22 percent, while railroads' fell from 61 percent to 41 percent. The gross operating revenue from the transportation of goods in trucking increased from $867 million to $12.4 billion, which represents a fourteenfold increase (without taking inflation into account). The share of total gross operating revenue going to trucking increased from 17 percent to 50 percent, while that of railroads feel fell from 75 percent to 41 percent, indicating that trucking's revenue per ton-mile was increasing more quickly than was railroads'. American Trucking Associations, *American Trucking Trends, 1969* (Washington, D.C.: American Trucking Association, 1969), 8–9. On federal regulation of the trucking industry and its effects on the IBT see Donald Garnel, *The Rise of Teamster Power in the West* (Berkeley and Los Angeles: University of California Press, 1972), 12–32; Perry, *Deregulation and the Decline of Unionized Trucking*, 9–59; William R. Childs, *Trucking and the Public Interest: The Emergence of Federal Regulation, 1914–1940* (Knoxville: University of Tennessee Press, 1985), 119–67.

20. Friedman, *Teamster Rank and File*, 116–20; James and James, *Hoffa and the Teamsters*, 98–100.

21. A. Belden Fields, *Trotskyism and Maoism: Theory and Practice in France and the United States* (Brooklyn, N.Y.: Autonomedia, 1988), 113–4.

22. Accounts of the 1934 Minneapolis teamster strikes are given in Dobbs, *Teamster Rebellion*; Charles Rumford Walker, *American City: A Rank and File History* (New York: Farrar and Rinehart, 1937); Arthur M. Schlesinger, Jr., *The Age of Roosevelt*, vol. 2: *The Coming of the New Deal* (Boston: Houghton Mifflin, 1959), 386–89; and Eric Sevareid, *Not So Wild a Dream* (New York: Atheneum, 1976), 57, which states "in the summer of 1934 the two cities were thrown into uproar by the famous truck drivers' strike, led by the Dunne brothers, Trotskyists, who organized the strike as none had been organized before in American labor history."

23. Dobbs, *Teamster Power*, 145–55; James and James, *Hoffa and the Teamsters*, 96–101.

24. Dobbs, *Teamster Power*, 236.

25. Dobbs, *Teamster Bureaucracy*, 137–63; Ralph James and Estelle James, "The Purge of the Trotskyites from the Teamsters," *Western Political Quarterly* 19 (1966): 5–15.

26. Quoted in James and James, *Hoffa and the Teamsters*, 83.

27. Garnel, *The Rise of Teamster Power in the West*, 67–77, 107; James and James, *Hoffa and the Teamsters*, 98–101; La Botz, *Rank and File Rebellion*, 107; Moldea, *The Hoffa Wars*, 32–34, 36–39.

28. Robert D. Leiter, *The Teamsters Union: A Study of Its Economic Impact* (New York: Bookman Associates, 1957), 39.

29. "The Racket-Ridden Longshoremen: A Functional Analysis of Crime," in *Labor and Trade Unionism: An Interdisciplinary Reader*, ed. Walter Galenson and Seymour Martin Lipsett (New York: John Wiley, 1960), 245–64.

30. Walter Galenson, foreword to *The International Brotherhood of Teamsters: Its Government and Structure*, by Sam Romer (New York: Wiley and Sons, 1962), vii.

31. Pete Camarata, interview with the author, Detroit, Michigan, 10 February 1989. Camarata is a former dock worker and current driver at Earl C. Smith, and former and current cochair of Teamsters for a Democratic Union.

32. See *Proceedings of the Fourth Annual National Forum on Trucking Industrial Relations and Proceedings of the Fifth Annual National Forum on Trucking Industrial Relations*, prepared and distributed by Industrial Relations Department, American Trucking Associations (Washington: D.C.: American Trucking Associations, 1953, 1954); Friedman, *Teamster Rank and File*, 60–69.

33. Peter Camarata, interview with the author, Detroit, Michigan, 10 February 1989.
34. Friedman, *Teamster Rank and File*, 53–64; Brill, *The Teamsters*, 262–71; Pete Camarata, interview with the author, Detroit, Michigan, 10 February 1989. Bob Janadia and Eileen Janadia, interview with the author, Detroit, Michigan, 8 February 1989. Bob Janadia is a grocery driver. During the 1960s and 1970s, he was a member of Detroit IBT Local 337. In 1976 and 1979 he ran for president of the local on the TDU platform. Eileen Janadia was a member of the TDU International Steering Committee.
35. Friedman, *Teamster Rank and File*, 62–64.
36. Grievances were handled by a series of local, area, and regional boards made up of an equal number of employers and union representatives. Deadlock at the highest level could result in either strike or lockout but not arbitration. Given division among the employers, the union could usually win any grievance it wished to pursue, provided it were willing to take the necessary steps. Most grievances were handled by some type of horse trading, but the threat of a strike was always present in any grievance. The unions won the right to veto any firm's proposed "change of operation" that might alter teamster job opportunities. An employer wishing, for example, to transfer work from one terminal to another had to request and receive union permission. *Proceedings of the Fifth Annual National Forum on Trucking Industrial Relations*; James and James, *Hoffa and the Teamsters*, 98.
37. American Trucking Associations, *American Trucking Trends, 1972* (Washington, D.C.: American Trucking Associations, 1972), 6; Perry, *Deregulation and the Decline of Unionized Trucking*, 12–13, 59–61, 87–105; Friedman, *Teamster Rank and File*, 116–23.
38. Steve Zeluck, "The TDU Convention—and the Fight against Givebacks," *Against the Current*, 1st ser., 1, no. 4 (Spring 1982): 36; Perry, *Deregulation and the Decline of Unionized Trucking*, 64–68.
39. Friedman, *Teamster Rank and File*, 116–20.
40. Brill, *The Teamsters*, 269–70; Friedman, *Teamster Rank and File*, 120; Ken Paff, interview with author, 9 February 1989.
41. "Tough Test for Labor," *Business Week*, 15 April 1967, pp. 33–35; Friedman, *Teamster Rank and File*, 120–23.
42. Ken Paff, interview with author, 9 February 1989; Pete Camarata, interview with author, 10 February 1989; Bob Janadia and Eileen Janadia, interview with author, 8 February 1989.
43. "White Line Slavery, *Convoy* no. 1: 2; Brill, *The Teamsters*, 269–70. It should be noted that the first twenty-four issues of *Convoy* did not list a date of publication on the masthead. It seems, however, that the first issue was produced in January 1976 and that the publication appeared on a more or less monthly basis thereafter.
44. "Tough Haul with Hoffa," *Business Week*, 28 January 1967, p. 114.
45. "The Bargaining Hurdles That Are Still Ahead," *Business Week*, 22 April 1967, p. 160.
46. "The U.S. Can't Afford What Labor Wants," *Business Week*, p. 104; "Crisis in the Teamsters, Part 2: The Rise and Decline of the Master Freight Agreement," *Convoy* no. 24: 4–5.
47. For example, wildcatting teamsters in Los Angeles in 1970 demanded sick leave, something some other teamsters already enjoyed.
48. Pete Camarata, interview with author, 10 February 1989; Perry, *Deregulation and the Decline of Unionized Trucking*, 57–58; "Crisis in the Teamsters," *Convoy* no. 24: 4–5.
49. "One-Man Rule Ends for the Teamsters," *Business Week*, 20 May 1967, pp. 152–54; James Neff, *Mobbed Up* (New York: Atlantic Monthly Press, 1989); Allen

Friedman and Ted Schwarz, *Power and Greed* (New York: Franklin Watts, 1989); Velie, *Desperate Bargain*; Brill, *The Teamsters*.

50. "Tough Man Ties Up Teamsters," *Business Week*, 6 May 1967, pp. 158–60.
51. Friedman, *Teamster Rank and File*, 136–68; Brecher, *Strike!*, 274–76; "Trucks Highball toward a Crisis," *Business Week*, 4 April 1970, 22–23.
52. The Teamsters for a Democratic Union Collection, Archives of Labor History and Urban Affairs, Wayne State University, Detroit, Michigan, *ALHUA*, holds a collection of various teamster rank-and-file newspapers.
53. The group's organizational and political genealogy began with the Communist League of America, a group expelled from the Communist Party in 1928 for supporting Trotsky's critique of Stalin. It was led by James Cannon, Max Shachtman, and Martin Abern. Farrell Dobbs joined the group in 1934, the year it merged with A. J. Muste's American Workers Party to form the Workers Party of the United States. In 1936 this group entered the Socialist Party (SP) and in 1938 it was expelled, creating the Socialist Workers Party (SWP), which still exists today. In 1940, Shachtman led a split from the SWP originally called the Workers Party but later called the Independent Socialist League (ISL). Shachtman's politics became more right-wing, and he eventually joined the SP. The left wing of the ISL, whose intellectual leadership came from Hal Draper, went on to create the Independent Socialist Clubs in 1967, based primarily on several university campuses. These became the International Socialists at a founding convention in 1969. A. Belden Fields, *Trotskyism and Maoism: Theory and Practice in France and the United States* (Brooklyn, N.Y.: Autonomedia, 1988), 131–42.
54. Dave Wolfinsohn, "TDU: Problems and Prospects," *Against the Current*, 1st ser., no. 1 (Fall 1980): 37.
55. In 1977 and 1979 the IS suffered splits. Both groups left in part because they believed IS activists in TDU were too reticent to raise explicitly socialist political ideas in the caucuses.
56. The analysis of IS politics and tactics relies primarily on numerous "perspective" documents in the IS Collections of *ALHUA* and TIL. From TIL, these include "Tasks and Perspectives: Convention Document from the Band," pamphlet, IS Not Dated Folder; "Tasks and Perspectives," photocopy, IS Convention 1970 Folder; "For a Workers Combat Organization—The Bolshevization of the IS," photocopy, IS Position Papers, Reports, 1975 Folder; "The Revolutionary Party," signed by John Weber, photocopy, IS Not Dated Folder; "For a Revolutionary Cadre Organization Based in the Working Class," signed by Joel Geier, photocopy, IS Not Dated Folder; "Labor Document," photocopy, IS Not Dated Folder; and "The State of the Unions and IS Work," pamphlet, signed by Kim Moody, IS Convention Material 1974 Folder. From *ALHUA*, see "A Guide to the Teamsters," pamphlet, Box 3-7-85.
57. "A Contract Worth Fighting For," TDC pamphlet, n.d., TDC Folder, Box 1-12-82, TDU Collection, *ALHUA*. Ken Paff, interview with the author, 9 February 1989.
58. "TDC Hits Fitz," *Convoy* no. 1: 1.
59. Information on the events leading up to and including the 1976 strike from Pete Camarata, interview with the author, 10 February 1989; also see "Talking Strike—Planning Sell-Out!" *Convoy Contract Bulletin*, 28 March 1976, p. 1; "Down to the Wire," *Convoy* no. 6: 1; "Talking Strike—Planning Sell-Out!" *Convoy* no. 7: 1; "Detroit Says: Turn It Down!" *Convoy* no. 8: 1; "The Teamsters Face a Wildcat Challenge," *Business Week*, 12 April 1976, p. 34; Moldea, *The Hoffa Wars*, 410; Agis Salpukas, "Gap of $1.40 an Hour Separates Negotiators in Teamster Talks," *New York Times*, 31 March 1976, p. 44.

60. Brill, *The Teamsters*, 314; Michael Ruby, "I Say to Them, Go to Hell," *Newsweek*, 28 June 1976, p. 49; Lee Dembart, "Teamsters Chief Scores Dissidents," *New York Times*, 15 June 1976, p. 17.

61. Pete Camarata, interview with the author, 10 February 1989; "IBT Convention," *Convoy* no. 9: 1.

62. "Report and Minutes of TDC Planning Meeting—June 5" (1976), Minutes— Steering Committee Folder, Box 2-7-80, 2 of 4, *ALHUA*; "A Cause Worth Truckin' For: TDU," pamphlet, Box 1-12-82, *ALHUA*.

63. Teamsters for a Democratic Union, "TDU Constitution" and "Resolutions" in "TDU Convention Bulletin, 1976," TDU 1970s Folder, TDU Collection, *ALHUA*.

64. Teamsters for a Democratic Union, "TDU Constitution," in "TDU Convention Bulletin, 1976," TDU 1970s Folder, TDU Collection, Archives of Labor History and Urban Affairs, Wayne State University, Detroit Michigan.

65. Ken Paff, interview with the author, 9 February 1989.

66. TDU, "TDU Convention Bulletin, 1976," *ALHUA*.

67. This is from one of the few signed articles in *Convoy*: Ken Paff, "Day in Court," *Convoy* no. 9: 2 (emphasis in the original).

68. Pete Camarata, interview with the author, 10 February 1989; "Right On S. Charley!" *Convoy* no. 8: 1; "Phone Time—On or Off?" *Convoy* no. 13: 1; "Solidarity Stops Safeway," *Convoy*, no. 20: 4.

69. In August 1976, even before the founding convention, TDU activists participated in a wildcat picket at McLean Trucking in West Middlesex, Pennsylvania, to re-instate teamster James Deeb, who had been fired after being accused of stealing fifteen stove bolts and six shirt buttons swept off the floor of an empty trailer. Not only did Deeb get his job back after the wildcat, but McLean teamsters won the elimination of forced inferior bids (through which high-seniority teamsters had to accept "worse" jobs than low-seniority teamsters) and "productivity letters" (warnings for low efficiency that almost always led to dismissal). The wildcat also resulted in the firing of "terminal manager-dictator" Charlie Mise and the rehiring of four teamsters fired during the wildcat. "Who's the Thief at McLean," *Convoy* no. 11: 1; and "Solidarity Brings Victory," *Convoy* no. 12: 1.

70. "Three Flint Bylaws Win," *Convoy* no. 19: 1.

71. Pete Camarata, interview with the author, 10 February 1989; Ken Paff, interview with the author, 9 February 1989. Bob Janadia and Eileen Janadia, interview with the author, 8 February 1989.

72. "Bylaws Vote Shakes Machine," *Convoy* no. 18: 1; "Three Flint Bylaws Win," *Convoy* no. 19: 1; "Green Bay Ranks Win," *Convoy* no. 24: 1.

6

Surprising Resilience:
The Steelworkers' Struggle
to Hang On to
the Fordist Bargain

Christoph Scherrer

INTRODUCTION

THE AMERICAN STEEL INDUSTRY has fallen on hard times. From 1981 to 1990, production tonnage decreased from 120 to 99 million tons, employment fell from 391,000 to 164,000, and the industry lost more than $8 billion. Management adopted an aggressive posture toward labor; nonetheless, the United Steel Workers of America (USW) held onto wages, pensions, and other fringe benefits at levels well above the manufacturing average (48 percent in 1990).[1]

The USW's hold on wages is also surprising because its postwar relationship with management, what I will call the "Fordist bargain," was often opposed by the rank and file, particularly in the integrated steel mills. The down side of the steel union's "success" was its failure to move beyond the Fordist bargain and develop more participatory labor relations. The steelworkers failed to draft their own vision of future work organization and they were thwarted in their attempts to establish meaningful forms of participation in management decision-making.

In this chapter I first discuss how the USW precariously hung on to the Fordist bargain. Second, I analyze why the union failed to achieve truly participatory labor relations. To address these problems I draw on three important theoretical perspectives. First, to understand the steel industry's economic dynamics, I draw on the insights of the French regulation theory. To analyze the union's response I follow the intermediary thesis that views unions as mediators between the interests of their members and those of the economic and political system.[2] And to grasp the behavior of the rank and file, I employ Richard Hyman's concept of "workplace legitimacy."[3]

Beginning with a description of the steel industry's Fordist phase, I examine chronologically the various responses of management, union, and workers to the unfolding crisis. I will conclude by interpreting these events in the light of the interpretive theories.

THE FORDIST PHASE IN THE U.S. STEEL INDUSTRY

Fordism[4] has been described as a regime of intensive accumulation with growing mass consumption under monopolistic regulation.[5] Mass production took place on the basis of the Taylorist,[6] Fordist production paradigm. The social habits and institutions (forms of regulation) that connect mass production and mass consumption were social security provisions, contractualization of labor, real wage increases tied to productivity gains, oligopolization or direct state regulation of major markets, credit money as legal tender, and Keynesian economic policies.[7] The mode of regulation of the steel industry mirrored the major characteristics of Fordism: seniority-oriented industrial relations, oligopolization of the markets, a high degree of vertical integration, antitrust regulation of monopoly power, financing through depreciation allowances, and selling primarily on the domestic market.[8]

With the formation of the United States Steel Corporation (USS) at the turn of the century, the structure of the U.S. steel industry began to look much like a textbook definition of an oligopoly. A few, highly vertically integrated firms organized most of the steel production and dominated the market. The practice of "oligopolistic cooperation" effectively suppressed the potential influence of demand fluctuations on the price structure. Prices moved along with long-run normal costs.[9] While this practice of "administered pricing"[10] subjected the steel industry to innumerable antitrust investigations by Congress, the courts, and economists, it proved to be essential for the growth dynamic of the mass production economy.

The relationship between capital concentration and unionization of the industry is intriguing. At the turn of the century, concentration led to the demise of craft control. In the famous Homestead Strike of 1893, Andrew Carnegie used his huge resources and political power to crush the union of skilled steel workers. In the aftermath of the Homestead Massacre, the industry mechanized quickly, further undermining the position of skilled labor. By 1909 the union had been driven out of the industry. The steel bosses' hard line in the unsuccessful steel strike of 1919 again manifested their power.[11] When in 1937 the steelworkers were finally able to challenge the corporations, the union won bargaining rights for almost half of the industry's workforce by gaining a contract with USS. Although the other companies were able to hold out against the union by violent means, once a court ordered the reinstatement of seven thousand union members at Republic in 1940, the USW was able to organize the rest of the industry quickly.[12]

The immediate postwar invention of linking wages and productivity through industrywide collective bargaining created a new level of mass consumption. In addition, the establishment of a social safety net allowed for increased individual consumption of durable goods.[13] The two commodities that typified the new consumption norm, the suburban home and the automobile, in turn had a profound influence on the steel industry. The greatly increased demand for sheet steel used in automobiles and home appliances filled the vacuum left by declining military orders.[14]

THE FORDIST BARGAIN

In the years between 1946 and 1952 through a series of lengthy strikes, lockouts, and President Truman's seizure of the mills, the basic contours of the Fordist bargain took shape. The companies recognized the unions as the legitimate and permanent representatives of their production workforces, and the union acknowledged management's right to manage. Collective bargaining was centralized (the companies formed a multiemployer bargaining unit) and followed a pattern whereby wages rose in accordance with productivity increases as well as inflation, and health care, pensions, and supplemental unemployment benefits were gradually extended. In a broader context, the USW subordinated the political struggle for social legislation for the benefit of all workers to the immediate interests of its members.

Although management was free to make basic entrepreneurial and managerial decisions, the discretionary power of the corporate hierarchy over the allocation of labor and the conditions of employment was severely restricted by the three pillars of the so-called job control unionism,[15] that is, legalistic conflict resolution, detailed job classifications, and a comprehensive seniority system.

Local collective bargaining agreements contained detailed lists of job classifications, which specified the individual tasks in production. In the tool and maintenance departments this codification of the division of labor among workers was accomplished by demarcations among the various skilled trades. The allocation of workers to these specified jobs was governed by the seniority system. It regulated the lines of succession in regard to hiring, firing, and internal promotions according to the length of service.[16] For the selection of workers, merit criteria, such as performance, qualification, and conduct, were ruled out. These rules were enforced by grievance persons who represented their union members in the grievance procedure. The allocative powers of management were further restricted by rules on production standards. Section 2-B of the collective bargaining agreement guaranteed that the traditional way of working would remain unchanged as long as the production technology stayed the same.[17]

Through these collective bargaining rules management lost important means for rewarding and punishing workers. Greater work efforts could be elicited neither through individual bonuses nor through promotion (except to a position outside the bargaining unit, that is, to supervisory positions). Thus management had to develop other forms of control. First among these was the incorporation of control into the labor process through machine pacing. Second, more time-study personnel were employed and the industrial engineering departments gained influence. Third, the number of supervisors was drastically increased. Fourth, group bonus systems tied workers' performance to incentive payments.[18]

How was it possible that U.S. management, known for its tough image, accepted such encroachments on its authority? Before management severely criticized the Fordist system of industrial relations in the 1980s, a number of authors stressed its economic functionality and its contributions to the maintenance of management's authority on the shop floor. The seniority system, for example, has been interpreted as a method for developing the skill levels of the workforce and for holding on to the most skilled workers during business downturns.[19] Or the rules were taken as instruments of capitalist domination, for they either led to a hierarchy among workers[20] or were an integral part of bureaucratic rule.[21] From a German perspective, however, these job controls were seen as a means by American unions to recapture some of their control lost through the Taylorist deskilling processes.[22] Building on both arguments, I want to put forward the thesis that management's acquiescence to job controls should be primarily interpreted as an attempt to legitimate and to strengthen management's rule on the shop floor, which had been partly lost during the struggles for union recognition. The diverse rules of job controls should not be exclusively viewed as means to fulfill certain functional requirements, but primarily as objects and instruments of a struggle between management and labor. If the balance of forces or the conditions for accumulation change, these rules can lose their original function. Thus the contractual limitations on management's power constituted a compromise, which took account of management's interest but was not necessarily considered by management optimal. The concrete form of the compromise was subjected to constant contention.[23]

Specifically, management assented to job control because it was compatible with its accumulation strategies and because alternatives to job control were less attractive. The rigid, codified division of work did not pose any major problems as long as the predominant production paradigm rested on an ever finer division of tasks and long production runs. Further, job controls reinforced interfirm wage equality. The rigid classification of jobs and the elimination of merit in the determination of individual paychecks allowed for the adoption of a uniform wage scale throughout the industry.[24] The seniority system provided for the smooth adjustment of employment to output, reducing the pressure to cut prices during periods of weak demand. Job controls were, therefore, functional for the industry's oligopolistic pricing strategies.

These protective rights of labor were, furthermore, preferable to the alternative of constant struggles on the shop floor. During unionization, workers in many companies had attained a high level of control over production standards and other issues of work organization and thus considered protest, wildcat action, and even sabotage as legitimate forms of resistance against any speedups.[25] Little steel's refusal to prepare itself for a permanent presence of the union by centralizing and professionalizing its personnel handling led to frequent walkouts and lower labor productivity. Eventually these companies had to imitate the more professional and consistent labor relations policies of big steel.[26]

Management could have also tried to pacify the shop floor by cooperating with the unions through Labor-Management Committees. As early as 1938 some SWOC leaders had offered to help steel mills in financial troubles through joint efforts to make plants more productive. These offers were tied to a number of stipulations: Management had to agree to the union shop, no worker could lose his job as a result of improvements in practices and technology, and the union had to be involved with management at every step. These conditions were set forth in a pamphlet called "Production Problems," which explained how union members could cooperate with management in improving the work process.[27] In 1940 Phil Murray emphasized the need for productivity increases in a speech: "As management and labor through strong labor unions become more nearly equal in bargaining power, they can either wage war to gain the spoils of production restriction and scarcity prices, or they can together devise improved production practices that increase social income."[28]

Soon after the end of World War II, however, efforts for shop floor cooperation were dropped. The USW's most forceful proponents of cooperation left for jobs in business and academe. Phil Murray had allegedly ceased to support them because he saw no point in pursuing a program management opposed.[29] Against the background of constant disruptions of authority on the shop floor, management considered these cooperation plans to be just another avenue for workers to raise their demands.[30] Furthermore, the rank and file showed little interest. The attitude among workers was "them against us." Militantly protecting their hard-won gains on the shop floor, workers looked with suspicion at joint productivity programs.[31]

In sum, in the immediate postwar years job controls were the smallest common denominator that workers, union, and management could agree on. In addition, the legalistic approach in defining the rights of workers was furthered by a series of arbitration rulings.[32]

The First Phase of Adjustment

Embedded in this Fordist mode of regulation, the steel industry participated in the postwar prosperity: It grew as quickly as the rest of the economy. The year 1966 marked a turning point in the growth path. The growth in steel output lagged along with the average growth of manufacturing.[33] At the same time the market share of foreign producers took a major leap forward: In steel this share grew from 7.3 percent in 1964 to 16.7 percent in 1968 (see figure 6.1).

The success of imports was a threat for a growth model that depended on corporate control of prices. In an initial response, the steel mills tried to renege on the Fordist wage compromise that had been put in place only ten years earlier. Most important, they sought to abolish rank-and-file control over

FIGURE 6.1   Import Shares, Steel Industry, 1955–1990

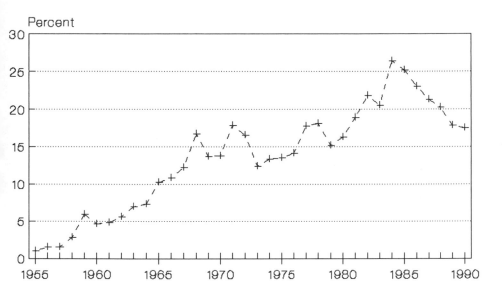

Source: *Annual Statistical Report* (Washington, DC: American Iron and Steel Institute, 1991).

local work practices (especially Section 2-B) as the key to increasing productivity. The resulting 116-day strike of 1959 ended in a standoff. The workers were too strong; their resistance also seemed legitimate in the light of workers' gains in other key industries. In addition, true to Keynesian principles, the Republican Eisenhower administration pressured (even if only reluctantly) management to end its offensive.[34]

After this first option was closed, the steel executives pursued a strategy of modernization. They spent huge sums on basic oxygen furnaces, but the return was disappointing. The rate of productivity growth actually decreased (see figures 6.2, 6:3). One of the causes of the failure of the modernization strategy was the fact that steel mill technology in general allowed only for small productivity increases and these came at the expense of a rise in capital intensity. A second cause was the high costs of construction[35] and a pessimistic assessment of future growth possibilities, which led the steel executives to prefer the modernization of existing facilities over the construction of new, efficient steel mills. While saving considerable money, the industry achieved only suboptimal efficiency gains. The piecemeal brownfield modernization that occurred led frequently to bottlenecks that made it impossible to reap the full benefits of the new installations.[36] The third reason for the failure of modernization was the fact that steel management's efforts were met by the collective as well as individual resistance of workers.

FIGURE 6.2   Production Volume and Level of Capital Investments, Index (1960–1989)

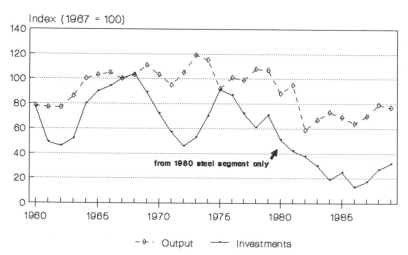

Index (1967 = 100)

- ◇ - Output   —•— Investments

Sources: Annual Statistical Report (Washington, D.C.: American Iron and Steel Institute, various years); U.S. Department of Commerce, Bureau of the Census, *Capital Goods Price Index: Statistical Abstract of the United States*, 110th ed. (Washington, D.C.: U.S. Government Printing Office, 1990.)

The standoff after the strike of 1959 had led to wage increases below those of the auto industry. These lower wage increases (see figure 6.4) and the willingness of USW president David McDonald to negotiate revisions of rules on work assignment and subcontracting stirred rank-and-file unrest in the early 1960s. In 1965, however, the protest was temporarily absorbed by a "palace revolt" by the secretary treasurer I. W. Abel, who promised in his successful bid for the union's presidency to take a more assertive stand against the companies and to "return the union to its members." Yet collective bargaining remained centralized, and the 1968 contract settlement fell well short of what was gained in other core industries. In fact, the 1968 agreement was followed by some of the first wildcat strikes of the 1960s. The extent of rank-and-file opposition in basic steel to Abel and his policies was revealed in the 1969 union elections. Emil Narick, a relatively unknown assistant general counsel of the union, received 40 percent of the votes cast and over 60 percent in the large basic steel locals with membership of five hundred or more.[37] Thereafter, wildcat strikes and individual forms of resisting factory discipline became common.[38]

However, the explanation for the "blue-collar blues" of the late 1960s in the literature on Fordism—that is, the exhaustion of the Taylorist-Fordist production paradigm[39]—is insufficient. On the one hand, the resistance was fueled by various social movements and the experience of the Vietnam War, which led to a general questioning of authority.[40] On the other hand, management's attempts to reassert its authority were severely restrained by the rules governing

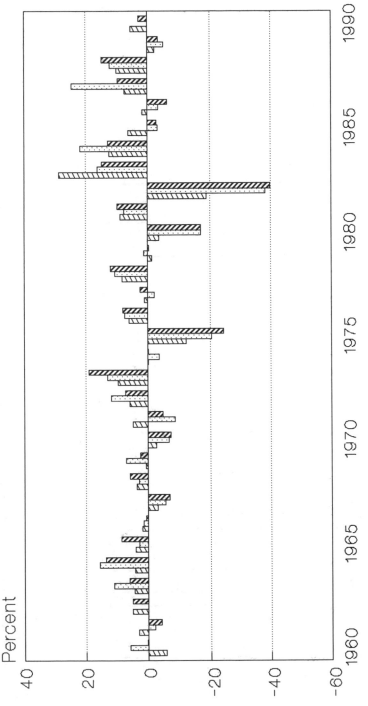

FIGURE 6.3 Productivity, Capacity Utilization, and Production Volume, yearly changes (1960–1990)

Sources: Unpublished Bureau of Labor Statistics data for 22 May 1985, 15 April 1991; American Iron and Steel Institute; U.S. Council on Wage and Price Stability, *Report to the President on Prices and Costs in the U.S. Steel Industry, 1977* (Washington, D.C.: U.S. Government Printing Office, 1977).

FIGURE 6.4　Real Wage, Fringe Benefits per Hour, Begin of Contract, Days on Strike (1950–1990)

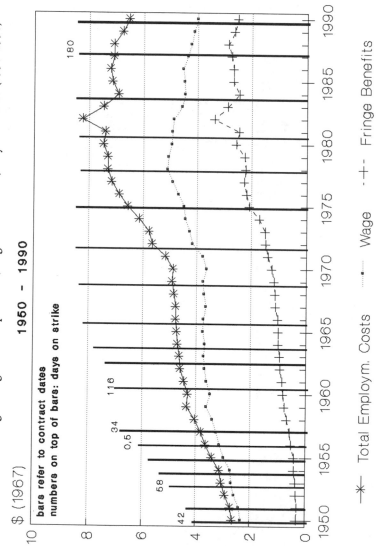

Note: The numbers on top of the bars refer to days on strike.
Sources: Authors calculation, based on American Iron and Steel Institute *Annual Statistical. Reports* and Bureau of Labor Statistics data.

shop floor relations. The detailed job classifications and the comprehensive seniority system removed from the management's hands both individual bonuses and nonsupervisory promotions, important tools for rewarding and punishing workers and thus for eliciting greater work efforts. Thus management chose to increase the number of supervisors, which often aggravated the shop floor confrontations and led to further job alienation.[41]

THE COMPLETION OF THE FORDIST WAGE COMPROMISE

Caught between rising imports and production cost increases, the steel industry's profitability declined precipitously throughout the 1960s. In response, the industry suspended its offensive approach to foreign competition. The new strategy aimed at preserving oligopolistic market control through trade protection. In 1968 the first steel import quotas (Voluntary Restraint Agreement [VRA]) were implemented. At the same time the volume of investments was reduced to a level that was no longer sufficient to reproduce the capital stock of the steel industry.[42] These steps, plus the worldwide boom in steel from 1972 to 1974, restored the profitability of the steel corporations. In this situation, management offered the USW a productivity pact. In exchange for the sacrifice of the right to strike and the willingness to participate in efficiency drives, the industry granted attractive wage increases of 3 percent per annum.[43] Thus the explicit recognition of the Fordist wage compromise took place in the steel industry when the decline of the industry was already written on the wall.

These defensive steps postponed only briefly the further decline of the industry. The sudden end of the steel boom destroyed the chances for achieving productivity increases by means of a high degree of capacity utilization and the self-financed modernization of the facilities. Nevertheless, management was committed to pay the 3 percent real wage increases. Even at the next contract negotiations in 1977, despite changed economic conditions, management was not able to insist on wage moderation. It felt it had to maintain this level of wage increases in order to maintain the cooperative leadership of the USW in power.[44] The latter was strongly challenged by a radical insurgent, District 31 director Edward Sadlowski, who criticized the undemocratic means by which the productivity pact had been forced on the membership.

Sadlowski received 43.1 percent of the 578,142 votes cast in the election for the union's presidency. He carried the locals of the integrated steel mills by a slim margin of 51.9 percent, which was not enough to offset the strong showing of Lloyd McBride, the candidate of the established union leadership, in the South, in Canada, and among members not working for steel-related businesses. While these results show that dissatisfaction with the accommodationist leadership of the union ran high among steel workers, the dissident campaign, called Fight Back, failed at broadening their appeal beyond big steel. The right-to-strike issue did not resonate with those union members who were less certain of being able to use the strike weapon successfully. The opposition to the dues increases proposed by the incumbent leadership, an issue that had been successfully used by past dissident movements, also failed to attract voters concerned with the threat of unemployment and stepped-up productivity pressures. The dissidents campaigned on a platform that reflected past conditions of an oligopolistic industry battling a militant work force. They did not respond to the first signs of the profound changes in the industrial environment of the coming years. Furthermore, Fight Back neglected to nominate candidates for district director in most districts. Given that Sadlowski did win the majority of votes in ten districts, it is highly likely that Fight Back could have gotten its candidates elected in five to ten districts instead of the two it did win. This organizational failure and the lack of foresight contributed heavily to the demise of the dissident camp on the national level thereafter.[45]

TRIPARTITE CRISIS MANAGEMENT

The worldwide steel recession in the wake of the first energy crisis and the decline in international competitiveness came to a conjunction in the fall of 1977. Within a few months fourteen steel works were closed and twenty thousand jobs were lost. USS furthermore threatened to lay off an additional 8,500 workers unless steps were taken "to stem the flow of foreign steel." These drastic cuts soon had an effect: About sixty steel towns formed the Steel Communities Coalition and by October of 1977 the newly established Congressional Steel Caucus counted more than 120 members. They called for the enforcement of "fair trade."[46]

The Carter administration responded to the mounting pressure by offering a mildly protectionist Trigger Price Mechanism (TPM) and a loan guarantee program and by establishing a Steel Tripartite Advisory Committee (STAC). The STAC was composed of representatives of the administration, the USW, and the major steel companies. As such it was a form of crisis management typical to Fordism.[47] Its objective was "to serve as a mechanism to ensure a continuing cooperative approach to the problems and prospects of the American steel industry."[48] While the TPM and the loan program were immediately implemented,[49] the STAC did not begin working before 1979.[50] In fact, its final report was released as late as September 1980, after the suspension of the TPM elicited new lobbying activism by the industry.[51] Accordingly, the report's principal recommendation was the reinstatement of the TPM.

Many of the proposals that went beyond the implementation of import restrictions met with resistance on the part of management. The leaders of the industry were especially opposed to any kind of state subsidies. Since, unlike the parallel case of Chrysler (which did come to a government-led bailout), the steel companies did not face a pressing liquidity crisis, cooperation with the USW would have meant continued consideration of the workers' interests, that is, maintenance of high employment levels at accustomed pay levels. Furthermore, any tripartite crisis management, as the case of Chrysler suggests (it was forced to sell off most of its nonauto related business), would have called into question the industry's diversification strategy. From management's point of view, then, tripartism would have perpetuated precisely what was perceived to be the main management problem: accommodation of labor's interests. In contrast, political action "against" the state held out the promise of improving the industry's condition of accumulation at the expense of the state as well as the liberty to pursue strategies to weaken labor—or if these failed, the promise of moving out of steel production altogether.

Ironically, the strongest supporter of this protectionist strategy was the USW. Not strong enough to impose its industrial policy concepts on the representatives of government and industry, the USW settled for protectionism as the easiest way to protect the jobs of its members.[52] In fact, at the time of the tripartite consultations, the USW leadership discouraged local initiatives to save plants with the help of government loans, wage concessions, and cooperative labor relations. It considered downsizing of the industry as inevitable. Any attempt to save obsolete capacity would undermine the uniform wage standard in the industry.[53]

Departure from the Fordist Mode of Regulation

The changed balance of forces in the political realm furthered the project of pushing back the Keynesian state. The election of Ronald Reagan expressed the new coalition between capital groups outside the Fordist regulation (especially in the South) and the capital groups in core industries. The tax revolt in California (which resulted in Proposition 13) had manifested the political strength of the "non-Fordist" capital factions.[54] This made them attractive to the capital-intensive corporations, which were increasingly pressured by international competition. International political events, such as the overthrow of the Shah of Iran and of Anastasio Somoza of Nicaragua, as well as the Soviet invasion in Afghanistan, brought multinationally oriented groups into this coalition.[55] This realignment of capital factions managed to gain popular support for a program to remove the state's responsibility for results of market processes. They thereby resorted to nationalist demagoguery and the invocation of the ideological tradition of individualism. At the same time they promised to cut taxes without eliminating major social security programs. The lack of institutional incorporation of labor and other nonbusiness groups in the political system, as well as their limited political coherence and ability to mobilize mass support, facilitated the attack on the postwar social accord.[56] Nonbusiness representatives were easily swept out of political power, allowing the Reagan administration to refute calls for full employment policies or structural adjustment aid during the monetarist-induced recession of 1981–1983.

This nonaction by the Reagan administration was sufficient to tip the balance of forces in favor of capital without resorting to legislative initiatives for

TABLE 6.1   Total Wage and Benefits Reductions per Hour, 1985–1987

COMPANY	DATE	NEW	EXPIRING	REDUCTION
Wheeling-Pittsburgh	8/85	$18.00	$21.40	$3.40
LTV	4/86	$18.09*	25.19	3.60
National	4/86	$22.21	23.72	1.51
Bethlehem	7/86	$22.50	24.84	2.34
Inland	8/86	$21.60	22.00	0.40
USX	2/87	$22.50	24.84	2.34

* Includes a $3.50 per hour reduction as a result of the Pension Benefit guarantee Corporation's assumption of pension liabilities
Sources: United States, International Trade Commission, 1987: *Annual Survey Concerning Competitive Conditions in the Steel Industry and Industry Efforts to Adjust and Modernize*, USITC Publication 2019, September, Washington DC, p. 22; *Business Week*, December 4, 1986, p. 26.

curbing union power. Without the power to regulate the capitalist mechanisms of competition politically, the unions fell victim to the logic of markets. Encouraged by the examples of other industries, the management of big steel used the severe recession of 1981–1983 to aggressively pursue a new, confrontational labor relations policy. It thereby was able to cash in on its Experimental Negotiating Agreement (ENA) investment because of the lack of strike experience and of a radical union leadership, as well as the previously prevailing spirit of social partnership.

CANCELLATION OF THE FORDIST WAGE BARGAIN

Aided by the examples of other industries (especially the auto industry) and by a sympathetic government, in 1983 the management of big steel succeeded in extracting considerable wage concessions ($1.4 billion) from a workforce whose jobs were disappearing under the combined impact of a severe recession and increasing import penetration.[57] After the disbandment of the industry's multiemployer bargaining unit in 1985, steel companies were able to extract further wage and benefit concessions from the USW on a one-by-one strategy (see table 6.1).[58]

The USW's leadership could not imagine any alternative to wage concessions. It feared that a refusal to acknowledge the dire financial circumstances of the steel mills would only further the political isolation of the union. The media and the government were not sympathetic to a workforce whose wages were more than 60 percent above the manufacturing average (my own calculation for 1981). Furthermore, the leadership believed that without concessions, the competitiveness of the companies would be at risk and would cause even larger job losses.[59] Ben Fischer, the former USW's arbitration expert, went even so far as to lose sight of traditional principles of union solidarity:

Differences between labor and management in a firm pale when compared with differences between companies, industries, and national economies . . . the people who make steel . . . have little in common with foreign workers. Even conflict between plants is unavoidable. . . . Workers can be comrades and also competitors. The nostalgia associated with historical labor culture cannot overcome harsh reality.[60]

Thus when the companies approached the USW for an early reopening of the contract, the leadership signaled its willingness to accept major concessions. However, the first concessionary contract proposal was voted down by the local presidents 241 to 131. One reason for the rejection of the proposal was that it would have meant that the locals outside of the integrated steel mills (for example, steel service centers) would be severed from the basic steel contract. Separate negotiations would have meant for these locals even higher wage concessions, since market conditions for steel centers were even more competitive. Furthermore, the dissident *Committee To Save Our Union* pointed out that management was not willing to guarantee job security in exchange for wage concessions. Its demand for "no concessions" found many supporters, especially among workers at USS, who were angered by the company's acquisition of Marathon Oil for $6 billion while it was demanding concessions from its workers.

The USW returned to the bargaining table with a slightly improved proposal that left the Cost of Living Allowance (COLA) principle intact, though modified, and contained an early retirement incentive. This time the concessions were ratified by the USW's bargaining conference 169 to 63. The local presidents outside basic steel had been excluded from voting on this pact. The main reason for ratification was probably that the local presidents had little hope for a revival of steel demand and thus were afraid to go on strike for a better settlement. It also reflected the disorganized state of the union's dissidents. In 1984, in the next election for the union's presidency, the dissidents' candidate, Ron Weisen, failed to even get on the ballot because he could not obtain the required 111 nominations by local unions.

In the bargaining round of 1986, which led to further concessions, no rank-and-file movement challenged the leadership, although members had gotten the right to vote on a contract for the first time in the history of the USW. The new president, Lynn Williams, undertook to link concessions with demands for better quid pro quo than in 1983. In addition, Williams took a tough position against USX (the name USS adopted after it had completed its profound diversification program), since this company was not willing to concede profit sharing in return for wage concessions. During the ensuing strike (or lockout), the workers demonstrated their militancy. The strike front remained solid throughout the following six months. USX had to settle along the lines of the contract with Bethlehem Steel. Massive job cuts, however, were not prevented.[61]

As early as 1985, the union under Williams's leadership demonstrated that it would act swiftly against major breaches of its bargaining principles and that it could count on the members' determination to fight against management even against great odds. When the bankruptcy judge allowed the Wheeling-Pittsburgh management to unilaterally suspend the contract (the company had filed for Chapter 11 protection), the workforce responded with a ninety-eight day-long strike. Although the strike did not prevent concessions, it limited their scope and even led to a change of management.[62] Again at LTV Corporation, another large steel producer in bankruptcy proceedings, workers spontaneously went on strike when the company wanted to terminate health and life-insurance benefits for its retirees. The leadership approved of the action, and after six days the benefits were reinstated.[63]

All in all, the membership remained rather passive in its protest against concessions and seldom engaged in militant forms of resistance on its own. It relied in most cases on the explicit support of the leadership. Resistance against plant closures remained similarly low keyed. Although the industry lost 290,000 jobs between 1978 and 1987 and many mills were permanently closed, a political struggle comparable to those in French Lothringen or in the German Rhein-Ruhr valleys did not ensue. The level of protest against the closure of the Youngstown mills in the late 1970s was later nowhere surpassed, although such local initiatives as the Mon Valley Unemployed Committee and the Tri-State Conference on Steel had done their best to wage campaigns to save specific mills and to support the unemployed. However, they failed in gaining broad, active support.[64]

WORK RULE CONCESSIONS

The efforts to overcome the restrictive job control focus of the traditional work organization were led by top management and the union leadership. Neither middle management nor rank and file showed any significant interest. If union members participated in any experiments, it was more for saving their jobs than for achieving workplace democracy. The union leadership's willingness to experiment with new forms of work organization rested in two traditions. The first was the long tradition of exchanging shop floor rights for material gains. The last efforts in this direction were the Joint Advisory Committees on Productivity of the 1971 contract. Second were the ideas of "industrial democracy" of the 1940s and the debates in the aftermath of the "blue-collar blues" of overcoming the degrading aspects of Taylorism. Since the 1970s both traditions, the accommodative and the emancipative, existed, but the former was clearly dominant. The main impetus was to help the companies regain their competitiveness.

A first step was taken in the 1980 contract. It established "labor-management participation teams" (LMPT) for the purpose of improving productivity in the steel mills. They were supposed to function like quality circles, resolving production problems without following traditional lines of authority and without changing contract language or its interpretation. Despite some initial enthusiasm on the part of the participating steelworkers, LMPTs did not become as widespread as in the auto industry.

In 1985 a more comprehensive attempt to restructure industrial relations took place at medium-sized Wheeling-Pittsburgh. After the already mentioned strike, the USW won a Cooperative Partnership Agreement, which provided the union with a role in what have traditionally been exclusively management decisions. The union gained two seats on the board of directors and equal representation on a Joint Strategic Decision Board, where investments, the introduction of new technologies and other strategic questions were supposed to be discussed. Similar boards have been established at the plant and department levels. They were not planned to substitute for the grievance procedure. They successfully tackled the problems of excessive overtime and contracting-out. However, management was not yet ready to discuss strategic decisions in the joint committees. Furthermore, the introduction of new forms of work organization were also met with resistance.[65]

In 1986 a similar contract was agreed upon at National Steel, but for a seat on the company's board. The position of a crew coordinator was established, which replaced first-line supervisors. The position was filled by union members. The contract introduced a gain sharing plan through which the workers could share in productivity gains and in the savings resulting from cuts in staffing levels.[66] The other, financially stronger companies did not copy the joint boards. They agreed only to the innovations of a crew coordinator and of productivity sharing.[67]

The Japanese team concept was first implemented at the Electro-Galvanizing Company, which is jointly owned by LTV and Sumitomo. Job classifications, seniority rights for in-plant transfers, and the grievance procedure were eliminated. The contract tied wages to a significant degree to profits, promised long-term job security, and introduced a "pay-for-knowledge" compensation system enabling workers to increase their pay by learning new skills. In return, the company recognized the USW as bargaining agent for the new employees even before they were hired.[68] In similar plants owned by other steel companies, which were built to satisfy the auto industry's demand for noncorrosive steels, the union was kept out.[69]

USX, the largest steel producer, stayed aloof from these cooperative endeavors but for a few, quickly abandoned efforts. Since the crisis of 1981–1983, management had decided that the best strategy to cut its workforce and increase productivity was the unilateral abrogation of workers' traditional rights. It moved aggressively in hiring outside contractors without consulting the union. By 1985 USX had contracted out the equivalent of two person-hours per ton (out of 7.5). It thereby created chaos and destroyed what little morale and incentive were left in the plant. The grievance backlog expanded rapidly.[70] While USX lost arbitration cases, it demonstrated to its employees that the union no longer had monopoly control of either labor supply or work practices.[71]

In addition to breaches of contract, USX tried to change local work practices through negotiation, that is, by using the technique of whipsawing. The crisis provided steel management with the liberty to decide which of their various mills would be closed. They thus had at their disposal a substitute for spatial capital mobility. The locals were confronted with the choice of either giving up their traditional work practices or losing jobs to other locals that were willing to make those changes.

For example, at Fairfield, Alabama, USX promised to reopen closed steelmaking units and got in return a contract that eliminated all past practices regarding manning, crew sizes, and job assignments and gave the management the unilateral right to establish new practices. It also authorized the company to contract out some services previously performed by USW members. It became U.S. Steel's model for negotiating at other plants.[72] However, the promise of new jobs was apparently not the only bargaining tactic. In 1990 USX was found guilty in court of having bribed the USW negotiators at Fairfield by enriching their pensions.[73] The practice of whipsawing was also perfected by other steel companies. Bethlehem Steel notified the union that it would modernize its structural-products division only if the union agreed to concessions.[74] This whipsawing of individual locals was more or less tolerated by the unions' top leadership, which did not lay down any guidelines for plant-level talks and which legitimated this practice by granting special concessions to those steel companies who could prove their financial crisis.[75]

After the long strike of 1986–1987, labor relations lost some of their previous antagonism, but management remained opposed to any joint decision-making committees. Said a top USX insider: "We want worker cooperation, but we don't want to broker it through the union."[76] USX did show some interest in team work concept but did not pressure the issue because it was apparently certain of having exploited the existing productivity potential to the fullest extent even without introducing the team concept.[77] The continued efforts of management to subcontract more work than allowed for in the contract kept labor relations tense.[78]

While in the 1990–1991 round of collective bargaining the USW was able to translate the steel boom of the late 1980s into contracts that regained some of the benefits and provisions lost in the previous rounds,[79] the steel recession of the early 1990s forced it again to offer concessions. For the bargaining round of 1993–1994 the USW expressed a willingness for "restructuring the workforce" and "reorganizing the way work is done." In exchange for this flexibility, it said it would allow "no concessions" in wages or benefits.[80]

SUCCESS AND COSTS OF PRIVATE MANAGEMENT

Management saw the strategy of opposing an "industrial policy" and fighting it out alone with the union as a success. The historic wage trend had been reversed, and productivity rose by a phenomenal 7.3 percent annually from

1981 to 1988, while spending on capital investments was cut in half (see figures 6.2 and 6.3).[81] A study by Thomas Dubois of the steel industry in northwest Indiana, which is today the center of U.S. steel production, revealed that new production facilities contributed only 6.5 percent to the productivity gains. Of much greater importance were the change in product mix (17.7 percent), increases in outsourcing (20.8 percent), closure of old facilities (23.3 percent) and the speedup of work (31.6 percent). Through these practices U.S. integrated steel mills caught up in 1987 with the productivity levels of the Japanese mills, despite their much older capital stock.[82] Thanks to the devaluation of the U.S. dollar, even their production costs were lower than for the Japanese.[83]

However, the limits of a strategy based on the exhaustion of the capital stock and combative personnel policies surfaced by the end of the decade. First, in the long run the exhaustion of the capital stock can be sustained only if the cash flow from the neglected facilities is reinvested in some core production sites. Yet this cash flow was partly used up by the substantial liabilities for early retirement costs that accrued because of plant closures. Therefore, a more extensive use of this strategy requires the socialization of pensions as a precondition. As early as 1987 the Pension Benefit Guaranty Corporation the public insurance company for private pension plans, had to take charge of $3 billion in steel-related pension liabilities.[84] The industry lobbied for public funding of pension liabilities in the case of plant closures, but as late as early 1995 had met with no success.[85] Unfunded pension liabilities also seemed to deter foreign investors. The two largest mill operations (the USS subsidiary of USX and LTV) were put up for sale, but without success to date because of the pension issue.[86]

Second, a rapid decline in the number of union members puts at risk the pensions of retired workers. The number of union workers has already shrunk out of proportion. At the LTV steel unit one worker supports three retirees. When LTV failed to meet its pension obligations, the federal Pension Benefit Guaranty Corporation had to take over temporarily, with dire consequences for some beneficiaries.[87]

Third, low levels of investments caused frequent equipment outages even at the industry's most efficient mills. These shutdowns for repairs prevented the integrated producers from taking full advantage of the improved demand for steel.[88] To prevent these equipment breakdowns, the steel corporations must increase their capital investments considerably.

Fourth, this strategy precludes any technology-driven competitive advantage. For many years now, every major investment project of steel mills in the United States has been supervised or carried out by foreign engineers. Most new steel mill facilities (especially the electro-galvanizing lines for auto body steel) have been established as joint ventures with foreign companies. Japanese steel mills have recently taken direct equity stakes in a number of major integrated steel corporations.[89]

Fifth, broken promises and gross offenses against traditional rights again and again incited rank-and-file protest. The bitterness created by USX's disregard for the contract became a powerful motivating force in the long strike against the company. In cases in which the management offensive threatened to endanger the survival of their organizations, the union leadership supported these protests. One instance was the strike of the USW against Wheeling-Pittsburgh, which prevented the bankruptcy court from unilaterally reneging on the contract. In another, the six-month-long strike against USX allowed the USW to limit the extent of wage cuts and force USX to reduce the volume of outsourcing to nonunion suppliers and maintenance crews.

Finally, it became evident that the success of the exhaustion strategy depended heavily on keeping foreign competition out. The sustained productivity gains were mainly due to high capacity utilization, resulting from retrenchment (about 40 million tons between 1977 and 1987)[90] and from the steel quotas that became effective after 1984. Their allegedly regained international competitiveness failed its true test when the steel quotas were terminated in early 1992. The industry resorted again to antidumping complaints to stem the flow of foreign steel.[91]

MINI-MILL CHALLENGE

Protectionism, however, will be only of limited help to the big steel corporations. A new challenge arose domestically. Mini-mills have increased their share of U.S. steel production from 3 percent in 1960 to a high of 21 percent in 1985. Their production concept of rigid specialization is characterized by a specialization in a limited range of low-value products, low skill requirements, and a flexible allocation of labor power within a Taylorist work organization. More than half of the mini-mills are nonunion, and the labor contracts at the rest of them are inferior to basic steel contracts.[92]

In those cases in which the USW has been favored by a strong minority or even a majority of workers, the mini-mill management has taken an aggressive anti-union stand. They threatened to relocate mills and frequently disregarded the laws governing the right to organize.[93] However, since the USW did not take the threat of the mini-mills seriously for a long time,[94] preventive measures proved sufficient most of the time. Some mini-mill chief executive officers, especially Kenneth Iverson of the extremely successful Nucor Corporation[95] and Gordon Forward from Chapparal Steel, were active proponents of "modern" personnel policies. Their "wide-open" management was supposed to create a familylike atmosphere for the production workers and management alike.

At least equally important for the avoidance of union organizing were the crisis dynamics at big steel. While in the 1960s small steel mills (usually also integrated) were inefficient operations and backward in their labor relations compared to the enlightened personnel policies of big steel (especially at USS), the relation between small and big steel producers reversed with the introduction of the electric furnace technology during the 1970s. Big steel lost market shares and closed complete complexes, and the USW was put on the defensive. In contrast, the mini-mills were able to point to increasing market shares, modern production equipment, increasing employment, and even rising wages. It is quite likely that this publicly debated contrast shaped the attitude of the workers in the mini-mills. Not by accident did a mini-mill pay the lowest wages where the decay of the integrated mills was most visible, that is, in the area of Youngstown, Ohio (McDonalds Steel).[96]

The rise of the minis put heavy pressures on those facilities (and their workforces) that competed in the same market segment (wire rod, reinforced bars, light shapes). Big steel tried to respond by modeling these divisions along the mini-mill line: Bethlehem Steel, for example, revamped its bar, rod, and wire division along mini-mill concepts. It abandoned the old coke ovens and blast furnaces and installed a large 1.2 million ton electric furnace. Hence the company succeeded in extracting major wage and work-rule concessions from its workforce. In return for the wage cuts, the employees received preference stocks that tied part of their labor compensation to the performance of this division. Within a year the easing of work rules contributed to reductions in staffing levels from 2,100 to 1,600 in production.[97] However, because of outdated rolling equipment, the division remained unprofitable. Except for one mill, Bethlehem therefore decided to sell its bar, rod, and wire division to an Indian steel company.[98]

The production paradigm of rigid specialization promises to be more enduring than the exhaustion strategy. Nevertheless, mini-mills encountered tougher competitive conditions by the mid 1980s. Specialization and substandard wage and work conditions were conducive to the growth of mini-mills only as long as prices and wages at the integrated mills were insulated from the volatility of demand. Once integrated producers engaged in price wars and began to cut costs by taking the above mentioned measures, and too many entrepreneurs followed the lure of high profits and entered the mini-mill sector, the minis began to feel strong competitive pressures. They reacted by moving into new product lines and by expanding their market range, but since their flexibility was limited, they lost their cost advantages.[99] Nevertheless, there are some indications that these limits can be overcome by placing variously specialized mini-mills under one command. The recent successful move of Nucor into flat-rolled steel products threatens the core business of the integrated mills.[100]

What is Left of the Fordist Bargain?

For the workers in the integrated steel sector, some basic elements of the Fordist bargain were left intact. So far, the USW has succeeded in defending the wage structure, pay scale, pensions, most fringe benefits, and in principle, the job control focus. But in other respects, the steel crisis has profoundly altered labor relations. The core idea of the Fordist bargain, the linkage between wages and productivity, has been lost. Even though labor productivity rose by 43 percent

FIGURE 6.5 Real Unit Wage Costs, Hourly Employees (1957–1989)

Note: The real unit wage costs are calculated by dividing the data series on real wage (as calculated in figure 6.4) with the index of productivity (unpublished Bureau of Labor Statistics Data, 22 May 1985; 15 April 1991).

between 1983 and 1990, real wages declined by 13 percent (see figure 6.5). In addition, some fringe benefits were cut, and paid vacation and holiday were trimmed. At most mills, the principle of job control was upheld. But in practice the basic elements of job control were seriously restricted, undercut, or disregarded. In a few places job classifications were abolished in exchange for the team concept, in many places they were substantially reduced, and in others they were simply disregarded. The seniority system has been respected for the distribution of benefits and organization of layoffs, but almost always ignored or severely restricted for regulating intraplant transfers. In some mills the grievance procedures have been complemented and in others replaced by joint committees, and in many mills they have lost their effectiveness. Most important, the number of workers enjoying the benefits of basic steel contracts have been reduced dramatically. In smaller steel mills and steel-related sectors during the 1980s, wages and benefits were cut drastically. And with the rise of the mini-mills the percentage of steelworkers organized by the USW fell.

In return, little was gained. The USW got the companies to reinvest what they saved in reduced wages, but while investments were greater than the savings they fell well short of what was necessary to comprehensively modernize the core steel mills. While joint committees were established at some mills, strategic decisions remained management's prerogative. The USW got seats on company boards only at steel mills suffering bankruptcy proceedings.[101]

THE DYNAMICS OF CHANGE

The difficulties of preserving the Fordist bargain can be readily explained in terms of the economic dynamics and macropolitical balance of forces. Fordism presupposed market control and steady productivity increases. The erosion of both conditions and management's determination to lower labor costs undermined the bargain. Management's opposition to a neocorporatist style of crisis management, however, was a product of the steelworkers' shop floor strength and of organized labor's general political weakness. The steelworkers' strength precluded drastic burden-shifting, but labor's political weakness more generally allowed market forces to determine the terms of collective bargaining.

The union's response was limited by three fundamental elements of the Fordist bargain: management prerogatives, the corporate focus, and the productivity deal. With the acceptance of management's exclusive right to determine product and investment strategies, the basis from which the union could have legitimately questioned management's decision to close plants was lost. The same holds true for the USW's dissidents. On the one hand, after three decades of struggle on the two fronts of management and union leadership, the dissidents' militancy had eroded. On the other, as their program had centered on improving the workers' living standards and defending their job rights, a general critique of capitalist exploitation had not been on their agenda. Therefore, they were unable to formulate a persuasive counterstrategy to plant closures resulting from the market society's logic.

The second fundamental aspect of the American Fordist bargain was its company-specific focus, that is, that bargains were struck company by company (or group of companies) and not on a national level. Consequently, the steelworkers were a very privileged group among manufacturing workers, with wages and benefits well above the average. Steeped in the tradition of business unionism, the USW leadership did not feel compelled to reach out to other social groups. In fact, during the leadership of Lloyd McBride, the union even rejected offers of community coalitions to engage in joint struggles to save steel industry jobs.[102] The USW's (and most other U.S. labor unions') ability to counter the political assault of the Reagan administration by broad-based political mobilizations was hamstrung from the start. Moreover, among the steelworkers themselves solidarity was limited. The proposal for a payroll deduction plan to support food banks drew little support.[103] No serious efforts were mounted to share work more evenly among the union members. In fact, the companies frequently imposed mandatory overtime to avoid recalling those laid-off workers who would have been re-entitled to benefits (such as health care) in a next round of layoffs. Without overtime, employment would have been 9.2 percent higher in August of 1985.[104] Seniority remained the mechanism determining who would work and who would become unemployed.

Third, the leadership's traditional preoccupation with imposing the productivity deal on a reluctant membership made it all too willing to accept the company's definition of what caused the industry's problems. Since in the early 1970s the leadership had failed to convince the rank and file of the necessity to improve productivity, and since labor costs had outpaced productivity gains during the 1970s (see figure 6.5), the union's leadership must have felt vindicated by the crisis of the early 1980s. It may be recalled that challenges to the leadership's authority had always come from the basic steel locals, which only a few years earlier had given Ed Sadlowski, in his bid for the union's presidency, the majority of their votes. Thus, Lloyd McBride must have considered the concessions asked for by management to be legitimate insofar as they corrected the "excesses" of the 1970s that had been caused in no small part by basic steel's irresponsible radicals.[105] Only when management's 1983 requests for ever more concessions started to threaten the basic tenets of the Fordist bargain and the union's survival did the union begin, under the leadership of Lynn Williams, to harness the remnants of rank-and-file militancy.

FORCES OF INERTIA

Compared to the auto industry, little institutional change in labor relations and work organization has been accomplished. LMPTs and joint committees were instituted only in bankrupt firms. For the principal industry players, USS and Bethlehem Steel, cooperative relations with the union were not a management objective. They believed they could achieve staffing level reductions and greater work allocation flexibility without cooperation. In terms of work organization, the gains of team work are in fact less obvious in process industries than in assembly industries. Furthermore, until the 1986 strike, USX had reason to expect that the union could be weakened to such a degree that it would become a negligible entity on the shop floor.

Management's opposition doomed any union moves toward participatory labor relations. Indeed, management easily dominated the shaping of post-Fordist industrial relations, since the union failed to mobilize effectively. Until the presidency of Lynn Williams, management defined the problems and developed appropriate solutions. But even if it had devised its own proactive solutions, union leadership would have lacked the moral authority to enlist the membership's support. Rank-and-file activism had always been motivated by the defense of work rules against the combined assault of management and the union leadership.

The leadership team of Lynn Williams, which enjoyed broader appeal among the rank and file in basic steel, developed a more sophisticated approach by offering the companies cooperation in return for certain safeguards or commitments. It achieved some successes, primarily at bankrupt firms. Among the rank and file, however, skepticism remained prevalent. It was fueled by the outrageous behavior of the USX management, but also by the following fundamental concerns: Since unions depend heavily on controlling the shop floor for their power and legitimacy, changes in shop floor relations risk endangering union survival. For example, if a union agrees to the broadening of job classifications and to a less-rigid enforcement of demarcation lines, members may no longer feel protected. In addition, if "team leaders," selected by the company or jointly, handle workers' complaints, in the members' eyes shop stewards may appear to be dispensable. Loosening the seniority system in exchange for more job security may have similar effects. Without legally mandated codetermination structures, the union faces the risk that once cooperation has undermined its legitimacy management will try to get rid of it altogether.[106] So far, even the legal status of current team work practices remains uncertain.[107] To avoid these risks, unions will have to educate and mobilize their membership continuously.[108]

In sum, while the stability of participatory labor relations apparently requires some state support, the U.S. political system denies unions institutional safeguards. Therefore, any attempts by the unions to move beyond Fordist labor relations and exert power on the shop floor rests on their linking of workplace struggles with other movements against capital's hegemony.

Notes

1. Total employment costs per hour worked (wage employees) were $25.62 in the steel industry (Washington D.C.: American Iron and Steel Institute 1991: 14) and $17.33 in manufacturing (Statistical Abstract 1991: Table 684).
2. Walter Müller-Jentsch, "Gewerkschaften als intermediäre Organisation," *Materialien zur Industriesoziologie, Kölner Zeitschrift für Soziologie und Sozialpsychologie*, Berlin: Sonderheft 24 (1982).
3. Richard Hyman, *Industrial Relations: A Marxist Introduction* (London: MacMillan, 1975).
4. The term *Fordism* has two connotations. First, in its use in industrial sociology it pertains to a method for pacing the rhythm of work (especially through the assembly line). Second, in social theory it connotes a phase of capitalism that is marked by mass production for mass consumption. I will use primarily the latter definition.
5. A *regime of accumulation* is a dynamically conceived scheme of production that takes into account both changes in the conditions of production and conditions of consumption. A *strategy of accumulation* describes the specific ways in which a single capital entity pursues its accumulation (work organization, marketing strategy, and so on). Within a regime of accumulation different strategies of accumulation can coexist. *Forms of regulation* are internalized rules and social procedures that incorporate social elements into individual behavior. A *mode of regulation* secures the compatibility among the different forms of regulation within a specific regime of accumulation; see Alain Lipietz, "Imperialism or the Beast of the Apocalypse," *Capital and Class*, Spring 1984: 81–110.
6. *Tayloristic* rationalization means strict separation of planning and carrying out of work as well as extreme division of labor.
7. Lipietz, "Imperialism or the Beast of the Apocalypse," 86.

8. For a detailed discussion of the Fordist mode of regulation in the auto and steel industries, see Christoph Scherrer, *Das Akkumulationsregime der USA im Umbruch: Die Suche nach neuen Regulationsformen in der Auto und Stahlindustrie* (Unveröffentlichte Dissertation, Fachbereich Gesellschaftswissenschaften, J. W. Goethe Universität, Frankfurt, 1988).

9. Zoltan J. Acs, *The Changing Structure of the U.S. Economy: Lessons from the Steel Industry* (New York: Praeger, 1984), 122.

10. M. A. Adelman, "Steel Administered Prices, and Inflation," *Quarterly Journal of Economics* 75 (February 1961): 16–40.

11. David Brody, *Steelworkers in America—The Nonunion Era* (Cambridge: Harvard University Press, 1960).

12. Mark McColloch, "Consolidating Industrial Citizenship: The USWA at War and Peace, 1939–46," in *Forging a Union of Steel: Philip Murray, SWOC, and the United Steelworkers*, ed. Paul F. Clark, Peter Gottlieb, and Donald Kennedy (Ithaca, N.Y.: ILR Press, 1987), 45–86.

13. Michel Aglietta, *A Theory of Capitalist Regulation: The US Experience* (New York: New Left Books, 1979).

14. William Hogan, *Economic History of the Iron and Steel Industry in the U.S.* (Lexington, Mass.: D. C. Heath, 1971), 1443.

15. Harry C. Katz, *Shifting Gears: Changing Labor Relations in the U.S. Automobile Industry* (Cambridge, Mass.: MIT Press, 1985). This term gives the misleading impression of craft control or workers' control. What is called job control emerged in those industries where the skilled workers had already lost their control over the work process and over the labor market (through hiring halls). Against the use of the term *job control unionism* for the practices of the USW there is also the fact that in the process of dismantling the informal controls of the workers over the work process, such as production standards and allocation rules, the Fordist *job controls* gained in importance. See Steve Jefferys, *Management and Managed: Fifty Years of Crisis at Chrysler* (New York: Cambridge University Press, 1986), 14; and Knut Dohse, with Ulrich Jürgens and Harald Russig, *Bestandsschutz durch Seniorität* (Berlin: International Institute for Comparative Social Research, Labor Policy, IIVG reprint, 1979), 79–221, 143.

16. Christoph Köhler and Werner Sengenberger, *Konjunktur und Personalanpassung: Betriebliche Beschäftigungspolitik in der Deutschen und Amerikanischen Automobil-industrie* (Frankfurt: Campus, 1983).

17. USS-USW, United States Steel Corporation and the United Steelworkers of America, 1980: Agreement Production and Maintenance Employees, 1 August, Pittsburgh, p. 11.

18. Jack Stieber, *The Steel Industry Wage Structure* (Cambridge, Mass.: Harvard University Press, 1959).

19. Peter B. Doeringer and Michael J. Piore, *Internal Labor Markets and Manpower Analysis* (Lexington, Mass.: Lexington Books, 1971).

20. Katherine Stone, "The Origin of Job Structures in the Steel Industry," *Radical America* 7, no. 6 (1973): 19–64; David Gordon, Richard Edwards, and Michael Reich, *Segmented Work, Divided Workers* (Cambridge, Eng.: Cambridge University Press, 1982).

21. Richard Edwards, *Contested Terrain: The Transformation of the Workplace in the Twentieth Century* (New York: Basic Books, 1979).

22. Dohse, with Jürgens and Russig, *Bestandsschutz durch Seniorität*; Richard Herding, *Kontrolle am Arbeitsplatz: Kapitalistische Arbeitsorganisation und Gewerkschaften in den USA* (Frankfurt: Campus, 1980); Christoph Köhler, *Betrieblicher Arbeitsmarkt und Gewerkschaftspolitik—Innerbetriebliche Mobilität und Arbeitsplatzrechte in der*

Amerikanischen Automobilindustrie (Frankfurt: Campus, 1981).

23. Carl Gersuny, "Origins of Seniority Provisions in Collective Bargaining," *Labor Law Journal*, August 1982: 518–24.

24. Robert Tilove, *Collective Bargaining in the Steel Industry* (Philadelphia: University of Pennsylvania Press, 1948).

25. Jens Peter Christiansen, "Labor Productivity in the Steel Industry: A Comparative Study of the Federal Republic of Germany and the United States of America" (Ph.D. diss., Stanford University, 1982); Charles R. Walker, *Toward the Automatic Factory: A Case Study of Men and Machines* (New Haven, Conn.: Yale University Press, 1976).

26. Jack Stieber, "Company Cooperation in Collective Bargaining in the Basic Steel Industry," *Labor Law Journal*, July 1960: 607–14.

27. John Hoerr, "Comments," in *Forging a Union of Steel*, ed. Clark, Gottlieb, and Kennedy, 118–25, 120–22.

28. As quoted in I. W. Abel, *Collective Bargaining, Labor Relations in Steel: Then and Now* (New York: Columbia University Press, 1976), 54.

29. Hoerr, "Comments," 124; Harold J. Ruttenberg, 1987: "Comments," in *Forging a Union of Steel*, ed. Clark, Gottlieb, and Kennedy, 126–30.

30. *Plant Labor-Management Committees* (Washington, D.C.: The Bureau of National Affairs, 1951).

31. Richard Betheil, "The ENA in Perspective: The Transformation of Collective Bargaining in the Steel Industry," *Review of Radical Political Economics* 10 (Summer 1978): 1–24.

32. John T. Dunlop, *Dispute Resolution, Negotiation, and Consensus Building* (Dover, Mass.: Auburn House, 1984).

33. *The U.S. Motor Vehicle and Equipment Industry since 1958* (Washington, D.C.: Department of Commerce, 1985), 143.

34. Paul A. Tiffany, *The Decline of American Steel: How Management, Labor, and Government Went Wrong* (New York: Oxford University Press, 1988), 149–66.

35. In the period from 1964 to 1967 the capital costs per ton of steel shipment capacity were $85 in Japan, $218 in the Federal Republic of Germany, and $399 in the United States. See Richard S. Thorn, *Changes in the International Cost Competitiveness of American Steel, 1966–1973* (Pittsburgh, Penn.: University of Pittsburgh, Working Paper no. 8, 1975), 8.

36. Donald F. Barnett and Robert W. Crandall, *Up from the Ashes: The Rise of the Steel Mini-Mill in the United States* (Washington, D.C.: Brookings Institution, 1986), 38, 49–52.

37. Betheil, "The ENA in Perspective," 12–16.

38. William Kornblum, *Blue Collar Community* (Chicago: University of Chicago Press, 1974), 40–42.

39. Aglietta, *A Theory of Capitalist Regulation*, 119–21.

40. Philip W. Nyden, *Steelworkers Rank-and-File: The Political Economy of a Union Reform Movement* (New York: Praeger, 1984).

41. Stanley Aronowitz, *False Promises* (New York: McGraw-Hill, 1973) 35.

42. Acs, *The Changing Structure of the U.S. Economy*, 143.

43. Betheil, "The ENA in Perspective."

44. Robert W. Crandall, *The U.S. Steel Industry in Recurrent Crisis: Policy Options in a Competitive World* (Washington, D.C.: Brookings Institution, 1981), 38.

45. Nyden, *Steelworkers Rank-and-File*, 84–90.

46. Michael Borrus, "Slow Growth and Competition Erosion in the U.S. Steel Industry," in *American Industry in International Competition*, ed. John Zysman and Laura Tyson (Ithaca, N.Y.: Cornell University Press, 1982), 60–105, 90.

47. Josef Esser, Wolfgang Fach, and Werner Väth, *Krisenregulierung: Zur politischen Durchsetzung ökonomischer Zwänge* (Frankfurt: Suhrkamp, 1983).
48. Steel Tripartite Advisory Committee, "Letter of Transmittal," (Washington, D.C.: STAC, 1980).
49. Robert S. Walters, *Patterns in the US Domestic Economic and Foreign Trade Policies: Industrial Crisis in Steel and Automobiles* (Pittsburgh, Penn.: University of Pittsburgh, 1982), 110f.
50. Joe Papovich, U.S. Department of Labor, interview, 30 August 1981.
51. Borrus, "Slow Growth and Competition Erosion in the U.S. Steel Industry," 103.
52. Christoph Scherrer, "Mini-Mills—A New Growth Path for the US Steel Industry," *Journal of Economic Issues* 22, no. 4 (December 1988): 1179–1200.
53. Staughton Lynd, *The Fight against Shutdowns: Youngstown's Steel Mill Closings* (San Pedro, Calif.: Singlejack Books, 1982).
54. Mike Davis, *Prisoners of the American Dream: Politics and Economy in the History of the U.S. Working Class* (London: Verso, 1986).
55. Thomas Ferguson and Joel Rogers, *Right Turn: The Decline of the Democrats and the Future of American Politics* (New York: Hill and Wang, 1986), 264–69.
56. Robert Kuttner, "Unions, Economic Power and the State," *Dissent*, Winter 1986: 33–44.
57. Steel wage employment dropped from 291,483 in 1980 to 168,852 in 1983. *Annual Statistical Report* (Washington, D.C.: American Iron and Steel Institute, 1985), 22.
58. John Hoerr, *And the Wolf Finally Came: The Decline of the American Steel Industry* (Pittsburgh, Penn.: University of Pittsburgh, 1988), 447–77.
59. Hoerr, *And the Wolf Finally Came*, 121–33.
60. Ben Fischer, "Impact of Transition on Steel's Labor Relations," *Labor Law Journal*, August 1986: 569–75, 573.
61. Hoerr, *And the Wolf Finally Came*, 556–66.
62. Hoerr, *And the Wolf Finally Came*, 455–63.
63. Hoerr, *And the Wolf Finally Came*, 508–9; John Sako, President, USW-Local 1011, East Chicago, Indiana, interview, 2 August 1988.
64. Hoerr, *And the Wolf Finally Came*, 577–88.
65. Paul Rusen, "Firing the Boss: The Steelworkers at Wheeling Pitt," *Labor Research Review* 6, no. 1 (1987): 63–77.
66. *Summary Proposed Agreement, United Steelworkers of America and National Steel Corporation* (Pittsburgh, Penn.: USW-United Steelworkers of America, 1986), 7, 10.
67. *Summary of the USWA/LTV Steel Corp: Proposed Agreement* (Pittsburgh, Penn.: USW-United Steelworkers of America, 1986).
68. USITC Publication 2019 (Washington, D.C.: U.S. International Trade Commission, 1987), 34–36.
69. *Industry Week*, 23 March 1987, p. 17.
70. The USWA Local 1397 Newsletter, *1397 Rank and File*, 6 September 1982, p. 6, described the situation dramatically: "When a Union Rep. or someone complains or objects, they're told, 'if you don't like it, file a grievance.' . . . On the average it takes two years to get a case through arbitration. . . . By the time we get the cases through the procedure, we'll have to send a search party out to find the grievant!"
71. Hoerr, *And the Wolf Finally Came*, 218.
72. Hoerr, *And the Wolf Finally Came*, 439.
73. *Wall Street Journal Europe*, 12 July 1992, p. 7.

74. *Wall Street Journal Europe*, 15–16 January 1993, p. 3.
75. Hoerr, *And the Wolf Finally Came*, 438.
76. *Business Week*, 26 June 1989, p. 83.
77. Larry Regan, President, USW-Local 1014, Gary, Indiana, interview, 2 August 1988.
78. *Business Week*, 26 June 1989, p. 83.
79. Michael Cimini, "Collective Bargaining in 1991," *Monthly Labor Review* 114, no. 1 (1991): 22–32, 25–26.
80. *Wall Street Journal Europe*, 7 January 1993, p. 5.
81. For a comparison of the period 1980–1985 and 1974–1980, see Scherrer, *Das Akkumulationsregime der U.S.A. in Umbruch*, 508.
82. By 1988, only 58.8 percent of U.S. mills had installed efficient continuous casters, compared to 93.3 percent in Japan. See *Iron and Steelmaking*, July 1988, p. 8.
83. USITC Publication 2115 (Washington, D.C.: U.S. International Trade Commission, 1988), 18, 36.
84. USITC Publication 2019, (Washington, D.C.: U.S. International Trade Commission, 1987), 29–31.
85. *Iron Age*, July 1987, p. 11.
86. *Wall Street Journal Europe*, 27 March 1990, p. 3; *Wall Street Journal Europe*, 16–17 November 1990, p. 5.
87. Especially early retirees, disabled persons, and widows. In this particular case the Pension Benefit Guaranty Corporation managed to return the pension obligations to LTV in a lengthy legal battle. However, since LTV has not moved out of Chapter 11 bankruptcy proceedings, the fate of the pension benefits remains uncertain. *Wall Street Journal Europe*, 8 November 1990, p. 10.
88. *Wall Street Journal Europe*, 13–14 October 1989, p. 7; *Wall Street Journal Europe*, 1 November 1990, p. 3.
89. *Annual Survey Concerning Competitive Conditions in the Steel Industry and Industry Efforts to Adjust and Modernize*, USITC Publication 2226 (Washington, D.C.: U.S. International Trade Commission, October 1989).
90. Tom Stundza, "Steel: Making More with Less," *Purchasing*, 12 February 1987, pp. 52–57, p. 53.
91. *Wall Street Journal Europe*, 22–23 January 1993.
92. Scherrer, *Das Akkumulationsregime der U.S.A. im Umbruch*.
93. Nyden, *Steelworkers Rank-and-File*, 59.
94. Dave Foster, President of USW-Local in St. Paul, Minnesota, interview, 24 August 1986.
95. Richard Preston, *American Steel: Hot Metal Men and the Resurrection of the Rust Belt* (New York: Prentice Hall Press, 1991).
96. "High Hurdles Ahead for U.S. Steel and National," *Business Week*, 20 February 1984, p. 39.
97. *Monthly Labor Review*, June 1985, p. 50.
98. *New York Times*, 12 November 1992, p. D4.
99. Scherrer, *Das Akkumulationsregime der U.S.A. im Umbruch*.
100. Martin Dickson, "How Nucor Is Stealing a March on the Big Mills," *Financial Times*, 29 May 1991, p. 12.
101. Christoph Scherrer, *Im Bann des Fordismus: Der Konkurrenzkampf der Auto und Stahlindustrie in den U.S.A.* (Berlin: Sigma Bohn, 1992), 272–86.
102. Lynd, *The Fight against Shutdowns*.
103. Hoerr, *And the Wolf Finally Came*, 357.
104. *Confronting the Crisis: The Challenge for Labor* (New York: Locker/Abrecht Associates, 1985), 11. Report to United Steelworkers of America.

105. Compare the description of McBride's bargaining strategy in Hoerr, *And the Wolf Finally Came*, 52–81, 215–23, 236–50, 333–89.
106. Tomasz Mroczkowski, "Is the American Labour-Management Relationship Changing?" *British Journal of Industrial Relations* 22, no. 1 (March 1984): 47–62, 56.
107. Charles Heckscher, *The New Unionism: Employee Involvement in the Changing Corporation* (New York: Basic Books, 1988), 134–36.
108. Mike Parker and Jane Slaughter, *Choosing Sides: Unions and the Team Concept* (Boston: South End Press, 1988), 76.

7

Leadership and Opposition in the United Automobile Workers

Glenn Perusek

UNTIL RECENTLY, MOST SOCIAL scientific and industrial relations studies approached American unions from within a broadly pluralist perspective. While important empirical studies of American unions were conducted from within this framework, these studies also tended to downplay certain features of union politics.[1] In particular, such studies neglected the interest division between union members and leaders and the impact of changing political and economic forces upon this division. As critics of pluralism have held, the assumption of internal democracy—accurate representation of member interests by full-time salaried officers—is hardly warranted in important cases.

This chapter examines the case of the United Automobile Workers (UAW), focusing on two discrete periods since the mid-1960s. After discussing the development of the union before 1967, conflict between oppositional membership groupings and the International union leadership (Solidarity House) during the late 1960s and early 1970s is examined. It is argued that the political and economic circumstances that fostered the development of these groupings changed dramatically after 1973, leading to an entirely new internal dynamic. Since the early 1980s, this dynamic has been characterized by relatively low levels of rank-and-file militancy, the pursuit of a conciliatory bargaining strategy by Solidarity House, and the growth of an opposition within the stratum of lower-level leaders that favored a more confrontational strategy.

THE UAW BEFORE 1967

The United Automobile Workers union was forged in sitdown strikes and other mass struggles in the late 1930s and 1940s. During its first decade, the union was characterized by a high level of rank-and-file participation, shop steward power, and unauthorized strike action. At high points of workers' militancy, stewards often orchestrated large-scale slowdowns and departmental work stoppages. Two strong caucuses vied for power at the top of the union, enhancing the democratic character of the whole organization. While processes of

169

centralization were already under way in the 1940s, questions of politics and economic strategy were openly debated in the union through World War II.[2]

The advent of full-time committeemen, the dues check-off, the incorporation of top union leaders into war planning, and the elimination of factionalism during and following the war all contributed to the centralization of the UAW. As Lichtenstein has shown, the rise of the Reuther leadership resulted in part from the changed political situation after the war.[3] Simultaneously, the long expansion of the American economy made a stable system of collective bargaining possible. Harry Katz has argued that in the auto industry three elements characterized this system: wage rules establishing formulalike structures for wage increases, "connective bargaining" structures limiting contract divergences between companies and between plants in single companies, and "job control" focus on bargaining over working conditions.[4] Under this system, the Reuther leadership could win significant, regular wage increases. But in return, auto contracts explicitly stipulated management's right to determine, maintain, and enforce work standards, which had been eroded during the UAW's first decade. For example, the no-strike clause in UAW contracts limited rank-and-file power to alter employment terms during contracts, just at the time when contracts were becoming multiyear agreements.[5] During the 1950s, the major American auto companies succeeded in weakening the power of shop stewards, substituting the formal, written grievance procedure for the old, informal shop floor system. As Lichtenstein points out, the increased number of written grievances through the 1960s was both an index of bureaucratization and a reflection of workers' continued dissatisfaction with deteriorating working conditions.[6] While the UAW leadership contended that the demands to "humanize" the auto plants were insoluble, they did use the situation to increase paid representation time for part-time committeemen, and full-time committeemen were installed for the first time at General Motors.[7]

Thus by the 1960s the UAW had developed into a large, bureaucratized organization. While the top leadership was elected at regular conventions, they wielded great organizational power through their appointment of the nearly one-thousand-strong bureaucracy of full-time, salaried International representatives. This layer of functionaries, which service the locals, could also withhold services from dissident locals, thus undercutting dissidents. Yet as long as the International leadership could deliver regular, significant wage increases, rank-and-file discontent could be deflected into such channels as the written grievance procedure. The eradication of radicals from positions of authority in the late 1940s and early 1950s meant that the organizational costs of launching any opposition to the International were very high.

THE RISE OF RANK-AND-FILE INSURGENCY
IN THE UAW, 1967–1973

Rank-and-file insurgency challenged the UAW's leadership bureaucracy during 1967–1973. Here I will discuss the growth of independent rank-and-file organizations, wildcat strikes, and the increased use of the grievance procedure. Rank-and-file organizations, which posed a programmatic and organizational alternative to official union leaders, grew up in nearly all major American unions in the late 1960s. The best known group in the UAW was the League of Revolutionary Black Workers (LRBW), an organization that counted probably 250 active militants in Detroit at its peak. The LRBW led wildcat strikes, ran oppositional candidates for local union office, and articulated a set of antiracist and rank-and-file demands. The league counted twelve to fifteen units at Detroit-area plants. Weekly Sunday meetings for workers at the Dodge Main plant (UAW Local 3) drew up to three hundred workers; at the Eldon Avenue Gear and Axle plant (UAW Local 961) up to four hundred—more than official local union meetings at this time. But many LRBW plant groups consisted of only a handful of activists; "a few bulletins or a single action might be the extent of their activities." Although more doctrinaire than other rank-and-file groups, the LRBW could still organize and lead workers far beyond their organization. This reflects the mood in the plants—workers were willing to follow a small group of revolutionary activists, even though they disagreed with them on a range of issues and even though it sometimes jeopardized their jobs.[8]

UAW leaders at the local and national level denounced the LRBW. The International Executive Board said the LRBW constituted a dual union threat and compared their influence to the Communist Party's in the 1930s.[9] In Mike Hamlin's (perhaps somewhat exaggerated) estimation of 250 active LRBW members, at its peak, we have another indication of LRBW influence. The LRBW was probably the most important threat to the UAW bureaucracy since its consolidation in the late 1940s.

A second important rank-and-file organization in the UAW, the United National Caucus (UNC), contrasts with the League of Revolutionary Black Workers in important respects. The UNC was less militant, in formal political terms and in actions. It provided no revolutionary critique of capitalism, nor did it base itself on leadership of wildcat strikes. On paper, the UNC was larger than the LRBW—it did have a truly national scope and at its peak counted more than one thousand members.

The UNC developed a comprehensive critique of the UAW leadership. While arguing that the leadership did not fight hard enough to win wage increases, the UNC focused their criticism on working condition issues. The plants were dangerous and production standards unreasonable. The UNC railed against the UAW's failure to provide real solutions to health and safety problems, work standards (speedup), and grievance procedure problems. Although based largely on skilled workers—who were disproportionately white men—the UNC argued strongly against company discrimination against both blacks and women.[10]

The UNC advanced proposals for sweeping reform in union structure. Instead of vesting power to appoint International representatives in top leaders, they advocated a system of labor counselors, elected in the plants, to serve the locals. Terms of office should be limited constitutionally; union functionaries should be required to return to their jobs periodically. Lastly, the UNC would restructure the dues system to diminish the International's power in relation to the locals and build up the strike fund.

The United National Caucus was the most consistent and perseverant opposition to the UAW bureaucracy during 1967–1973. Although less militant than the League of Revolutionary Black Workers, and thus of somewhat less immediate concern to the leadership, it was the sole *national* opposition organization in the UAW. The UNC articulated a criticism of the bureaucracy, and in some instances it put this opposition into practice. Although its dues-paying membership probably never rose above a thousand, UNC influence was wider than this. It could, for example, organize demonstrations of much larger numbers. Its papers and publications reached tens of thousands of UAW members. Other single plant organizations, such as the Linden Auto Workers and the United Black Brothers in New Jersey, or groupings around individual militants existed throughout the union.

Yet, strike and grievance statistics suggest that rank-and-file unrest existed well beyond the influence of such groups. During the 1950s grievances were not a serious problem. So few grievances were filed against General Motors in 1954 that committeemen used only 36 percent of their representation time, leading to cuts in contractual representation time in 1958.[11] But the total number of grievances rose by 240 percent during the 1960s. Grievances per worker increased 176 percent in these years. According to General Motors, by 1970 "the Umpire Step of the procedure has become overloaded to the point where it has not been possible to schedule hearings with sufficient frequency and regularity to meet the needs of all plants. In 1969, 2,498 cases were appealed to the Umpire compared to an average of about 1,500 per year since 1964."[12]

General Motors officials complained that the whole procedure had broken down at many locations. Blaming "irresponsible" committeemen for failing to limit the number of grievances filed, GM urged the UAW leadership to intervene. Both the companies and the UAW leadership desired to constrict the grievance procedure. To this end they agreed in 1967 to a system of full-time committeemen and union work centers in GM plants for the first time. By 1969 there were 491 full-time committeemen in GM plants. Creating a layer of full-time committeemen, company and union officials hoped, would insulate them from rank-and-file pressure. But GM officials said in 1970 that the liberalized representation system failed to yield "results predicted by the International Union and expected by management."[13]

Another indicator of heightened conflict between workers and management and between workers and UAW officials during the years 1967–1973 is the trend of strikes. The most complete information concerns strikes against Chrysler Corporation. The number of strikes during 1967–1973 is incomparably higher than in the periods directly before and after. An average of 66.1 strikes per year were conducted against Chrysler during 1967–1973. In 1960–1966 it was only 20.4, and by 1980–1985 it had returned to a low of just 29 strikes per year. (A transition period, 1974–1979, witnessed 39.8 strikes per year.) The ratio of unauthorized strikes to all strikes increased somewhat during 1967–1973 as well. It was 88.8 percent in 1960–1966, but rose to 94.3 percent in 1967–1973, then dropped to 76.6 percent in the years 1974–1985. Another important indicator of the rise in militancy is hours lost to unauthorized strikes. In 1960–1966, a yearly average of 84.8 million man-hours were lost to unauthorized strikes. This ballooned to 425.5 million man-hours per year during 1967–1973, then dropped to 250.1 in 1974–1978 and to 60.5 million in 1979–1985. A similar, although less pronounced, pattern can be seen in figures for General Motors. Strikes numbered 25.1 yearly against General Motors from 1960 to 1966. Then in 1967–1973, they rose to 36.9 per year, returning to 17.5 per year in 1974–1979. Man-hours lost to unauthorized strikes against GM rose from 184.5 million per year in 1960–1966 to 286.1 million in 1967–1973 and dropped to 111.0 in 1974–1978.[14] For American industry as a whole, the growing proportion of contract rejections in this period further confirms the trend of rising militancy.[15]

This trend should be understood within the economic and wider political context of late 1960s–early 1970s social protest. The late 1960s economic expansion, in part spurred by the Vietnam War, led American auto plants to run near capacity. This brought large numbers of (often more militant) young and black workers into the auto plants. At all major American auto producers, more than 25 percent of workers were under age thirty; at Chrysler the figure was over 30 percent. Similarly, the black proportion of the workforce at many major urban-area plants was high. By 1968 the UAW as a whole was at least 30 percent black. At the Chrysler Eldon Avenue Gear and Axle plant, location of a strong LRBW chapter, 75 percent of production workers were black or other minorities; more than half the production workers at Dodge Main were black.[16]

Full employment also made all workers more confident of their position in the production process. This confidence was the necessary precondition for rising militancy—workers felt they could strike or engage in other unauthorized actions with relative impunity. Because the corporations introduced little productivity-improving technology in these years, production speedups and deteriorating safety conditions were salient protest issues.

But the political context is perhaps even more important in accounting for the unrest. The five years starting in 1967 witnessed militant protest activity unprecedented in the postwar United States, centered on the black rebellion (both the organized Black Power movement and unorganized ghetto rioting) and antiwar protests. Rebellion inside the UAW may best be conceived of as a component of the general rebellion against racism and the status quo. Many workers entered the plants after a radicalizing experience in Vietnam. Young workers who opposed the war and who supported the demands of student and black militants were the new workers of the late 1960s. Indeed, Harlan Hahn presents data indicating that, particularly after the Tet Offensive in early 1968, the majority of American workers probably opposed the war—and were more likely to do so than college graduates and members of higher-income groups.[17] A large proportion of the new, young, black workers sympathized with the demands and tactics of nationally known radical black nationalist organizations—they would be most likely to engage in militant action inside the plants, too.[18]

Societal protest affected protest within the UAW and other unions in many ways. In the widest sense, union members learned from the examples set by the wider militancy. They were swept up in the mood of protest. Because an ideology and acceptance of militant protest existed, the cost of embarking on such action was reduced. More concretely, some student and black militants directly entered the car plants with the explicit intention of organizing workers. LRBW leaders had received some orthodox Marxist training from Detroit followers of C. L. R. James, which pointed them in this direction; a small number of other student socialists (Maoists, Trotskyists, and others) "industrialized," entering the plants with plans to lead activity. For all these reasons, rank-and-file insurgency in the auto plants in 1967–1973 should be seen as interwoven into the whole environment of protest that existed in the black community and among young people.

THE YEARS AFTER 1973:
A NEW PATTERN OF CONFLICT IN THE UAW

The political and economic factors responsible for the rank-and-file revolt changed dramatically after 1973. By January 1975, economic recession idled 164,050 workers—nearly one quarter of all UAW members for the big three were on indefinite layoff.[19] Recession and unemployment strangled the viability of all opposition activity. "When the economy is faltering, workers in any shop might be more concerned about having a job at all and will temper their militancy accordingly."[20] Wildcat strikes dropped off sharply after 1973. Similarly, the external political fillip to rank-and-file protest also evaporated with the end of the Vietnam War and the militant Black Power phase of the black movement. Rank-and-file militancy would not reemerge after 1974. Nearly all the shop floor militants who began organizing in the late 1960s and early 1970s failed to gauge the impact that the recession would have. Instead of anticipating the conservatizing effect it would have on the rank and file, they believed that economic crisis would increase radicalism and interest in protest.

With rising oil prices during the 1970s, American auto producers found themselves at a significant disadvantage against foreign competitors, particularly the Japanese, who were developing inexpensive, high-quality small cars. In 1979, Chrysler obtained concessions from workers and financial assistance from the federal government. Starting in 1982, Ford and GM also obtained concessions. In part, the major car producers' drive for concessions was an effort to finance massive investment programs. International competition forced American producers to invest in costly, productivity-improving technologies, even as they were suffering huge losses. All told, the American auto companies spent a total of $70 billion between 1979 and 1985 to convert to smaller cars and front-wheel drive. This was the largest privately funded investment program in history.[21]

Computer Integrated Manufacture (CIM), the cutting edge of the technological advances, has affected unionized autoworkers in two major ways. First, it required great reductions in the numbers of unskilled workers.[22] Second, it has created the single most important conflict between the auto makers and their employees in the 1980s: the conflict over work rules. Companies want to consolidate job classifications so that workers perform several tasks instead of a single one and to pay workers for the different jobs they can perform ("pay for knowledge") instead of a negotiated rate for each job category.

Quality of Work Life (QWL) and employee involvement programs are spreading the new organization of production to existing auto plants. In QWL programs, the companies offer workers and union officers involvement in small-scale decision-making about the production process. In return, workers discuss ways to improve productivity and product quality, through such organizations as quality circles. In essence, quality of work life programs prepare workers to become "general purpose resources" by breaking down the "job control unionism" that had defined shop floor relations since the 1940s.[23]

American auto companies began the earnest drive for drastic work-rule changes in 1981, using outsourcing threats and whipsawing to force UAW locals to change work organization.[24] In 1982, Solidarity House reopened national Ford and GM contracts to offer the companies concessions. In addition to wage freezes, elimination of some holidays, and deferment of cost-of-living increases, the 1982 contracts included pledges that the national UAW leadership would agree that work rules should be drastically altered in local contracts.[25]

Many locals declared there would be no local concessions—management had already gotten more than they deserved in the national contract concessions. In part, local leaders' resistance at assembly plants was predicated on workers' relatively strong bargaining position. These plants were least susceptible to closing; the companies could not compare them to nonunion outside suppliers as easily as could parts plants. In twenty-two large General Motors Assembly Division (GMAD) plants, workers rejected the 1982 contract by 29,640 to 17,551—these workers were least likely to agree to work-rule concessions in local negotiations.[26] Yet in many instances, local officers opposed concessions more militantly than their members. Concessions threatened to destroy their own prerogatives even as they made work more difficult. While workers often believed effective opposition to concessions was impossible, and thus invested nothing in the effort, some local officers came to see the battle as all-important.

By the mid-1980s, the auto companies had drastically cut the number of production workers. In 1984, GM's blue-collar workforce in the United States was down to 375,000 from its peak of 502,000 in 1979.[27] The UAW International leadership emphasized job security in 1984. UAW members, frustrated with concessions, voted out numerous local officials. Workers who in the 1967–1973 period would probably have expressed discontent through wildcat strikes or other unauthorized action now had only the instrument of local union ballots.

The centerpiece of the 1984 GM contract was a $1 billion jointly administered job bank program to retrain and place in new jobs workers displaced by new technology. Importantly, GM reportedly offered the UAW leadership higher wages than were eventually accepted.[28] The International union *turned down* company offers for higher wages to gain the job bank. The UAW leadership enthusiastically hailed the job bank as an unprecedented job security measure.

Experts on the impact of automation on manufacturing jobs were less enthusiastic. The $1 billion spread over the six-year job bank agreement amounted to just $167 million per year, "about the cost of one new paint shop in one new auto plant."[29] Workers displaced by imports or other "market-related" factors would not even enter the bank. In any event, fewer than four thousand workers per year could be accommodated in the program—and they would be all-purpose utility workers, part of the cutting edge of GM's drive to eliminate job classifications. GM had already announced projected job cuts five to ten times that great. The 1984 Ford contract included a similar "job bank" provision.[30] Importantly, the GM and Ford national contracts allowed the companies to press for factory-floor efficiencies until 1990 regardless of provisions in local agreements, through joint development of proposals to "improve operational efficiencies."

CONFLICT BETWEEN LAYERS OF THE UAW BUREAUCRACY

The character of conflict inside the UAW changed after the 1967–1973 period of rank-and-file militancy. Rank-and-file militancy has diminished greatly since the mid-1970s. In 1982, workers opposed further concessions to Chrysler but also opposed striking. While in 1967–1973 workers struck over more trivial matters, now they refused to strike against massive concessions. In 1982 and again in 1984, the union's leadership used the prospect of striking a rejected contract as a stick against workers. Dire economic conditions made autoworkers susceptible to such arguments.

In 1967–1973, the bureaucracy was relatively unified in the face of rank-and-file militancy. In part, this indicates that the UAW's top leadership maintained control over the whole bureaucracy. Pressure from below raised administration costs by creating governance problems for local officers. Local officers generally opposed wildcat strikes and grievance procedure overload, which made their jobs more difficult. But the companies' drive against protective work rules since the early 1980s constitutes the main challenge to local officers. Thoroughgoing work-rules changes would render local leaders superfluous. In any event, they promise to diminish local leaders' power and prerogatives. The companies forced some local officials to accept concessions under the threat of plant closures. While local leaders often acceded to concessions to save jobs, and thus their own positions, some of these employer attacks occasioned the most important militant action in the UAW during the 1980s—action initiated by lower levels of the union bureaucracy.

Under these conditions, top UAW leaders' interests diverged from local officers'. Central to the top leaders' strategy was to seek joint program administration with the companies. The top UAW leadership would accept significant concessions as long as they could be part of administering them. They participated with GM in planning the Saturn program, even though it constituted a potentially disastrous precedent for autoworkers and local officers. They administered the job bank programs stipulated in 1984 contracts with GM and Ford and declared the contracts to be a historic step toward genuine job security for autoworkers—even though fewer than twenty-five thousand GM workers could be accommodated in the program and GM had already predicted job cuts up to five times that high. After reopening Ford and GM contracts in 1982, the International, alongside the companies, pursued concessions at the local level. The bureaucracy's interest in administration—preserving and extending its prerogatives in joint management of programs—appeared to override member concerns that the union was bargaining away important protections. Top leaders were relatively free to pursue concessions that would preserve the union's dues base. The electoral process, which effectively insulated top leaders from opposition from below, afforded no real channel to check the top leaders' authority; recession's effects choked off more militant, extra-electoral action.

The top UAW leadership's acceptance of concessions in 1982 produced opposition from below, but its character illustrates how different industrial relations in the post-1973 period were from those of the 1967–1973 years: The opposition to concessions was centered on local presidents and other full-time officers, in midwestern UAW locals. While some local leaders against concessions were able to bring large portions of their memberships along with them (in voting on the 1982 national contracts), in other cases they acted without support from their members.

The threat to the union has affected different levels of the bureaucracy in different ways. Harry Katz and Charles Sabel argue that International leaders can be threatened with an increasingly chaotic system, as the implementation of vastly varied local agreements could undermine their authority. But local officials felt the attack on their prerogatives most sharply. Once the defining feature of the union's role in production was its bargaining and administration of the job classification system. Changes in work rules now under way promise to destroy this system. "The more work organization itself prevents . . . conflicts [over work rules] from occurring in the first place or allows for their informal resolution, the harder it becomes for American-style unions to justify themselves as daily guarantors of the workers' rights."[31] International leaders can bargain away the power of committeemen and local officers to administer local contracts without affecting their own prerogatives, but such concessions threaten to touch off conflict between layers of the union leadership.

The most important expression of subnational opposition to International leadership policy during the 1980s was the New Directions movement, which began in 1985 in the UAW's Region 5 (southwestern states). Local presidents, dissatisfied with concessions, complained that the national leadership was offering no effective opposition to whipsawing and employer concession demands. The New Directions Steering Committee pressed assistant regional director Jerry Tucker, with whom they had worked, to run for regional director. When Tucker announced his candidacy, the International Executive Board immediately fired him, charging that he had violated administration caucus rules by declaring his candidacy less than ninety days before the convention. At the convention, top leaders pressured Region 5 delegates to vote for Ken Worley. International representatives told local officers that they would get no assistance in local negotiations should they oppose Worley. Worley won a close, contested election.[32] The Tucker versus Worley battle reflected the debate over concessions and cooperation with management. Tucker and the New Directions movement represented the position of a minority of local leaders—against concessions and cooperation. Essentially, the insurgents called for a confrontational stance to company plans for concessions and work-rule changes.[33] They successfully implemented this approach in "work-to-rule campaigns" in Region 5, at Moog Automotive, Inc. (UAW Local 282) in St. Louis (1981–1982), the Schwitzer cooling fan plant in Rolla, Missouri (1983), Bell Helicopter in Texas (1984), and the Grand Prairie, Texas, LTV-Vought aerospace defense systems plant in 1984–1985.[34]

The conflict between layers of the UAW bureaucracy also expressed itself in the 1984 split of the Canadian region of the union from the International. Canada's bargaining conditions in the 1980s made concessions less warranted—Canadian autoworkers fell behind their American counterparts. In 1984 GM–Canadian UAW negotiations, the top UAW leadership sought to curtail efforts by Robert White, director of the Canadian region, to gain a better settlement than they had negotiated in the United States. This led White to initiate a move for greater autonomy, or independence, for the Canadians. In part, White was responding to membership pressure for stronger bargaining over wages. In addition, the Canadian leadership felt constrained by their association with the UAW—political conditions in Canada presented them with an opportunity to pursue a more aggressive organizational strategy, such as the foundation of a Canadian metalworkers' federation (amalgamating autoworkers to steelworkers, machinists, and others into a larger organization). The UAW leadership in Detroit viewed the Canadians' continued association as problematic. The Canadians represented a potential pole of attraction for a larger and much more effective anticoncession movement within the UAW. Such a movement would threaten their incumbency. While from a strict bargaining perspective, the UAW leadership might have preferred that their Canadian affiliate strive to equalize real wage rates across the border, their fear of the impact of an aggressive partner on the internal stability of the American union was an overriding concern.[35]

During the 1980s, lower-level UAW leaders have undertaken oppositional activity without significant membership pressure. In 1967–1973 the central cleavage in the union was between the relatively unified bureaucracy—from the International to the local level—and rank-and-file militants who attempted to organize a portion of members behind them. But by the 1980s, the central cleavage was *within* the bureaucracy—between the International and local layers. In part, the locus of the employers' attack determined this fragmentation. Concessions, which threatened to alter long-standing shop floor relations, were far more problematic for local full-time officers than for national leaders. Even wage concessions and mass layoffs did not constitute inroads on the national union's financial or organizational stability. Most union members, devastated by unemployment and concessions, opted for individualistic or passive conceptions of strategies to advance their interests. Between these, some local leaders understood management attacks to constitute a life-or-death threat to their own prerogatives. They acted, sometimes quite militantly, without significant pressure from below. Their problem was to convince their own members that militant action is both necessary and viable—a difficult task indeed, given conditions.

Top UAW leaders argued that their main concern during the 1980s was job preservation. This included the failed attempt to press for "domestic content legislation," requiring all companies selling a significant number of cars in the United States to build a certain portion here. Critics of the UAW leadership have suggested that contractual job security gains have been ineffectual. Harley Shaiken argues that in the age of super-automation, wage and work-rule concessions, while saving companies money, will not necessarily save workers' jobs. That concessions were reinvested in new technology, only further displacing workers, bolsters this argument. Additionally, low autoworker wages in Britain, Italy, and France do not of themselves create internationally competitive auto firms. And even if UAW members give concessions, they may not gain an advantage over workers in supplier industries—with whom they are in direct, company-fostered competition. "The much-noted differential between autoworkers' wages and those of workers in related industries may not be reduced; the proportions may remain the same as everyone's wages are ratcheted down." Shaiken estimates the elimination of twenty-six holidays in the 1982 Ford and GM contracts destroyed eighteen thousand jobs. Furthermore, when the auto industry recovered after the 1982 recession, auto makers relied on massive overtime

TABLE 7.1   U.S. Automobile Industry, Hourly Manufacturing Employment
(1978–2000) (in thousands)

	1978	1990	2000 (est.)
Assembly plants			
Big Three	263	199	150–75
Transplants, unionized	—	11	15
Transplants, nonunionized	—	19	35
Parts plants			
Big Three parts	428	258	150–75
Independent, unionized	155	85	50
Independent, nonunionized	141	242	200–250
Percentage of auto industry			
workers belonging to unions	86%	68%	58%

Source: Steve Herzenberg, U.S. Congress, Office of Technology Assessment, in *Detroit Free Press*, 13 September 1992, A9.

rather than hiring back most workers on indefinite layoff. This is a common, economical practice. But the lack of leadership response on the issue seems to belie their concern for job security. The UAW leadership's safety net for their membership seems to contain sizable holes.[36]

Thus, rather than actually preserve jobs, Solidarity House has pursued a risk-averse strategy that has amounted to presiding over a significant decline in numbers of unionized autoworkers in the United States. The UAW has been able to organize only about eight thousand of the hundred thousand workers at Japanese transplants. Overall, the unionization rate for the American automobile industry has declined from about 86 percent in 1978 to 68 percent by 1990 (see table 7.1). Even when confronted with attacks on their own power, Solidarity House has preferred defeat to engaging in the bold tactics that would provide the only viable strategy for preserving jobs, wages, and work rules.

In the present environment, faced with aggressive firms' bargaining posture, union leaders cannot maintain existing contractual conditions—let alone improve conditions—without organizing a concerted struggle. In the 1992 Caterpillar strike, the company sought to break a pattern agreement the UAW had established with Deere as part of a thoroughgoing modernization plan. After a five-month strike, management played on workers' fear for their jobs by threatening to replace them permanently. The UAW's leadership was faced with a choice of escalating the conflict or capitulating. Escalation was necessarily a risk-laden strategy, but the only way to preserve pattern-bargaining. With proper preparation and the willingness to carry the strike to its logical conclusion, the union could have pursued the escalatory strategy with a reasonable chance of success.

This is precisely what the Canadian Auto Workers (CAW) did in the fall 1992 CAMI strike. The CAW staged a successful five-week strike against CAMI, the four-year-old Ontario GM-Suzuki plant, forcing alterations in the so-called management by stress system. The CAW won the right for workers to elect team leaders (who had been appointed by management, protection for workers who stop the assembly line for quality reasons, a pool of replacement workers, an improved representation ratio, and other gains. Jane Slaughter argues that the CAW's willingness to mobilize GM workers throughout Canada bolstered their bargaining position, making the victory possible.[37]

Similarly, as Jim Woodward has argued in *Labor Notes*, in the 1989 Pittston strike, the United Mine Workers mobilized resources of whole communities, occupied buildings, built Camp Solidarity, and encouraged sympathy strikes. "It's not any one tactic the Pittston miners used that was key, but their overall approach. They were daring and creative. They took risks. They pulled off dramatic actions to inspire their supporters. . . . In short, they turned their strike into a cause." These are precisely the risk-laden tactics that Solidarity House was unwilling to employ. Surely such tactics bear great costs and are dangerous. But, Woodward contends, while Pittstonlike tactics may not guarantee victory, "the old ones guarantee defeat."[38]

At the end of 1992, Caterpillar was adding insult to injury by unilaterally imposing its final offer (the contract offer the UAW had initially struck over). It ceased the long-standing practice of paying union committeemen, arguing that it should not be responsible for the compensation of union officials who were orchestrating the work-to-rule campaign that sought to bring the company back to the bargaining table.[39]

CONCLUSIONS

This chapter has argued explicitly for a conception of bureaucratized unions that distinguishes the international leadership, local leaders, rank-and-file militants, and ordinary union members as distinctive actors with distinctive interests. Additionally, it has argued that the relations between these different actors changed under different economic and political circumstances.

The UAW became a bureaucratized union in the post–World War II period. Until the late 1940s, the UAW negotiated annual contracts, but since the late 1940s the UAW leadership has negotiated long-term contracts, which contained no-strike clauses. Such mechanisms as the dues check-off widened the division between members and full-time officers. By the early 1950s, the leadership around Walter Reuther had the financial and organizational resources of the International at its disposal. Top leaders maintained their own tenure through International staff, whose members served at the pleasure of top leaders.

For the UAW since the 1960s, two sharply differentiable periods can be distinguished. In 1967–1973, conflict within the UAW confirms the Michelsian thesis that union leaders are more conservative than are their members in pursuit of union aims. The UAW leadership conceived of rank-and-file militancy as a potential threat to bargaining stability and to their own prerogatives.

In lockstep fashion, the UAW bureaucracy—from the International leadership down to the local level—opposed the insurgency from below.

During this period, the UAW leadership also worked to reduce costs associated with striking. In 1970 pressure from below led the UAW leadership to call a national strike against GM. The strike depleted the UAW's strike fund, leading the union into debt for a time. In 1972, the UAW also suffered long local strikes at several GMAD locations. Determined to avoid any more such costly strikes, top leaders devised a creative tactic to accommodate pressure from below without unduly taxing the strike fund—mini-strikes. In fall 1972 the national leadership called individual GMAD plants out one at a time over long weekends. UAW leaders believed this would disrupt GM production enough to force the company to settle local production standard issues. At the same time, the union paid out no strike benefits.[40]

Careful examination of the period since 1973 in the UAW shows counterevidence to the Michelsian thesis. The UAW rank and file was decimated by high levels of unemployment after 1973. This did not heighten worker militancy—it destroyed it. Instead of more dramatic, collective solutions to more desperate problems, workers turned inward. Increasingly, they conceived of their problems in individual terms—concerned with their own job security, workers put their heads down and thought a fight against concessions was hopeless.

Interestingly, the most militant part of the UAW during the 1980s was a minority of local and regional leaders, the lower levels of the bureaucracy. In part, this was determined by the locus of employers' attack. If successful, employers' attempts to transform shop floor work organization would eliminate a large part of local leaders' function—the administration of the grievance procedure and negotiation over work rules.

The major challenge to the UAW's leadership in 1967–1973 came from rank-and-file protest. Pressure from below constrained the leadership to bargain for significant improvements in national contracts. Simultaneously, the leadership devoted resources to quelling unauthorized job actions. A qualitatively different pattern of relations between members and leaders obtained during the 1980s, when UAW leadership policy was divided between layers of the bureaucracy. At the national level, the leadership was willing to bargain concessions in an effort to preserve the union's dues base. But at the local level, union officers' prerogatives were threatened by the drive to transform work rules. While this drive also threatened to undermine workers' job protections, it is important that the militant reaction of a section of lower-level union officers has occurred in the absence of pressure from below.

This chapter has focused on the relations between full-time union leaders, at the national, regional, and local levels, and the rank and file. Relations between these actors can be interpreted as including a great deal of strain and interest conflict. Union leaders have vested interests that in different economic and political circumstances lead them to behave in different ways. They are not necessarily bound by the wishes and demands of their members, especially when their members are forced by economic hardship into quiescence.

This suggests that the critique of pluralist theory as a description of politics in advanced capitalist democracies might be served by an increased focus on relations between members and leaders in large membership organizations. A fundamental assumption of the pluralists—that we can assume coincidence of interest between leaders and members of such organizations—may not be as universally true as the pluralists contend. A comprehensive critique of pluralist theory—one that can provide a positive theoretical alternative—will probably have to completely reinterpret the internal group life of membership organizations.

We have attempted to show the linkage between extra-organizational economic and political factors and the pattern of conflict within the UAW. Under conditions of full-employment and widespread societal protest in 1967–1973, a significant rank-and-file insurgency grew up within the union. Because this threatened the stable governance of the union, the international leadership consistently opposed this movement. When the political and economic situation changed drastically after 1973, this insurgency evaporated, giving way to a cautious, defensive mood on the shop floor. This destroyed the base for the militant rank-and-file groupings of the earlier period.

By the early 1980s, pressure from foreign competition led the American automobile companies to seek concessions from the UAW. In addition to wage and benefit demands, they launched a drive against protective work rules. Because this attack affected the International leadership and local leadership differently, these actors' response was fragmented. The International leadership proclaimed their central concern was for job security. This was predicated on their organizational interest in maintaining the UAW's dues base. The International was willing to make any number of concessions to the car companies as long as the companies would continue to treat the UAW leadership as a partner— joint programs illustrated how willing the companies were to do this. But along with this cautious bargaining strategy, the UAW leadership transformed the financial structure of the union: They made the organization increasingly independent of dues income. To some extent, this insulates the organizational leadership from adverse effects of continued membership decline.

Most UAW local leaders followed Solidarity House uncritically in this strategy. But some local leaders chose to embark on a strategy of confrontation— against both the companies and the UAW's top leadership. Some of these leaders were in a safer position because of their stronger base in assembly plants not threatened by closure. Others saw no option but to fight because their prerogatives in the production process, their role in the grievance procedure, would be wiped out if the companies achieved all they sought. Local oppositionists crystallized into the New Directions movement in the mid-1980s.

Intra-union conflict is qualitatively different in the two periods examined here. The radicalism of the League of Revolutionary Black Workers was based first and foremost on its ability to mobilize workers in wildcat strikes. This contrasts sharply with the movement of local and regional leaders in New Directions: Theirs is primarily an electoral challenge to Solidarity House. More than anything else, this is probably a result of the different mood of rank-and-file workers in these two periods. Rank-and-file confidence, born of full employment and societal protest, characterized 1967–1973. Rank-and-file demoralization—although strongly tinged with bitterness— characterized the 1980s. The changed character of oppositional organizations reflected this changed rank-and-file mood.

Notes

1. Seymour Martin Lipset, *Political Man: The Social Bases of Politics* (Garden City, N.Y.: Doubleday, 1960), is perhaps the most systematic statement of the pluralist theoretical perspective as applied to trade unionism, and Seymour Martin Lipset, Martin Trow, and James Coleman, *Union Democracy: The Internal Politics of the International Typographical Union* (Glencoe, Ill.: Free Press, 1956), is among the most rigorous empirical studies. Jack Stieber, *Governing the UAW* (New York: Wiley, 1962), applies this perspective to the UAW.
2. Nelson Lichtenstein, "Conflict over Workers' Control: The Automobile Industry in World War Two," in *Working Class America: Essays on Labor, Community, and American Society*, ed. Michael Frisch and Daniel Walkowitz (Urbana: University of Illinois Press, 1983); Stieber, *Governing the UAW*.
3. Nelson Lichtenstein, "UAW Bargaining Strategy and Shop-Floor Conflict: 1946–1970," *Industrial Relations* 24 (Fall 1985): 360–81.
4. Harry C. Katz, *Shifting Gears: Changing Labor Relations in the U.S. Automobile Industry* (Cambridge: MIT Press, 1985), 28.
5. The "Treaty of Detroit," the 1950 UAW-GM contract, was typical of the move to multiyear contracts that guaranteed wage increases in return for reassertion of managerial prerogatives. Of this pact, the editors of *Fortune* suggested that "GM may have paid a billion for peace, but it got a bargain. General Motors has regained control over one of the crucial management functions . . . long range scheduling of production, model changes, and tool and plant investment." Quoted in John Barnard, *Walter Reuther and the Rise of the Auto Workers* (Boston: Little, Brown and Company, 1983), 143.
6. Lichtenstein, "UAW Bargaining Strategy."
7. Leonard Woodcock: "The question of how to perform work should not be a matter of confrontation in collective bargaining, because you can only have a confrontation in collective bargaining if you have in sight a solution to the problem which has produced the conflict. And as matters stand, we do not have—no one has—the ready answers to the question of how best the work can be done in a humane way." Quoted in *Workers Power* 75 (30 March 1973). By 1969 there were 491 full-time committeemen at GM, according to "Statement of General Motors to the UAW," 21 July 1970, in Ernest Moran Collection, Box 2, Archives of Labor History and Urban Affairs, Wayne State University, Detroit, Michigan. Subsequent references to collections, unless otherwise noted, are to materials housed at the Archives of Labor History and Urban Affairs, Wayne State University, Detroit, Michigan.
8. Dan Georgakas and Marvin Surkin, *Detroit: I Do Mind Dying* (New York: St. Martin's Press, 1975), 88, 112–113; *Dodge Main News*, 15 June 1968, p. 1, and 31 August 1968, p. 1.

9. *Dodge Main News*, 15 February 1969, p. 1; UAW International Executive Board, "Administrative Letter on Black Revolutionaries," 10 March 1969, in Detroit Revolutionary Movements Collection, Box 4; James A. Geschwender, *Class, Race, and Worker Insurgency: The League of Revolutionary Black Workers* (Cambridge: Cambridge University Press, 1977), 114; O. D. McQueen, Letter to Tony Connole, 14 March 1969, in Arthur Hughes Collection, Box 47; Bill Beckham, Letter to WPR [Walter P. Reuther], 13 February 1969, in Walter P. Reuther Collection, Box 74; William H. Oliver, Letter to Walter P. Reuther, 11 April 1969, in Walter P. Reuther Collection, Box 213; Carl Sheier, Letter to Doug Fraser, 7 January 1969, in Walter P. Reuther Collection, Box 213. Members of the Communist Party (and other socialists and radicals) were, in fact, instrumental in the formation of many CIO unions. In 1937 the Communist Party counted some 550 members in the UAW, according to Bert Cochran, *Labor and Communism: The Struggle That Shaped American Unions* (Princeton, N.J.: Princeton University Press, 1977), 124.

10. Glenn Perusek, "The Internal Politics of the United Automobile Workers, 1967–1985" (Ph.D. diss., University of Chicago, 1988), 228–43; "United National Caucus," introductory pamphlet, 1973, in Arthur Hughes Collection, Box 47, 5; CKLW-TV, "United National Caucus," transcript of program, 8 Novermber 1970, in Ken Bannon Collection, Box 65; Pete Kelly, "Chairman's Report," *The United National Caucus* 2 (15 April 1971), in Arthur Hughes Collection, Box 47.

11. Robert M. MacDonald, *Collective Bargaining in the Automobile Industry: A Study of Wage Structure and Competitive Relations* (New Haven, Conn.: Yale University Press, 1963), 331.

12. "Statement of General Motors to the UAW," 21 July 1970, in Ernest Moran Collection, Box 2. See also Theodore St. Antoine, "Dispute Resolution between the General Motors Corporation and the United Automobile Workers, 1970–1982," in *Industrial Conflict Resolution in Market Economies: A Study of Australia, the Federal Republic of Germany, Italy, Japan, and the UAW*, ed. T. Hanami and R. Blanpain (Deventer, The Netherlands: Kluwer Law and Taxation Publishers, 1984), 297–316.

13. "Statement of General Motors to the UAW," 17.

14. Chrysler Corporation, Wage and Salary Administration, Industrial Relations Office, "Authorized and Unauthorized Strikes, Chrysler, U.S. Locations, 1960–1985," mimeo, 1986, in author's possession; Sean Flaherty, "Strike Activity and Productivity Change: The U.S. Auto Industry," *Industrial Relations* 26 (1987): 174–85; General Motors, Corporate Labor Relations, "Man Hours Lost Due to Authorized Strikes, General Motors—U.S. Operations, All Unions," mimeo, 1986, in author's possession; United Automobile Workers, International Executive Board, "Letters of Intent to Authorize a Strike," in Leonard Woodcock Collection, Box 26.

15. Lou Carliner, Statement to UAW Region 9 Staff Meeting, January 1969, in Walter P. Reuther Collection, Box 221.

16. Georgakas and Surkin, *Detroit: I Do Mind Dying*, 40, 102; Steve Jefferys, *Management and Managed: Fifty Years of Crisis at Chrysler* (Cambridge: Cambridge University Press, 1986); General Motors, *General Motors Public Interest Report* (Detroit: General Motors, 1985), 60; Ford Motor Company, *Annual Report* (Dearborn, Mich.: Ford Motor Company, 1985), 42.

17. Harlan Hahn, "Correlates of Public Sentiments about War: Local Referenda on the Vietnam Issue," *American Political Science Review* 64 (December 1970): 1186–98; and "Dove Sentiment among Blue-Collar Workers," *Dissent* 17 (May/June 1970): 202–5.

18. Georgakas and Surkin, *Detroit: I Do Mind Dying*; Geschwender, *Class, Race, and Worker Insurgency*. Poll data showing the great popularity of the militant Black Panther Party is instructive of the general mood in the black community in the late 1960s. According to a Harris poll taken in 1970, fully 9 percent of blacks believed that violence would be necessary to bring about black equality; 25 percent "greatly admired" the Black Panthers. Only the NAACP was admired more. See Philip Foner, *The Black Panthers Speak* (Philadelphia: Lippincott, 1970), xiv.

19. Jack Weinberg, "UAW Response to the Economic Crisis," *Network* 1 (1975): n.p.

20. Harley Shaiken, *Work Transformed: Automation and Labor in the Computer Age* (New York: Holt, Rinehart and Winston, 1984), 42.

21. Norman S. Fieleke, "The Automobile Industry," *Annals of the American Academy of Political and Social Sciences* 460 (1982): 83. See also Christopher Wood, "Another Turn of the Wheel," *The Economist*, 2 March 1985 (supplement), p. 8; Amal Nag, "Tricky Technology: Auto Makers Discover 'Factory of the Future' Is Headache Just Now," *Wall Street Journal*, 13 May 1986, p. 1; Alan Altshuler, Martin Anderson, Daniel Jones, Daniel Roos, and James Womack, *The Future of the Automobile* (Cambridge: MIT Press, 1984), 136; Shaiken, *Work Transformed*, 168.

22. Jack Thornton, "Robots—Is Long Expected Boom Underway?" *American Metal Market*, 12 October 1981, p. 12; Organization for Economic Cooperation and Development, *Long Term Outlook for the World Automobile Industry* (Paris: OECD, 1983), 99; H. Allen Hunt and Timothy L. Hunt, *Human Resource Implications of Robotics* (Kalamazoo, Mich.: Upjohn Institute for Employment Research, 1983), 3.

23. Harry C. Katz and Charles Sabel, "Industrial Relations and Industrial Adjustment," *Industrial Relations* 24 (1985): 298.

24. Dale D. Buss, "Unions Say Auto Firms Use Interplant Rivalry to Raise Work Quotas," *Wall Street Journal*, 7 November 1983, p. 1; "Detroit Gets a Break from UAW," *Business Week*, 30 November 1981, pp. 94–96; Iver Peterson, "Auto Workers Divide on Demands for Concessions," *New York Times*, 8 January 1982, p. 10. Management whipsawing threats played production facilities against each other. GM threatened two of six Fisher Body hardware plants with closure, unless it got work-rule changes amounting to a 20 percent productivity increase. Once these were conceded, the company threatened the other four plants with closure unless similar gains were conceded. Whipsawing touched off open bickering between local officials about who would get future work. Threatened with loss of their jobs, workers were often the most willing to make concessions. Such confrontations were repeated in plants throughout North America. See Alfonso A. Narvaez, "Linden, N.J., Local to Challenge Auto Pact Votes," *New York Times*, 10 April 1982, p. 9; *Assembler* [UAW Local 595], September 1982, p. 1.

25. Alfred S. Warren, Jr., to the UAW, letter of 21 March 1982, reprinted in *Assembler*, April 1982, p. 2.

26. For examples, see Frank Locricchio, "Shop Committee Chairman's Report," *Fleetwood Organizer*, May 1982; Tony Fernandez, "UAW 595: The President's Report," *Assembler*, March 1982, p. 2; Dave Yettaw, "Common Sense Killed GM Pact?" *Headlight* [UAW Local 599], 3 February 1982, p. 2.

27. Michael Brody, "Labor Showdown of the Decade," *Fortune*, 7 September 1984, p. 128.

28. Dale D. Buss and Melinda Grenier Guiles, "GM Pact Has Job-Security Gains but Isn't Assured of Ratification," *Wall Street Journal*, 24 September 1984, p. 3.

29. Donald Woutat, "Auto Pact Could Help to Keep Inflation Low," *Wall Street Journal*, 24 September 1984, p. 1.

30. Wood, "Another Turn of the Wheel," 7.
31. Katz and Sabel, "Industrial Relations," 310.
32. Victor Reuther, "Confrontation at Two Union Conventions: Auto Workers." *Union Democracy Review* 54 (1986); Jane Slaughter, "UAW Convention Debates 'Saturnization,'" *Labor Notes,* July 1986: 16.
33. See Paul Wagman, "Labor Department Sues to Force New UAW Election," *St. Louis Post-Dispatch,* 13 September 1986, p. 11A; Paul Wagman, "Vote Fraud Charged in UAW Election," *St. Louis Post-Dispatch,* 3 August 1986; David Moberg, "Democracy at Issue for UAW," *In These Times,* 22–28 October 1986, p. 2.
34. Jack Metzgar, "'Running the Plant Backwards' in UAW Region 5," *Labor Research Review* 7 (1985): 35–43; Dave Elsila, "Moog: The Saga of a Shop-Floor Victory," *Solidarity,* June 1982: 12–16; Joe Smith, Speech at Labor Notes conference, 15 November 1986, Dearborn, Michigan.
35. Glenn Perusek, "The U.S.–Canada Split in the United Automobile Workers," in *Proceedings of the 41st Annual Meeting of the Industrial Relations Research Association,* ed. Barbara Dennis (Madison, Wisc.: Industrial Relations Research Association, 1989), 272–78; Jane Slaughter, "Canadian UAW Severes Ties with International," *Labor Notes,* October 1985: 1, 12.
36. Harley Shaiken, "At Stake in Detroit," *New York Times,* 21 January 1982 p. 23; Dennis Farney, "House Clears 'Domestic Content' Measure for Autos Again," *Wall Street Journal,* 4 November 1983, p. 2; Howell Raines, "Move to Curb Competitiveness of Imports Rises as Focus at End of Campaign," *New York Times,* 25 October 1982, pp. II, 6; John Holusha, "Auto Unionists Narrowly Favor New G.M. Pact," *New York Times,* 10 April 1982, p. 1; Dale D. Buss, "Auto Makers Scheduling Overtime Instead of Recalling Idled Workers," *Wall Street Journal,* 9 August 1983, p. 35.
37. Jane Slaughter, "A Big Win for Auto Workers—in Canada," *Labor Notes,* December 1992: 1, 13.
38. Jim Woodward, "The Rules Have Changed; Our Unions Must Change, Too," *Labor Notes,* May 1992: 12.
39. "Caterpillar Seeks Approval for Halting Wages for Full-Time Union Officials," *Walls Street Journal,* 24 December 1992, p. 10.
40. John Fillion, Memo to Irving Bluestone, UAW Inter-Office Communication, 12 November 1973, in Leonard Woodcock Collection, Box 26.

8

The Airline Industry and Airline Unionism in the 1970s and 1980s

Andy Pollack

LIKE EVERY OTHER NATIONALLY prominent strike in the 1980s, the Eastern Airlines strike was going to be the one to turn the labor movement around. But in the end, Eastern's owner, Frank Lorenzo, was driven out of business. Eastern workers all lost their jobs, and generally, no new strategy was found in the course of the strike to translate militancy into success.

How did this happen? How much is this strike symptomatic of the peculiarities of the airline industry and its unions, and how much symptomatic of the general crisis of labor? How much was the loss due to objective difficulties, and how much to strategic failings? This chapter assesses the relative importance of these factors. It outlines the industry's structural features, both historically and in the more recent deregulated period. It also looks at the conscious decisions and actions of labor officials and rank and filers in relating to those structures. Finally, it evaluates the extent to which the results of this interaction between the industry's structures and union activity are unique to airline labor, as opposed to being symptomatic of the failings of the broader labor movement.

THE ATTACK ON AIRLINE LABOR UNDER DEREGULATION

Airline labor struggles in the 1980s set the stage for the Eastern strike in a most inauspicious manner. Hard on the heels of the 1981 defeat of the Professional Air Traffic Controllers (PATCO) strike came Lorenzo's busting of the unions at Continental in 1983. This strike occurred as concessions were becoming a nationwide trend and as strikes using routine tactics to resist concessions were proving to be ineffective (when they were resisted, which wasn't often). Next, in 1986, came the strike of the Independent Federation of Flight Attendants at TWA against Lorenzo's twin in piracy, Carl Icahn—a strike that failed in part because of the refusal of the International Association of Machinists (IAM) to walk out in sympathy.

During this same period, equally massive concessions were gained without strikes by the biggest, most profitable carriers—United and American. United got the Air Line Pilots' Association (ALPA) to agree in 1981 to reduce flight crew size from three to two. Two years later, American won the agreement of the Transport Workers Union to a two-tier wage system for mechanics, and soon such systems swept the industry—although American remained the carrier throughout the decade with the most B-scale workers. By 1985 *Fortune* magazine estimated that the two-tier wage system was bringing American $100 million a year.[1]

These concessions received less attention not only from the media but also, because of the industry's fragmented union structures, from workers in the rest of the industry. No identifiable villain à la Icahn or Lorenzo gained notoriety at these profitable carriers, yet the concessions extracted were just as large. The lack of attention to what was happening at the successful carriers helped reinforce the notion among workers at the weaker carriers that their problem stemmed from individual villains such as Lorenzo or Icahn.

The American and United agreements set off a wave of givebacks throughout the industry in the 1980s. ALPA gave concessions forty-five times between 1980 and 1984, and by the end of 1981 Continental, Pan Am, Republic, and Western (the last two soon to go out of business) had won 10 percent pay cuts and work-rule changes from most of their unions.[2]

Behind these concession demands lay a mixture of industry and societywide trends. The industry, on the one hand, went first through a headlong expansion after deregulation, then through a renewed consolidation. This occurred in the context of an economy in a steady decline—interrupted by an occasional "recovery" fueled by the same speculative manias sweeping the airline industry. Airlines were battling for survival in a newly competitive market, one shrinking due to the economy's crisis. At the same time, they had to pay off billions in debt acquired during the prior decades of expansion—as well as new debt incurred through leveraged buyouts (LBOs) used by corporate raiders taking advantage of the deregulated market.

Labor's response to the attack on Continental's unions is typical of the narrowness of its worldview. Lorenzo's tactics were seen as a direct outgrowth of deregulation, but the fight against Lorenzo was never conceived of as a jumping-off point for a union response to deregulation across the industry. The fight at Continental—and later at Eastern—thus remained an isolated one. Union officials paid lip service to its importance for all of labor, and workers could see how its outcome would affect their fates. But turning this awareness beyond the stage of moral or symbolic support and organizing it into effective solidarity actions would have required two steps that the union leadership was unwilling to take. First, it would require the creation of cross-union, cross-company solidarity structures to involve the ranks elsewhere in support for the strikers. Second, it would require fostering a discussion about industrywide goals in the fight against deregulation-era union-busting, thus making concrete the otherwise abstract sense that this strike had some relevance for workers at other carriers.

The Eastern Strike

After the 1983 defeat at Continental came struggles against demands for concessions at Eastern, then headed by Frank Borman. Like unions in other industries, the IAM participated in Quality of Work Life programs at Eastern in the mid-1980s and won seats on its board of directors.[3]

Union-management collaboration proved to be a one-way street. After the IAM official responsible for voting over four million shares of stock began using his power in the interests of the union members, Eastern went to court and got a ruling that the official was "conspiring with the union members on the board of directors"; as a result voting rights were taken away from the IAM and handed over to an "independent trust."[4] Meanwhile Borman began renewing concessions demands in November 1985, after a decade in which $10 billion in concessions had already been granted. There was some resistance to Borman; a rally of twelve thousand in Florida in July 1987 uniting all area unions against Eastern led to the formation of Jobs with Justice, a nationwide group that seeks to mobilize cross-union, cross-industry solidarity.[5] When Borman failed to gain concessions, Eastern was sold to Lorenzo.[6]

Until the bitter end of the strike, unionists remained loyal to Charlie Bryan, the innovative District 100 IAM leader. Bryan led in both the collaborative efforts and the resistance to management. When Bryan, despite his attempt to collaborate with management, put his foot down over further demands from Borman, the latter sold Eastern to Frank Lorenzo, who had already built a solid anti-union track record in the early 1980s at Continental, New York Air, and Peoples' Express.

For fifteen months the IAM resisted concession demands from Lorenzo, including wage and benefits cuts of 28 percent, totaling $150 million. In March 1989 the Machinists finally walked out and were joined in sympathy walkouts by the flight attendants, represented by the Transport Workers Union (TWU), and the pilots, represented by ALPA. An initial threat by IAM officials to shut down the East Coast's rail system was abandoned after a court issued an injunction against it; a similar threat to picket other airlines was dropped by IAM officials, who claimed that the traveling public would turn against the strikers.[7]

Had the IAM challenged the court's injunction—either in the streets or in court—it very well may not have stood up. Nothing in the Railway Labor Act (RLA) forbids secondary picketing of nonstruck carriers or railroads. In this sense the RLA is superior to the National Labor Relations Act which governs most U.S. workers. Even the Presidential Emergency Board, which is set up when the RLA-established National Mediation Board cannot achieve a settlement, can only make nonbinding recommendations to the parties involved. Nevertheless, judges, presidents, and Congress have time and again used concepts such as "national emergency" or vague threats presented by strikes to the public's convenience to issue injunctions, executive orders, or special legislation overriding the act.[8]

Throughout the strike few strikers went back to work, and much verbal support came from other unions—but nothing in the way of effective solidarity. This was due in part to the striking unions' focus on finding a new owner for Eastern and on securing federal intervention against Lorenzo rather than on organizing action to expand the strike. It was also due to the disinterest of labor officials in such action, a disinterest manifested in every landmark strike of the 1980s. Thus, for instance, when the Denver chapter of Jobs with Justice shut down that city's airport with a car caravan, they were ordered by the AFL-CIO to cease and desist from such actions. (They were accused of "dual unionism" for usurping the functions of the city's Central Labor Council— functions the latter never carried out!)[9]

Pilots voted to end their strike on 23 November and the flight attendants— who had stayed out all these months with no strike benefits from their unions, relying on skimpy handouts from the AFL-CIO Emergency Fund—followed suit the next day. The IAM stayed out until Eastern itself died in January 1991, when the carrier was dissolved in an auction of its remaining routes and gates.

The Eastern strike stands out as the airline struggle with the highest degree of cross-union unity, of resistance to management demands, and of awareness, if only in words, throughout the labor movement of the struggle's broader significance (including, unlike in the P-9 or Watsonville struggles, awareness by the top of the AFL-CIO hierarchy).[10] Industry-specific problems of craft divisions—most strikes in the industry heretofore had been by only one craft at one carrier—and the general hesitancy to strike at all, or for very long, were evident throughout the country. Strikers fought under two banners: resistance to the evil Lorenzo, and setting an example for a besieged labor movement. As we will see below, this dichotomy in goals proved to be telling.

This strike, like other landmark strikes in the 1980s, showed that a willingness to strike was not enough to win in this period. Precisely because all unions at the carrier hung together, in contrast to normal industry practice, the inadequacy of the routine strike strategy stands out most starkly. One cannot blame the strike's failure on betrayal by a sector of the leadership, or a failure of one part of the struck company's workforce to support the rest, or a lack of awareness of the strike's significance. Why, then, couldn't "normal" strike tactics not work?

First, Lorenzo and other owners, each for different reasons, were willing to let Eastern go out of business rather than give in to the strikers. Lorenzo, as the strikers correctly pointed out, is not an "airline man"; that is, his attachment is to the bottom line and not to the industry. Even within the industry, his interests were spread across the Texas Air empire, which included not only Eastern and its Boston–New York–D.C. shuttle but also Continental—all controlled through his holding company, Jet Capital Corporation. One of the provocations leading to the strike in fact was Lorenzo's shifting of assets away from Eastern to his other, nonunion, companies. The other owners, because of their desire to use deregulation to squeeze out the weaker carriers, were perfectly happy to see Eastern fail—especially since the strike clearly wasn't going to be brought to their doors.

This shakeout of the weaker carriers was only the particular form taken in this industry by various nationwide trends: concessions, deregulation, plant closures, and so on—all within an economywide, decades-long decline in profitability.[11] As such, the battle at Eastern could have been used both to develop strategies for fights against these broader trends both within and outside the industry. Instead, the leaders of both the IAM and AFL-CIO chose to pose the strike merely as a fight against the crimes of a particularly crude union buster.

The strikers' attitude toward Lorenzo captured the limitations of this approach. On the one hand, they were willing to see the carrier and their jobs go under rather than submit to his demands. On the other hand, they were willing to give more concessions than Lorenzo was asking to several potential "white knights" because, for lack of an industrywide approach, they believed their jobs depended on the survival of Eastern as a unit. With one exception (described below) there has never been multicarrier bargaining or strike action, even though both are legal under the RLA. Workers who for decades pursued better contracts on a company-by-company basis are now understandably viewing their job survival as tied to the fate of their company.

This was not inevitable. In 1966 the IAM launched a strike against five carriers, winning most of their demands. Yet this example was never repeated, much less developed into industrywide pattern or joint bargaining. In fact, many workers I talked to during the Eastern strike had never heard of the 1966 strike and were under the erroneous impression that multicarrier strikes are illegal under the Railway Labor Act.[12]

Both at the very beginning of the Eastern strike and near the end, the specter of industrial action by non-Eastern workers was raised and quickly abandoned. Plans had been laid to put up picket lines not only around other airlines but around railroads on the East Coast. This action, entirely legal under the Railway Labor Act,[13] was called off at the last minute, allegedly for fear of "alienating the public"—despite the fact that some of the rail unions involved were themselves in negotiations and were eager for a chance to walk out. Before the strike, the IAM newspaper had even pledged to pull out its members at other carriers—a pledge not only never carried out, but one that many members never even knew had been made.

In August 1989, as the strike was sputtering out, ALPA's Eastern Master Executive Council (MEC) unanimously asked its parent body to organize a one-day suspension of service (that is, a nationwide strike) in support of a legislative investigation into the fitness of Frank Lorenzo to continue operating both Eastern and Continental Airlines. This action, too, had a fair chance of succeeding: Three-quarters of ALPA members industrywide were in negotiations at that time.[14] Some IAM locals, led by Local Lodge 796 in Washington, D.C., began circulating this resolution to other IAM locals. But the national

ALPA leadership refused to put this motion up for a vote by the MECs at other carriers.[15]

The call for the suspension of service was focused solely on the situation at Eastern, and even more narrowly on the fitness of Lorenzo to run the carrier. The call was not made in support of specific wage or work-rule demands against Lorenzo's concessions drive. By this point in the strike, all the unions had offered to make concessions to a sought-for white knight twice as large as those Lorenzo was seeking. The most prominent partisan of this white-knight strategy was Charlie Bryan, who throughout the strike was frequently heard announcing that he had just come from, or was going to, meetings with potential buyers for the carrier. Bryan also announced plans for an "acquisition trust" to buy the carrier, to which he donated $100,000 of his own money.[16]

This white-knight strategy derives from the tendency of airline unions to mimic ALPA's lead in seeking to out-lawyer and out-invest management. We shall see below how this strategy flows from both industry peculiarities as well as classwide conservatism.

Complementing this strategy was another, equally doomed: the attempt to force Lorenzo into bankruptcy court, which kept the struggle on the terrain of who owned Eastern rather than on the strikers' jobs, wages, and working conditions. Later, the unions sought a congressional bill for federal intervention into the strike. Congress refused to call for the requested emergency board, instead proposing a bipartisan commission to recommend settlement terms. When even this was vetoed by President Bush, the pilots voted to return to work. Neither the bankruptcy court nor congressional avenues were useless as secondary tactics—but for lack of effective strike action, there was no reason to think that governmental officials in either sphere would be scared enough of labor's clout to meet their demands.

Even as a tactic, however, the congressional approach had problems. Congress has repeatedly used its alleged emergency powers under the RLA to impose management's final offers on railroad workers, precedents that airline union officials should have made clear to their own ranks. Unlike in other countries, where all transport workers are in one union, rail and airline workers in the United States are separated from each other—and isolated by craft and company even within their own industry. This fragmentation limits workers' knowledge of and ability to act on such basic history lessons as Congress's strikebreaking record.

Also near the end of the strike came the linkage of the flight attendants' union, TWU Local 553, with Ray Rogers's Corporate Campaign. Among other activities, including a consumer boycott of Lorenzo's other carrier, Continental (as well as SAS, part-owner of Continental), Rogers led a caravan from Miami to New York—a caravan not joined by ALPA and IAM, who instead started their own independent caravan.

Shortly after the Eastern strike was defeated, Pan Am and Braniff went out of business, and TWA, Northwest, and Continental were headed either for death or absorption—in either case certainly leading to further job loss and concessions. The Eastern unions claimed the strike shows an employer would pay the price for busting strikes, but this is a rather Pyrrhic victory, and one, moreover, that has done nothing to generalize the courage and militancy of the strikers into an industrywide trend.

How did labor come to such a pass? How much is due to the specifics of the industry and its unions, how much to the general problems of U.S. labor, and how much to the conscious formation of policy and strategy—especially the lack of any leadership pursuing either industrywide or classwide strategy?

THE UNIONS

Airline unions are governed by the Railway Labor Act. This means, on the one hand, that they do not enjoy access to the National Labor Relations Board— for example, they cannot file unfair labor practice charges or call upon any of the precedents set by the board. On the other hand, the RLA frees airline unions to take actions that are illegal for unions governed by the National Labor Relations Act (NLRA), such as secondary boycotts and picketing of nonstruck carriers.

When the first airline union, the Airline Pilots Association, was established in the 1930s, labor leaders and management agreed to put the industry under the strictures of the RLA instead of the brand-new National Labor Relations Act. The RLA says in so many words that the procedures in the act to authorize a strike are purposely designed to slow the process and to minimize the number of strikes. The act lists as one of its purposes "avoid[ing] any interruption to commerce or to the operation of any carrier."

The RLA was first written in response to the nationwide rail strikes of 1920s, which came as a climax to a movement for amalgamation of the rail unions led by the Trade Union Educational League. This movement in turn drew inspiration from Eugene V. Debs's earlier attempt to unify these unions into his American Railway Union after the defeat of the Pullman strike of 1894 (and before that of the nationwide general strike of 1877 sparked by a rail strike). Each of these upsurges in rail threw up new, more militant leaderships with broader strategies—something yet to evolve in the air.[17]

ALPA's request at its birth that airline unionism be governed by the Railway Labor Act rather than the recently enacted National Labor Relations Act set the stage for decades ahead, fostering craft unionism, occupational segregation, and infrequent strikes. The RLA declares a preference for single-company, single-craft bargaining—although it doesn't forbid multicarrier or multicraft bargaining and even refers in passing to strikes that can legally arise from the latter. But it has steered all-too-willing union officials toward the narrower bargaining forms.

Another consequence of the act's encouragement of such fragmented bargaining is its impact in reinforcing segregation of occupations, thus hindering the development of industrywide consciousness. Unlike in steel or auto, there is no bidding and training for promotion up the craft ladder: Flight attendants don't become pilots, ramp service workers don't become mechanics, and so on. This occupational segregation reinforces (and is reinforced by) the race and gender discrepancies between crafts.

Unions in the industry include ALPA, representing all pilots except those at American (who are represented by the Allied Pilots Association); the International Association of Machinists and the Transport Workers Union, representing mechanics and ramp service workers; and a variety of flight attendants' unions. Less prominent are the handful of unions representing reservations and ticket agents and clerical workers at some of the carriers (this is the only occupational sector of the workforce not thoroughly organized. Also unorganized is Delta–except for its pilots—and the ramp service workers at USAir, whose Teamster local was decertified in 1991).

ALPA represents an extreme case of craft unionism, both in terms of the job's skill and training requirements and in the type of attitudes and unionism the job has fostered. Many ALPA members are former Navy and Air Force pilots, and they carry with them the extreme chauvinism of the military. As such, they are often the butts of jokes by flight attendants responding to their elitism and sexism. The solidarity displayed during the Eastern strike by ALPA toward its fellow unions on the property was deemed notable by the latter precisely because such solidarity represented a break with ALPA's historic go-it-alone ethos.

Like other skilled trades unions, ALPA is almost exclusively white and male, and also like those unions, its high dues enables it to spend lavishly on showy, if not necessarily politically consequential, organizing projects. ALPA was the innovator in recorded messages, computer hookups, nationwide videoconferences, and so on. More significantly, ALPA has spent enormous amounts of dues money on high-priced legal and investment advice in its efforts to go head-to-head with airline owners in attempts to purchase carriers in trouble or in contract disputes. In other words, its craft mentality and opportunities have meant that even at its most militant—during the Eastern strike—its strategy mimicked that of the airline bosses and sought to play on their turf. That strategy was in turn mimicked by other unions in the industry.

Whereas ALPA can be viewed as the industry's "natural" AFL-type union, the mechanics and ramp service workers can be seen as the industry's "natural" CIO-type constituency, that is, a mixture of skilled, semiskilled, and unskilled blue-collar workers like that found in the industries organized by various CIO unions in the 1930s and 1940s. And in fact much of this sector was organized during that period—but with two twists hindering their effectiveness.

First, they were not organized by one union—some were organized by an old AFL union, the IAM, and some by a newer CIO union, the TWU. Second, neither of these were industrial unions in the sense that most CIO unions were.

The IAM, originally an AFL craft union for mechanics, began to expand during the 1930s, as did other AFL unions feeling the heat of CIO competition, and it organized in new industries in a new way, gathering mechanics as well as the unskilled into the same local lodges. The TWU started out as a typical CIO union based in one industry—municipal transport workers—and with a militant leadership drawn from the Communist Party milieu. But ironically, this industrial character failed to benefit the airline workers who became an appendage to that traditional base—especially as the bureaucracy ruling that base increasingly divorced itself from its original leftist traditions.[18]

The end result for both unions, because of the eventual dovetailing in both strategy and organizational form of the AFL and CIO, was the formation of conglomerate unions, thus diluting the common political interests of members in any particular industry.[19] This conglomerate, nonindustrial nature took shape during the period when the militancy that had achieved the original breakthrough—industrywide organizing—was dying. Many thought that, after organizing whole industries, the CIO unions would move on to various social and political tasks. Instead, they reverted to a more conservative, routine state even while their conglomerate nature meant that they embraced workers in many industries.

A final irony is that, although today the IAM is more reflective than the TWU of the liberal business unionism of former CIO unions like the United Auto Workers, this liberalism proved to be inadequate to the tasks posed by the Continental and Eastern strikes (as it has for the UAW in its battles, or rather lack thereof, against auto manufacturers' concessions drives).

There is another peculiarity facing those unions organizing the airline's "natural" CIO-type constituency. In most industrial unions a wide range of jobs and skill levels coexisted, and while there has been tension between, say, the skilled trades in the UAW and the semiskilled and unskilled members, the range of jobs is large enough to make their differences less obvious than their difference from the common management enemy. For the IAM and TWU, in contrast, given the inordinate dependence of the industry on mechanical maintenance, there are only two major occupations in this part of the workforce, mechanics and ramp service workers, with relatively unimportant subgradations. This has sometimes created tension, a tension currently being exploited by a new craft union, the American Mechanics Fraternal Association, which has conducted numerous raids. This tension is a microcosm of the extreme occupational segregation between the industry's other crafts.

The flight attendants are, in job characteristics and demographics, representative of the new, predominantly female, service sectors partially organized in the last three decades. They are represented by seven different unions: Association of Flight Attendants, Association of Professional Flight Attendants, Independent Union of Flight Attendants, Independent Federation of Flight Attendants, Union of Flight Attendants, Transport Workers Union, and International Brotherhood of Teamsters. This organizational chaos came from a series of splits from sexist parent unions (ALPA and TWU) in the 1960s and 1970s. But this process reached fruition at different times and in different ways at each company. For lack of an organization seeking to regroup these splitoffs into one union for all flight attendants, the common battle against sexism and the rise in militancy that accompanied the birth of new flight attendant unions have been splintered across organizational lines.

The departure from parent unions happened in several ways. First, the Association of Flight Attendants, which has the franchise from the AFL-CIO, split from ALPA. Second, the Independent Union of Flight Attendants (that is, until the demise of Pan Am, its sole carrier) and the Independent Federation of Flight Attendants at TWA split from the TWU. Third, there was a political but not organizational dissent from the TWU: most leaders and members of TWU Local 553, representing Eastern flight attendants, drew the same conclusions as had other carriers' flight attendants about the conservatism and sexism of their International's leadership, but these conclusions were manifested in alternative policies and behavior within the union rather than splitting from it. Local 553 displayed a militancy on strike against Eastern wholly foreign to today's parent body; what's more, 553 delegates voted with reformers at the union's convention in 1989 in the midst of the strike, when the local had the most to fear by way of retribution from the International leadership (and in fact as the strike fell apart Local 553 was put into receivership and its leadership marginalized).[20]

All these splits, fueled by recognition of male unionists' sexism, occurred during a period of rising militancy among women in the country in general, and flight attendant battles often provided further fuel for the broader women's movement. Many flight attendants became activists in groups such as the Coalition of Labor Union Women and the National Organization for Women (the latter is currently headed by a former Pan Am flight attendant). Yet the "double burden" faced by flight attendants—as underrepresented workers and discriminated-against women—has not yet produced a unified organizational response to this burden, in the form, for instance, of one union for all flight attendants that could consolidate the fight on both fronts (although sporadic networking efforts have sprung up).

Despite extreme racial segregation, there has never been a parallel movement among black workers seeking justice within their unions. Reinforcing racial discrimination in the industry, beyond the occupational segregation already described, are the two-tier wage system and the various low-wage fueling, maintenance, and catering firms that service the carriers; these are disproportionately staffed by people of color.[21]

Clerks and reservations and ticket agents were represented by the Teamsters at Pan Am; the IAM represents those at TWA. Those at other carriers have never been successfully organized.

The result of this organizational fragmentation has been the absence of industrywide bargaining, whether in the form of multiemployer contracts or even pattern-bargaining. The only exception to this disunity in bargaining was the 1966 IAM five-carrier strike. This fragmentation was formed during the days of regulation, a period that also, because of a less intense competitive atmosphere and decades of expansion of the industry, provided relatively easier bargaining opportunities for airline labor. This situation paralleled that of unions in unregulated but heavily concentrated or otherwise unusually stable industries. By the same token airline unions suffered from the same inability experienced by other unions in failing to figure out strategic responses to their particular woes when that hegemony ended, and regulation, concentration, and stable profits vanished. Thus the "leapfrogging" over regulation, which allowed unions to gain one-by-one successively better contracts, has turned into a reverse leapfrogging of more and more concessions and jobs lost.

Consciousness of this parallel between airline labor's woes and the classwide situation was reflected in what workers said about the Eastern strike. This was the one, they hoped, that would turn around the fortunes of airline workers in particular and the country's labor movement in general. We learned from our mistake in not supporting PATCO, thousands of strikers and their supporters said. Yet this consciousness of the broader stakes of the strike was constrained by the organizational limits described above—as was also the case in strikes in other industries in the 1990s, each of which in turn had been looked to as the long-hoped-for end to the movement's decline, the one that would turn the labor movement around. But although the strikes at Eastern (and earlier at TWA) were fought with a militancy and determination reflecting those stakes, the tactics and goals chosen reflected instead the particular organizational divisions of the industry's unions. They also reflected a shaping of that legacy by the industry's characteristics, which I will discuss next.

This peculiar fragmentation of airline labor highlights a broader sociological peculiarity of labor movements. When the industrial unionism of the CIO ran out of steam and then converged with the traditions of the AFL, it left several of its tasks uncompleted—including the elimination of craft unionism, which survives in a sense as a vestige, that is, as organizational forms that have been proven to be less effective and advanced—and this is true in industries such as the airline industry, where the objective necessity for an industrial approach has long been obvious.

THE INDUSTRY

Regulation, which existed from the industry's origins until 1978, encouraged union passivity, as relatively secure profits led to a relatively stable bargaining field. Labor failed to develop either a general strategy for the deregulated environment as a whole or special tactics for the weakest carriers, which went under first in the second phase of deregulation, the reconsolidation of the industry. And of course airline labor functioned within a labor movement unable to develop responses to macroeconomic assaults on its standards.

The relatively new (in a historical sense) airline industry experienced its first major and prolonged slump in the 1970s. Until that decade, recessions were less significant in determining labor's fate than were the stronger expansionary tendencies of this relatively new industry. The nonstop growth of markets, of equipment innovation and of organizational advances was more salient for its growth rates than were macroeconomic events such as recessions. By the same token, this meant that labor, from the birth of the industry until deregulation, was on a generally upward curve, organizing new sectors and achieving new contract gains as it sought to catch up to previously organized sectors of the economy. The 1966 IAM strike, for instance, was posed as a chance to catch up to mechanics' wages in other industries. The organization of flight attendants in the 1960s and 1970s reflected a twofold process: on the one hand a part of a nationwide trend of organization of predominantly female sectors, on the other hand the completion of an unfulfilled task within the airline industry, as comparisons were made with contracts and rights achieved earlier in "male" crafts.

Thus airline labor, when deregulation hit in 1979, had never suffered through a major depression or industrywide cutback, had no legacy of struggle against such an occurrence to fall back on, and had no organized rank-and-file opposition to import such lessons from other industries. This meant in particular that no leadership interpreted deregulation as a symptom of societywide trends, thus enhancing the tendency to interpret concessions demands as the work of individual "villains" like Lorenzo or Icahn.

Within this context, two peculiar technological and organizational structures of the airlines shaped labor's lack of response to deregulation.

First the occupational segregation described above, although structured by management, was never challenged by union leaders. No fight was ever launched for the contractual right to advance by seniority from one craft to another. Ironically the limited number of crafts, four or five, versus the ten, twenty, or more in other industries, makes their rigid separation seem more "natural." The notion that unions would fight for the right of flight attendants to become pilots or reservations agents to become mechanics is simply never discussed.

And second, the success or failure of carriers—and thus their demands for labor concessions—are played out in a unique marketing structure, which itself is shaped by a unique range of technological and financial concerns.

Airlines are constantly adding and shedding routes, and in the deregulation period were consolidating their hold on a given route structure by centralizing these routes through particular airport hubs. But when routes get sold or carriers merge, the workers servicing those routes don't go with them, for lack of effective labor protective provisions (LPPs) or national legislation.[22]

How carriers change their route structure depends on some factors that are common to other industries, such as product differentiation (in this case better service or more comfortable planes), economies in costs, and price wars (although these are unusual given the tight oligopoly in the industry). But most significant is the economies of scale that benefit the biggest carriers. What has proven to be key in the post-1979 period is the extent of a carrier's domestic route system; the weakest carriers have been those such as Pan Am, TWA, and Eastern, whose strength before 1979 was primarily overseas.

Finally, the tools with which carriers battle over routes are also unique. At one end in time frame and expense are the industry's biggest capital investment, its aircraft. Planes must be ordered years in advance, and designs for new models are developed years before that. Billions of dollars must be set aside across a similarly long time span to purchase aircraft, making the industry more dependent than most on loans from banks, insurance companies, aircraft and engine manufacturers or leasing companies, and so on.

In the middle range in price and time frame are the carrier's routes. Entry and exit into particular routes involves not only their purchase, and gaining approval from the Departments of Transportation and Justice, but also buying gate and terminal space from airport authorities, supplying and staffing those facilities with workers and equipment, and similar considerations.

In the short term—in this case an extremely short term—are price changes. Because of the computerization of reservations and ticket sales, airlines juggle dozens of fare categories on each of the hundreds of routes they service. Every day these Computerized Reservations Systems (CRSs) change back and forth the number of seats available for purchase in each of these categories on all of those routes. Overlaying this process is the regular announcement of discount sales covering all or most categories of fares; most significantly, a sale announced by one carrier, typically covering most of its routes, is immediately matched by most or all of the others—or if not matched, is dropped within days by the initiator for fear of retaliation (and in fact sometimes price changes are signaled in the CRSs even though there is no intention to implement them: They serve instead as warning signs to a competitor to stop considering entry into a market).

The successful carriers, that is, the ones that can consolidate strong route structures, are those whose managements can juggle the various strategies to deal with these extremely different needs: long-term investment in aircraft, medium-term route transfers, and short-term fare changes. Unfortunately, unions have bought into management's claim that labor costs, rather than the exigencies of management strategy, are to blame for carrier success or failure.

Management uses a variety of technological and organizational tools to enhance its survival strategy, that is, as a way of balancing its short-, medium-, and long-term constraints. These include frequent flyer programs and expanding their monopolization of hubs and of CRSs. In 1990 a congressional study showed that eight major carriers held 95 percent of the landing slots, with 20- to 40-year leases on gates. This was before the death of Pan Am and Eastern.

The main winners in the deregulated period, then, are those who started with a solid domestic route system and added to it foreign routes, as well as associated equipment (both CRSs and aircraft), in a slow, incremental fashion.

These winners, which include American, United and Delta, also forced concessions on their workers, but in a similarly low-key—and tactically wiser—fashion. Although the first concessions in the industry were granted at Braniff, United was next when it got ALPA to agree in 1981 to reduce flight crew size from three to two. This set off the concessions wave described earlier.

The industry leaders set off a trend of givebacks. ALPA gave concessions forty-five times between 1980 and 1984, and by the end of 1981 Continental, Pan Am, Republic, and Western (in the second and third tiers of the industries) had won 10 percent pay cuts and work-rule changes from most of their unions.

Yet neither United nor American adopted the across-the-board, openly union-busting tactics often used by those in the next category—those who have failed or are on the verge of doing so. This category includes those with a primarily foreign base who were unable to add sufficient domestic routes to feed that base, such as TWA and Pan Am.[23] It also includes Frank Lorenzo, whose empire included Eastern, which had both a domestic and foreign route structure—although less so in both spheres than those dominant in only one of these sectors. It also included—most significantly from a management tactical perspective—Continental, which declared bankruptcy in order to get out of union contracts when it was trying to compete with the new, low-fare carriers of early deregulation days. That is, Continental chose not to try to become a fourth wheel to the big three (United, Delta, and American).

Perhaps the most visible result of competition between airlines is the relatively more rapid entry and exit, birth and death, of carriers. This reinforces the notion that union survival means carrier survival, and thus fosters strategies geared toward finding white knight buyers. However, this same firm instability could, with an alternative strategy and set of goals, lead to a diametrically opposite consciousness; that is, the instability of the industry's firms could become a rationale for unions to fight for industrywide demands such as LPPs, thus taking jobs and wages "out of competition."

Union structures thus failed in two respects. First, they failed to educate their members that the exigencies of management strategy, and not labor costs, determined carrier success, thus leaving members' prey to a belief that concessions were needed to make "their" carrier survive. Second, they failed to fight against concessions at the strong carriers, which even by management's own arguments were "unnecessary."

In these two respects the airline labor story parallels that elsewhere. The first failing resembles that of the UAW at Chrysler, the second of the UAW at GM. In some ways it should have been easier for unions to argue against concessions at weak carriers, since passengers continued to fly on the routes abandoned by weak or dead carriers.[24] But to do so would have required an industrywide approach—an approach that could then have led to development of a strategy for dealing with macroeconomic shifts affecting both strong and weak carriers.

Unions did rail against "mismanagement," poor service, and so on at the weaker carriers, demonizing owners like Icahn and Lorenzo. But the particular way in which they argued that labor should not pay the price for their mistakes doomed their efforts: Rather than fighting for LPPs, they pursued white knight buyers or even employee ownership; that is, they sought to find a "good" or "successful" manager. This even though the unions railed against deregulation as a whole. In this failure they shared the fate of labor elsewhere who fought for Employee Stock Ownership Plans (ESOPs) instead of nationalization, or pursued Quality of Work Life or team concept schemes, in either case assuming the survival of the firm was key to labor's survival. The airlines are only a more extreme example, given the more rapid entry and exit of firms and owners from the industry—a rapidity that forced the question of ownership and management "quality" into the consciousness of workers.

Management and government strategies in the air overlapped with those used in other industries. Deregulation occurred in this same period in trucking, energy, banking, and telecommunications. And it was obviously not just airlines which experienced LBOs and debt-fueled mergers. All the unions in the industry were aware of the multi-industry nature of these trends and often reported on them in their publications. Some, especially the social democratic ones like the IAM with large, efficient research departments, tried to inform members about such industry- and economywide phenomena. Often, too, they would call for legislative restrictions on debt-financed purchases of airlines, use of bankruptcy to evade unions, reversal of Reagan's tax breaks for the rich, and so on. But this recognition on paper of the need for broader solutions was never framed in either contractual or legislative goals—again reinforcing the narrow focus on the use of LBOs, for instance, by the "bad managers," while ignoring the equally exploitive two-tier wage systems instituted by the "good managers" at carriers like American.

SOME OBJECTIVE BASES FOR INDUSTRYWIDE STRATEGIES

Is this picture unique to the airline industry and its unions? I believe not; the extreme fragmentation of its unions, the instability of its firms, its peculiar technology and organizational structure highlight trends found in other industries and perhaps make more visible the sources of labor's difficulties. Airline workers share with other workers the difficulty of learning, through proper organizational and political strategies, how to see the forest for the trees, how to integrate the awareness of its tasks at a particular carrier with its fate in the industry and the economy as a whole.

Such a broader vision, if adopted by unions at the outset of deregulation, would have meant turning fights at particular carriers in the lower tier into broader industrywide fights. Unions could have developed joint movements to take wages, conditions, benefits, and especially employment levels "out of competition." Through pattern-bargaining or through legislative demands, they could have sought to establish standards on an industrywide basis not subject to the vicissitudes of a particular company's profitability.

Frequent flyer programs, the hub-and-spoke system, and limited gate facilities at airports are tools used by management to reconcentrate the industry. Yet the strategic opportunities presented by this reconcentration have yet to be realized by the industry's unions. By the same token, the cost of aircraft, which makes airlines as a group dependent on a handful of financial institutions—in fact making several airlines often dependent on the same ones—presents labor with a strategic target rarely taken advantage of. Thus when Corporate Campaign went after the banks and insurance companies behind American or Eastern, they pointed out the interwoven threads linking Wall Street and the carriers, the implication being that these threads proved the need for a solidaristic strategy among unions at different airlines and between airline workers and workers in other industries (such as steel) affected by LBOs and similar management/Wall Street strategies.

Computerized Reservations Systems are the clearest example of the industry's technological unity. There are only a handful of major CRSs, and the biggest are shared by three or more carriers. The majority of travel agents purchase access to the biggest of this handful. (The travel agency industry is itself increasingly concentrated, with most of the business dominated by the three major agencies, Thomas Cook, Liberty, and American Express. Labor needs to begin exploring the possibilities of organizing these outfits.) Most importantly each CRS carries all the essential information carried on all the others. Times, costs, and capacity for all flights on all carriers are accessible to any CRS user regardless of which system one is accessing; there might be a difference in which carrier's flight appears first on your screen and how much information on that flight is available (such discrepancies frequently being the subject of lawsuits). But no seller of seats on an aircraft can afford to not know what all competitors are doing on any given route.[25]

Some liberal trustbusters have argued that ownership of these systems be separated from the carriers as a means of lessening the oligopolistic outcome of deregulation.[26] I believe instead that the objective socialization represented by these systems—and the wealth of information that reservations and travel agents glean every day from them—could be used to demonstrate the rationality of industrywide strategies for pattern-bargaining, legislative protection, even nationalization.[27] By virtue of its access to computerized displays of patterns of industry sales, pricing, traffic, and so on, labor can easily document its case for industrywide demands; that is, in some senses thanks to these computers labor does not need to demand of management that it "open the books"—many of the chapters are already open! (Reservations agents I worked with at Pan Am frequently referred to statistics on their screens to document their opinions about such things as the injustice of particular management policies or the state of the industry's economics.)

The Railway Labor Act itself poses both industrywide opportunities and problems. As mentioned above, secondary boycotts and picketing of nonstruck carriers is permitted by the RLA; workers in the air thus have a weapon not available (at least legally) to workers governed by the NLRA. Of course this legal right has been undercut by congressional strikebreaking in both 1991 and 1992, when Congress ordered railworkers back to work. However, like management abuse of the NLRB, this strikebreaking could not have happened had Congress not sensed that labor was unwilling to use the power available to it under the law; a defiance of Congress's back-to-work order might have enabled the unions to prove to the public that it was Congress that was breaking the provisions of the act. On the other hand, the RLA's strike-delaying features should long ago have become a focus for an industrywide effort to change the law.[28]

An example of this industrywide approach to job retention had already been provided by the government when it crafted deregulation—and was quickly ignored, even by the unions. The Deregulation Act contained a provision for a "National Hiring Hall" to find jobs for workers displaced by deregulation. This provision was never implemented for two reasons: first, because industry hiring boomed in the immediate post-deregulation period, and second, because those jobs that were lost were claimed by the carriers and the government to have fallen prey to "market forces" and not to deregulation, that is, to the "natural" outcome of competition and not to some defect in the deregulation act. (Neither management nor the government explained this distinction without a difference, which is odd considering that deregulation was justified as a pro-market act.)

By the mid-1980s, strikes, layoffs, and carrier failures had put many unemployed airline workers on the labor market. Yet unions never demanded, for instance, that those strikers fired from Continental or TWA have access to this National Hiring Hall. In any case the provision had a ten-year limit—which is about when it began to really be needed to deal with jobs lost during the industry's reconsolidation.

One final example of an objective opportunity foregone by union fragmentation: the failure of unions representing pilots or mechanics to benefit from industrywide increases in demand for their labor in the 1980s. The shibboleth about the correlation between the size of the reserve army of labor and labor quiescence, while containing some truth, ignores how that correlation gets played out organizationally at particular firms by particular unions in the face of particular management strategies. A mechanic on strike at Eastern, for instance, may know he can get a job at American or Delta—but with no seniority at second-tier wages.

WHERE WILL A NEW STRATEGY COME FROM?

Above I outlined some of the objective bases provided by the industry structure for cross-carrier goals. Taking advantage of these presumes creating union structures to mobilize for these goals.

Examples of cross-craft, cross-carrier solidarity are not unheard of even in existing union structures. Pilots in ALPA have a Master Executive Council with representatives from each carrier. During the Eastern strike this MEC levied contributions from non-Eastern pilots to support strikers, and this was the body that considered (but unfortunately rejected) the motion by Eastern pilots for an industrywide pilots' strike. This was also the body that took polls of all ALPA members on whether to continue such contributions. Hostility from pilots toward MEC leaders who proposed calling off the contributions and then the strike led to a turnover in national ALPA leadership near the end of the strike—a hostility not only from Eastern pilots but also from those at other carriers who saw the handwriting on the wall for themselves if such lack of solidarity prevailed. The new leadership, however, soon proved to be no more militant.

The point is that new, consciously crafted broader structures can develop what Rick Fantasia calls "cultures of solidarity."[29] That is, these broader structures become the setting for discussions of industrywide problems that otherwise get relegated to informal griping sessions among isolated friends or work groups. These structures can then become the setting for proposals of alternative policies and tactics. In one sense this statement is nothing more than a commonplace; the whole point of unions in the abstract is a recognition of the relationship between unity in structure and joint cultural beliefs (in this case solidarity). This chapter simply explains how this commonplace has manifested itself in the airline industry given its peculiarities. But whether looking at the choice of ALPA leaders to foist the RLA on the new industry; of the IAM to call a five-carrier strike; of sexist unions to ignore flight attendant concerns, and of the flight attendants to form several new unions; each of these decisions, constrained by industry peculiarities, was also consciously chosen from among several alternatives.

A final example: In April 1990 (by which point the Eastern strike was withering) the Air Transport Industry Division of the IAM proposed several structural reforms to enhance solidarity, including a multicarrier master agreement and multiunion coalitions at each carrier. Halting steps toward the last goal were taken during negotiations later that year with United, but in general the proposal seems not to have been seriously implemented.

What is needed then is a new, rank-and-file-led movement to begin proposing and creating broader structures. Some of the measures such a movement would advocate are listed in an article by Kim Moody in *Labor Notes*: coordinated bargaining, synchronized expiration dates, respecting other unions' picket lines, use of the secondary boycott, and standardization of wages, benefits, and work rules. Fighting for these would necessitate forming cross-craft, cross-carrier mobilizing structures, for instance, airport-based strike committees open to all workers at each airport, which could then forge links to surrounding communities and other unions.[30]

A new strategy would also entail a new political approach. For lack of same, even the choice of who gets labeled villains in the industry has been rather peculiar. The architect in Congress of deregulation was Ted Kennedy, a political ally of IAM head William Winpisinger. Kennedy's aide in crafting the legislation, Phil Bakes, went on to become Lorenzo's right-hand man. Yet the role of Kennedy and the Democratic Party in general never became an issue during the Eastern strike.

Finally, although the theme of this chapter has been the failure of an industrywide perspective and how this failure is symptomatic of general classwide problems, I would argue that airline labor cannot advance by simply "going back" to an industrial approach. Already they are faced with the globalization of the industry and the need for international solidarity, when they have yet to forge solidarity within the United States. More generally, unions must begin to develop a new strategy based as much on a social as on an industrial analysis. Put another way, an industrial perspective would have already posed some social questions. Most obvious are the race and gender segregations obscured by the lack of an industrial bargaining structure. Also, answering the questions of who runs the industry as a whole and how labor can stand up to them will pose multi-industry questions that soon become social and political: Who, and why, determined in the past and today whether passengers and freight are transported by air, rail, or car? What social needs are met by such transport?

Addressing such questions would eventually lead to the crafting of legislative demands for public control and financing of the transport sector; the first step down that road will come through solidarity actions between militants fighting in any one industry within that sector. Taking that first step will raise again the unresolved task set by the creation of the CIO: the translation of militancy in particular industries into classwide militancy, and solidarity across industry lines.

Notes

1. For an overview of these events and their relationship to the fate of the broader labor movement, see Kim Moody, *An Injury to All: The Decline of American Unionism* (New York: Verso, 1988), chap. 8; and Kim Moody, *Airlines: An Industry in Crisis* (Detroit: Labor Notes Pamphlet, 1991).
2. See Moody, *Airlines: An Industry in Crisis.*
3. See Paul J. Baicich, "'Worker Participation' Doesn't End Eastern's Concession Demands," *Labor Notes*, January 1986: 1.
4. See Paul J. Baicich and W. R. Brown, "Labor Cooperation Experiment Collapses at Eastern Airlines," *Labor Notes*, January 1987.
5. The rally featured rank and filers and officials from the three unions at Eastern, as well as the heads of the National Rainbow Coalition, National Organization for Women, Southern Christian Leadership Conference, and the Florida Consumers Federation.

   The activities of Jobs with Justice vary by area, with some local chapters taking initiative in support of ongoing strikes, others passing out literature, others doing little or nothing at all. The degree of activism depends on local and national labor leaderships' attitudes toward the group's perspective. The UAW, for instance, side-tracked what was supposed to be Jobs with Justice's first rally, which would have protested layoffs in Detroit as well as attacks on Service Employees International Union (SEIU) janitors. See Andrew R. Banks, "Jobs with Justice: Florida's Fight against Worker Abuse," in *Building Bridges: The Emerging Grassroots Coalition of Labor and Community*, ed. Jeremy Brecher and Tim Costello (New York: Monthly Review Press, 1990).

6. See Paul J. Baicich, "Machinists Reject Concessions at Eastern," *Labor Notes*, April 1986: 3; and Baicich and Brown, "Labor Cooperation Experiment Collapses at Eastern Airlines," 1.

7. See Agis Salpukas, "High-Stake Strike: Seeking Control," *New York Times*, 6 March 1989, p. B8; Louis Uchitelle, "Rare Labor Unity," *New York Times*, 9 March 1989, p. B15; and Bureau of National Affairs, *Daily Report*, 20 March 1989.

8. See John W. Gohmann, ed., *Air and Railway Labor Relations* (Dubuque, Iowa: Kendall/Hunt, 1979); and Benjamin Aaron, ed., *The Railway Labor Act at Fifty: Collective Bargaining in the Railroad and Airline Industries* (Washington, D.C.: National Mediation Board, 1977). A *New York Times* editorial on 8 March 1989 used the possibility of an industrywide airline strike or an extension to the railroads to argue for repeal of the Railway Labor Act. See Lynn Henderson, "How We Got to Where We Are Today," *Straight Track*, June 1992: 6, for an analysis of government intervention in the railroads. (*Straight Track* is a rank-and-file railroad workers' newsletter, available by writing to the Intercraft Association of Minnesota, 3948 Central Ave., N. E., Minneapolis, Minn., 55421.)

9. See Kim Moody, "Striking Eastern Workers Fire Lorenzo, but He Won't Clear His Desk," *Labor Notes*, May 1989: 3.

10. See Salpukas, "High-Stake Strike"; and Louis Uchitelle, "Rare Labor Unity."

11. See Moody, *An Injury to All*, chap. 5; Anwar Shaikh, "The Falling Rate of Profit and the Economic Crisis in the U.S.," in *The Imperiled Economy*, book 1 (New York: Union for Radical Political Economy, 1987); Arthur MacEwan, *Debt and Disorder: International Economic Instability and U.S. Imperial Decline* (New York: Monthly Review Press, 1990).

12. On this strike see Andy Pollack, "The Crippling Legacy of Airline Craft Unionism," *Against the Current*, November/December 1989: 14.

13. Airline unions are governed by the Railway Labor Act, not the National Labor Relations Act (NLRA).

14. Under the RLA bargaining often goes on for years; contracts don't expire, they become "amendable." Furthermore, the RLA is designed to prolong bargaining in order to avoid strikes.

15. See Kim Moody, "Eastern: An SOS Few Heard or Heeded," *Labor Notes*, September 1989: 3.

16. Moody, "Eastern: An SOS Few Heard or Heeded."

17. See Daniel Guerin, *100 Years of Labor in the USA* (London: InkLinks, 1979); and Philip Foner, *History of the U.S. Labor Movement*, vol. 2, chap. 17, 18, and vol. 9, chap. 9 (New York: International Publishers, 1981).

18. See Joshua Freeman, *In Transit: The Transport Workers Union in New York City, 1933–1966* (New York: Oxford University Press, 1989).

19. See Moody, *An Injury to All*, chap. 3; and Art Preis, *Labor's Giant Step* (New York: Pathfinder, 1972), 512–21.

20. A similar intraunion reform effort occurred within the Teamsters, as Northwest flight attendants formed Flight Attendants for a Democratic Voice.

21. See Herbert Northrup, *The Negro and the Airline Industry* (Philadelphia: University of Pennsylvania Press, 1971).

22. "Labor protective provisions" is the term for provisions that protect the right of a worker to go with the route when it is sold between carriers or that determine

whether and how seniority lists will be merged when carriers merged. Before de-regulation the Civil Aeronautics Board (CAB) decided whether to uphold this right in each case, usually deciding against it. The CAB said explicitly that it supported LPPs only when it appeared the union was ready to strike to gain them—which usually was not the case. Since deregulation, unions have said they will fight for contractual LPPs but have done little to win them.

23. Among the reasons for the greater ease in adding foreign routes to domestic rather than vice versa are the more stable nature of domestic routes (which are less de-pendent on swings in tourism, economic ups and downs, and so on) and the relatively more self-contained nature of a domestic route system (which depends on both leisure and business travel). In this the industry is a microcosm of na-tional economies in general, which despite the internationalization of capital still derive most of their trade and production internally rather than externally. In sum, there's a basic asymmetry: A carrier needs a domestic route structure to feed its foreign routes, but not necessarily vice versa—until recently, that is. With the internationalization of the industry, as megacarriers' sphere of competition be-comes crossnational, they will need both strong domestic and foreign route struc-tures (and labor will need a strategy taking this into account).

24. Autoworkers might think about the flip side of this argument: Since declining Chrysler sales went in part to GM or Japanese manufacturers, a truly industrial UAW would argue for retention of Chrysler workers elsewhere in the industry—or in new, publicly financed mass transit industries.

25. See "Complicated Kinships: Mergers and Coalitions Are Changing CRSs from Airline Marketing Tools into Cooperative Information Platforms," *Air Transport World*, August 1992; U.S. Transportation Department, *Airline Marketing Prac-tices: Travel Agencies, Frequent Flyer Programs, and Computer Reservations Systems*, Washington, D.C., 1990; Joan Feldman, "Global CRS: Choosing Up Sides," *Air Transport World*, August 1989; Committee on Public Works, U.S. House of Rep-resentatives, "Hearings on Airline Computer Reservation Systems," Washington, D.C., 14 September 1988. The last article focuses on potentially monopolistic interaction between CRSs and travel agents; the marketing end of the airline busi-ness has been the subject of frequent Justice Department antitrust investigations and lawsuits in recent years.

26. Such trustbusters have also proposed that frequent flyer programs be outlawed. For a typical example of the trust-busting approach see Paul Dempsey, *The Social and Economic Consequences of Deregulation: The Transportation Industry in Transi-tion* (New York: Quorum Books, 1989).

27. No one has yet developed a counterpart for airlines of the Plumb Plan developed in the 1920s for nationalization of the railroads and approved by the AFL and all the railroad brotherhoods. Perhaps the place to start is by digging up the history of a now-forgotten bill introduced in Congress in 1948 to create an "All-American For-eign Carrier" in 1948 (until the 1980s, most other countries had always had one, nationalized flag carrier; during the latter decade many of these were privatized).

28. See *The Plane Truth*, August 1992, for an analysis of this aspect of the RLA.

29. See Rick Fantasia, *Cultures of Solidarity* (Berkeley and Los Angeles: University of California Press, 1988).

30. See Kim Moody, "Searching the Skies for Solidarity," *Labor Notes*, June 1987: 8–9; and Kim Moody, "Airlines: A Two-Tiered Industry in Trouble," special *Labor Notes* report, 1991. These suggestions have been dealt with in a rank-and-file news-letter, *The Plane Truth*, started after the Eastern strike. For copies contact the author. See also Steve Downs, "The Confrontation at Eastern Airlines: What Needs to Be Learned from the Strike?" *Against the Current*, November/December 1989.

9

Reflections on the "European Model"

Kent Worcester

INTRODUCTION

ONE OF THE HALLMARKS of American progressive discourse is a keen appreciation for what is sometimes referred to as the "European model." This term is used by different actors on the left and in the labor movement to connote specific arrangements as well as to refer to a climate of opinion that is favorable to extensive public services, negotiated industrial relations, and popular interests more generally. The term is also used to highlight the contrast between northern Europe's putatively enlightened, symmetrical, and cooperative system(s) of labor relations with the hyper-capitalist hierarchies of American manufacturing. Reference is sometimes made to a third model of industrial and social relations—the so-called developmental capitalist model favored by Japan and other dynamic Asian economies, which is state-capitalist, paternalistic, and nationalistic in character.[1]

The rhetoric of the European model is often used to advance a broadly social democratic conception of politics, production, and state intervention in the economy in the context of a markedly anticommunist polity.[2] In this sense it has an elective affinity to, and can be used as a substitute for, the ideology of socialism and state planning that gave relative depth to labor's discourse in the 1930s and 1940s. Throughout the twentieth century, efforts to introduce "foreign" notions of behavior and institution-building into the governance of industrial relations and the provision of collective services have been deployed as a wedge against the apparent parochialism of political discourse and policy-making in the United States.

Rather than looking to indigenous models of alternative unionism and collective action—such as the friendly societies of the early nineteenth century, the Industrial Workers of the World of the early twentieth century, the rank-and-file movements of the 1970s, and so on—those who cite developments in Scandinavia, Germany, and elsewhere are likely to see the solution for labor's impasse taking the form of new patterns of state activity that would insert "European" modes of corporate representation onto the American landscape.

One popular scenario would have reform-minded Democrats working in tandem with a revitalized AFL-CIO and the Rainbow Coalition to produce a New Deal for the 1990s. A key problem, however, with this scenario is that the impetus for pro-labor reforms within the Democratic Party essentially evaporated in the period following the fiscal crisis of the 1970s.[3]

Although it remains unlikely that a Democratic administration would introduce anything resembling a social democratic legislative agenda, "European" proposals and arrangements will continue to inspire democratic and progressive politics for the foreseeable future. For this reason, it may be helpful to "unpack" the concept and locate it within a specific political and historical context. The main sections of this chapter seek to do this by tracing the rise and fall of the social compact of the postwar era. Promising comprehensive public services, full employment through neo-Keynesian demand management, and industrial cooperation through neocorporatist interest-group intermediation,[4] the so-called postwar settlement marked a major advance on earlier systems of negotiated class compromise.[5] While the institutional pillars of the postwar order have undergone considerable erosion during the transition to a global market economy (1980s onward), enthusiasm for "European" arrangements remains a conspicuous component of nonconservative thought in the United States.

The chapter also provides an overview of the European Community (EC) and the recent controversy over the Maastricht Treaty. While the social and industrial policies of the postwar settlement should be regarded as the cornerstone of a European mode of advanced capitalism, the emergence of the EC as an instrument of social reform and as an autonomous power center in the sphere of international relations has generated considerable interest in North America and elsewhere. As I suggest, however, Community policy is simultaneously geared toward undermining the macroeconomic capacity of national states and enhancing the power of autonomous financial institutions. In addition, the Community's very organization may preclude it from advancing a pro-labor or democratic agenda. At the very least, it should be evident that pro-labor forces are operating at a considerable disadvantage within the Community as it is presently constituted.

In closing I take note of the fact that attempts to import European-style programs of industrial reform and social "concertation," or formal negotiated cooperation between organized interests, would undoubtedly encounter tremendous opposition from powerful business and professional interests. Business groups as well as "free market" and New Right groups are far better organized than they were fifteen or twenty years ago, and their capacity to mobilize sizable sections of public opinion against union rights, higher taxes, and new government programs is striking. While this fact should not justify scaling back leftist agendas, it may have implications for the kinds of strategies that pro-labor organizations should adopt in order to challenge the hegemony of pro-capital ideology. Issues of political strategy aside, it should also be noted that the implementation of European arrangements could have an adverse impact on political dynamics within the labor movement. For reasons that I spell out later on, neocorporatist bargaining arrangements could well exacerbate one of the central contradictions facing organized labor in the United States—the wide disparity between the experiences and interests of the labor bureaucracy and those of the rank and file.

THE HISTORICAL PARAMETERS OF THE EUROPEAN MODEL

Even at the level of political rhetoric, the notion of a European model can only be applied to a relatively narrow band of countries—for example, Austria, Belgium, Britain, Germany, the Netherlands, Norway, and Sweden. In the postwar period, elites in southern Europe (Greece, Portugal, Spain) and central Europe (Czechoslovakia, Poland, Hungary) developed coercive forms of labor and social control that differed dramatically from those that emerged in the more prosperous northern tier. In addition, there are a number of countries and regions that cannot be readily subsumed under the model, such as Finland, Ireland, and Northern Ireland. Finally, France and Italy constitute atypical cases from a comparative perspective. With its weak unions, *dirigiste* state, and syndicalist traditions, Gaullist France cannot easily be located within social democratic, authoritarian, or communist archetypes.[6] At the same time, the "overloaded" Italian system constitutes a peculiar combination of political immobilism, regional differentiation, and complex socioeconomic coordination.[7]

Thus the notion of a European model has its origins in a generalized appreciation for the great strides that a select group of European countries made in applying neo-Keynesian policies to the major political and economic challenges of the postwar period. That these countries have, to varying degrees, been unable to sustain the social and political coalitions that girded specific policies has only partially diminished the model's appeal. For heuristic purposes, it may be useful to highlight five key features of the European model:

- the incorporation of producer interests in policy-making processes in a manner that enhances the public authority of the trade unions;
- the effort to generate full employment through job creation programs and other interventionist labor market policies;
- the taxation of consumption and income to finance public services (such as education, health, welfare) targeted at the population at large;
- the emergence of social democratic parties as central to the formulation of public policy and as the guarantors or anchors of neocorporatism and the welfare state; and
- the mobilization of public sentiment around egalitarian and inclusivist norms that both facilitate high levels of public expenditure and inhibit purely capitalist norms.

Policies of universal welfare provision and industrial cooperation were rooted in popular opinion as policy-makers sought to forestall a return of the global slump of the 1930s and the nationalist violence of the 1940s. During the "golden age" of the postwar settlement, economic growth and full employment policies generated rising real wages and increased levels of unionization across industrial and public employment sectors.[8] Union federations were often able to translate economic leverage into civic access as state leaders invited labor representatives into the policy-making process. The incorporation of union leaders into state structures enhanced their macroeconomic role and provided further stimulus to the expansion of the welfare state. The unionized working class served as an important constituent of pro-growth alliances that favored both private investment and redistributive public spending.[9] What John Ruggie has described as the "compromise of embedded liberalism"[10]—domestic interventionism combined with unprotected international trade—allowed domestic elites considerable latitude in adjusting their response to subaltern demands for social rights and economic security. New taxes on consumption and middle-class income further fueled an expansion of a welfarist-inclusionist state sector.

Concertation among producer interests and between peak organizations and the state took a variety of forms in this period.[11] Patterns of decision-making came to reflect the goal of promoting social harmony among stable corporate interests. This aim became formalized through the creation of "tripartite" institutions and other regulatory bodies that augmented or displaced parliamentary and/or executive governance structures.[12] In a handful of cases, such as Austria and Sweden, peak organizations worked with government actors in setting wages, prices, and public expenditure levels. In other cases, such as Britain and the Netherlands, union representatives were granted privileged access to high-level civil servants and were consulted in areas such as training and education. In West Germany, employee representatives played an active role in legally sanctioned work councils established across manufacturing.

During the postwar era employer groups and union federations also engaged in collective bargaining at industrywide levels. Thus unions became significant institutional players and were regarded as forces to be consulted and cajoled. This became especially true in the late 1960s and 1970s, as union leaders were brought into the policy-making process in response to rising levels of public and industrial unrest. However, even prior to the late 1960s, regulated labor markets became the norm as the percentage of the workforce belonging to trade unions crept steadily upward.

From the late 1970s onward, however, organized labor found itself on the defensive on a variety of fronts. This reflected a newfound willingness of some employers to engage in more confrontational forms of industrial relations. At the same time, it also disclosed a hardening of anti-union and antitax sentiments among middle-class sectors even in typically pacific societies such as Norway and Switzerland. The most extreme manifestation of the new spirit of opposition to collective rights emerged in Britain, where Thatcher and her allies secured power within the Conservative Party in 1975 and electoral power from 1979 through the 1980s. At the root of these developments lay the collapse of the conditions that had facilitated the emergence of the postwar settlement. The international slump of the late 1970s and early 1980s, which signaled the exhaustion of the postwar Keynesian accumulation strategy,[13] also represented the point at which political and economic elites in Western Europe began to reconsider their once-protective stance toward union organization. To bring the difficulties facing European organized labor in the 1990s into focus, we must recognize the ways in which the declining fortunes of organized labor were closely entangled with the decay of the so-called Keynesian revolution and the postwar settlement.

With others, Mark Kesselman and Joel Krieger locate the postwar settlement between the end of World War II and the stagflation and oil shocks of the early 1970s. They emphasize the role that economic prosperity played in enabling divergent producer and sectoral interests to accept the social compromise embedded in consultative processes and in the welfare state. As prosperity eroded, the glue of social harmony became less adhesive. Kesselman and Krieger suggest that the fall of the postwar settlement occurred in "three acts." The first act, which they date from the late 1960s to the early 1970s, was a turbulent period when rising expectations and the U.S. intervention in Indochina generated extraordinarily high levels of civic protest. With social instability raising the specter of "ungovernability," a New Right was galvanized into action. The second act took place from the mid-1970s to the mid-1980s, when European governments of both left and right adopted a range of policies in a futile attempt to restore the socioeconomic equilibrium of the postwar settlement. "Political momentum shifted toward the Right," they conclude, "as it became apparent that . . . the possibilities were sharply limited for deepening those features of the postwar settlement that involved extending direct state economic management and increasing welfare benefits."[14]

They describe the third act as a transitional period in which socialist and laborist energies had largely dissipated but in which new social movements, particularly environmental and other so-called postmaterialist groups, renewed their push onto the political agenda. This transitional period has been characterized by the growing impact of international economic processes on domestic policy-making and political coalition-building. A critical development is the unwillingness of key portions of the electorate to see taxation rise beyond approximately 50 percent of the gross domestic product. As a result of this "tax revolt," there has emerged a damaging clash of interests between private and public-sector workers, which has obstructed the formation of political coalitions based on broadly working-class constituencies.

In this transitional period, political leaders have continued to encounter major difficulties in attempting to stimulate national economies through Keynesian means. As Jonas Pontussan has written, "the internationalization of capital and the growing interdependence of the advanced capitalist countries have undermined the regulatory capacities of national governments."[15] This is a particularly

consequential development for social democratic forces, which have traditionally relied on Keynesian spending to differentiate themselves from their more
fiscally cautious conservative and Christian Democratic counterparts. The closing off of the deficit-spending option has left public authorities unable to effectively respond to the specter of mass unemployment, which during the
early 1990s has hovered above 10 percent of the labor force within the European Community and which poses a major challenge to the long-term stability
of the European system.

Yet despite the array of forces mobilized against it—from advocates of limited government to nationalist and anti-immigrant parties—the consultative
and redistributive aims of the postwar settlement continued to guide state and
labor actors in a number of key countries, such as Germany and Sweden, and
to inform social democratic discourse in Britain and elsewhere. Rightist governments have sought to modify or revise the original goals of the postwar
settlement but have been reluctant or unable to dismantle the welfare state
altogether. The political economist Peter A. Hall finds that

> European welfare states remain highly funded and developed, relative to the
> American one; in many European nations, the trade unions remain stronger,
> especially at local levels, than their American counterparts; levels of taxation
> for collective consumption remain relatively high; and activist labor market
> policies have been a feature even of conservative regimes e.g. in France and
> Britain.[16]

Even as the centralized institutions of organized labor found themselves
marginalized within the policy-making process, trade unions have retained support
among significant layers of workers in the private and particularly the public
sectors. At the same time, however, job growth became concentrated in services and small-scale manufacturing, where unions have been traditionally weak
on the ground. Partly as a result of economic restructuring, unions are increasingly significant as sectoral actors rather than as national (let alone international) institutions. In a diverse array of cases, peak level bargaining has been
replaced by plant or sectoral level negotiations. In and of itself, this may not
be a bad thing from the standpoint of organized labor. But as Kathleen Thelen
has warned, the "danger labor faces in the 1990s is not just that central unions
grow weak, but rather that weak defenses at the plant level could render their
central successes irrelevant."[17]

This discussion outlines the general parameters of the rise and fall of the
postwar settlement. We will be able to obtain a more finely grained sense of
recent developments by looking at three critically important cases: Germany,
Sweden, and Britain.

Germany

Patterned by the electoral rivalry of the Christian Democrats and their one-
time coalition partners, the Social Democrats, the postwar West German state

assumed responsibility for the overall development of a relatively efficient industrial and social system that nevertheless eschewed the redistributive aims of the Scandinavian welfare states.[18] This system could be characterized as highly stable throughout the postwar period. Even during the 1970s, when rising levels of political violence sent shock waves through the upper reaches of the society, the electorate as a whole appeared firmly wedded to postwar democratic institutions.

While he can be dismissive of his leftist opponents, Chancellor Helmut Kohl appears to accept the broad parameters of the postwar settlement. Under Kohl's tumid leadership, the Christian Democrats have maintained a productivist strategy encompassing three dimensions: investment in primary industries such as engineering, chemicals, and automobiles; the integration of financial and manufacturing oligopolies at the expense of consumers and stockholders; and worker-management "codetermination" through works councils and other consultative forums. In the period following reunification, Kohl adopted the slogan "*Standort Deutschland*" ("Germany as an Industrial Site") to suggest that he supported the productivist strategy and opposed the drift toward a service-based economy.

At stake is the maintenance of an internationally competitive system characterized by high-quality apprenticeship programs, high worker productivity, enviable wages and employment levels, relatively short working hours, and comparatively safe working conditions. However, new challenges—such as the high costs of reunification, a protracted economic downturn coupled with mass unemployment, and the complex segmentation of the labor market—have begun to erode the foundations of Germany's vaunted "social market economy." Kohl's rhetorical backing for manufacturing industry is no match for the enormous pressures being generated both within the new Germany and in the context of the global economy.

Kohl is perhaps best known for his stewardship of the reunification of the two Germanies in 1990–1991. While his hurried approach to unification initially proved electorally popular, the costs of rebuilding eastern Germany have placed an enormous strain on the federal budget.[19] In addition, the cost of readjustment has fueled an anti-immigrant backlash that has sparked nationalist violence and counterprotest throughout much of the country. Neither of the major political parties appears capable of providing the quality of leadership necessary to stem the tide of racism and revanchism. The result is a resurgence of civic activism combined with mounting public alienation from the political process. Faced with internal factionalism and the exhaustion of its cadres, Europe's best-known alternative party, *Die Grunen* (the Green Party), has been unable to capitalize on the masses' antipathy to traditional politics.[20]

Despite a structural recession that has scarred German and European industry, the country's currency remains reasonably strong and the prospects for growth by the mid-1990s appears moderate to good.[21] Whether eastern Germany can catch up with its more prosperous sibling remains highly uncertain, however. At the time of unification, West German unionists hoped that generous federal assistance and mass membership drives could ease the transition to market capitalism and elevate living standards in the east. However, in light of recent trends—a precipitous decline in manufacturing output, the prevalence of low-paid and unskilled employment, uneven levels of uhionization in the region, and so on—it is perhaps unsurprising that "eastern Germany threatens to export its harsher labour practices to the west."[22] Many employers have called on the government to abolish or reduce social benefits that have cushioned the shock of unification and fueled public spending deficits, in the interests of lowering the costs of production.[23]

The troubled conditions in the east further complicate the difficult situation facing Germany's politically incorporated union movement as international competition and tertiary sector growth generate severe pressure on postwar institutions. The practice of negotiating a single wage standard for each industry has come under attack as employers have experimented with single-company contracts. In a few cases, "firms have reached agreements to cut workers' pay below the level set in their contract, a practice that is illegal in Germany. Unwilling to drive these firms out of business, unions have ignored the breach."[24] More significant, perhaps, is the gradual shift toward service-sector employment, where unionization levels have been far lower and where the attitude of workers to union organizations may be more heterogeneous than in manufacturing. Structural change has been accompanied by a new willingness on the part of employers to penetrate shop floor culture through American-style "Quality of Work circles" and "human resources management." As two industrial relations specialists note, "contemporary management strategies tend towards an ideological subordination of the core blue- and white-collar workers; they are expected to commit themselves emotionally and totally to company objectives in order to ensure their security and integration into the company."[25]

Leaders of such unions as the metal workers' union, I.G. Metall, are faced with the task of appeasing the unionized third of the workforce even as they attempt to recruit from nonunion sectors. As a postunification system of industrial relations establishes a new institutional equilibrium between producer interests and the state, union organizations will be compelled to demonstrate their relevance to younger employees who may be unmoved by appeals to postwar social solidarity. The "incorporation of unions into the state"[26] will be likely to come under increasing criticism from opponents of accommodationist strategies on both the left and right. A climate of flux and uncertainty may continue to shape the politics of German industrial and social relations throughout the remainder of the decade.[27]

Sweden

That Germany's militaristic past renders it suspect as an export model helps explain why a country with roughly one-tenth of Germany's population, Sweden, has acquired such an extraordinary reputation as *the* exemplary case of postwar enlightenment. The basis for this reputation may be traced to three main factors. First, from the late 1930s onward, the Swedish Social Democrats have pursued one of the most sweeping programs of egalitarian social reform in the history of Europe.[28] Second, Sweden achieved a remarkable degree of political stability in the prewar and postwar periods. Between 1932 and 1976 the country had three prime ministers—all Social Democrats. As Jonas Pontusson has written, "the Swedish Social Democrats have enjoyed a longer and more stable tenure in government than any other party operating in the context of free and competitive elections."[29] Third, producer interests are entrenched players in the nation's political process. Over 90 percent of the nation's workforce is unionized, and a majority of employers belong to similarly well-organized and centralized federations. Sweden remains one of the most highly corporatized societies in the world.[30]

In the postwar era, Western intellectuals praised Sweden and other Scandinavian welfare states for pioneering a "third way" between capitalism and communism.[31] Active labor market policies, distributive equity, ever-narrower wage differentials, and high levels of collective consumption offered a uniquely peaceable alternative to unfettered market liberty or coercive state planning. Through generous child care and unemployment benefit schemes, extensive retraining progams, world-class public transport systems, and other valuable social services, the country's political system helped eradicate most forms of poverty and provided a measure of real equality between the social classes. While financial and commercial interests remained in private hands, government policies and collectivist institutions constrained capital from engaging in socially predatory actions. Many of the country's larger firms, such as Volvo, Saab, and Electrolux, successfully combined high-tech, export-driven, high-profit operations with negotiated labor pacts and generous in-house programs. An ethos of social awareness permeated political discourse and helped shape the programs of the centrist or "bourgeois" People's Party and the Moderate Unity Party, which sought to soften but not reverse the egalitarian policies of the left.

With its electoral base protected by a mass membership and a stable alliance with rural producers forged in the prewar era, the Social Democrats regained political power in 1982 and held office until the early 1990s. While the election of 1991 seemed at first to constitute an antileftist critical realignment of the country's political system, the Social Democrats have bounced back in the opinion polls and seem likely to be returned to office in the next election. At present, a center-right coalition government is attempting to reduce public spending and privatize a number of state-owned firms. This government has come under fire not only from the newly revived left but also from the populist right. Appropriating the power-to-the-people rhetoric of the 1960s, an organization called New Democracy defiantly assails the high-tax/high-productivity policies of the welfare state. In combination with the once-moribund Christian Democratic Party, which vigorously opposes abortion rights, New Democracy represents a major challenge to the institutions and value orientation of the Scandinavian postwar settlement. In light of recent evidence of political instability—as manifested by tax revolts, public sector strikes, and the unsolved 1986 murder of prime minister Olaf Palme—not a few observers have posed the question of whether the Swedish "third way" is sustainable under conditions of global competitive capitalism.[32]

The atmosphere of political uncertainty has contributed to, but also reflects, the country's economic difficulties. Throughout the 1980s, inflation crept upward as macroeconomic policies failed to squeeze excess demand or curb spiraling labor costs and as regional stagflationary pressures played themselves out at the domestic level. The deregulation of financial services in the mid-1980s symbolized the welfare state's partial accommodation with the international investment community, but, as in Britain, deregulation spawned a credit boom and deepened the inflationary cycle. In addition, as in other European countries, substantial gains in the output of labor have been difficult to achieve in light of the gradual shift from manufacturing to service employment. A "productivity crisis" has encouraged more ambitious firms to "rationalize" the labor process in an attempt to raise individual worker productivity and factory output.[33] Under conditions of inflation, deregulation, productivity drives, and heightened international competition, employer-employee relations, as well as negotiated relations among producer interests, have soured in comparison to the recent past.

The sheer complexity of Sweden's economic situation has placed an enormous burden on the trade unions. The movement has long been divided into two federations, one representing blue-collar workers (LO), and one representing white (TCO); by tradition, the former is closely aligned with the Social Democrats and is more militant than its white-collar counterpart.[34] Recent developments have generated new tensions within and between the two union federations, as generational, occupational, and political cleavages threaten to tear at the fabric of social and class harmony. In particular, solidarity between public and private-sector workers has eroded as the divisive issue of taxation has reconfigured the politics of nongovernmental employees. "Solidaristic wage bargaining"—a notable legacy of the postwar settlement in which more powerful unions offered pay restraint as a trade-off for labor peace and higher wages in less well organized sectors—has been criticized not only on economic grounds but on populist-libertarian grounds as well.[35] In addition, industrial concertation and centralized wage bargaining have partially unraveled as a result of the decay of postwar institutions and a backlash against neocorporatist arrangements.[36] A policy of active labor market intervention, in which the government provides extensive retraining and job programs, is one of the few anchors of the industrial and social system to retain widespread popular support.[37]

The controversy surrounding the so-called wage-earner funds nicely captures the partial decomposition of the postwar system of class compromise.[38] In the 1970s, economists attached to LO urged that companies be required to issue new stocks and place a percentage of after-tax profits into union-managed trusts that would combine profit-sharing schemes with socially beneficial investments. By the early 1980s, their proposal had been revised as a result of pressure from entrepreneurs, the TCO, and sections of the Social Democrats. "Under the new proposal," writes Pontusson, "collective profit-sharing would . . . take the form of a profits tax, the revenues of which would be used by regionally organized wage-earner funds to purchase corporate shares."[39] Even this watered-down version aroused the animosity of business groups, which chafed under the "paternalism" of the welfare state and which sought to mobilize public opposition against any deepening of the social democratic project.[40] Hereafter the government's program was dominated by efforts to encourage private investment and lower inflation (and therefore job growth) rather than to enhance the political and market power of working-class institutions.

Britain

The British experience offers an interesting contrast with the Swedish experience. Whereas Swedish political elites have gradually retreated from the more radical implications of the social democratic project, British elites have lurched from the tripartism of the postwar era to the "enterprise culture" of the Thatcher years. Prior to the emergence and consolidation of the Thatcherite project, union leaders had come to assume that history had an essentially progressive dynamic and that policies of inclusion and unionization could push Britain steadily toward an equitable, harmonious, and social democratic future.[41] By setting out to weaken the power of union leaders, reduce public spending, and empower entrepreneurial interests, Thatcherite policy-makers shattered this laborist complacency. Ministers openly mocked union prerogatives and took steps to reduce the legitimacy of union leaders as participants in national political life. In the absence of a coordinated macroeconomic policy, the government encouraged job losses in unproductive sectors and promoted flexible work environments and the rapid introduction of new technologies. While union leaders viewed the collapse of tripartism with horror, the reform of labor law and economic policy made a far greater impression on shop floor relations than did the disintegration of negotiated policy-making.[42]

While several of the initiatives taken by the Thatcher government helped to stimulate export-led growth and dampen inflationary pressures, the government's economic program also ensured that the country remained trapped in a "low-skills equilibrium," where "the majority of companies produce low quality goods or services using workers and managers whose education and training is relatively poor by the standards of the advanced industrial countries."[43] The government's hostility to organized labor was matched by its assault on state regulatory institutions protecting the wages and conditions of the bottom end of the labor market. In addition, the government actively sought to attract overseas investment on the basis of its relatively low-wage scales and newly pacified workforce. At the same time, training policy under the Conservatives veered erratically as the government introduced a succession of indifferently managed schemes designed to provide minimum skills training and to bring down the official tallies of the unemployed.[44]

Throughout the 1980s, the government expended enormous resources in order to demonstrate its political and economic resolve. The length (356 days) and cost to the state (over £7 billion in policing and energy imports) of the 1984–1985 miners' strike indicates the degree to which government ministers were prepared to impress the "demonstration effect"[45] on militant unions and other civic institutions. The government's refusal to subsidize failing companies or increase public spending to stimulate private investment constituted perhaps the most powerful expression of the demonstration effect. In a number of industries, such as printing, steel, and shipping, employers took advantage of government policy to impose major reforms.[46] Specialists called attention to the increasing tendency of employers to insist on more flexible work practices (that is, fewer rules concerning occupational demarcation, and the introduction of new technology), so that workers could carry out a wider array of tasks as part of their assigned duties.[47] At the same time, studies suggested that most employers were anxious to avoid conflict with union negotiators.[48]

Union membership declined every year following the all-time record high of the 1980s, wiping away the membership gains of the 1960s–1970s. With union membership as of 1990 below 40 percent of the labor force, one author justifiably claimed that nonunionism "is now dominant in Britain."[49] At the same time, few employers seemed eager to withdraw recognition from existing unions.[50] Michael Fogarty and Douglas Brooks conclude that union membership had fallen "largely as a result of the fall in the number of employees in employment, and with variations from sector to sector, union density—membership as a percentage of the number of employees—has been impressively well maintained."[51] During this period there was also a marked decline in strike activity,[52] suggesting that the combined effect of mass unemployment and fiscal conservatism was to dampen working-class militancy and the willingness and capacity of union leaders to take members out on strike.

The government's antipathy toward union organizations provoked angry rebuttals from Britain's labor leaders. One Trades Union Congress leader spoke in 1980 about the "inevitable progress of the democratic forces which are at work in industry and in every other part of our society," progress which even "the present Government" could not "continue indefinitely to withstand."[53] By the end of the decade, however, most observers had concluded that the capacity of unions to exercise "their traditional functions" had been severely constrained by the actions of the Thatcher government. The paralysis of organized labor was accompanied by the failure of the social democratic Labour Party to recover substantial electoral ground in the general elections of 1983, 1987, or 1992. Even with Labour's recent resurgence in the opinion polls, the prospects for a wholesale revitalization of the labor movement seem slim. In conjunction with the deinstitutionalization and rationalization of European capitalism, the onslaughts of the Thatcher decade decisively altered the political and economic terrain upon which organized labor operates.

As we have seen, the transformation of European politics has taken different forms in different countries. The degree to which labor movements have been marginalized or placed on the defensive as a result of state policies, employer strategies, and/or the reallocation of power on the shop floor varies between countries and across sectors. While the expansion of welfare services under the postwar settlement has been checked or reversed in virtually every case, the pace of change and the degree to which union leaders retain influence in the area of social policy may differ depending on the preferences and strategies pursued by political elites as they exercise state power. From a social democratic perspective, the Swedish case remains perhaps the most hopeful, despite the erosion of leftist hegemony, while the German case represents the problematic reproduction of selected elements of the postwar settlement under conditions of Christian Democratic rule. If recent developments seem discouraging in Scandinavia and Germany, the British example offers a worst-case scenario, where social decay and economic decline march hand-in-hand with the consolidation of Conservative power and the elimination of many of the key signposts of the welfare state. While this necessarily partial sketch hardly exhausts the full range of real-world experiences, it can perhaps provide us with an appreciation for some of the constraints that pro-labor and leftist actors confront in the current period.

THE EUROPEAN COMMUNITY

The appeal of the European model reflects the legacy of the postwar settlement. But it is also bound up in the emergence of the European Community as a creative, modernizing force in regional and international affairs. Despite the Community's famous "democratic deficit"—the byproduct of the disproportionate contribution that foreign ministers (and upper-echelon EC administrators, or "Eurocrats") make to the formulation and implementation of Community policy—sympathetic observers have noted the pink-and-green hue of the European Parliament, which contains an ample number of social democrats and ecologists as well as left-leaning regionalists. The European Parliament plays an important role in providing aid to underdeveloped regions, and helps enact EC-wide standards in such areas as environmental standards and women's rights. Many specialists expect that the European Parliament will gain new powers, and some observers hope the EC can play a responsible role in global politics and can help restrain the U.S. tendency to use military force in the resolution of international crises.[54]

The political storm over the exchange rate mechanism (ERM) and the Maastricht Treaty raises important questions about the capacity of European elites to reconcile national sovereignty, popular demands for economic security, and the European ideal. The treaty was intended to mark a third stage in the Community's consolidation.[55] The first stage was the founding of the European Economic Community under terms specified by the Treaty of Rome, which was signed by six member nations in 1957. Over time, the signatories to the treaty achieved modest success in establishing a customs-free trade zone across much of Western Europe. The second stage was the effort, inaugurated in 1986, to forge a single market of goods, services, capital, and labor across the EC (numbering by now twelve member states). Although the single market was to have been in effect by the end of 1992, negotiations over a range of complex issues are ongoing. The third stage was intended to lay the basis for an Economic and Monetary Union, which was to have established (by 1999) a central European bank (modeled on the inflation-phobic German Bundesbank), a common European currency, and a common foreign policy. Had the original Maastricht Treaty been ratified and accepted by the Community's constituent members in 1992–1993, Europe would have been launched on the road to a "super-state."

One of the undeclared aims of the third phase was to establish an economic zone where the capacity of individual states to set macroeconomic policies would be greatly diminished. As Chris Toulouse has written, governments "which already look to Bonn [the German capital] and Brussels [the Community's capital] for the lead on interest and exchange rate policy, will gradually dilute their sovereignty in matters of taxation, public spending levels and industrial policy."[56] Anxieties connected with the intensification of international economic competition (emanating in particular from the United States and Japan) helped lay the basis for a treaty that was to have substituted autonomous (and largely anonymous) steering mechanisms for democratic consideration of alternative economic strategies. In retrospect, it seems unsurprising that such a centralist conception would arouse misgivings among various European publics. Yet few observers anticipated the rapidity with which the treaty came under assault, nor the adverse impact that currency upheavals could have on the fragile environment within which politicians, financiers, and Eurocrats alike operate.

The inconclusive results of the public referenda on Maastricht partly reflects political pressures having little to do with the terms of the treaty. Yet the surge of anti-Maastricht sentiment also revealed popular misgivings about the asymmetrical power relations that the treaty attempted to lock into place.[57] In devising a union that would make its highest priority the fight against inflation—rather than, say, against unemployment or shallow economic growth—the Community sought, in effect, to empower the interests of finance (which is particularly sensitive to inflation) over manufacturing and labor. Even as the treaty brushed aside questions of economic convergence, the social dimension, or the democratization of EC's institutions, it placed price stability over growth and social expenditure and valorized a monetarist economic agenda. Viewed in this light, the position of leftist defenders of the treaty looks highly problematic,[58] and the hope that a renegotiated Maastricht could create, in the words of *The Economist*, "the promise of more democratic openness"[59] is likely to remain unfulfilled. Yet there may be additional problems, which are highlighted by ongoing debates over the social dimension, an aspect of the Community's development that constitutes the fundamental test of the EC's relationship to organized labor and to the moderate egalitarianism of the postwar settlement.

The framers of the European Community had intended that the EC would exhibit a special concern for the health and well-being of Europe's peoples. During the 1980s, much of the impetus for expanding the Community's social role came from Jacques Delors and other French socialists who believed that a united Europe could advance French national interests as well as protect low-wage workers and other disadvantaged groups. As proposals for a European union were being thrashed out at the Dutch town of Maastricht, the Thatcher government strenuously objected to the inclusion of a "social charter," with the result that all references to social rights and collective bargaining were grafted onto the treaty in the form of a "protocol" lacking the status of EC law.[60] Efforts to enhance the Community's social dimension were impeded not only by the recalcitrant British but also by the vigorous representations that employers' associations (such as the Europe-wide employers' confederation, UNICE) made within the EC's policy-making bodies.

In the aftermath of the Maastricht controversy, it might be expected that the EC would move to strengthen its social and regulatory component in order to placate its working-class critics. Yet such moves could be viewed as being largely cosmetic or symbolic in nature. As Christiane Lemke and Gary Marks have argued, unions are at a distinct disadvantage at the pan-European level. It is one thing, they point out, "for a company to span Europe and quite another thing for a union." As they note, firms are "minimally based on the pursuit of material gain, and this logic travels without difficulty across western borders. Unions, by contrast, provide a collective good, and they are unable to do this simply by appealing to individual economic interest." Because unions are "more intensively nationally rooted than corporations, they find it far more difficult to develop supranational organization."[61] Consequently, the European Trades Union Congress (ETUC) has been far less effective than UNICE in defending its interests inside EC chambers. The ETUC's position has been further complicated by the fact that many union movements (in France, Italy, Spain, and elsewhere) are divided along institutional and ideological lines. Only in Britain and Germany do unions belong to a single labor congress, and the British Trades Union Congress has found it difficult to maintain even the semblance of intra-union unity in recent years.

In addition, as a result of the institutional dominance of territorial politics as filtered through the Council of Ministers, the EC's very structure may hamper supranational interest representation, even on the part of employers. Alberta Sbragia notes that although organized interests "are not insignificant in the Community, they typically must use, and will need to keep using, channels provided by national governments in order to maximize their influence."[62] As a result, "the social policies of the EC are likely to be fragmented, partial, and piecemeal, responding more to complex configurations of special interests than to any broad principle developed by stable political and social coalitions."[63] The preponderance of these special interests—which are most often grounded in territorial politics and divided along lines of region, class, and nation—will be highly sensitive to the impact of social measures on economic competitiveness. Peter Lange has noted that labor itself may be divided on issues of harmonization, since "potential conflicts of interest . . . [may] arise among firms that operate in the same sector but have different social costs, technologies, and production techniques."[64]

All of this helps to place the concept of a European model into proper perspective. With the erosion of the welfare state and the apparent paralysis of social democracy[65] the long-range survival of the institutions of the postwar settlement may be in doubt. The decentralization of wage bargaining and the emergence of the middle-class tax revolt are just two symptoms of a larger process. While the unions have managed to hold the line in many cases, particularly at the local level, their leaders have failed to advance recruitment and bargaining strategies that can revitalize their internal structures, attract new layers of members, or push employers onto the strategic defensive. Thus the famous "crisis of the left" goes well beyond intellectual culture to encompass mainstream, left-of-center politics. And while the European Community has made moves in the direction of regional aid and environmental protection, it is ill equipped to serve as a vehicle of grass-roots, social democratic, or leftist aspirations. From the perspective of pro-labor politics, then, the overall picture is decidedly mixed, if disheartening.

DISCUSSION

The 1992 Clinton victory against an incumbent Republican president represented a major boon to an AFL-CIO leadership that had seen its member organizations besieged (and union membership shrink) throughout the 1980s. Despite Clinton's well-established connection to the neoliberal Democratic Leadership Council, the new administration appeared to adopt a cooperative and even friendly relationship with the trade unions. Union leaders were encouraged by Clinton's emphasis on investment in infrastructure and health care and by the appointment of political economist Robert Reich as Secretary of Labor. Union chiefs who attended the pre-inaugural Economic Summit were clearly gratified to be included in high-level economic and social policy deliberations. Clinton's appointments to the National Labor Relations Board represented a fresh start after the laissez-faire approach of the Reagan and Bush administrations, and his administration's decision to allow PATCO members to apply for jobs as air traffic controllers was a welcome measure, if long overdue. For a section of the union bureaucracy, the chief task before the labor movement was that of working with congressional allies to ensure that Clinton fulfilled his campaign promise of combining a deficit reduction package with bold new initiatives to stimulate job growth. The unions also made the passage of a striker replacement bill a top legislative priority. Labor's opposition to the North American Free Trade Agreement (NAFTA) represented perhaps the single most important political issue separating union leaders—and, for the most part, union members—from the administration.

As the labor journalist Kim Moody has noted, however, the political and economic climate had changed dramatically since the Democrats were last in the White House. Moody writes:

> The crisis of profitability had proved chronic and incurable, even with shock treatment, and spawned a storm of global competitiveness that confounded new and old policy options alike. In boom and in bust, unemployment levels remained twice what they were when Jimmy Carter took the oath of office. Indeed, the boom of the 1980s was more like a bust in the 1950s than a real expansion. The shape of business organization, entire systems of production, the rules of world trade, the flow of humanity in search of peace and jobs, the functioning of financial markets: all these and more changed—sometimes beyond recognition. With these changes crumbled the very foundation of liberal economic policy on which the Democratic Party of yesteryear—the party of big-city bosses, power-brokering labor leaders, and patrician liberals—was based.[66]

What Moody describes as "liberal economic policy" was only rarely as ambitious as the more redistributive programs of the European postwar settlement. In the United States, "single-payer" health care initiatives and full employment legislation stalled as suburban and Republican legislators successfully resisted the tide of the welfare state. As a sop to the prevailing ideological and political winds, the bulk of union elites mounted a well-publicized retreat on the issue of health care and offered their support for the Clinton administration's neoliberal program of "managed care." The call for full employment, which had been central to postwar union politics, had been placed on the back burner in the late 1970s and hardly surfaced at all during Clinton's first year of office. Thus the political retreat of European social democracy in the 1980s and early 1990s was more or less matched by the eclipse of traditional liberalism in the Democratic Party and the rise of pro-business pragmatic moderation in the United States.

Historical and institutional differences between northern Europe and the United States remained as important as any similarities, however. In particular, the system of federalism, which cedes considerable power to state and local authorities to set social policy objectives and spending limits, helped generate a patchwork system that encouraged employers to withdraw their operations from comparatively generous states such as New York and Massachusetts. Yet New Deal liberalism bore a certain familial resemblance to its European counterpart, even as it lacked the specific mechanism of a labor-based political party. The reasons for this relative convergence of program and ideology seem fairly straightforward—shared experiences such as the Depression of the 1930s and efforts to eradicate poverty in the 1960s come to mind—just as the logic guiding the combined shift away from liberalism and social democracy seems broadly comprehensible. In the absence of a labor-based party, however, social programs are even more vulnerable to a rightist backlash, and the position of labor organizations is less secure. Bill Clinton may be better informed, more energetic, and more articulate than his predecessor, George Bush, but he has shown little interest in empowering the unions or in defying the "civil religion" of "money and class in America."[67]

With the decomposition of the New Deal social coalition, calls for the consolidation of a welfare state or for a civic movement favoring union rights and rank-and-file power have become steadily fainter. This has only emboldened groups on the right that combine pro-market rhetoric with an antilibertarian offensive against unsanctioned expressions of individual freedom. While the Clinton victory may have disappointed many on the political and religious right (especially critics of abortion), it hardly derailed their movement. Most significantly, the right's capacity to mobilize against pro-labor and leftist initiatives appears undiminished. Those who espouse ideas that are "outside of the mainstream" may need to find ways of addressing the fears and anxieties of a mass public that has imbibed the language and values of hyper-capitalism. Of necessity, this will involve tackling the right's synthesis of free market and strong state ideology[68] in a manner that may be incompatible with a sustained commitment to either the Democratic Party or the Clinton administration.

Whether power brokering by labor leaders should be restored and even enhanced through the introduction of neocorporatist arrangements is of course debatable. At the very least, it is a separate question from that of building support for the collective provision of social services or for developing stronger and more democratic trade unions. The establishment of formal processes of concertation may represent one means of safeguarding social programs and empowering union organizations, but for this option to even be considered the labor movement would have to reverse its current decline and somehow represent itself as working on behalf of millions of American workers. It may be years before unions are able to achieve the membership growth and accumulated political authority that would be required to pursue this strategy. The discussions that have taken place between union leaders and the Clinton administration—sporadic meetings about subcabinet appointments, brief encounters at fund-raising dinners, and so on—are a far cry from the formal negotiations offered by a number of European political systems in the postwar period.

It should be noted that the potential drawbacks of a neocorporatist strategy are considerable. Interest groups that are excluded from the neocorporatist decision-making process (such as, for example, small business) would probably seek to ignite a political firestorm over the issue, and conservative groups would no doubt view the introduction of neocorporatist arrangements as a fundamental assault on the American way of life. Furthermore, in exchange for a "seat at the table" and other concessions, union leaders would in all likelihood be encouraged to discipline their members in the interests of worker-management harmony and economic competitiveness. This discipline could take the form of promoting government policies, dampening strike activity, and/or imposing new technologies and new labor processes and practices on reluctant groups of workers. Yet many union leaders have a demonstrated propensity to engage in these kinds of activity even without the incentive of power-broker status. Their willingness to "carry water for management" may be one reason why unions have lost support among core sectors of the labor force in the first place.

As I suggested at the outset of this chapter, the establishment and maintenance of neocorporatist arrangements could serve to further estrange union members from the union bureaucracy. Neocorporatist "bargains" could prove far more appealing to union leaders than to the rank and file. Union leaders, for example, could promise labor quiescence and lower wage demands in exchange for specific legislative gains or a more sympathetic NLRB—a bargain, perhaps, for those operating in an environment that is decisively shaped by legislative and judicial considerations, but possibly less attractive to, say, assembly-line workers. In addition, an enhanced policy-making role for union leaders could further isolate the labor bureaucracy from the experiences and needs of ordinary union members. Organizations that are already oriented toward developments in Washington, D.C., might further concentrate resources on the executive and legislative branches of government, while paying less attention to recruitment, leadership training, and local union structures. The tendency to "leave things in the hands of the leaders"—already dominant in the American labor movement—would be strengthened, and union leaders would be further encouraged to see themselves as accountable to the political system and the Democratic Party rather than to the membership of particular unions or to popular interests more generally.

Of course, a full-fledged neocorporatist system is unlikely to emerge in the United States. But the fantasy of active involvement in the inner councils of the state remains a constituent feature of the labor bureaucracy's ideological and political makeup. The same can be said about the bureaucracy's overall attachment to the European model. While many aspects of the postwar European experience may seem appealing from the vantage point of organized labor in the United States, their wholesale introduction would undoubtedly engender new social contradictions.

Notes

1. The term *developmental capitalism* has been coined by the political economist Chalmers Johnson. In paraphrasing Johnson's views, the *New York Times* described the Japanese state as organized "almost solely for the purpose of making Japanese industry and exporters more competitive, and the apparatus for achieving this goal is one that no trade negotiations can dismantle." See James Sterngold, "A New President Finds the Trade Combatants Acting Up," *New York Times*, 31 January 1993, p. D18.

This chapter will be exclusively concerned with the European model, which I judge to be more influential within trade union circles than the Japanese model. The situation may be reversed among employers' groups.

2. *Social democracy* is a key term in the comparative analysis of labor-based parties committed to social reform and economic redistribution within the context of Western capitalism. While Europe's social democrats have played a critical role in the construction of pro-labor, pro-welfare policies, *social democracy* should not be seen as synonymous with the *European model*, which is a somewhat looser term referring to a range of policies and institutional arrangements rather than to a specific political or ideological movement.

3. An exemplary study of the modern sociological and political transformation of the Democratic Party remains Thomas Byrne Edsall, *The New Politics of Inequality* (New York: Norton, 1984).

4. For the past two decades social scientists have debated the relevance of the term *corporatism* in distinguishing formal structures of interest intermediation from pluralist forms. Its use here is intended simply to connote the structured participation of select interest groups in public policy-making, and I do not accept the claim that there is a corporatist "drift" or "bias" inherent in the organization of advanced industrial societies. The classic statement of the corporatist thesis is Philippe Schmitter, "Still the Century of Corporatism?" *Review of Politics* 36 (1974). See also Alan Cawson, *Corporatism and Political Theory* (Oxford: Blackwell, 1986); Wyn Grant, ed., *The Political Economy of Corporatism* (New York: St. Martin's Press, 1985); and Wolfgang Streeck and Philippe Schmitter, eds., *Private Interest Government: Between Market and State* (London: Sage, 1985). Two pluralist challenges to the corporatist thesis are Andrew Cox, "Corporatism as Reductionism: The Analytical Limits of the Corporatist Thesis," *Government and Opposition* 16, no. 1 (1981); and Ross Martin, "Pluralism and the New Corporatism," *Political Studies* 31, no. 1 (1983).

5. Kesselman and Krieger describe the postwar settlement as a period when "the welfare state was consolidated; high levels of employment achieved; anti-capitalist forces marginalized; and an unusual degree of social, industrial, and political consent for mainstream (and reformist) policies secured." See Mark Kesselman and Joel Krieger, eds., "Introduction," *European Politics in Transition* (Lexington, MA: D. C. Heath, 1987), 11.

6. Reliable studies include Stephen S. Cohen, *Modern French Planning: The French Model* (Berkeley and Los Angeles: University of California Press, 1977); Peter A. Hall, *Governing the Economy: The Politics of State Intervention in Britain and France* (New York: Oxford University Press, 1986); Chris Howell, *Regulating Labor: The State and Industrial Relations Reform in Postwar France* (Princeton, N.J.: Princeton University Press, 1992); and John Zysman, *Political Strategies for Industrial Order: State, Market, and Industry in France* (Berkeley and Los Angeles: University of California Press, 1977).

7. Two specialists have drawn a distinction between an "overloaded" Italian system, which inhibits "methods of concerted governing of industrial relations," and the "greater solidity of certain middle and north European social pacts." They suggest that the "overload depends to a great extent on institutional and government weaknesses. But it has affected both the unions and the system." See Gian Primo Cella and Tiziano Treu, "Collective and Political Bargaining," in *Economic Crisis, Trade Unions, and the State*, ed. Otto Jacobi, Bob Jessop, Hans Kastendiek, and Marino Regini (London: Croom Helm, 1986), 186. Also see, *inter alia*, Joanne Barkan, *Visions of Emancipation: The Italian Workers' Movement since 1945* (New York: Praeger, 1984); Miriam Golden, *Labor Divided: Austerity and Working-Class*

Politics in Contemporary Italy (Ithaca, N.Y.: Cornell University Press, 1988); and Carol A. Mershon, "The Crisis of the CGIL," in *Italian Politics: A Review*, ed. Stephen Hellman and Gianfranco Pasquino (London: Pinter Publishers, 1992), 87–109.

8. For a sophisticated analysis of the dynamics of the postwar settlement, see Andrew Glyn, Alan Hughes, Alain Lipietz, and Ajit Singh, "The Rise and Fall of the Golden Age," in *The Golden Age of Capitalism: Reinterpreting the Postwar Experience*, ed. Stephen A. Marglin and Juliet B. Schor (Oxford: Oxford University Press, 1991), 39–125.

9. The concept of a postwar "growth alliance" is developed in Otto Jacobi, "Economic Development and Trade Union Collective Bargaining Policy since the Middle of the 1970s," in *Economic Crisis, Trade Unions, and the State*, ed. Jacobi et al., 213–35.

10. Ruggie describes how "multilateralism [that is, unprotected international trade] and the quest for domestic stability were coupled and even conditioned by one another" in his article "International Regimes, Transactions, and Change: Embedded Liberalism in the Postwar Economic Order," in *International Regimes*, ed. Stephen D. Krasner (Ithaca, N.Y.: Cornell University Press, 1983), 195–231.

11. A useful overview is provided by Gerhard Lehmbruch, "Concertation and the Structure of Corporatist Networks," in *Order and Conflict in Contemporary Capitalism: Studies in the Political Economy of Western European Nations*, ed. John Goldthorpe (Oxford: Oxford University Press, 1984), 60–80.

12. On "tripartism," that is, formalized bargaining relations between representatives of state, labor, and employer groups, see Kent Worcester, "From Tripartism to the Enterprise Culture: The Trade Unions, Training Policy, and the Thatcher Government, 1979–1988" (Ph.D. diss., Columbia University, 1990), 11–20.

13. Colin Leys, "Thatcherism and Manufacturing: A Question of Hegemony," *New Left Review* 151 (1985): 5–25.

14. Mark Kesselman and Joel Krieger, eds., *European Politics in Transition*, 2nd ed. (Lexington, Mass.: D. C. Heath, 1992), 19.

15. Jonas Pontusson, "Introduction," in *Bargaining for Change: Union Politics in North America and Europe*, ed. Miriam Golden and Jonas Pontusson (Ithaca, N.Y.: Cornell University Press, 1992), 37.

16. Personal correspondence with the author, 7 July 1993.

17. Kathleen Thelen, "The Politics of Flexibility in the German Metalworking Industries," in *Bargaining for Change*, ed. Golden and Pontusson, 246.

18. See Gosta Esping-Andersen and Walter Korpi, "Social Policy as Class Politics in Post-War Capitalism: Scandinavia, Austria, and Germany," in *Order and Conflict in Contemporary Capitalism*, ed. Goldthorpe, 195–205.

19. Kohl has admitted that unification "brought with it enormous problems, more than many people, myself included, had expected." Quoted in Roger Cohen, "Paying for the Fall of Communism," *New York Times*, 27 September 1992, p. D1.

20. Environmentalists everywhere were shocked and saddened by the apparent murder of party cofounder Petra Kelly, who served in the German Bundestag from 1983 to 1990. See Jennifer Scarlott, "Petra Kelly, 1942–1992," *New Politics* 4, no. 2 (1993): 193.

21. See *The Economist*'s survey, "Not as Grimm as It Looks," 23 May 1992.

22. "Germany Labours On," *The Economist*, 23 January 1993, p. 64.

23. "To cut government spending by $11.8 billion next year, Bonn plans to reduce unemployment payments, which now start at 68 percent of a recently employed worker's after-tax wages, to 64 percent. The government also wants to change the law to make it possible for most factories to operate on Sundays and holidays and

to allow companies to require employees to work overtime, to a total of 10 hours a day." Craig Whitney, "Western Europe's Dreams Turning to Nightmares," *New York Times*, 8 August 1993, p. 16.

24. "Germany Labours On," 64.

25. Otto Jacobi and Walther Muller-Jentsch, "West Germany: Continuity and Structural Change," in *European Industrial Relations: The Challenge of Flexibility*, ed. Guido Baglioni and Colin Crouch (London: Sage, 1991), 151.

26. See Hans Kastendiek, Hella Kastendiek, and Hugo Reister, "Institutional Strategies for Trade Union Participation: An Assessment of the Incorporation Thesis," in *Economic Crisis, Trade Unions, and the State*, ed. Otto Jacobi et al., 258.

27. For more detailed analyses of the German trade unions, see, *inter alia*, Peter J. Katzenstein, ed., *Industry and Politics in West Germany: Toward the Third Republic* (Ithaca, N.Y.: Cornell University Press, 1989); Horst Kern and Charles Sabel, "Trade Unions and Decentralized Production: A Sketch of the Strategic Problems in the West German Labor Movement," *Politics and Society* 19, no. 4 (1991); Peter Swenson, "Union Politics, the Welfare State, and Intraclass Conflict in Sweden and Germany," in *Bargaining for Change*, ed. Golden and Pontusson, 45–76; and Kathleen Thelen, *Union of Parts: Labor Politics in Postwar Germany* (Ithaca, N.Y.: Cornell University Press, 1991). A good overview is Andrei S. Markovits, *The Politics of the West German Trade Unions: Strategies of Class and Interest Representation in Growth and Crisis* (Cambridge: Cambridge University Press, 1986).

28. For theoretical assessments of Sweden's social policies see, *inter alia*, Gosta Esping-Andersen, *The Three Worlds of Welfare Capitalism* (Princeton, N.J.: Princeton University Press, 1990); Hugh Heclo, *Modern Social Politics in Britain and Sweden* (New Haven, Conn.: Yale University Press, 1974); Mary Ruggie, *The State and Working Women: A Comparative Study of Britain and Sweden* (Princeton, N.J.: Princeton University Press, 1984); and Timothy Tilton, *The Political Theory of Swedish Social Democracy: Through the Welfare State to Socialism* (Oxford: Clarendon Press, 1990).

29. Jonas Pontusson, "The Emergence of the Modern Swedish State," in *European Politics in Transition*, ed. Kesselman and Krieger, 427.

30. See, *inter alia*, Eric Einhorn and John Logue, *Modern Welfare States: Politics and Policies in Social Democratic Scandinavia* (New York: Praeger, 1989); and Hugh Heclo and Henrik Madsen, *Policy and Politics in Sweden: Principled Pragmatism* (Philadelphia, Penn.: Temple University Press, 1987).

31. As one historian has written: "Socialism remains a beautiful dream. In real life it has been proven unnecessary by the welfare states of Scandinavia. In combining some socialism with a great deal of private ownership, they have reached levels of prosperity, equity, and personal freedom that the founders of socialism thought only a revolution could achieve. These just societies are unexciting. The militant young of the world do not sing their praises. They are to be cherished all the same." See William L. O'Neill, *The Last Romantic: The Life of Max Eastman* (Oxford: Oxford University Press, 1978), 206.

32. An early expression of this debate is Marquis Childs, *Sweden: The Middle Way on Trial* (New Haven, Conn.: Yale University Press, 1980). See also Eric Lundberg, "The Rise and Fall of the Swedish Model," *Journal of Economic Literature* 23 (1985); and Jonas Pontusson, "Radicalization and Retreat in Swedish Social Democracy," *New Left Review*, no. 165 (1987): 5–33.

33. See Barry Bosworth and Alice Rivlin, eds., *The Swedish Economy* (Washington, D.C.: Brookings Institution, 1987).

34. LO stands for Landsorganisationen, while TCO stands for the Tjanstemannens centralorganisation.

35. See Gosta Rehn and Birger Viklund, "Changes in the Swedish Model," in *European Industrial Relations*, ed. Baglioni and Crouch, 304–5; and Scott Lash and John Urry, *The End of Organized Capitalism* (Madison: University of Wisconsin Press, 1987), chap. 8.

36. See Scott Lash, "The End of Neo-Corporatism? The Breakdown of Centralized Bargaining in Sweden," *British Journal of Industrial Relations* 23 (1985).

37. On Sweden's labor market policies, see, *inter alia*, Gosta Esping-Andersen, *Politics against Markets: The Social Democratic Road to Power* (Princeton, N.J.: Princeton University Press, 1985); Walter Korpi, *The Democratic Class Struggle* (London: Routledge, 1983); and Gosta Rehn, "Swedish Active Labor Market Policy: Retrospect and Prospect," *Industrial Relations* 24 (1985).

38. The definitive study of the politics of investment and economic redistribution in Sweden is Jonas Pontusson, *The Limits of Social Democracy: Investment Politics in Sweden* (Ithaca, N.Y.: Cornell University Press, 1992).

39. Pontusson, "The Rise and Fall of the Postwar Settlement," in *European Politics in Transition*, ed. Kesselman and Krieger, 455.

40. When the Social Democrats returned to office in 1982, they invited twenty-five organizations "to participate in consultations over wage-earner funds and related issues." Not only did business groups decline the invitation, but the opposition parties "announced beforehand that they were not about to engage in any form of negotiations, and the TCO leadership showed up only to inform the government that it would neither support nor oppose any forthcoming legislation." See Pontusson, "The Rise and Fall of the Postwar Settlement," in *European Politics in Transition*, ed. Kesselman and Krieger, 456.

41. See, for example, several of the contributions to Martin Jacques and Francis Mulhern, eds., *The Forward March of Labour Halted?* (London: Verso, 1981).

42. For an adept discussion of these issues see Colin Crouch, "Conservative Industrial Relations Policy: Towards Labour Exclusion?" in *Economic Crisis, Trade Unions, and the State*, ed. Jacobi et. al, 131–53.

43. David Finegold, "Institutional Incentives and Skill Creation: Preconditions for a High-Skill Equilibrium," in *International Comparisons of Vocational Education and Training for Intermediate Skills*, ed. Paul Ryan (London: Falmer Press, 1991), 113, note 1. See also David Finegold and David Soskice, "The Failure of British Training: Analysis and Prescription," *Oxford Review of Economic Policy* 4, no. 3 (Autumn 1988): 21–53.

44. See Worcester, "From Tripartism to the Enterprise Culture," chap. 2.

45. The phrase is taken from Hugo Young, *The Iron Lady: A Biography of Margaret Thatcher* (New York: Farrar, Straus, Giroux, 1989).

46. One management consultant complained that for "twenty years executives had received a buffeting and bashing from government and unions. . . . We have an opportunity that will last for two or three years, then the unions will get themselves together again and the government, like all governments, will run out of steam. So grab it now. We have had a pounding and we are all fed up with it. I think it would be fair to say it's almost vengeance." Len Collinson, quoted in John MacInnes, *Thatcherism at Work* (Milton Keynes, Britain: Open University Press, 1987), 92.

47. See, *inter alia*, Philip Bassett, *Strike Free: New Industrial Relations in Britain* (Basingstoke: Macmillan, 1989); and P. K. Edwards, *Managing the Factory* (Oxford: Blackwell, 1987).

48. A 1985 survey found that personnel managers believed that industrial relations had improved because there was "greater management skill and commitment to employee relations," and "improved employee involvement." Some respondents

also noted that a generalized "fear of unemployment" had made their job considerably easier. See MacInnes, *Thatcherism at Work* (Milton Keynes, Britain: Open University Press, 1987), 109.

49. Philip Bassett, "Non-Unionism's Growing Ranks," *Personnel Management*, March 1988: 45.

50. As John Kelly notes, "establishments which recognized trade unions in 1980 were almost certain to do so in 1984." See John Kelly, "Trade Unions through the Recession," *British Journal of Industrial Relations*, July 1987: 275.

51. Michael Fogarty, with Douglas Brooks, *Trade Unions and British Industrial Development* (London: Policy Studies Institute, 1986), 89.

52. See John Kelly, *Trade Unions and Socialist Politics* (London: Verso, 1988), 262.

53. "Governments which treat unions as responsible organisations are entitled in return to expect unions to act responsibly. But if Governments treat unions as unworthy to share, or incapable of accepting, responsibility then unions will be driven back to exercising their traditional functions of defending their basic rights, defending living standards, defending jobs—on which incomes depend—and defending the social wage." Lionel Murray, "The Democratic Bargain," in *The Role of the Trade Unions: The Granada Guildhall Lectures*, ed. James Prior, Tony Benn, Lionel Murray (London: Granada, 1980), 88.

54. This "Europhoric" reading of the European Community's potential is reflected in the writings of John Palmer, who argues that a united Europe could "exercise a greater influence on world affairs. . . . For the first time in generations the peoples of Europe—all of Europe—are feeling their way to play their part in the creation of a better future. That, in the final analysis, is the true relevance of the debate which 1992 has made possible." See John Palmer, *1992 and Beyond* (Luxembourg: Office for Official Publications of the European Communities, 1989), 95.

55. This section draws on Chris Toulouse, "Europe after Maastricht: Into the Twilight Zone," *New Political Science* 24–25 (Summer 1993): 175–92.

56. Toulouse, "Europe after Maastricht," unpublished early draft, 1.

57. See Niels Finn Christiansen, "The Danish No to Maastricht," *New Left Review*, no. 195 (September/October 1992): 97–101.

58. One editor, writing just after the currency crisis of September 1992 had knocked the British pound (and the Italian lira) out of ERM, wanly maintained that "Maastricht does at least provide for some form of democratic control over the financial institutions that hold effective sway over the economies of Europe. The proposed European central bank, for example, would be accountable to Ecofin, the council of economic and finance ministers of the member states. Limited and inadequate though this accountability may be, it is more than exists among the currency market speculators whose dealings have picked off one currency after another over the past two weeks." See Steve Platt, "Euro-Buckers," *New Statesman and Society*, 25 September 1992, p. 5.

59. "Half-Maastricht," *The Economist*, 26 September 1992, p. 15.

60. For the Conservatives, the EC's social component is best confined to a narrow set of concerns (such as protecting children in the workplace) and should avoid advancing more far-reaching goals.

61. Christiane Lemke and Gary Marks, "From Decline to Demise? The Fate of Socialism in Europe," in *The Crisis of Socialism in Europe*, ed. Christiane Lemke and Gary Marks (Durham, N.C.: Duke University Press, 1992), 16.

62. Alberta M. Sbragia, "Thinking about the European Future: The Uses of Comparison," in *Euro-Politics: Institutions and Policymaking in the "New" European Community*, ed. Alberta M. Sbragia (Washington, D.C.: Brookings Institution, 1992), 290.

63. Peter Lange, "Politics of the Social Dimension," in *Euro-Politics*, ed. Sbragia, 229.
64. Lange, "The Politics of the Social Dimension," 236–37. He writes: "The complexity of interests on the social dimension arises from the direct and indirect social costs that firms incur in order to employ workers, as well as from the rules and regulations that constrain employers' prerogatives. . . . In the European and international marketplaces, it is likely that firms in different countries and regions, operating under different social-cost regimes and institutionalized constraints (as well as diverse infrastructural and other conditions outside their control), have developed unique internal equilibria with regard to how they employ workers and capital in order to remain competitive" (p. 236). Workers and unions are likely to be as sensitive to changes in these "internal equilibria" as are employers.
65. As our survey of developments in Germany, Sweden, and Britain suggests, social democratic parties have been placed on the electoral and political defensive in a number of countries. Whether this condition is insurmountable is the subject of an extensive scholarly debate. Key contributions include Stuart Hall, *The Hard Road to Renewal: Thatcherism and the Crisis of the Left* (London: Verso, 1988); Wolfgang Merkel, "After the Golden Age: Is Social Democracy Doomed to Decline?" in *The Crisis of Socialism in Europe*, ed. Lemke and Marks, 136–70; Leo Panitch, *Working Class Politics in Crisis: Essays on Labour and the State* (London: Verso, 1986); Adam Przeworski, *Capitalism and Social Democracy* (New York: Cambridge, 1986); Adam Przeworski and John Sprague, *Paper Stones: A History of Electoral Socialism* (Chicago: University of Chicago Press, 1986); and Fritz W. Scharpf, *Crisis and Choice in European Social Democracy* (Ithaca, N.Y.: Cornell University Press, 1991). A useful overview is provided by Gosta Esping-Andersen and Kees van Kersbergen, "Contemporary Research on Social Democracy," *Annual Review of Sociology* 18 (1992): 187–208.
66. Kim Moody, "Labor under Clinton: In Training to Compete," *Against the Current*, no. 43 (March/April 1993): 7.
67. See Lewis Lapham's unfairly neglected study, *Money and Class in America: Notes and Observations on Our Civil Religion* (New York: Weidenfeld and Nicolson, 1988).
68. Despite its British focus, Andrew Gamble's *The Free Economy and the Strong State: The Politics of Thatcherism* (London: Macmillan, 1988) has considerable relevance in this context.

10

Conclusion

Staughton Lynd

I

THE ESSAYS IN THIS book set forth a political economy of union decline in the United States. The reappearance of international competition in the 1960s is seen as the driving force. "Global restructuring," writes Chris Toulouse, "has broken the back of organized labor."

As a result of renewed competition between capitalist firms and nations, real wages in the United States began to fall in the early 1970s and are now at the level of the early 1960s. The implicit post–World War II social compact in Great Britain and the United States, whereby the national government "underwrote the cost of old age, housing and education," came under attack as well. What Toulouse and Kent Worcester term hyper-capitalist administrations in Great Britain and the United States set out to challenge these arrangements. The result, by the end of the 1980s, was the erosion of working-class social mobility and the attrition of union organization.

International economic forces, however, are only part of the story. Hard times may not automatically lead to greater working-class radicalism, but neither is it inevitable that they should produce social quiescence. Plant closings, for example, offer difficult terrain for organizers and tend to push workers into individual survival strategies, but they have also produced an effective boycott campaign at the General Motors Van Nuys plant, the inspired use of eminent domain at the Morse Cutting Tool plant in New Bedford, and plant occupations, as well as a movement for worker-community ownership, in Youngstown.[1] Significantly, each of these radicalizing struggles was led by *local* unions and had community support. There can be no adequate explanation of the collapse of organized labor in the decade of the 1980s that does not include, along with an analysis of international economic forces, the pathetically inept misleadership of bureaucratized national unions.

Glenn Perusek offers a refreshing assessment of bureaucratic unionism in his essay on the classical sociology of Webbs, Michels, and Lenin. Clearly he is on to something. The words of Sidney and Beatrice Webb about the main craft societies' leaders in Great Britain during the 1860s and 1870s (that they were

234

preoccupied with preserving their dues income, that their "distinctive policy . . . was the combination of extreme caution in trade matters and energetic agitation for political reforms" that would solidify their own leadership positions, and that their "trade policy was . . . restricted to securing for every workman those terms which the best employers were willing voluntarily to grant") fit equally well the AFL-CIO leadership in the 1980s.

The Webbs and Robert Michels agreed that democracy was possible only in small groups and that the necessary creation of national trade unions and political parties inevitably brought with it organizational conservatism. Left labor organizers have yet to respond adequately to this critique. Indeed, as Perusek points out, communist organizers helped along the bureaucratizing trend in the early CIO by fighting for full-time committeemen and the dues check-off.

Lenin, like the Webbs and Michels, expressed in his own way the labor bureaucrat's belief in what Perusek calls "the incompetence of the masses." In his *What Is to Be Done?*, Lenin argued that without input from a vanguard political party the working class would spontaneously pursue only opportunistic, "economist" goals. And Perusek might have added that Lenin came to this conclusion about the young Russian working class with the Webbs' analysis of the mature British working class before him. Lenin, according to Eric Hobsbawm, was well aware when he wrote *What Is to Be Done?* of

> the fullest and best-informed work on the "aristocratic" trade unions of the nineteenth century, Sidney and Beatrice Webb's *Industrial Democracy*. This important book he knew intimately, having translated it in his Siberian exile. It provided him, incidentally, with an immediate understanding of the links between the British Fabians and Bernstein: "The original source of a number of Bernstein's contentions and ideas," he wrote on 13 September 1899, to a correspondent, "is in the latest books written by the Webbs." Lenin continued to quote information drawn from the Webbs many years later, and specifically refers to *Industrial Democracy* in the course of his argument in *What Is to Be Done?*[2]

Fascinatingly, the passage in *What Is to Be Done?* in which Lenin mentions the Webbs is precisely the one in which Lenin pours scorn on direct or "primitive" democracy:

> It must also be observed that [there is] a confusion of ideas concerning the meaning of democracy. In Mr. and Mrs. Webb's book on trade unionism [here Lenin cites not *Industrial Democracy* but *The History of Trade Unionism*], there is an interesting section on "Primitive Democracy." In this section, the authors relate how, in the first period of existence of their unions, the British workers thought that in the interests of democracy all the members must take part in the work of managing the unions; not only were all questions decided by the vote of all the members, but all official duties were fulfilled by all the members in turn. A long period of historical experience was required to teach these workers how absurd such a conception of democracy was and to make them understand the necessity for representative

institutions on the one hand, and of full-time professional officials on the other.[3]

Scholars and activists ought now to feel forced to reexamine these classical ideas, for the CIO in the half century from its founding in 1935 to the mid-1980s has traversed precisely the trajectory mapped out by the Webbs, Michels, and Lenin. Explanations (judicial conservatism, World War II, McCarthyism) and excuses (the difference between labor laws in the United States and Canada) abound as to why the CIO has come to its present sorry pass.[4] These essays suggest a longer view. The bureaucratization of the CIO differs very little from the bureaucratization of British unions in the late nineteenth century, as chronicled by the Webbs, and of the German unions and Social Democratic Party in the early years of the twentieth century, the subject of Michels' analysis. The British and German experiences led Lenin, first in *What Is to Be Done?* and then in *Imperialism*, to posit an inherent conservatism in the working classes of advanced capitalist societies and, additionally, to suggest a distinction between the "lower stratum" of the working class in such societies and an "upper stratum" or "labor aristocracy."[5] Lenin's analysis, whatever its imperfections, adds to the insular critique of the Webbs and Michels a sense of the connection between working-class conservatism and capitalist imperialism. There is or has been in certain periods a sizable number of workers who have benefited from imperialist super-profits and from what some have termed "white skin privilege." We are led to the question of whether the entire project of a radical working class, capable of self-transformation from a "class in itself" to a "class for itself" and of taking the lead in the *Aufhebung* of capitalist society as a whole, is an illusion.

II

The essays in this volume by Aaron Brenner, Christoph Scherrer, and Andy Pollack, together with Glenn Perusek's essay on the UAW, probe the unionism of the 1960s and 1970s for signs of new life. The most hopeful story is that of the Teamsters, and Brenner adds to the many journalistic accounts the important insight that the decentralized character of the trucking history (and subjectively, the truck driver's existential experience of himself or herself as an industrial cowboy) made possible organizing "on an incremental basis": the winning of small victories through direct action, the slow building of a movement from the bottom up.

But even in the trucking industry, hard times and concession bargaining in the 1980s caused direct action to slack off. "The balance shifted toward electoral politics" within the union. As in the larger society, powerlessness was masked by the periodic ritual of choosing someone else to make decisions. Moreover, the national electoral victory of Ron Carey would probably not have come about without federal intervention to a degree profoundly inconsistent with labor traditions of autonomy and self-government. Having elected

Ron Carey—a decent man who voted for Nixon and who told a *Labor Notes* convention in 1991 that he wanted to get back to the good old days in the Teamsters union—the radicals organized in Teamsters for a Democratic Union were unsure what to do next.

In other trades and unions the scene was even more depressing. The United Steel Workers of America continued "the long tradition of exchanging shop floor rights for material gains." The most active and militant steelworkers were retirees, who, altogether unrepresented in union decision-making and unrestricted by contractual no-strike language, experienced both the necessity and the possibility of direct action. Their protests sometimes succeeded in restoring the promised pension and medical insurance rights for which, when they were working, they had given up present income in the form of wages. But the contradictions of capitalism in the steel industry ground on remorselessly: Worldwide excess capacity forced companies in the United States, Great Britain, France, Germany, and elsewhere to close mills; a smaller number of active workers could not produce the cash flow necessary to fund the fringe benefits of an ever-increasing number of retirees; corporations themselves turned to the government for help (as in taking over pension liabilities), but not, of course, to public ownership.[6]

Perusek's essay on the UAW sets forth a view shared by other essayists in this volume, namely, that the last upsurge of labor militancy in the United States was in the late 1960s and early 1970s, specifically from 1967 to 1973. Why then? he asks, answering paradoxically (from the standpoint of traditional Marxism as exemplified by Trotsky) that workers rebelled in the Vietnam War period partly because these were good times and they did not fear for their jobs. Other sources of radicalism were the hiring of more blacks and young people, and the "general rebellion against racism and the status quo."

But auto workers, like teamsters, eschewed direct action in the late 1970s and 1980s. As in the Teamsters union, so in the UAW the project of union dissidents came to be running for union office, not solving problems through wildcat strikes. Indeed, Perusek finds, the dissidents themselves came to be lower-level union officers rather than informal shop floor leaders. The latter were paralyzed by fear: fear engendered by capital flight, plant shutdowns, and the whipsawing of one plant against another that often preceded shutdowns, especially in General Motors.

Andy Pollack's thoughtful essay about the airlines industry stresses the inadequacy of Big Labor's analysis of the causes of excess capacity, capital flight, and facility shutdowns. There was a tendency to blame what was happening to a given airline on a particular capitalist (Icahn, Lorenzo) and to conjure up fantasies of so-called worker ownership and rescue by entrepreneurial white knights. Because even the IAM did not face up to the "objective socialization" of the airlines industry and the need not just for public reregulation but for public ownership, strike strategies floundered and corporate campaigns failed to come off.

Pollack and his colleagues are not quite sure about the alternative to what is. His essay invokes both the pattern-bargaining called for by Kim Moody in his *An Injury To All*[7] and the local direct action lovingly narrated by Rick Fantasia in his *Cultures of Solidarity*.[8] But these are quite different concepts. The culture of solidarity that can be created in an airport-based strike committee of all trades, for which Pollack quite properly calls, is the product of an essentially local experience. How to achieve the same experience nationwide is somewhere, to paraphrase e. e. cummings, that the labor movement of the United States has not recently traveled.

We are back to the dilemma posed by the Webbs and Michels: The democracy that is possible in a small group seems difficult or impossible to bring about on a larger scale.

III

Is there a political economy of hope, a political economy of labor revival? I will venture some suggestions.

To begin with, we should put aside the notion of returning to some hypothetical point in the history of the CIO where things went wrong. The question that prefaces Michael Goldfield's important essay, "Was There a Golden Age of the CIO?," leads on to other questions: Was the CIO *from the beginning* a semipublic institution, licensed by the state?[9] Did CIO national unions *from the beginning* practice top-down decision-making, and seek to regulate shop floor activity from above? Did the CIO *from the beginning* discourage independent labor politics? And finally, did there exist an alternative unionism of the early 1930s to which we can now return in seeking a new beginning? Summarizing the work of a number of younger historians on particular places and trades, I have suggested that

> the alternative union paradigm to be found in the struggles of the early 1930s is rank-and-file based, democratic, politically independent, and deeply rooted in inter-craft solidarity. Its common organizational form is the inclusive and independent city labor movement. Historians have supposed that the local general strikes in Toledo, Minneapolis, and San Francisco in 1934 were atypical. We suggest that, on the contrary, these local general strikes of 1934 were characteristic of what Rose Feurer and Gary Gerstle call the "mobilizations" of working-class communities in the early 1930s. Still more fundamentally, the organizing principle of the alternative unionism of the early 1930s—distinguishing it from CIO unionism in every period of the CIO's history—was its reliance on the *horizontal* rather *than vertical bonding of working people*.[10]

The self-organization of the rank and file in the early 1930s was at least as effective as the top-down efforts of the CIO a few years later. In June 1933 the Amalgamated Association of Iron, Steel, and Tin Workers reported less than five thousand members. By the time of the Amalgamated's national conven-

tion in April 1934 its membership had increased to a number variously estimated at 50,000 to 200,000. In a comparable period of time, from June 1936
to March 1937, the Steel Workers Organizing Committee using two hundred
full-time organizers enrolled about the same number of workers.[11]

The picture was similar in other industries. By June 1935 there were one
hundred federal labor unions in Summit County, Ohio, including the city of
Akron, with 60,000 members.[12] In Flint, the citywide council of federal labor
unions claimed 42,000 members in March 1934, and AFL records indicate
that there were 14,000 members who paid dues. These numbers are roughly
equivalent to the 25,000 UAW members claimed by organizer Bob Travis
immediately after the sitdown strike.[13] Similarly, the United Textile Workers
Union witnessed an extraordinary increase in southern membership from only
a few thousand in July 1933 to between 85,000 and 135,000 in July 1934.[14]
The Independent Textile Union in Woonsocket, a single local union in a small
industrial city, had 15,449 members by 1943.[15]

To be sure, mere numbers do not in themselves make an effective organization. In all the mentioned situations—steel, rubber, auto, and textiles—an essentially similar drama played itself out in the early 1930s. The federal
government's overriding concern to avoid strikes and the AFL's failure to offer
militant national leadership led to meaningless agreements between the government and AFL leaders, the defusing of gathering strike sentiment at the
grass-roots level, and subsequent demoralization. Uncoordinated local distur-
bances could not take the place of a national movement.[16] Alternative means
were needed to coordinate local efforts on a regional and national scale.

National radical parties could have provided the resources and professional
skills (lawyering, public relations, fund-raising) that local groups of rank-and-
file workers needed to coordinate their efforts regionally and nationally. The
organization of the International Longshoremen's and Warehousemen's Union, uniting a variety of crafts over a thousand miles of coast under strong
Communist Party influence, shows that this model is hardly hypothetical. It,
too, actually happened. But on reflection I believe that such parties were (and
are) themselves so vertically organized, resembling in this respect the national
CIO and its unions rather than local "solidarity unions," that they could not
have played the needed coordinating role and would have tried to dominate
for their own purposes.[17]

Alternatively, local unions could have coordinated (and can today coordinate)
their efforts in a variety of ways without belonging to the same organization
and without sacrificing their freedom of action to the heavy-handed topdown
governance that seems so often to accompany industrywide pattern-bargaining.

John Sargent's account of bargaining at Inland Steel under his presidency in
the late 1930s suggests one such mechanism. The local had an agreement with
management that the company would match the highest wage rate for a particular line of work that steelworkers established anywhere in the country.[18]
The experience of Barberton, Ohio, during the half century following the early

1930s, narrated by John Borsos,[19] indicates that such mechanisms can function effectively over a long period of time. Barberton workers created industry- or corporationwide conferences, consisting of members of the same union working for the same company in different locations (the boilermakers), or of members of different unions all employed by the same company (the chemical workers), or of members of different unions in different companies of the same industry (the insulator workers).[20]

In Spain in the 1930s,[21] in Poland in the early 1980s,[22] and in the present functioning of the Spanish longshoremen's union,[23] workers in other countries have more fully developed coordinating mechanisms like those at Inland Steel or in Barberton.

Moreover, as Michael Kozura shows in his account of "bootleg" coal mining in the anthracite region of Pennsylvania in the 1930s, local groups that come into being primarily for self-defense can also provide a setting where workers organize themselves to operate the means of production. "Bootleg unions set coal prices, organized rescue teams, taught first aid, hired lawyers for legal defense, and resolved disputes." When mining companies and the United Mine Workers union sought to reverse the local victories of bootleggers by new state laws, the bootleg locals united the region's miners and truckers in one big association, and on 7 April 1935 convened the first regionwide convention of the bootleggers' union. Three weeks later ten thousand miners rode into Harrisburg in the backs of coal trucks, marched through the streets to the Capitol, and blocked passage of the owners' legislative agenda.[24]

Were local unions in the United States in ways like these able to be "all leaders," without resorting to top-down national union structures patterned on the corporation, it would extend into working-class reality the participatory democracy envisioned both by the IWW and by the student movement of the 1960s. We will not know if it is possible unless we try.

Notes

1. See, for example, Eric Mann, *Taking On General Motors: A Case Study of the UAW Campaign to Keep GM Van Nuys Open* (Los Angeles: Institute of Industrial Relations Publications, 1987); Staughton Lynd, *The Fight against Shutdowns: Youngstown's Steel Mill Closings, 1977–1980* (San Pedro, Calif.: Singlejack Books, 1982); Staughton Lynd, "The Genesis of the Idea of a Community Right to Industrial Property in Youngstown and Pittsburgh, 1977–1987," in *The Constitution and American Life*, ed. David Thelen (Ithaca, N.Y.: Cornell University Press, 1987).
2. Eric Hobsbawm, *Revolutionaries: Contemporary Essays* (New York: Pantheon, 1973), 122–23.
3. Vladimir Ilyich Lenin, *What Is to Be Done? Burning Questions of Our Movement* (New York: International Publishers, 1929), 131–32.
4. Some of the most interesting work along these lines has been done not by labor historians but by legal historians, notably Karl Klare, "The Judicial Deradicalization of the Wagner Act and the Origins of Modern Legal Consciousness, 1937–1941," *Minnesota Law Review* 62 (1978): 265–332, and James Atleson. Atleson's work,

still for the most part unpublished, includes the most detailed examination to date of the activity of the War Labor Board and an exhaustive comparison of union organization in the United States and Canada.

5. Vladimir Ilyich Lenin, *Imperialism: The Highest Stages of Capitalism* (New York: International Publishers, 1939), 105–8.

6. See generally, Staughton Lynd and Alice Lynd, "Labor in the Era of Multinationalism: The Crisis in Bargained-For Fringe Benefits," *West Virginia Law Review* 93 (1991): 907–44.

7. Kim Moody, *An Injury to All: The Decline of American Unionism* (London: Verso, 1988).

8. Rick Fantasia, *Cultures of Solidarity: Consciousness, Action, and Contemporary American Workers* (Berkeley and Los Angeles: University of California Press, 1988).

9. In this connection one should take note of Trotsky's view, as quoted by Perusek, in chap. 3, note 34, that common to all modern trade unions "is their drawing closely together with the state power."

10. Staughton Lynd, "We Are All Leaders: The Alternative Unionism of the Early 1930s," unpublished paper presented at the North American Labor History Conference, October 1992, and citing Rose Feurer, "The Nutpickers Union, 1933–1934: Crossing the Boundaries of Community and Workplace," unpublished paper; and Gary Gerstle, *Working-Class Americanism: The Politics of Labor in a Textile City, 1914–1960* (Cambridge: Cambridge University Press, 1991), chap. 4, "Citywide Mobilization, 1934–1936."

11. For estimates of Amalgamated membership in the first part of 1934 of 50,000, 150,000, and 200,000, see Staughton Lynd, "The Possibility of Radicalism in the Early 1930s: The Case of Steel," *Radical America*, 6 (1972): 37–64, 191, 205 note 6. David J. McDonald, treasurer of SWOC, estimates SWOC membership at the end of 1936 as a "shaky 82,000" and states that when U.S. Steel signed a contract with SWOC in March 1937 SWOC had signed up only 7 percent of its employees. Lynd, "The Possibility of Radicalism in the Early 1930s," 191–92, 205 note 11.

12. Daniel Nelson, *American Rubber Worker and Organized Labor, 1900–1941* (Princeton; N.J.: Princeton University Press, 1988), 145. Sidney Hillman told biographer Mathew Josephson that during the NRA period over forty thousand rubber workers had been organized. David Brody, "Emergence of Mass-Production Unionism," in *Workers in Industrial America: Essays on the Twentieth Century Struggle* (New York: Oxford University Press, 1980), 90.

13. Ronald Edsforth, *Class Conflict and Cultural Consensus: The Making of a Mass Consumer Society in Flint, Michigan* (New Brunswick, N.J.: Rutgers University Press, 1987), 162, 265 note 11, 176.

14. Janet Irons, "A New Deal for Labor? Southern Cotton Mill Workers and the General Textile Strike of 1934," unpublished paper presented at the 1989 annual meeting of the Organization of American Historians, 9–10.

15. Gerstle, *Working-Class Americanism*, 269–70.

16. I agree with a great deal that is said in Frances Fox Piven and Richard Cloward, *Poor People's Movements: Why They Succeed, How They Fail* (New York: Pantheon, 1977), 96–180. However, I disagree with their statement on page 96: "Factory workers had their greatest influence and were able to extract their most substantial concessions from government during the early years of the Great Depression *before they were organized into unions*" (emphasis in original). Workers were organized into unions in the early 1930s, as the evidence cited throughout this essay proves. They were unions of a different kind than the CIO unions that succeeded them. Had Piven and Cloward written, "before they were organized into *CIO*

unions," I would agree. Rather than thinking that workers should not be organized or should not belong to unions, I believe that they should organize themselves *in a different way* and should form unions *of a different kind.*

17. An example of such domination occurred in organizing New York City transit
workers: "TWU elections were always two-stage affairs, with one voting period for
day workers and another the next morning for the night shift. In this case, after
the day-shift vote, [Michael] Quill, who was living at the union hall, decided to
check the ballots. He discovered that O'Shea was leading Santo by a considerable
margin, enough to almost guarantee his victory. If the inner core of the union—
the delegates council—had been convinced of O'Shea's failings, the membership
at large remained loyal to the man the union itself had carefully built up. . . .
Believing that O'Shea's election would be disastrous, Quill approached another
left-wing TWU leader and the two men took the ballot box up to Quill's room.
Without consulting others, they stuffed the box with enough ballots to ensure
Santo's victory." Joshua B. Freeman, *In Transit: The Transport Workers Union in
New York City, 1933–1966* (New York: Oxford University Press, 1989), 88–89.
At the time Quill had moved into the Communist Party orbit, was attending
meetings of party members, and had probably become a party member; Freeman,
In Transit, 57.

18. According to Sargent: "We made an agreement with Inland Steel way back in '38
or '39 that the company would not pay less than any of its competitors throughout the country. We never had it so good. . . . All you had to do as a union
representative was come into the company and say, 'Look, we have a group of
people working in the pickle line, and at Youngstown, Ohio or Youngstown Sheet
and Tube in East Chicago people are getting more money that we're getting for
the same job.' And if that was a fact, we were given an increase in wages at
Inland. In those departments where we had a strong group of union members,
where they were most active, we had the highest rates in the country. We were
never able to secure conditions of this kind after we secured contracts." John
Sargent, "Your Dog Don't Bark No More," in *Rank and File: Personal Histories by
Working-Class Organizers,* ed. Staughton Lynd and Alice Lynd (New York: Monthly
Review Press, 1988), 100.

19. John Borsos, "Talking Union: The Labor Movement in Barberton, Ohio, 1891–
1991" (Ph.D. diss., Indiana University, 1992).

20. There have been similar efforts recently to form confederations of autonomous
local unions among paperworkers and meatpackers. United Paperworkers Local 20
in Kaukana, Wisconsin, initiated a "coordinated bargaining pool" after losing a
bitter eighteen-month strike against International Paper in 1987–1988. Locals that
joined the pool were to make common demands during their local negotiations,
seal their ballots after the final contract vote, and work without a contract rather
than take individual action or sign a concessionary agreement. When the pool felt
it had sufficient strength, the ballots would be counted. If a majority voted against
the local agreements, the union would take nationwide action. The strategy was
intended to create a common contract expiration date, and ideally, one contract
for all International Paper locations. By June 1991, the pool included 60 percent
of International Papers's seventeen thousand workers in thirty-five locals. The strategy
failed not because of any substantive defect but because in December 1991 the
NLRB declared it illegal. Phil Kwik, "Bargaining Pool Collapses at International
Paper; 'The Fight Isn't Over,' Activists Declare," *Labor Notes* no. 159 (June 1992).
Similarly, after the defeat of the strike against Hormel led by United Food and
Commercial Workers Local P-9 in Austin, Minnesota, former P-9 activists estab-
lished the North American Meatpackers Union (NAMPU) in June 1986. NAMPU

was intended to be a confederation of autonomous locals. According to a NAMPU founder: "Each local would be *autonomous* and each local would have control of its strike funds. It would be more or less a 'one plant, one local' philosophy that builds the union. That's the way the packing industry used to be. . . . Local people can take care of local problems, what we need is a national support effort, and a federation of locals that are willing to support each other. . . . The federation of locals would be a support group that would help a local union in any way they could in their negotiations, and that's about the only way we're going to stop this downward spiral of concessions." George DeMartino, "Trade-Union Isolation and the Catechism of the Left," *Rethinking Marxism* 4 (Fall 1991): 41, quoting *Industrial Worker* (March 1987): 3.

21. See Sam Dolgoff, ed., *The Anarchist Collectives: Workers Self-Management in the Spanish Revolution 1936–1939* (Montreal: Black Rose Books, 1990). The Central Labor Bank in Barcelona channeled funds from more prosperous to less prosperous collectives, charging 1 percent interest (pp. 68–69). Purchasing, packing, and exporting of the Valencia orange crop, 90 percent of which was exported, was managed through 270 committees in towns and villages (p. 76). Barcelona longshoremen abolished racketeers who had acted as go-betweens, brought about higher wages, better working conditions, and "by setting aside a certain sum for each ton of cargo handled, unemployment, health, and accident prevention" (pp. 90–91). On agrarian collectives each work group elected a delegate, and delegates met weekly with the collective's "delegate for agriculture"; the collective as a whole met weekly, bi-weekly, or monthly (p. 167). The fundamental principles were (1) faith in the constructive and creative capacity of the masses, (2) autonomy (self-rule), and (3) "decentralization and coordination through the free agreement of federalism" (p. 174).

22. Polish Solidarity was the result of a spreading solidarity process, involving the creation of workplace committees, with elected representatives from all departments, then of regional interfactory committees, and finally, in September 1980, of a national coordinating committee but *not* a hierarchical national organization. At each stage workers challenged one another to recognize that "if the workers at these other factories were defeated, we wouldn't be safe either." Anna Walentynowicz, quoted in Staughton Lynd, *Solidarity Unionism: Rebuilding the Labor Movement from Below* (Chicago: Charles H. Kerr, 1992), 35. Roman Laba argues persuasively that workers in the north coast cities of Gdansk, Gydnia, and Szczecin improvised the first two steps in this process in December 1970–January 1971, without significant input from intellectuals. Roman Laba, *The Roots of Solidarity* (Princeton, N.J.: Princeton University Press, 1991), chap. 2, 3, especially pp. 66–67 (elected workplace committee at Warski Shipyard) and 68–69 (inter-factory strike committee). Workers built on this experience in the great upheaval of August 1980. At a meeting of rank-and-file delegates from all over Poland, held on 17 September at the Seaman's Hotel in Wrzeszcz, there was fierce debate between intellectuals associated with the workers' defense committee (KOR) who wanted a centralized national structure like the state with which the movement would have to do combat, and workers led by Lech Walesa, who wanted "a decentralized structure grounded in many unions and many statutes" (chap. 5, especially pp. 106–12, where Laba bases his discussion on a tape recording made of the meeting). The workers prevailed: Solidarity was to consist of loosely coordinated "spreading horizontal structures" (p. 112).

23. The Spanish longshoremen's union, La Coordinadora, was brought to the attention of the labor movement in the United States by Stan Weir, who visited Spain in 1982 and described the movement in "Rank and File Networks: A Way to

Fight Concessions," *Labor Notes*, 27 January 1983. The most accessible account is by Don Fitz, "La Coordinadora: A Union without Bureaucrats," in *Within the Shell of the Old: Essays on Workers' Self-Organization*, ed. Don Fitz and David Roediger (Chicago: Charles H. Kerr, 1990), 88–96, based on Fitz's own visit in 1987–1988. As in the case of West Coast longshoremen from the mid-1930s until 1960, the heart of the Spanish system is the hiring hall: "Both in Barcelona and Verona . . . dockers pointed with great pride to the rows and columns of tags which each bear one longshoreman's number. Those at the top of the list receive the first jobs that come in. Job dispatchers of the Office for Port Labor (OTP), a division of the Spanish Labor Ministry, then move the tags of those who are hired to the bottom of the list. . . . With work evenly distributed, there is no group of unemployed longshoremen who might step in when others were on strike. Their hiring halls include every docker—rank and file longshoremen, *delegados*, local president, and national officers" (pp. 88–89).

La Coordinadora operates out of a building a few blocks from the Barcelona hiring hall. Owned by the anarchist union before the Spanish Civil War, it was seized by Franco in 1939. After Franco's death in 1975, dockers asked for the return of the building. When the government hesitated, dockers occupied the building and have remained there since (pp. 89–90).

With eight thousand members, representing 80 percent of the nation's longshoremen, La Coordinadora is the largest of several Spanish longshoremen's unions and currently Spain's only industrial union. Local *delegados* and national officers work on the docks and make the same pay as other longshoremen. There are only two full-time union staff persons; they are not officers, have no power other than answering letters, and receive longshoremen's wages (pp. 92, 95).

Elected *delegados* do a great deal of work for the union, but decisions are made only by periodic assemblies, which can be attended by any member and at which any member can vote. Each local union is autonomous. "The only way a national port strike can occur is for each autonomous union to recognize that a threat to another port is a threat to itself" (pp. 93–94).

24. Michael E. Kozura, "Disinvestment and Defiance: Anthracite Miners and the Challenge to Corporate Property, 1930–1940," unpublished paper presented at the North American Labor History Conference, October 1992, especially pp. 15–25.

INDEX

245